P9-BEE-536

Encyclopedia of
American
Indian
Wars
1492–1890

LIBRARY
WINDSOR LOCKS HIGH SCHOOL
58 SOUTH ELM STREET
WINDSOR LOCKS, CT 06096

DISCARD

DISCARD

Encyclopedia of

American
Indian
Wars
1492–1890

Jerry Keenan

W. W. Norton & Company

New York • London

All illustrations courtesy of the Library of Congress

First published as a Norton paperback 1999
Copyright © 1997 by Jerry Keenan

Printed in the United States of America
All rights reserved. No part of this publication may be reproduced, stored in a retrieval system, or transmitted, in any form or by any means, electronic, mechanical, photocopying, recording, or otherwise, except for the inclusion of brief quotations in a review, without prior permission in writing from the publishers.

Library of Congress Cataloging-in-Publication Data
Keenan, Jerry.
  Encyclopedia of American Indian wars, 1492–1890 / Jerry Keenan.
    p.   cm.
  Includes bibliographical references and index.
  1. Indians of North America—Wars—Encyclopedias.   I. Title.
E81.K44   1997
973—dc21   97-13841
                                                                                     CIP

ISBN 0-393-31915-6

W. W. Norton & Company, Inc., 500 Fifth Avenue, New York, N.Y. 10110
www.wwnorton.com

W. W. Norton & Company Ltd., 10 Coptic Street, London WC1A 1PU

1 2 3 4 5 6 7 8 9 0

For Carol
Nunc scio quid sit Amor

Contents

Preface, ix

Encyclopedia of
American Indian Wars,
1492–1890, 1

References and Selected Readings, 259
Index, 269

Preface

Clashes between European powers and the indigenous peoples of the Americas began almost immediately upon the arrival of the first Europeans on the shores of the New World. Such conflict seems inevitable in retrospect, and perhaps it should have been expected at the outset as well. The great disparity between the two cultures, particularly their differing concepts of land ownership, made peaceful coexistence virtually impossible.

Although they may have rued the arrival of the Europeans, Indians (the name I have chosen to identify native peoples purely for the sake of simplicity) quickly discovered that these interlopers did not arrive empty-handed. Whiskey and diseases such as smallpox certainly had no redeeming features, but other possessions of the fair-skinned peoples proved more than a little appealing. Iron implements and firearms soon came to be recognized as measures of wealth and power. Tribes who possessed these things, especially firearms, held a decided advantage over traditional enemies. Suddenly the ground rules were changed. The balance of power in many instances shifted dramatically. Equations that had been in place for generations were abruptly altered. White traders, settlers, and government officials wasted little time in exploiting what soon evolved into a dependent condition by forging helpful and protective alliances with neighboring tribes. These pacts not only reinforced a community's defensive capability but also served as a means to acquire land for the rapidly expanding colonies.

Many of the so-called Indian wars were not really wars per se but simply continuations or extensions of campaigns or battles temporarily ended by weather or lack of necessary resources. In a sense it might be thought of as one war with a great many smaller splinter wars and campaigns that lasted nearly four centuries. This work is intended to fill a niche as a work of general reference, wherein the reader will have quick access to a wide range of basic information pertaining to the four centuries of conflict between Indians and European colonists. The challenge in creating a work such as this is twofold: what topics to include and how much to say about each. My aim was to present a broad coverage of the Indian wars, to provide a more or less complete picture—albeit one that would necessarily be brief in recounting complex events and personalities.

In selecting a topic as an entry, one of three standards was applied. The first was relative importance in the overall history of the Indian wars (King Philip's War, the war for the Old Northwest, and the Great Sioux War of 1876). The second included events of somewhat lesser import that nevertheless served to mirror the struggles of a particular region in a particular time period (the Gnaddenhutten Massacre, the fight at Piqua Town, and the Fetterman Disaster). Individuals were chosen for their special impact on a given time and place (Joseph Brant, Andrew Jackson, Sitting Bull). Others were deemed representative of a particular type of individual whose presence was so much a part of the Indian wars as to call for representation in a work such as this. Examples here include Simon Girty, Robert Rogers, and Yellowstone Kelly. Finally, some general reference entries were chosen purely to provide additional information and insight to other entries. Weapons, forts, treaties, military units, and practices such as scalping make up this category.

Preface

Geographically, this work is limited to that part of North America that eventually evolved into the United States. Accordingly, events that occurred in Canada or Mexico fall outside the scope of this study and are not included, except for a very few instances. Selecting entries necessarily involved a certain subjectivity on my part. Some readers will question why certain topics were included and not others, and why some entries were not treated in more detail. This is to be expected. Meeting the editorial challenge in a way that would prove most useful to the most readers was my foremost objective. The end result, I hope, is a work that proves as beneficial to the user as it was satisfying to the author in its creation.

I could not possibly consider this undertaking complete without acknowledging those whose help and support enabled me to ever press on. Thanks are due the following: Henry Rasof, formerly of ABC-CLIO, who responded to my original proposal with enthusiasm and who patiently guided me through the initial phase of the project's development. Longtime friend Mike Koury, of Fort Collins, Colorado, who graciously loaned me books from his extensive library. Many friends in the Order of Indian Wars and the Boulder Corral of Westerners. Finally, loving thanks are tendered to my wife, Carol, who helped in countless ways and was always there to buoy the flagging spirit with support and encouragement.

Jerry Keenan
Boulder, Colorado

A

Abnaki War

See King William's War

Abnakis (Abenakis)

First discovered by the earliest European traders and explorers, the Abnakis were a powerful Algonquian confederation located in Maine. Early on, they formed alliances with the French, primarily as a result of missionary contact. Thus, the Abnakis were often in conflict with the English during the French-English wars, particularly during King William's War.

As pressure from expanding English settlements grew, many Abnakis gradually withdrew to Canada, where descendants of the tribe still live today. In addition to their coverage in standard histories of the colonial wars period, Abnakis are also featured in the historical novels of Kenneth Roberts, notably *Arundel.*

See also: King William's War
Further Reading: Leach, *Arms for Empire;* Steele, *Warpaths*

Acoma Pueblo, Fight at

January 1599

A pueblo community situated atop a 350-foot-high mesa some 50 miles west of present-day Albuquerque, New Mexico, Acoma ("People of the White Rock") is said to be the oldest continuously inhabited settlement in the United States.

Although there was Spanish contact with Acoma at least as early as 1539, the most noteworthy encounter between the two cultures took place in 1598, when Don Juan de Oñate led a self-financed expedition from Mexico to protect Spain's northern colonial frontier. As a result of conflicts farther south, in central and northern Mexico, this region was in need of attention. Oñate probably viewed this expedition as an opportunity to enlarge his own already substantial fortune.

Approaching Acoma, which was estimated to contain some 200 dwellings and a like number of warriors, Oñate sent an advance party under the command of his nephew, Juan de Zaldivar, to notify the inhabitants that they were now Spanish subjects and would be required to renounce their heathen ways. The Acomans, however, had a reputation for hostility toward neighboring tribes and made no exception for the Spanish. In a surprise move they attacked Zaldivar's column and drove it off, killing 14 of his men.

Angered by the repulse, Oñate dispatched a stronger column commanded by Zaldivar's brother, Vicente. In a fierce struggle, the Spanish fought their way up the rocky trail to the mesa top, eventually overwhelming and killing most of the defenders. In retaliation for the Acomans' resistance Oñate took some 500 women and children captive. Additionally, 80 surviving men were sentenced to lose one foot and to serve as slaves for 20 years. Even a pair of innocent Hopi bystanders were not spared. Oñate ordered a hand cut off each of these particularly unfortunate observers, then sent them back to their own communities to serve as an object lesson—a reminder of the fate that awaited those who resisted Spanish advances.

See also: Pueblo Indians; Spain
Further Reading: Forbes, *Apache, Navaho, and Spaniard;* Hodge, *Handbook of American Indians,* vol. 1

Adobe Walls, First Battle of
25 November 1864

In the fall of 1864 Gen. James Henry Carleton, commanding the Department of New Mexico and having largely destroyed the Navajo capacity to wage war, was directed to take action against Indian raiders on the Santa Fe Trail. Wagon trains along the famous overland route had been subjected to deadly raids by Kiowas and Comanches. Even large, well-organized trains had been hard-hit. Many travelers were killed and much livestock was captured by the raiders. In response to these raids Col. Christopher (Kit) Carson was directed to assemble an expedition and sweep through the Canadian River valley, located in the Texas Panhandle, to destroy Indian villages.

Accordingly, Carson departed from Cimarron, New Mexico, in November 1864 with a force of 300 mounted volunteers from California and New Mexico supported by a contingent of Ute and Jicarilla scouts, a pair of 12-pounder mountain howitzers, and a large wagon train. Late on 24 November Carson's scouts reported a large Kiowa-Apache encampment not far from the site of the abandoned Bent–St. Vrain trading post, known as Adobe Walls, so called because some of the walls were standing. The area was favored by Indians because of the large buffalo herd that wintered there.

Leaving his wagon train in camp under a 50-man guard, Carson executed a 15-mile forced night march to be in position for a dawn attack on the village, estimated to contain about 175 tipis.

Carson's attack on 25 November was carried out mostly as planned, despite a premature foray by his hired scouts to capture the village horse herd. The village was largely destroyed and its inhabitants were routed. Carson's cavalry pursued the survivors for 4 miles. When Carson reached Adobe Walls, however, he was forced to halt, as the Indians seemed to be increasing in number and resistance was stiffening. Unknown to Carson, the villagers he had just attacked were being reinforced by hundreds of Comanches from a much larger village located down-

stream. These new arrivals also seemed to be well armed, with many carrying weapons obtained from the Comancheros (a group of unscrupulous traders and brigands that did business in the Llano Estacado, or Staked Plains, of Texas and New Mexico). Carson had never before seen so many Indians at one time—and the numbers appeared to be increasing, with estimates ranging from 1,000 to 3,000. However, the two mountain howitzers kept the growing Indian force in check.

Having obviously lost the initiative, Carson decided to withdraw. The movement was ably supported by the howitzers and was inadvertently aided by the Indians themselves, who started a grass fire intended to hinder the withdrawal but that actually helped to cloak the movement. Thanks to his own good judgment, the effect of the howitzers, and the screen thrown up by the grass fire, Carson was able to extricate his men from what could have been a tactical disaster. Back in New Mexico, he officially touted his campaign as a success but privately felt it had fallen far short of its goal to chastise the Indians, who continued to raid through the area, largely with impunity.

See also: Carleton, Gen. James Henry; Carson, Christopher Houston (Kit); Comanches; Kiowas; Navajos
Further Reading: Fehrenbach, *Comanches;* Leckie, *The Military Conquest of the Southern Plains*

Adobe Walls, Second Battle of
27 June 1874

The second fight at Adobe Walls was part of the Red River, or Buffalo, War of 1874. The Treaty of Medicine Lodge (1867) had set aside a large part of the Texas Panhandle exclusively for Indian use. In violation of this treaty hide-hunters from Dodge City, Kansas, moved into the area to take advantage of the large buffalo herd found there. The hunters were accompanied by traders and merchants who established a small settlement on the site of the old Bent–St. Vrain trading post. In 1864 the site, so called because walls from the original structure were still standing, had been the scene of a fight between a large force of Comanches and an army column led by Col. Kit Carson.

The Indians, already upset at the increasing toll taken on the buffalo herd by hide-hunters, as well as at white horse thieves who raided their pony herds, were further angered by the nonarrival of their regular annuities, delayed by weather. At this time an Indian prophet appeared named Ee-shatai, or Isa-Tai (literally, "coyote droppings"), who declared that he had special powers to protect Indians from the white man's bullets. Given the bellicose mood of the moment, Isa-Tai was able to unite the Comanches and introduce them to the sun dance, a long-standing religious ceremony of the northern Plains tribes, but one that had not previously been part of Comanche tradition.

Accordingly, after four days of intense religious preparation a large war party set out to attack the hunters' settlement at Adobe Walls. The principal leader of the war party was renowned war chief Quanah Parker, the son of a Comanche chief, Nawkohnee, and a white woman, Cynthia Ann Parker, who had been taken captive by the Comanches about 1835.

The Comanches launched their attack on Adobe Walls near dawn on 27 June 1874. Inside the settlement were 28 hunters and one woman. Despite overwhelming numbers, the attackers were held off by the accurate shooting of the buffalo hunters, who were armed with long-range Sharps .50-caliber rifles, with which they inflicted many Indian casualties. The Indians chose not to rush the settlement, which they probably could have easily overrun. Disillusioned by the failure of Isa-Tai's medicine to protect them and by the unexpectedly accurate return fire, the Indians were eventually driven off. In fact one hunter, Billy Dixon, well known as a crack shot, hit an Indian seated on his horse some 1,500 yards away; as it turned out, the victim was next to Isa-Tai.

The second fight at Adobe Walls, although not decisive one way or the other, foreshadowed several months of hard fighting and campaigning before hostilities on the Southern Plains were resolved.

See also: Parker, Quanah; Red River War; Treaties and Agreements, Medicine Lodge, Treaty of
Further Reading: Dixon, *Life of Billy Dixon;* Fehrenbach, *Comanches;* Leckie, *The Military Conquest of the Southern Plains*

Alexander
See Wamsutta (Alexander)

Algonquian

One of the principal linguistic divisions of North American Indians, the Algonquian family was large in number and geographically extensive. At one time its member tribes ranged northward from Virginia to Canada along the Atlantic Coast and westward beyond the Mississippi. Algonquian-speaking tribes were the first to have contact with the early English settlements in Virginia and Massachusetts. The Algonquian family included the Delawares, Ottawas, Sauks and Foxes, Shawnees, Kickapoos, Wyandots, and Potawatomis.

See also: specific tribes
Further Reading: Debo, *A History of the Indians of the United States*

Allen, Samuel, Jr.

Samuel Allen Jr. served as an example that not every person captured by Indians found it to be a disagreeable experience. Allen was captured in an August 1746 raid on Deerfield, Massachusetts, during King George's War. Taken to Canada, he took to the Indian way of life, and after nearly two years of captivity he was repatriated—against his will. Years later he recalled this episode with the Indians as the happiest period of his life.

See also: King George's War
Further Reading: Axelrod, *Chronicle of the Indian Wars;* Leach, *Arms for Empire*

Alliances, Indian-White

War among Indian tribes was an established practice long before the appearance of whites, but the arrival of European powers in North America altered the balance of power considerably. Smaller tribes soon found that by allying themselves with the English they were better able to defend themselves against powerful and aggressive neighbors—particularly if they were able to acquire firearms. However, Indian-white alliances were complex and unstable arrangements at best. The quid pro quo was to help your own cause by aiding the group who could best help you at the moment. For whites and Indians, alliances offered a strengthening of military capability, economic betterment through trade, and certain assurances of territorial integrity.

Some tribes, such as the Hurons, fiercely resented the English and their permanent settlements and so allied with the French, who were less interested in planting colonies than in harvesting fur. Without question, the French and Indian War was the most savage and brutal example of Indians allying against one another as well as Europeans. Indian-white alliances were common as white settlements marched westward. Pawnees, hereditary enemies of the Sioux, fought with white soldiers against their old enemies, as did Crows and Shoshones. Apache scouts tracked Apache raiders, and Tonkawas fought with the cavalry against their enemies, the Comanches.

See also: Apache Wars; Horseshoe Bend, Battle of; Sioux War (All are examples of campaigns and battles in which Indian alliances played an important role.)
Further Reading: Dowd, *A Spirited Resistance;* Hoxie, *Parading through History;* Steele, *Warpaths;* Worcester, *The Apaches*

Amherst's Decree
1761

In February 1761 Gen. Jeffrey Amherst, commander of British forces in North America, refused to perpetuate the longstanding practice of issuing gifts, especially powder and lead, to Indian leaders when they visited a fort or outpost. The practice, seen by most as a needed diplomatic gesture of good faith, was viewed by Amherst as excessive coddling and unnecessarily

Gen. Jeffrey Amherst

costly to the Crown. Amherst's Decree, which halted the practice of dispensing gifts to Indians, is considered by many historians to have been the act that eventually led to Pontiac's uprising.

See also: Pontiac's War/Rebellion/Uprising
Further Reading: Leach, *Arms for Empire;* Peckham, *Pontiac and the Indian Uprising*

Apache Pass, Battle of
15 July 1862

On 15 July 1862, a detachment of Union volunteers under the command of Capt. Thomas Roberts was ambushed by a large force of Apaches led by Cochise, Mangas Coloradas, and other prominent leaders. The ambush took place at Apache Pass in southeastern Arizona, east of present-day Willcox. Formerly a stop on the old Butterfield Stage Line, the pass was strategically located, and its fresh water springs made it important to travelers.

As Captain Roberts moved into the pass, his command came under fire from Indians positioned behind rocks and in gullies along both sides of the pass. Needing water, the troops were forced to fight their way to the springs. Although outnumbered, Roberts had two howitzers, which he used to shell the Indians out of their positions and eventually win the battle. As a result of the fight, Gen. James Henry Carleton, commanding the California Column, of which Roberts's force was a part, ordered that a fort be built on Apache Pass to help control the Apaches and to ensure travelers' access to the all-important springs. Fort Bowie, named for one of the officers in the column, became a pivotal post during the later Indian wars in the Southwest.

See also: Apache Wars; Carleton, Gen. James Henry; Cochise; Mangas Coloradas; Victorio
Further Reading: Sweeney, *Cochise*; Thrapp, *The Conquest of Apacheria*; Utley, *Frontiersmen in Blue*

Apache Wars

Anglo-European wars with the Apaches began early and were among the very last to end. For convenience, the Apache wars can be divided into two phases. The first phase, that with the Spanish, commenced in the seventeenth century and continued with the Mexicans after Spain's presence in the region had ended. Phase two involved hostilities with the United States.

The 1835 passage of a scalp bounty law by the Mexican state of Sonora in retaliation for Apache raids greatly exacerbated a situation that had worsened over the years. A bounty of 100 pesos (equal to 100 Yankee dollars) was offered for the scalp of an Apache warrior. Harmful enough in and of itself, the law was made still worse by unscrupulous bounty hunters who were not choosy about whose scalp they turned in. Many scalp hunters were American trappers whose ruthless participation in the hunting of Apaches, together with ill treatment of them by unscrupulous prospectors and traders, led to a steadily deteriorating relationship between Apaches and Americans. Probably the most prominent incident in this regard occurred about 1835, when a party of Missouri fur trappers—in company with a trader and scalp hunter named Johnson—betrayed and murdered the Mimbres Apache chief, Juan Jose Compa.

Geronimo and his warriors, 1886

During the next half-century on-again off-again hostilities marked the relationship between Apaches and Americans, who moved to the Southwest in steadily increasing numbers. In addition, the Apaches continued their traditional forays into Mexico, thereby aggravating the situation there. As a result of the Gadsden Treaty (1854) the United States officially acquired territory that comprises present-day Arizona and New Mexico. However, boundaries recognized by the United States and Mexico meant nothing to the Apaches, who continued to raid south of the border. These raids posed a political problem for the United States, who was obliged by virtue of the treaty to control Apache movements.

Under the leadership of such able warriors as Mangas Coloradas, Cochise, Juh, Nana, Victorio, and Geronimo, the Apaches struck fear throughout the Southwest. During the last half of the nineteenth century a number of peace agreements were signed, but none proved meaningfully effective. Unscrupulous traders and a vacillating peace policy on the part of the U.S. government created an adversarial climate. Incidents such as the Bascom Affair and the Camp Grant Massacre inflamed both sides and perpetuated hostilities. It was not until the surrender of Geronimo to Gen. Nelson A. Miles in September 1886 that the Apache wars finally came to an end.

See also: Bascom Affair; Camp Grant Massacre; Cochise; Crook, Gen. George; Geronimo; Mangas Coloradas; Miles, Gen. Nelson Appleton; Victorio
Further Reading: Thrapp, *The Conquest of Apacheria;* Worcester, *The Apaches*

Apaches

An Indian tribe of the American Southwest, the Apaches are members of the Athapascan linguistic family and are closely related to but distinct from Navajos. Apaches call themselves *Diné,* or "the people." The most notable Apaches lived in New Mexico, Arizona, and northwestern Mexico—*Apacheria,* as it was called. In addition, the related Kiowa Apaches and Lipans dwelled on the Southern Plains. The main tribal entities occupying the Southwest were divided into two basic groups: eastern and western. The eastern tribes were Jicarillas, Mescaleros, Mimbrenos, Mogollones, and Chiricahuas; western tribes included Tontos, Coyoteros, and Pinalones. The basic tribal groupings were further divided into smaller bands and sub-bands.

The Apaches seem to have been present in the Southwest since at least the seventeenth century. They developed a reputation as fierce warriors to whom raiding, particularly in Mexico, was part of life. Of all the Indian foes the U.S. Army had to contend with, the Apaches may have been the most difficult.

See also: Apache Wars; Bascom Affair; *specific leaders, e.g.,* Cochise, Geronimo, Mangas Coloradas, Victorio
Further Reading: Thrapp, *The Conquest of Apacheria;* Worcester, *The Apaches*

Arapahos

An Indian tribe belonging to the Algonquian linguistic family, the Arapahos are closely related to the Cheyennes. A small tribe, the Arapahos numbered approximately 3,000 during the nineteenth century. They migrated west from the woodlands of Minnesota to the region drained by the South Platte River, where they were located when the whites moved across the Great Plains. Like other Plains tribes, the Arapahos were converted by the acquisition of the horse to a seminomadic people dependent on buffalo to sustain their way of life.

During the Indian War of 1864–1865, while most Union troops were fighting the Civil War back east, Cheyenne and Arapaho war parties raided throughout southwestern Nebraska and northwestern Kansas. The Treaty of Medicine Lodge (1867) placed many of the Arapahos on a new reservation in Indian Territory, but dissatisfaction with the location and the failure of the U.S. government to fulfill the treaty's terms soon caused many Arapahos to go on the warpath.

During the 1870s some Arapahos farther north continued their militancy, joining with Sioux and Cheyennes to resist white efforts to subjugate them. After the Indian coalition that defeated Custer on the Little Bighorn in June 1876 dissolved, about 1,000 Arapahos were placed on the Wind River Reservation in Wyoming; others were re-relocated to Oklahoma.

See also: Cheyennes; Indian War (1867–1869); Sioux War
Further Reading: Trenholm and Carley, *The Arapahoes*

Arikaras

An Indian tribe belonging to the Caddoan linguistic family, the Arikaras are closely related to the Pawnees. By the seventeenth century they lived in the Missouri River valley in present-day North Dakota and South Dakota. Although at one time they were a numerous people, their population was drastically reduced by a smallpox epidemic about 1780. They were among the first tribes encountered by Lewis and Clark on their western expedition in 1804.

Traditional enemies of the Sioux, the Arikaras, or Rees, as they were sometimes known, furnished scouts to the U.S. Army during the Indian wars on the northern Plains. Custer's favorite scout was said to have been Bloody Knife, who was killed with Reno's detachment during the Battle of the Little Bighorn.

See also: Custer, Lt. Col. George Armstrong; Sioux War
Further Reading: Debo, *History of the Indians of the United States*; Hodge, *Handbook of American Indians*; Innis, *Bloody Knife*

Artillery

During the Indian wars of the colonial period, forts and defensive bastions nearly always featured one or more cannons for use as defensive weapons. Their weight and size, however, made it difficult to employ them in the field against Indians.

By the nineteenth century, however, artillery had become more mobile, and so army columns often carried several field pieces on Indian campaigns. In the West the mountain howitzer proved most adaptable. Capable of firing a 9-pound shell nearly a mile, it was often used with great effective-ness against Indians. At the Battle of Apache Pass in 1862 Union artillery meant the difference between victory and defeat.

See also: Apache Pass, Battle of; Connor's Powder River Expedition
Further Reading: Hafen, *Powder River Campaigns;* Leach, *Arms for Empire;* Utley, *Frontiersmen in Blue*

Athapascan

One of the principal linguistic divisions among North American Indians, the Athapascan family includes many of the southwestern tribes, including several of the Apache bands and Navajos, as well as a number of Alaskan tribes.

Further Reading: Debo, *History of the Indians of the United States*

Atkinson, Gen. Henry
1782–1842

Born in North Carolina, Henry Atkinson was commissioned a captain in the Third Infantry in 1808; during the next six years he rose to the rank of colonel. In 1815 and again in 1825 he organized and led expeditions to the Yellowstone country. From 1826 until the time of his death in 1842 he was involved in the pacification and removal of the Winnebagos and the Sauks and Foxes from Wisconsin to Iowa. During the spring and summer of 1832 Atkinson led the campaign against Black Hawk, which culminated in the Battle of Bad Axe on 2 August. Fort Atkinson, Iowa, is named for Henry Atkinson.

See also: Bad Axe, Battle of; Black Hawk; Black Hawk War
Further Reading: Nichols, *General Henry Atkinson*

Augur, Gen. Christopher Columbus
1821–1898

Born in New York, Augur's family moved to Michigan, from which state he entered West Point in 1839, graduating in 1843. After service in the Mexican War he was stationed on the western frontier, seeing action against Yakimas and Rogue Indians in Washington and Oregon during the 1850s. During the first months of the Civil War Augur served as commandant of cadets at West Point, followed by two years of field service during which he suffered a severe wound at the Battle of Cedar Mountain. During the last part of the Civil War he commanded the Department of Washington and ended the war with a fine record.

From 1867 to 1871 he commanded the Department of the Platte; he commanded the Department of Texas from 1871 to 1874. He played key roles in the treaties of Medicine Lodge (1867) and Fort Laramie (1868). Unlike some of his contemporaries, Augur was not a high-profile military figure but was known throughout the army as an able soldier.

See also: Indian War (1867–1869); Treaties and Agreements, Fort Laramie, Treaty of; Treaties and Agreements, Medicine Lodge, Treaty of
Further Reading: Utley, *Frontier Regulars*

B

Bacon's Rebellion
1676–1677

A controversial episode in Virginia history, Bacon's Rebellion was actually an outgrowth of the Indian War of 1675–1676, which began as a dispute between some Maryland Nanticoke (Doeg) Indians and a Virginia planter named Thomas Mathew. Convinced that the planter had cheated them, the Indians murdered him, thereby triggering reprisals from both sides, including an accidental attack on a friendly Susquehannock village, which was actually a pallisaded settlement located on Piscataway Creek and called Fort Piscataway. This attack, known as the siege of Fort Piscataway, was carried out by Virginia militia and caused the death of five Susquehannock chiefs under a flag of truce.

A full-scale investigation was immediately launched by Virginia's governor, William Berkeley, who feared that the situation might escalate into a broader conflict like King Philip's War, then raging in New England. Berkeley addressed the crisis by adopting a defensive strategy, which included constructing a series of forts into which colonists could retire when threatened. Berkeley also prohibited unauthorized campaigns against the Indians, a departure from the more aggressive posture he adopted during the Powhatan War. Berkeley drew the ire of many colonists with this order forbidding independent campaigns, which some chose to ignore regardless. This set the stage for one Nathaniel Bacon, a wealthy young planter from Henrico County and member of the Virginia Council who was related to the governor by marriage.

In the spring of 1676 Bacon presented himself to the governor in Jamestown, requesting a commission and offering to lead an expedition against the Indians. The request was denied, but Bacon nevertheless organized and led a force of 200 against some alleged Susquehannock raiders. Unsuccessful in locating his quarry, Bacon then entered an alliance of sorts with some Occaneechees who offered to attack their old enemy, the Susquehannocks. They subsequently did, capturing some 30 in the process. After torturing the Susquehannocks Bacon suddenly turned on the Occaneechees, apparently in a dispute over captured booty, killing 50 while losing 12 himself. As a result, Berkeley declared Bacon to be in rebellion and removed him from the Virginia Council. Notwithstanding his public censure, Bacon savored the adulation accorded a popular hero.

Although he had been elected to the new Virginia Council, Bacon was captured by Berkeley and persuaded to admit the error of his ways, whereupon he was pardoned. Berkeley's victory, however, was only temporary, because Bacon returned to Jamestown in June accompanied by 500 followers. Confronted by this show of support for Bacon, Berkeley reluctantly issued him a commission. Now backed by the force of a coerced commission, Bacon launched a campaign against area Indians, even attacking a village of friendly Pamunkeys, killing many. Although Bacon's ruthless and indiscriminate behavior was supported by some council members who favored enslaving the Indians, Governor Berkeley repudiated the act and repealed Bacon's commission. Learning of the governor's action against him, Bacon returned and laid siege to Jamestown. Using hostages, he forced Berkeley out of the stockaded settlement and into exile on Virginia's Eastern Shore, then put Jamestown to the torch.

In October Bacon succumbed to the effects of dysentery, and without his leadership the movement lost much of its impetus. By January Berkeley had mustered enough support to end what was left of the rebellion. Bacon's leaders were executed and their property confiscated. Any servant who was found guilty of aiding the rebellion had his term of indenture extended.

The effects of Bacon's uprising were far-reaching. For all practical purposes, the Occaneechees ceased to be a presence of any importance in the area, and as a consequence the Virginia settlements now had direct access to the Cherokee villages to the south. The rebellion also prompted an inquiry that subsequently resulted in Berkeley's dismissal as governor. In 1676 the Virginia Council had authorized the sale of Indian lands to underwrite the cost of the war and also sanctioned the sale and enslavement of Indians. These laws were repealed by the Treaty of Middle Plantation (1677).

See also: Berkeley, Gov. Sir William; Jamestown, Virginia; King Philip's War; Susquehannock War; Susquehannocks (Susquehannas); Treaties and Agreements, Middle Plantation, Treaty of
Further Reading: Axelrod, *Chronicle of the Indian Wars;* Steele, *Warpaths*

Bad Axe, Battle of
1 August 1832

Fleeing westward across southern Wisconsin to escape the pursuing troops under Gen. Henry Atkinson, a band of Sauks (Sac) and Foxes—called the "British band" to distinguish them from others who were pro-American—reached the confluence of the Bad Axe and Mississippi Rivers near present-day Victory, Wisconsin. The Indians intended to escape across the Mississippi but, lacking boats, were forced to build rafts, a time-consuming process that tribal leader Black Hawk counseled against, advising instead that they head north and try to hide among the Winnebagos. Overruled by the majority, Black Hawk, with a few followers, headed upriver while the others set about constructing rafts.

While the rafts were being built the steamboat *Warrior* arrived with a compliment of troops aboard. Given little choice, the Indians tried to surrender, but their offer was misunderstood by the commander of the troops, who opened fire, initiating the battle. By the time the *Warrior* was forced to withdraw two hours later because of lack of fuel some 23 Indians had been killed. Other Indians managed somehow to escape across the river just before General Atkinson's troops arrived to initiate a second attack. In the melee it was difficult to distinguish warriors from noncombatants, and by the time the second phase of the fight had ended about 150 Indians lay dead; nearly half that number were taken prisoner. Army losses were low.

The Sauks and Foxes who did reach the west bank of the Mississippi River fared no better, as they were soon attacked by Sioux war parties. Black Hawk himself was later captured and imprisoned.

See also: Atkinson, Gen. Henry; Black Hawk; Dodge, Col. Henry
Further Reading: Jackson, *Black Hawk;* Prucha, *Sword of the Republic*

Baker's Attack on the Piegans
23 January 1870

Pres. Ulysses S. Grant's peace policy, introduced in 1869, was barely in place when two squadrons of the Second Cavalry under Maj. Eugene Baker struck a Piegan village on the Marias River in northern Montana. The surprise attack resulted in the destruction of the village and the deaths of some 173 Piegans, including more than 50 women and children. Baker's rationale for the attack was to punish the Piegans, a tribe of the Blackfoot Confederacy, for past raids and depredations. Fully aware of the plan to attack the village, Lt. Gen. Philip H. Sheridan, commanding the Military Division of the Missouri, had ordered Baker to "strike them hard." Like the

Fleeing bands of Sauk and Fox Indians were caught and attacked by American troops in Wisconsin, resulting in the Battle of Bad Axe.

massacres at Sand Creek and Camp Grant, Baker's attack on the Piegans produced considerable controversy and derailed the plan to have army officers serve as Indian agents.

See also: Blackfoot; Peace Policy, President Grant's
Further Reading: Ege, *Tell Baker to Strike Them Hard*; Utley, *Frontier Regulars*; Welch, *Killing Custer*

Bannock War
1878

The Bannocks living near the Fort Hall agency in southeastern Idaho had become restless during the Nez Perce uprising and soon found cause for their own rebellion. In the spring of 1878 settlers' livestock had destroyed much of the Camas Prairie of southeastern Idaho, an area favored by the Bannocks and other tribes for its abundance of Camas roots, an important dietary ingredient. Thus, when the Bannocks arrived to harvest roots that spring they were angered to discover the damage that had been done to the area by grazing livestock. Two white men were killed, setting the stage for an armed clash.

Most of the other tribes who had come to the area—Paiutes, Lemhis, and Umatillas—quickly returned to their agencies. However, the Bannocks, under Buffalo Horn, a young war chief who had previously given excellent service as a scout for the army, concluded that they might as well strike back to redress past wrongs since they were certain to be punished for killing the two white men. Raiding across southern Idaho, the Bannocks killed some ten whites before a fight at Silver City on 8 June 1878, resulted in the death of Buffalo Horn. Despite the loss of their leader the Bannocks, now led by chief Egan, continued west to Oregon's Steens Mountain. Here, prior efforts to draw Paiutes into the Bannock fold paid dividends when a band of Paiutes bolted from Malheur Reservation to join them, swelling the number of warriors to 500.

Just as he had the previous year against the Nez Perce, Gen. O. O. Howard, commanding the Department of Columbia, promptly organized a force to move against the recalcitrants. A troop of the First Cavalry commanded by Capt. Reuben Bernard, a veteran and very capable Indian fighter, had already been in pursuit of the hostiles, reaching a sheep ranch on the Jordan River when General Howard arrived to take personal command. In the meantime, Sarah Winnemucca, daughter of a Paiute chief, volunteered to act as emissary, an offer that Captain Bernard accepted. However, the hostiles were so fired up that Sarah and her followers barely escaped with their lives.

Although Howard had issued mobilization orders for troops throughout the department, his immediate superior, Gen. Irvin McDowell, commanding the Department of Pacific, directed Howard to first try to resolve the problem by negotiation. Howard now approached Steens Mountain with three columns of troops only to discover that the Indians had moved on to Silver Creek, where Captain Bernard located them and attacked with three companies of cavalry on 23 June. As Bernard's horsemen swept through the village, the Indians retreated to steep bluffs across the creek. Bernard chose not to pursue, and the Indians managed to

escape after nightfall. Although his quarry had escaped, Bernard must have known that his destruction of the village and its supplies had been a blow to the Indians.

Howard resumed the pursuit with a mixed force of 500 infantry and cavalry. Bernard's horsemen led the advance through rugged country drained by the John Day River, pursuing the hostiles all the way to the Blue Mountains. In the meantime, Bernard had augmented his force with troops drawn from posts to the north and now commanded seven companies of cavalry, despite the fact that an officer of his rank would normally command only a single company (Bernard had earned the brevet rank of colonel during the Civil War).

On 8 July scouts located the hostiles strongly positioned on Birch Creek near Pilot Butte, the slopes of which Howard later described as steeper than Missionary Ridge, the site of an important battle during the Civil War. Bernard's troopers nevertheless stormed the heights and eventually drove the Indians from their positions. Horses and men were exhausted, however, and Bernard was unable to offer immediate pursuit.

The Indians now headed south, eventually pursued by Howard and Bernard's rested cavalry. Suddenly reversing course, however, the hostiles turned north toward the Umatilla Reservation and a possible rendezvous with the Umatillas, who until now had remained largely neutral. Howard responded quickly to this threat. A column of 500 men under Capt. Evan Miles reached the Umatilla Reservation ahead of the hostiles, now led by Oytes following the death of Egan on 22 June.

On 13 July Miles's command engaged the hostiles in a sharp, all-day battle that was observed by the Umatillas, who were dressed for war but had apparently elected to defer joining the hostiles, depending on the outcome of this fight. Although the hostiles had initiated the attack, the troops eventually carried the day, driving them back into the mountains. Later, the Umatillas came in to negotiate a settlement with the army.

During the next two weeks the army skirmished frequently with the hostiles, but rough country prevented a decisive engagement from taking place. Tired of fighting, the Paiutes split off, but the Bannocks continued on, raiding settlements as they fled from the pursuing troops. Like the Nez Perce had done earlier, the Bannocks soon sought the safety of Canada. At this juncture troops under the command of Col. Nelson A. Miles, who had been victorious in the fight with the Nez Perce, intercepted the Bannocks east of Yellowstone Park and drove them back. On 12 September, in a final engagement, the Bannocks were defeated, bringing the war to an end.

Many of the original group that had followed Buffalo Horn were now gone, and only 131 surrendered. After being held as temporary prisoners through the winter of 1878–1879 they were returned to their agency at Fort Hall.

See also: Buffalo Horn; Howard, Gen. Oliver Otis; Miles, Gen. Nelson Appleton
Further Reading: Arnold, *The Indian Wars of Idaho;* Corless, *The Weiser Indians;* Howard, *My Life and Experiences among Our Hostile Indians;* Russell, *One Hundred and Three Fights and Scrimmages*

Barbancito
ca. 1820–1871

A Navajo subchief, Barbancito was noted for a fine singing voice and his ability as a speaker. This latter gift no doubt proved an asset in his efforts to reach a harmonious relationship with the whites. During the 1850s he met several times with white representatives, seeking to establish an acceptable peace treaty. Mostly, these efforts produced little success. Raids and counterraids persisted. In 1860 Barbancito was wounded in a skirmish with New Mexican volunteers.

In 1861 Barbancito reluctantly signed a treaty that severely restricted his tribe's activities but that, not surprisingly, did little to end Navajo raids. During Kit Carson's 1864 campaign that penetrated the remote vastness of Canyon de Chelly, Barbancito's band was the last to surrender. Following the Navajos' infamous Long Walk and internment at Bosque Redondo, Barbancito escaped but was subsequently captured and returned to the hated place in eastern New Mexico. When a new treaty was proposed in 1868 that allowed the Navajos to return to their homeland, Barbancito was among the first to sign, even though he was not a head chief. Barbancito died at Canyon de Chelly three years later.

See also: Canby's Campaign; Canyon de Chelly, Arizona; Carleton, Gen. James Henry; Carson, Christopher Houston (Kit)
Further Reading: L. Kelly, *Navajo Roundup;* McNitt, *Navajo Wars*

Bascom Affair
February 1861

A tragic event resulting from a misunderstanding, the Bascom Affair was important to the history of Indian-white relations in Arizona. In the fall of 1860 a band of Coyotero Apaches captured the stepson of an Arizona rancher named John Ward, as well as some of Ward's livestock. The army, however, was unable to send troops to investigate the incident until January 1861, when a detachment under the command of Lt. George Bascom was sent from Fort Buchanan in southwestern New Mexico. Bascom's orders were to proceed to Apache Pass, near present-day Willcox, Arizona, and to demand the return of the boy and the livestock from Cochise, a Chiricahua leader who—mistakenly, as it turned out—was believed to be responsible.

At a parley with Bascom held at the Butterfield Overland Stage station, Cochise said he was not holding the boy or the livestock and categorically denied having been involved in the incident. Dissatisfied with this explanation, Bascom took five Apache hostages including Cochise, who later managed to escape. In retaliation Cochise captured an employee of the stage station, whom he offered to release in exchange for the Apache hostages. Bascom, however, refused to release the hostages without the boy and the livestock. Cochise then laid siege to the stage station's corral for a week. Additionally, he blocked Apache Pass, through which ran the main east-west route to California. He also attacked a stagecoach and wagon train, burning the teamsters to death. Two relief columns reached the scene several days later only to discover that after executing the hostage Cochise had crossed the border into Mexico. Returning to Fort Buchanan, the troops found the burned bodies of the teamsters and summarily hung several of their Chiricahua hostages in retaliation.

The Bascom Affair, as it came to be known, was an incident upon which the course of future events would hinge. It severely undermined Apache-white relations, and 25 years of bloody warfare would ensue as a result.

See also: Apache Wars; Cochise
Further Reading: Sweeney, *Cochise;* Utley, *Frontiersmen in Blue;* Worcester, *The Apaches*

Bear Paw Mountains, Battle of
30 September–5 October 1877

The Battle of Bear Paw Mountains marked the dramatic conclusion of the long-running fight with the Nez Perce Indians and their epic flight for freedom. After successfully maneuvering their way to the threshold of the U.S.-Canada border—some 1,200 miles from their Oregon-Idaho homeland—and defeating U.S. Army columns on three separate occasions, the Nez Perce were finally caught, surrounded, and forced to surrender—though not until after a fierce fight in which they inflicted heavy casualties on their attackers.

The Nez Perce were pursued by troops under Gen. O. O. Howard who, fearing his quarry would elude him without assistance, telegraphed Col. Nelson A. Miles of the Fifth Infantry at Fort Keogh, Montana (later Miles City), requesting his help. Miles promptly took after the Nez Perce with a strong column. The Nez Perce, meanwhile, believing they were far enough ahead of their pursuers, slowed their desperate sprint for the border and made camp on the north end of

the Bear Paw Mountains, about 40 miles from Canada.

On the clear, cold morning of 30 September Miles launched a surprise attack on the village. A detachment of the Seventh Cavalry under Capt. Owen Hale charged directly on the Nez Perce camp while a detachment of the Second Cavalry under Capt. George Tyler went after the pony herd. After overcoming brisk resistance, Tyler's troopers managed to capture most of the horses, but Nez Perce warriors, finding strong defensive positions along the stream banks and numerous gullies, inflicted heavy casualties on Hale's men. A high number of officers and noncoms were hit, forcing Miles to reluctantly call off the assault.

Given the fierce resistance and the high number of casualties he had suffered, Miles elected to lay siege. During the next five days the troops and Indians exchanged desultory fire, to which was added the occasional salvo from Miles's single field piece. Finally, on 5 October, their supplies nearly gone and having suffered many casualties, the Nez Perce elected to surrender. It was in accepting the terms offered by Miles that the Nez Perce leader, Joseph, made this famous statement: "From where the sun now stands, I will fight no more forever." Although most of the Nez Perce surrendered, a few escaped across the border into Canada.

See also: Howard, Gen. Oliver Otis; Joseph; Kelly, Luther S. (Yellowstone); Looking Glass; Miles, Gen. Nelson Appleton; Nez Perce
Further Reading: M. Brown, *The Flight of the Nez Perce;* Hampton, *Children of Grace*

Bear River, Battle of
27 January 1863

During the Civil War, as large battles raged east of the Mississippi River, military commanders in the far western territories were compelled to address increasing Indian attacks, often with fewer resources than their better-supplied counterparts back east. To punish Indian raiders for depredations committed against travelers on the trails to Oregon and California and the Montana gold camps further north, Col. Patrick Edward Connor, a Mexican War veteran, launched a midwinter campaign against the Bannocks and Shoshones. In brutally cold weather Connor marched out of Fort Douglas, Utah, at the head of some 300 cavalry and aiming to strike the village of Bear Hunter, believed to be located on the Bear River about 150 miles north of Salt Lake City.

Finding the village early on 23 January, Connor started his command across the Bear River's icy waters. Once across, the advance elements charged the village, which was located in a large, deep ravine into which the Indians had cut steps. From their prepared positions the Indians quickly threw back the initial attack, inflicting heavy casualties in the process. At this juncture Connor, having now reached the opposite shore, elected to move against the village on both flanks. From the ravine's heights the troops were able to pour a deadly fire down upon the defenders.

Although their prepared positions had initially served them well, the Indians found they now had no escape. Soon the fight was carried out at close quarters, with many on both sides killed in hand-to-hand combat. By midmorning the battle was over. Connor's troops reportedly counted in excess of 200 Indian bodies, including that of Bear Hunter. Army casualties were also high, though far less than those of the Indians. Because of the high number of Indian casualties and the fact that many were thought to have been killed unnecessarily, the battle is sometimes referred to as the Bear River Massacre.

The affair was considered an important victory to an army that had difficulty keeping open routes of travel in the western territories. For his part in the Battle of Bear River, Connor was promoted to brigadier general.

See also: Connor, Gen. Patrick Edward; Shoshones (Shoshonis)
Further Reading: Hunt, *Army of the Pacific*; Madsen, *The Shoshoni Frontier*; Utley, *Frontiersmen in Blue*

Beaver Wars

The so-called Beaver Wars were a continuing series of conflicts that spanned nearly five decades in the middle of the seventeenth century. The lure of firearms and iron goods that could be had from European traders in exchange for fur pelts, especially beaver, pitted Indian against Indian in a bloody struggle for control of a beaver supply that would soon be exhausted in the New England region. On one side was the Iroquois Confederacy (the Five Nations), which aligned against the Hurons, Tobaccos, Eries, Ottawas, Mahicans, Illinois, Miami, Susquehannocks, Nipissings, Potawatomis, Delawares, and Sokokis.

Although strictly speaking this was a running war among Indian tribes, it had its roots in the European impact on the Indians' culture and way of life. Tribal competition for fur created an adversarial situation that led to war, which in turn was instrumental in establishing a balance of power among Indian tribes that would play an important role in future conflicts involving European powers.

See also: Dutch; England; France; Iroquois Confederacy
Further Reading: Jennings, *The Invasion of America*; Steele, *Warpaths*

Beecher Island, Battle of
17–25 September 1868

The Battle of Beecher Island was one of the celebrated events of the western Indian wars. In an effort to counter increasing Indian raids in the Central and Southern Plains, Lt. Gen. Philip H. Sheridan, limited by the number of regular army troops at his disposal, authorized a member of his staff, Maj. George A. (Sandy) Forsyth, to organize a company of civilian scouts to fight Indians.

Forsyth, a Civil War veteran, encountered little difficulty enlisting men anxious to join his elite company, and he soon filled his quota of 50. Most, though not all, were experienced frontiersmen, and some were veterans of the Civil War. Each man was armed with a 7-shot Spencer breech-loading carbine and a Colt revolver. For those who furnished their own horse the pay was $75 per month, $50 if the army provided the animal.

Forsyth's second in command was young Lt. Frederick H. Beecher, nephew of the famous abolitionist Henry Ward Beecher.

On 29 August Forsyth's Scouts marched out of Fort Hays, Kansas. On 14 September they picked up a large Indian trail, which they followed up the Republican River valley in northeastern Colorado. On the evening of 16 September the scouts camped along the Arickaree Fork of the Republican, near present-day Wray, Colorado. At dawn on 17 September the scouts were attacked by a large war party of Cheyennes, Dog Soldiers, Sioux, and Arapahos.

At the outset of the fighting the scouts took up a defensive position on a spit of land about 75 yards by 30 yards in the mostly dry riverbed. After surviving the first assault the men feverishly scooped holes in the sandy earth using cups, knives, or whatever was handy. Using their Spencers, the scouts repulsed several more assaults but suffered heavy casualties; Forsyth was wounded three times. The company's surgeon, J. H. Mooers, and young Lieutenant Beecher were both killed. To honor the fallen officer the site would thereafter be known as Beecher Island. Among the Indians, the prominent Cheyenne war chief Roman Nose had also taken a fatal wound.

After the first day's fighting the Indians laid siege to the island, cutting off escape, which would have been all but impossible anyway because the Indians had run off or killed the scouts' horses. The eight days that followed became an unforgettable ordeal—for the survivors. Reduced to eating whatever they could find, including the flesh of dead horses, and with the wounded suffering terribly, Forsyth's men continued to hold off their attackers. In an effort to get help Forsyth called for volunteers and separately sent three pairs of scouts to Fort Wallace, some 100 miles distant. The second pair was unable to get through the Indian lines and was forced to return to the island. The first pair of scouts, Jack Stillwell and Pierre Trudeau, eventually got through to report the plight of Forsyth's command, as did Jack Donovan and Allison Pliley.

On 25 September, after a nine-day ordeal, Forsyth's scouts were relieved by a column of buffalo soldiers from the Tenth Cavalry at Fort Wallace under the command of Forsyth's one-time Civil War comrade, Capt. Louis Carpenter. The scouts had survived—but only barely. Forsyth's casualties amounted to five killed and 18 wounded. Estimates of Indian losses are contradictory, with one report stating as few as nine. Although many of the scouts were experienced Indian fighters and had given a good account of themselves, Sheridan's idea had certainly not produced the kind of results he had envisioned at the outset, and as a result he abandoned the concept of enlisting companies of civilian scouts.

See also: Forsyth, Maj. George Alexander (Sandy); Indian War (1867–1869)

Further Reading: Grinnell, *The Fighting Cheyennes;* Monnett, *The Battle of Beecher Island;* White, *Hostiles and Horse Soldiers*

Benteen, Capt. Frederick William
1834–1898

A Virginian by birth, Frederick Benteen was appointed a lieutenant in the Tenth Missouri Cavalry in 1861 and served with distinction throughout the Civil War, reaching the brevet rank of lieutenant colonel by 1865. After the war Benteen chose to remain in the army and was appointed captain in the Seventh Cavalry, the regiment he would be associated with thereafter. His general dislike of George Armstrong Custer, the de facto commander of the regiment, became intense after the Battle of the Washita. Benteen believed Custer had abandoned, without just cause, a detachment under Maj. Joel Elliott that was subsequently wiped out.

At the Battle of the Little Bighorn, Benteen's role, along with that of Maj. Marcus Reno, came under intense criticism. Both officers have been vilified by Custer supporters for failing to support the ill-fated battalion, thereby ensuring its ultimate destruction.

In 1877 Benteen saw action against the Nez Perce. He was later transferred to the

Ninth Cavalry. In 1882 he was charged with drunkenness. A court-martial sentenced him to dismissal from the army, but Pres. Chester Arthur reduced the sentence to suspension. He retired in 1888 and died ten years later.

See also: Custer, Lt. Col. George Armstrong; Little Bighorn, Battle of the (Custer's Last Stand); Reno, Maj. Marcus Albert (Alfred); Washita, Battle of the
Further Reading: Graham, *The Custer Myth;* Mills, *Harvest of Barren Regrets;* Utley, *Cavalier in Buckskin*

Berkeley, Gov. Sir William
1606–1677

Sir William Berkeley was governor of the Virginia Colony twice (1642–1652, 1660–1677). He was not always appreciated by some colonists, who felt he favored large tobacco planters. Berkeley employed harsh measures to bring the Powhatan War to an end, launching a series of strikes against the tribes of the Powhatan Confederacy. He personally was involved in the capture of the aged chief Opechancanough, whose hatred and mistrust of the English had fueled the fires of resistance for nearly three decades.

After serving as governor for a decade, Berkeley was supplanted in 1652, becoming one of several royal officials to be replaced during the English civil war. However, in 1660 he was restored to office by a new administration. During his two terms as governor, which spanned an often violent and unsettled period of Virginia's early history, Berkeley was closely involved in wars with the Dutch and the Indian War of 1675–1676. He also played a key role in Bacon's Rebellion, the event for which he is perhaps best remembered. In 1676 he was relieved of the governorship at his request and returned to England, where he died the following year.

See also: Bacon's Rebellion; Opechancanough; Powhatan War; Susquehannock War
Further Reading: Jennings, *The Invasion of America;* Steele, *Warpaths*

Big Bend, Battle of
12 May 1860

One of two engagements of the Paiute War, the Battle of Big Bend came about as a result of an incident on the California Trail in Nevada's Carson Valley. When white traders kidnapped and raped two Indian girls, the Paiutes retaliated by attacking a stage station and killing five inhabitants. Fearing a major Indian war, angry miners organized an army drawn from various mining camps. This first effort petered out once the miners sobered up, but a second, under the command of Maj. William Ormsby, was more successful. Numbering about 100, the citizen army marched to Paiute country near Pyramid Lake. The Paiutes were not anxious for war but were nevertheless ready to defend themselves.

Using arrows tipped in poison the Paiutes ambushed the citizen army as it approached the Big Bend of the Truckee River, killing nearly half. Word of the incident spread, and the governor of California sent troops, which defeated the Paiutes near Pinnacle Mountain at the end of May, bringing the brief war to a close.

Further Reading: Paher, *Fort Churchill*

Big Hole, Battle of the
9 August 1877

During their epic flight from army troops the Nez Perce reached the Big Hole River in southwestern Montana on 6 August 1877. Believing they were temporarily safe from the pursuing soldiers, who were still far behind them, the Nez Perce decided to spend time there, resting up from the rigors of their flight. Unknown to the Indians, however, a second army column under Col. John Gibbon, commanding the District of Montana, was rapidly closing in. With a force of 150 troops from the Seventh Infantry, reinforced by 45 civilian volunteers, Gibbon reached the Big Hole Valley on 8 August, his approach unobserved.

At dawn on 9 August Gibbon attacked, catching the Indians completely by surprise, and in a short time he had taken control of the village. The Nez Perce, having at first fled in disorder at the surprise attack, rallied and began to fight back, forcing Gibbon's troops to retire from the village and take up a defensive position. Pinned down for several hours, the soldiers suffered heavy casualties from the accurate Indian fire. Gibbon himself was badly wounded. On the afternoon of 10 August the Nez Perce, having derailed the army's pursuit, resumed their flight, leaving a few warriors behind to worry Gibbon's soldiers.

By the following day the advance troops of Gen. O. O. Howard, whose command had been pursuing the Nez Perce across Idaho, arrived to relieve the besieged Gibbon, thereby bringing an official end to the fight. Army casualties amounted to 30 killed and 39 wounded. Estimates of Indian losses range from 40 to 80.

See also: Gibbon, Col. John; Howard, Gen. Oliver Otis; Nez Perce War
Further Reading: Brown, *The Flight of the Nez Perce*; Haines, *An Elusive Victory*; Hampton, *Children of Grace*

Birch Coulee, Battle of
2 September 1862

In the weeks following the bloody Sioux uprising in southern Minnesota in August 1862, an army of sorts—consisting mainly of home guards, volunteers, and others—was mobilized at Fort Ridgely under the command of Col. Henry Hastings Sibley. Sibley's orders from the new department commander, Gen. John Pope, were to punish the Sioux and secure the release of the captives they were holding.

On 31 August, advised that no Sioux were in the area, Sibley sent a detachment of 170 men from the Sixth Minnesota and the Cullen Guards. The former were under Capt. Hiram Grant; Capt. Joseph Anderson commanded the Cullen Guards. Overall command of the burial party was vested in Maj. Joseph Brown, a former Indian agent. The detachment's orders were to move upriver and bury victims, most of whom were still lying where they had been killed. Proceeding as ordered, the detachment moved up the river burying any bodies they came across, making camp for the night near Birch Coulee Creek.

On 1 September the command split. Brown, with the cavalry (Cullen Guards),

crossed the Minnesota River and continued along its south bank. Capt. Hiram Grant, with the Sixth Minnesota, remained on the north side. Both columns continued to find and bury a number of bodies. By evening the two forces had reunited and bivouacked near Birch Coulee, having buried some 54 bodies. Neither column had discovered any sign of Sioux, who were believed to have fallen back beyond Yellow Medicine River but in fact were much closer at hand than the troops realized.

At dawn on 2 September a strong force of Indians led by Mankato, Big Eagle, Red Legs, and others suddenly struck the camp. Taking good advantage of the surprise factor, the Indians raked the camp with a deadly fire. For their part, the troops rushed to create defensive positions. Most of the cavalry horses were killed early on, and the troops used the dead animals as barricades. Others dug in using any tool they could find. As the sound of the fight reached Fort Ridgely, Sibley immediately dispatched a relief column of 240 men, but as they approached the battle zone they too came under attack. Col. Samuel McPhail, commanding the relief force, quickly concluded that additional help was needed and so informed Sibley by courier.

Upon receipt of this distressing news, Sibley promptly marched out of Fort Ridgely with everything he had left—eight companies of infantry and some artillery. By midnight Sibley had reached McPhail's position, and at daylight the combined force moved to relieve Brown's command, which had been under siege for more than 30 hours without food and water. Sibley and McPhail finally reached Birch Coulee about noon after using artillery to disperse the Indians.

What had begun as a burial detail had unexpectedly evolved into the costliest battle of the Minnesota uprising for the army, which suffered casualties of 13 killed and 47 wounded.

See also: Little Crow; Minnesota Sioux Uprising; Sibley, Gen. Henry Hastings; Wood Lake, Battle of
Further Reading: Carley, *The Sioux Uprising of 1862*

Birch Creek, Battle of
8 July 1878

During the spring and early summer of 1878 some 200 Bannocks who had taken to raiding for perceived treaty violations fled pursuing army troops under the command of Gen. O. O. Howard. On 8 July Capt. Reuben Bernard, with seven companies of cavalry, located the Indians on Birch Creek and Pilot Butte, near present-day Pendleton, Oregon. The Indians were strongly positioned along the bluffs, the slopes of which "were steeper than those of Missionary Ridge," according to General Howard. Nevertheless, Bernard's troopers advanced up the slopes, driving the defenders still higher while taking heavy casualties. The Indians were finally defeated by a two-pronged flank attack that drove them from the field.

See also: Bannock War; Buffalo Horn; Howard, Gen. Oliver Otis
Further Reading: Brimlow, *The Bannock Indian War of 1878*; Russell, *One Hundred and Three Fights and Scrimmages*

Black Hawk
1767–1838

Black Hawk was a leader of the Sauks (or Sacs), known by his people as Ma-ka-tai-me-she-kia-kiak. He was born in what is now Illinois, somewhere near the Rock River confluence with the Mississippi. As a young man, Black Hawk won a reputation for bravery, and upon his father's death he inherited the elder's tribal responsibilities.

Black Hawk fought with Tecumseh on the British side during the War of 1812. A believer in Indian unity, he supported Tecumseh's efforts and tried in vain to forge a union among his own people. The Sauks and Foxes had split into two factions, however, one under Keokuk that was pro-American, the other under Black Hawk, which supported the British and was known as the "British band." Black Hawk and his followers were opposed to white expansion into areas regarded as Indian land, and since the British posed no threat in this direction the choice was relatively clear-cut.

Sauk brave Black Hawk

In 1832 Black Hawk led his people in the Black Hawk War, a conflict that lasted only 15 weeks but virtually ended his people's power as a tribal entity. Black Hawk himself was captured shortly after the end of the war and was imprisoned for a time in Fortress Monroe, Virginia. He was later released, and eventually he returned to Iowa after touring eastern cities. His autobiography was dictated to a French interpreter and published in 1833. The book was later edited and reissued by the University of Illinois Press in 1955.

See also: Black Hawk War; Sauks and Foxes
Further Reading: Jackson, *Black Hawk*

Black Hawk War
1832

The Black Hawk War was an outgrowth of the Treaty of 1804, in which the Sauks (sometimes known as Sacs) and Foxes conceded all of their land east of the Mississippi River for a small price. The Sauks were closely allied with the Mesquakie, whom the French erroneously called Fox. During the nineteenth century the United States often tried to deal with the two tribes as one entity, which led to confused and strained relations.

However, it was not until after the War of 1812, when southwestern Wisconsin and northeastern Illinois were opened to settlement, that trouble began to develop. As settlers began to move into the area, Black Hawk, a young Sauk warrior who had fought alongside Tecumseh in the War of 1812, grew increasingly disturbed over the loss of Indian lands and attempted to organize Indian opposition to lands lost by the treaty.

By 1831 white settlement had begun to take over Black Hawk's own village near present-day Rock Island, Illinois. Furious, Black Hawk prepared to resist, but army troops finally forced him to move his people to the west bank of the Mississippi. In defiance of orders, however, he returned the following spring, taking his people to a Winnebago village whose leader was sympathetic to Black Hawk's cause.

Not all Sauks and Foxes sided with Black Hawk, however. One faction under Keokuk continued to be pro-American, and the followers of Black Hawk were known as the "British band" because of their support for the British. Like other Indian leaders, notably Tecumseh, Black Hawk viewed the British as less threatening to the Indian way of life. It was the Americans, not the British, who sought Indian land, and since the British were the enemies of the Americans support for the British made sense.

Upon returning to the eastern side of the Mississippi, Black Hawk soon found himself pursued by Gen. Henry Atkinson with a mixed force of regular army troops and volunteers, which included Abraham Lincoln. When it became clear he could not count on any real support from other Indians or from the British, Black Hawk decided to surrender. In attempting to negotiate a settlement, however, two of Black Hawk's five emissaries were slain by unruly militia. Alerted by the three who had escaped, Black Hawk prepared to defend his position against the militia, who greatly outnumbered him. Atkinson and his officers were unable to ef-

fect much control over the militia, many of whom were rowdy and drunk as they rushed toward the Indians. Firing from positions of concealment, the Indians struck first, quickly dispersing the suddenly panic-stricken militia, who fled back toward their camp. This incident came to be known as the Battle of Stillmans Run.

Encouraged by his success, Black Hawk launched other attacks throughout the spring of 1832, managing to evade the often incompetent bands of militia sent against him. By the end of June a strong force of federal troops under General Atkinson and Gen. Winfield Scott had joined the pursuit, though Black Hawk managed to evade these columns as well. However, supplies were running low, and with the troops in pursuit it was becoming riskier to raid settlements. By midsummer Black Hawk had moved north into southern Wisconsin and concluded that the only safety lay in crossing the Mississippi once again. Accordingly, with the river as his objective, Black Hawk urged his people across southwestern Wisconsin, pursued now by a force under Atkinson and Col. Henry Dodge.

On 1 August Black Hawk reached the confluence of the Bad Axe and Mississippi Rivers, but with no way of crossing and fearing the approach of the troops Black Hawk counseled moving north to perhaps find help among the Winnebagos. He was overruled, and most of the band proceeded to build rafts to cross the river. Black Hawk and a few followers, meanwhile, proceeded upriver.

While the rafts were being built the steamboat *Warrior* arrived with a compliment of troops aboard. Left with little choice the Indians tried to surrender, but their offer was misunderstood by the commander of the troops, who opened fire, initiating the Battle of Bad Axe. By the time the *Warrior* was forced to withdraw two hours later because of lack of fuel, 23 Indians had been killed. Some 200 others managed somehow to escape across the river just before Atkinson's troops arrived to initiate a second attack, which was later supported by the refueled *Warrior.* In the melee it was difficult to distinguish warriors from noncombatants, and by the end of the second fight about 150 Indians lay dead; nearly half that number were taken prisoner. Army losses were low. Those who did reach the west bank of the Mississippi fared no better, as they were attacked by Sioux war parties.

The Black Hawk War was brief, as wars go, lasting only 15 weeks. However, it was an especially costly war for the Indians, who suffered 400 to 500 casualties. On the other side, some 70 soldiers and civilians were killed. Black Hawk was later captured and imprisoned for a year in Fortress Monroe, Virginia. After his release he was taken on a tour of eastern cities, and he later dictated his autobiography to a French interpreter. The story was published in book form. As a result of the Black Hawk War the Sauks and Foxes were forced to cede an additional block of land some 50 miles wide that runs the length of present-day Iowa.

Further Reading: Jackson, *Black Hawk;* Prucha, *Sword of the Republic*

Black Hills, South Dakota

Covering more than 5,000 square miles in western South Dakota, the Black Hills played a pivotal role in the Sioux Indian War of 1876. Called *Paha Sapa* by the Lakota Sioux, the area is known to whites as the Black Hills because its thickly timbered hills appear dark from a distance.

The Sioux regarded the Black Hills as sacred, the dwelling place of spirits. Until 1874 white traffic had largely skirted the Black Hills, although a few explorers and trappers had undoubtedly penetrated the region early on. However, when Lt. Col. George Armstrong Custer's reconnaissance expedition revealed the presence of gold in 1874, the Black Hills became a mecca for prospectors and opportunists overnight.

The swarms of prospectors pouring into the Black Hills posed a problem for the U.S. government, since the area had been declared off-limits to whites by the Laramie Treaty

(1868). The army, accordingly, was ordered to enforce the terms of the treaty and expel all white trespassers discovered by its patrols. Not surprisingly, the Indians retaliated with raids on the miners, whose demands for military protection soon resulted in the government's bowing to the cries of its constituents rather than honoring its treaty. Thus the invasion of the Black Hills may be viewed as a prime factor, more than any other single event, in initiating the war of 1876.

Further Reading: Gray, *Centennial Campaign;* Jackson, *Custer's Gold;* Stewart, *Custer's Luck;* Utley, *Frontier Regulars*

Black Kettle
ca. 1803–1868

A Cheyenne peace chief, Black Kettle (Moketa-ve-to) was born in present-day South Dakota. As a leader he was inclined early on toward harmonious relations with the whites. Notwithstanding his nonmilitant approach, Black Kettle's village was the target of Chivington's brutal attack at Sand Creek, Colorado, in 1864. Black Kettle himself survived this tragedy only to be killed by Custer's troops at the Washita nearly four years to the day after Sand Creek.

See also: Chivington, Col. John M.; Evans, Gov. John; Sand Creek Massacre; Washita, Battle of the
Further Reading: Grinnell, *Fighting Cheyennes;* Hoig, *The Sand Creek Massacre;* ———, *Battle of the Washita*

Black Robes

Black Robes was the name given to Roman Catholic priests who performed missionary work in the New World, seeking to convert to Christianity the Native American tribes with whom they were able to make contact. Originally, the name referred to priests of the Jesuit order, though in later years it was universally applied to all Catholic priests without regard to their specific order. As the frontier moved west, so did the Black Robes. Some, such as Father Jean Pierre De Smet, exercised considerable influence among the Indians and acted as mediators when conflicts arose.

Further Reading: Killoren, *Come Black Robe*

Blackfoot

An Algonquian tribe composed of Piegan, Blood, and northern Blackfeet bands, the Blackfoot were a warlike, buffalo-hunting people of the upper Missouri River region. A poor relationship with whites began when a member of the Lewis and Clark Expedition killed a Piegan. For more than half a century thereafter, trappers and missionaries who ventured into Blackfoot territory did so at the risk of their lives. In 1870 the Baker Massacre on the Marias River effectively ended Blackfoot resistance, and by the end of the decade most of the tribe had moved to Canada.

See also: Baker's Attack on the Piegans
Further Reading: Ege, *Tell Baker to Strike Them Hard;* Ewers, *The Blackfeet: Raiders of the Northern Plains*

Blockhouses

Blockhouses were log structures, often two stories high, with embrasures and loopholes that permitted the defenders to return hostile fire with a high degree of safety. Blockhouses tended to be centrally located so as to provide settlers with refuge in time of attack. Usually, the interior of the blockhouse was provisioned with water and supplies to take care of the defenders' needs until help arrived.

Blue Licks, Battle of
19 August 1782

In July 1782 Indian raiders threatened Wheeling, Virginia (which is now in West Virginia), then attempted to surprise the garrison at Bryan's Station near Lexington, in present-day Kentucky. The Kentucky militia, having been drawn away by a diversionary attack, returned in time to surprise the Bryan's Station besiegers from behind.

Suddenly finding themselves threatened, the Indians withdrew to Blue Licks Springs on the Middle Fork of the Licking River. Daniel Boone and others counseled against a pursuit, advising to wait for reinforcements. Their advice, however, went unheeded.

Plunging ahead, the militia ran straight into an ambush prepared by the renegade Simon Girty, which killed 70 and routed the remainder of the column.

Further Reading: Bakeless, *Background to Glory*

Blue Water, Battle of
2 September 1855

Following the Grattan Massacre (19 August 1854), Brig. Gen. William S. Harney was recalled from a vacation in Paris by Secretary of War Jefferson Davis (who would later head the Confederate States of America in the Civil War), with orders to punish the Sioux who were responsible. Accordingly, in August Harney led a 700-man force of infantry, cavalry, and artillery north out of Fort Leavenworth, Kansas, and on 2 September located the Brulé Sioux village of Little Thunder on Blue Water Creek near Ash Hollow, Nebraska.

Harney is reported to have said, "By God, I'm for battle—no peace." Thus, when Little Thunder offered to surrender Harney rejected the overture and attacked, destroying the village and killing more than 100 inhabitants. The wisdom of Harney's philosophy was borne out in the aftermath of the Blue Water attack, when he met with Sioux leaders at Fort Laramie. He warned the chiefs to not interfere with traffic along the Overland Trail—and they were to surrender those individuals involved in the Grattan Massacre. The Sioux had little choice but to accede to Harney's demands.

See also: Grattan Massacre; Harney, Gen. William Selby
Further Reading: Utley, *Frontiersmen in Blue;* Werner, *The Blue Water*

Boone, Daniel
1734–1820

Perhaps the most famous frontiersman and Indian fighter in U.S. history, Daniel Boone, along with Davy Crockett and others, has assumed a mythic-hero status in the public consciousness. Boone was born in Berks County, Pennsylvania, but his family moved to Yadkin

Daniel Boone and friends rescue Betsey and Francis Calloway as well as their daughter, who had been carried off by Indians while crossing a river in Kentucky.

Valley, North Carolina, when he was a boy because of a conflict arising from his sister's marrying outside the Quaker religion.

As a young man Boone became deeply interested in hunting and woods lore and soon became an expert marksman. A surveyor by trade, Boone was afflicted with a wanderlust, and early travels took him to Florida. As a teamster on the ill-fated Braddock expedition he heard enticing stories about Kentucky, which he visited in 1769 with his brother, Squire, passing through the famous Cumberland Gap. After two years exploring the land called "Kaintuck" the brothers returned to North Carolina, and in 1773 Boone gathered his own family and organized a party of adventurous souls to establish a new settlement in Kentucky.

In 1775 he established a wilderness road from Cumberland Gap to Boonesboro, the second settlement in the state (the first was Harrodsburg). Boone's wilderness road was variously called Boone's Trace, the Virginia Road, and the Kentucky Road. The next three years represented a bloody period in Kentucky history (giving rise to the "dark and bloody ground" depicted in history books), and no one was more involved in the struggle for this land than Daniel Boone. Captured by Shawnees, he was held captive for three months before managing to escape. Following his escape he conducted a successful defense of Boonesboro, which he had learned during captivity was going to be attacked. In 1782 he was involved in the disastrous defeat at Blue Licks, Kentucky. Boone and a few others counseled against an attack but were overruled.

Although best known as a woodsman and Indian fighter, Boone was also active in civic affairs despite the fact that he was barely literate. In 1798 Boone lost much of his substantial land holdings due to improper registration; some were later restored. About 1799 Boone crossed the Mississippi and relocated to Missouri, where he had been given a large Spanish grant. He died there in 1820.

Of medium height and build and possessing an unusually large forehead, Boone was said to have been an honest and remarkably serene man. Boone was not the first white man to see Kentucky or the first to explore the region, although he is often credited for doing so. He did, however, leave a mark on the country as few others have.

See also: Blue Licks, Battle of; Boonesboro, Kentucky
Further Reading: Bakeless, *Daniel Boone: Master of the Wilderness;* Faragher, *Daniel Boone*

Boonesboro, Kentucky

A famous site in early American history, Boonesboro was built in 1775 by Richard Henderson's Transylvania Company near the south bank of the Kentucky River south of present-day Lexington. The structure was named in honor of Daniel Boone, who established a western corridor through Cumberland Gap and helped select the site for Boonesboro. The second oldest settlement in Kentucky (Harrodsburg was the first), Boonesboro was subjected to many Indian attacks during the early years of its existence.

See also: Boone, Daniel; Harrodsburg, Kentucky
Further Reading: Bakeless, *Daniel Boone: Master of the Wilderness;* Faragher, *Daniel Boone*

Bosque Redondo

As a part of Gen. James H. Carleton's campaign of 1863, Col. Christopher (Kit) Carson led a strong military column into the heart of Navajo country, penetrating even the formidable Canyon de Chelly, destroying crops, villages, and livestock. By early 1864 many Navajos had surrendered to Carson and were subsequently marched east to Fort Sumner, New Mexico, some 300 miles from their homeland, where they were held prisoner at the Bosque Redondo reservation on the Pecos River. Known as the Long Walk in

Navajo history, the march to Bosque Redondo is a western version of the Trail of Tears. In 1868 a treaty between the Navajos and the U.S. government allowed the Navajos to return to their homeland.

Further Reading: Kelly, *Navajo Roundup;* McNitt, *Navajo Wars*

Boyer, Minton (Mitch)
ca. 1846–1876

The son of a French trader and a Crow Indian woman, Mitch Boyer was the protégé of famous frontiersman Jim Bridger. Some said that Boyer was the best scout between Bozeman, Montana, and the Platte River, aside from Bridger himself. He was also said to have been the only scout of mixed race heritage able to accurately estimate distance in terms of miles.

Boyer served as a scout for Gen. Patrick Edward Connor's column from Fort Laramie to the Tongue River in 1865. He began the 1876 campaign against the Sioux by serving as guide and interpreter for Col. John Gibbon's Montana Column. Later, he was loaned to Custer because of his specific knowledge of the country over which the Seventh Cavalry would pass. Boyer was killed with the Custer battalion in the Battle of the Little Bighorn. He is reported to have warned Custer just prior to the battle that if they attacked the Indian village that lay ahead they would never come out alive.

A far-fetched but intriguing theory is that arrangements had been made with Boyer to assassinate Custer.

See also: Custer, Lt. Col. George Armstrong; Little Bighorn, Battle of the (Custer's Last Stand)
Further Reading: Gray, *Custer's Last Campaign;* Weibert, *Sixty-six Years in Custer's Shadow*

Bozeman Trail

The discovery of gold in southern Montana during the early 1860s attracted prospectors and opportunists to the area. At first those arriving from the east journeyed by steamboat up the Missouri River as far as Fort Benton then overland to the gold camps at

Bannack, Alder Gulch, and Virginia City. River travel, however, was limited to the warm months of the year when the river was free of ice.

In 1863 a man named John Bozeman and his partner, John Jacobs, pioneered a route that split off from the Great Overland Trail to Oregon and California near present-day Casper, Wyoming, and went north, roughly following what is today Interstate 25 along the eastern flank of the Big Horn Mountains before finally turning west to the gold camps. The route thus came to be known as the Bozeman Trail, or Bozeman Road. The attraction of the route was that it was shorter than traveling via the river and could be traveled year-round, although few attempted the journey during winter.

The drawback was that it passed through the Powder River country of the Sioux and Cheyennes, who resented intrusions into their territory and retaliated by attacking travelers. As a result of the Indian resistance, the army established three forts along the trail during the summer of 1866: Fort Reno, east of present-day Kaycee, Wyoming; Fort Phil Kearny, south of Sheridan; and Fort C. F. Smith, on the Big Horn River in Montana.

Despite the presence of the three forts, travel over the Bozeman Trail during the next two years was a dangerous proposition because of what became known as Red Cloud's War. Nevertheless, the trail remained in use until the Treaty of Fort Laramie (April 1868), which resulted in the abandonment of the three forts and the closure of the Bozeman Trail itself.

Further Reading: Hebard and Brininstool, *The Bozeman Trail*; Murray, *The Bozeman Trail*

Braddock, Gen. Edward
1695–1755

The son of a general officer in the British army, Edward Braddock followed in his father's footsteps and became an officer in the Coldstream Guards in 1710 at age 15. Braddock's career moved ahead nicely. He saw service during the War of the Austrian Suc-

cession and in 1755 was named commander of British forces in North America.

Brave but arrogant is a fitting way to describe this officer, whose name has become synonymous with defeat. From March to July 1755 Braddock led a column against Fort Duquesne, building a wagon road across the Allegheny Mountains in the process. Failing to heed the advice of colonial subordinates, one of whom was George Washington, Braddock and his column were ambushed by French and Indian forces near Fort Duquesne. Although the British troops acquitted themselves well, they were off-balance against the elusive backwoods tactics of the French and their Indian allies. Braddock himself was mortally wounded, and his command was salvaged only by the skill of Washington and others.

Further Reading: Leach, *Arms for Empire;* ———, *Roots of Conflict*

Braddock's Campaign
1755

The campaign conducted by Gen. Edward Braddock was one of two major thrusts to expel French forces from North America. One was launched against Fort Niagara (New York); the second, led by Braddock, intended to attack the key post of Fort Duquesne, the capture of which would give the British control of the vital Three Forks region.

Braddock's column assembled during the spring at Fort Cumberland on the upper Potomac River. The 44th and 48th Regiments of Foot were considered the heart of the command, which was augmented by some colonial troops and a few Indian scouts. Rivalries precluded major Indian support for the expedition. Col. George Washington served as Braddock's aide-de-camp. The British column also featured heavy siege guns, which Braddock planned to use to batter down the walls of Fort Duquesne. The disadvantage of hauling heavy artillery was that it required the construction of a road across the mountains.

The campaign got under way in mid-June. Braddock's approach to his objective

Gen. Edward Braddock lies dying on a caisson during his army's hasty retreat after a surprise attack by French and Indian forces in 1755.

was careful and cautious, with scouts out on all quarters. By 8 July the advance had reached the confluence of Turtle Creek with the Monongahela River. The French, meanwhile, had moved out to confront Braddock, hoping to defeat the British before the heavy guns, which they had learned of, could be brought to bear against the fort.

Battle between the two forces was joined in a heavily wooded area. The French forces were at first driven back but eventually recovered and counterattacked, moving silently through the wooded terrain along the British flanks and taking the surrounding high ground. The tide of battle shifted quickly. Unprepared to fight in this style, the British position quickly deteriorated. Defensive organization broke down, and Braddock himself was mortally wounded. He died on 13 July and was buried by Washington.

Guided now by Washington and others, the British fell back, destroying their artillery and anything else of value to the French.

Survivors finally reached the safety of Fort Cumberland, from whence they had started so confidently. The expedition had been a disaster, with more than 600 killed, including the commander. To make matters even worse, the French also captured Braddock's official papers, containing information about the British northern campaign.

Further Reading: Brookhiser, *Founding Father;* Leach, *Roots of Conflict*

Brant, Joseph (Thayendanega)
1742–1807

A powerful and dynamic Mohawk chief, Brant's Indian name was Thayendanega, or He sets or places together two bets. Brant was born along the Ohio River during a hunting trip. Following his father's early death, his mother married an Indian known to the whites as Brant. Exactly when he adopted the name Joseph is not known, though it may have been about this time.

At age 13 young Brant joined Sir William Johnson's expedition to Lake George. Johnson, who was the common-law husband of Brant's older sister, Molly, took a liking to the young man and sent him to school in Connecticut, where he learned to read and write. In 1765 Brant joined the Episcopal Church, married, and fathered a son and daughter. Following the death of his wife, he married her half-sister.

A protégé of Johnson, Brant accompanied him during his Niagara expedition of 1759. No doubt due largely to his mentor's influence, Brant became a staunch supporter of the British, on whose side he fought during Pontiac's uprising. Brant's loyalty to the Crown never wavered. During the American Revolution he persuaded four of six nations in the Iroquois Confederacy to support the British cause (the Tuscaroras and Oneidas elected to ally themselves with the American colonies). Under Brant's charismatic leadership, the four nations of the Iroquois Confederacy inflicted a reign of terror across the northeastern frontier throughout the Revolution. Brant himself played a prominent role in the Cherry Valley Massacre and at Minnisink, Orange County, New York, in 1779.

Joseph Brant died on 24 November 1807, on the Grand River in Ontario. He was one of the most influential Indian leaders of his day.

See also: Iroquois Confederacy; Johnson, Sir William; Revolutionary War
Further Reading: Bakeless, *Background to Glory;* Hodge, *Handbook of American Indians,* vol. 1; Hurt, *The Ohio Frontier;* Stone, *Life of Joseph Brant;* Wood, *War Chief of the Six Nations*

Brodhead's Campaign
1779

As part of General Washington's retaliatory measures against raiding Indians, Col. Daniel Brodhead was directed to march up the Allegheny River with a force of 600 men, uniting with the larger command of Gen. John Sullivan at Genesee on the New York–Pennsylvania border. An aggressive commander, Brodhead led his column on a month-long raid along the river, destroying a number of Indian villages and many acres of corn. Brodhead's campaign, like those of Sullivan and Gen. James Clinton in the north, although destroying much Indian property, seemed to spur the tribes into making further raids on the frontier communities.

Further Reading: Dowd, *A Spirited Resistance*

Buffalo (Bison)

Buffalo, or, more correctly, bison, once roamed the Great Plains from Canada to Mexico and as far east as the Mississippi River. It is estimated that at their peak, around 1800, there were 40 million buffalo in the United States. The principal source of food for the Plains Indian tribes, the buffalo was also a resource in other ways. Robes, shields, and drums, among other things, were made from the hide. The sinews were used for bowstrings, hooves could be converted to glue, and hair was used for headdresses.

The unbelievably swift destruction of the herds by white hide-hunters during the last half of the nineteenth century exacerbated tension between the Indians and whites. Although it was never official military policy to eliminate the buffalo, unofficially some military leaders were convinced that the destruction of the buffalo herds would expedite the subjugation of the Indians and, accordingly, encouraged the systematic destruction of the herds. Thus, the buffalo is closely linked to the Indian wars of the Great Plains region.

Further Reading: Dary, *The Buffalo Book*

Buffalo Horn
?–1878

A highly regarded Bannock chief, Buffalo Horn served as an army scout during the Indian wars of the 1870s. His last term of service as a scout was for Col. Nelson A. Miles during the Nez Perce Campaign in 1877. When trouble developed between Bannocks and white settlers in the spring of

L. T. Bowen lithograph, Hunting the Buffaloe

1878, however, Buffalo Horn reversed his earlier role and led a party of warriors on a raid. Near Silver City, Idaho, the Bannocks encountered a force of volunteers, and in the ensuing fight Buffalo Horn was killed. Famous scout Luther S. (Yellowstone) Kelly once remarked that "Buffalo Horn was one of the bravest Indians I ever had anything to do with."

Further Reading: L. Kelly, *Yellowstone Kelly;* Utley, *Frontier Regulars*

Buffalo Soldiers

Black soldiers who served on the Western frontier came to be called buffalo soldiers by the Indians, supposedly because the soldiers' hair reminded the Indians of the buffalo's kinky fur. Four regiments of buffalo soldiers served on the frontier during the post–Civil War period—the Ninth and Tenth Cavalry regiments and the Twenty-Fourth and Twenty-Fifth Infantry regiments.

Further Reading: Billington, *New Mexico's Buffalo Soldiers, 1866–1900;* Carroll, *The Black Military Experience in the West*

Buffalo War
See Red River War

Burnt Corn Creek, Battle of
27 July 1813

During the War of 1812 militant Red Stick Creeks, under their leader, Peter McQueen, of mixed race heritage, were returning home from a meeting with Spanish officials in Florida, where they had hoped to obtain firearms and ammunition but only managed some of the latter. At Burnt Corn Creek, some 80 miles north of Pensacola, they were surprised by a force of American militia. Although confused at first, the Red Sticks rallied and counterattacked, driving back the militia. Casualties were light on both sides. The fight was insignificant in and of itself, but in the larger picture it turned what had been an internal fight among the Creeks into the Red Stick War with the Americans.

See also: Chickamaugas; Creek Campaigns; Red Sticks
Further Reading: Dowd, *A Spirited Resistance;* Prucha, *Sword of the Republic*

A Campfire Sketch, *line drawing by Frederic Remington*

Bushy Run, Battle of
5 August 1763

In July 1763 a British relief column nearly 500 strong under the command of Col. Henry Bouquet gathered at Carlisle, Pennsylvania, and set out to relieve Fort Pitt, which was then perceived to be in some danger from Indian attacks. At a place called Edge Hill, approximately 25 miles east of Fort Pitt, Bouquet suddenly came under attack by a large mixed force of Delawares, Shawnees, Mingos, and Hurons. The fighting was intense through the day as Indian strength seemed to increase. With darkness, the troops established a circular defensive perimeter atop a hill, with their wounded and livestock placed in the center.

The next morning, 5 August, when a portion of the troops defending the line appeared to be retiring, the Indians attacked, only to be themselves unexpectedly struck in the flank by the troops they had thought to be retiring. Caught off-guard, the Indians fell back in some disorder, pursued by Bou-

quet's troops. With the attackers dispersed, Bouquet moved his command to a place called Bushy Run, about a mile distant, where desperately needed water was available. The fight is identified with this locale rather than with Edge Hill, where it was actually fought.

Eventually, Bouquet reached Fort Pitt, where he discovered the situation not as desperate as earlier believed. The Battle of Bushy Run, although a victory for the British, was costly, resulting in 50 killed. Indian losses were also heavy, however, with two prominent Delaware chiefs among those killed.

Further Reading: Peckham, *Pontiac and the Indian Uprising*

Butterfield Overland Mail Route

This was a famed route named for John Butterfield (1801–1869), who with associates was awarded a U.S. government contract in

1857 to create an overland mail route to the West Coast. Some 2,800 miles in length, the route ran from St. Louis to San Francisco via El Paso, Tucson, and Los Angeles. The route itself was known as the Butterfield Trail. Service commenced in 1858 and essentially ended with the outbreak of the Civil War in 1861. Portions of the route, particularly the sections across southern New Mexico and Arizona, were often subject to Indian attack.

See also: Apache Pass, Battle of

Further Reading: Conkling, *The Butterfield Overland Mail*

C

Camas Meadows, Battle of
19 August 1877

Following the Battle of the Big Hole, Gen. O. O. Howard took up pursuit of the fleeing Nez Perce, who reversed course, crossed the Continental Divide, and moved down Idaho's Lemhi Valley. Howard correctly guessed that the Nez Perce would move south then turn east through Yellowstone Park in order to reach the plains beyond, and he moved to intercept.

On 19 August Howard's tired command camped at a place called Camas Meadows, so named because the camas root, which was a staple of the Nez Perce diet, grew there in great abundance. Howard knew he was close, because the Nez Perce had camped there just 24 hours earlier. The one thing Howard did not anticipate was that the Indians would come looking for him—which they did. That night a war party estimated at 200 crept in and managed to run off a number of the army's pack mules. Fortunately, Howard's cavalry mounts were picketed. In the morning a detachment pursued the raiders and managed to recover part of the stolen stock. However, the Nez Perce then counterattacked, forcing the troops to retreat. They were rescued when Howard arrived with the main body.

As battles go, Camas Meadows was a minor encounter. Howard had one killed and seven wounded, but once again the Nez Perce had managed to embarrass the army pursuers and continue their epic flight.

See also: Big Hole, Battle of the; Gibbon, Col. John; Howard, Gen. Oliver Otis; Joseph; Looking Glass; Nez Perce War
Further Reading: Brown, *The Flight of the Nez Perce;* Hampton, *Children of Grace*

Camp Grant Massacre
30 April 1871

At dawn on 30 April 1871, a band of vigilantes attacked an Apache village, or *rancheria*, near Camp Grant, northeast of Tucson. The band, numbering about 150, was composed mainly of Papago Indians and Mexicans, together with a handful of white men. Despite efforts by the U.S. government and Army to resolve the Apache problem, raids and depredations had continued. Frustrated by the government's failure to punish the raiders, the vigilantes elected to take matters into their own hands. A target for their anger was a band of peaceful Apaches, who were being fed and otherwise provided for by the army at Camp Grant, northeast of Tucson. The vigilantes were convinced that these Apaches were in fact the raiders and accordingly decided to attack.

Organizing in secret, the group rendezvoused at a prearranged location then proceeded toward the unsuspecting Apache camp and attacked at dawn, killing an estimated 80 to 150, most of whom were women and children. Additionally, some 25 to 30 children were taken into slavery. The Camp Grant Massacre is regarded as one of the most opprobrious incidents of the western Indian wars.

Further Reading: Schellie, *Vast Domain of Blood;* Thrapp, *The Conquest of Apacheria;* Worcester, *The Apaches*

Canby, Gen. Edward Richard Sprigg
1817–1873

Born in Kentucky, E.R.S. Canby graduated next to last in his class at West Point in 1839.

The Modoc's murder of General Canby

Despite his academic underachievement, however, Canby went on to enjoy a solid career as a professional soldier.

Following graduation, he saw action in the Second Seminole War and subsequently participated in the removal of Indians to Arkansas under the government program. After service in the Mexican War he was assigned to duty in the Pacific Northwest and then in New Mexico, where he was engaged in fighting the Navajos. During the early part of the Civil War he was appointed head of the Department of New Mexico, which he successfully defended against the 1862 Confederate invasion. Canby's subsequent Civil War service included the capture of Mobile, Alabama, and the acceptance of the surrender of the last two major Confederate armies.

At the close of the Civil War Canby was promoted to brigadier general in the regular army and appointed to the command of the Department of Columbia in 1870 and, three years later, the Department of the Pacific. In 1873, while attempting to negotiate a peace settlement with the Modocs of northern California, Canby was brutally murdered by the Modoc leader, Captain Jack. Canby was the only general officer of the regular army to lose his life during the Indian wars. Canby was an able if not a dramatic leader and a man of honor. Ulysses S. Grant called him "a prudent soldier."

Further Reading: Heyman, *Prudent Soldier;* Murray, *The Modocs and Their War*

Canby's Campaign
1860–1861

During the late 1850s and early 1860s increasing Navajo depredations resulted in military reprisals. In January 1860 the Navajos attacked supply trains moving across western New Mexico, and at the end of April a large war party attacked Fort Defiance and nearly overran the post before finally being repulsed.

In response the Department of New Mexico received substantial reinforcements that summer to prosecute a campaign against the Navajos. The newly arrived units included the Fifth and Seventh Infantry regiments as well as part of the Tenth Infantry and the Second Dragoons. Selected to lead the campaign was Maj. E.R.S. Canby, a solid if unspectacular soldier.

Canby departed Fort Defiance in November 1860 with more than 600 men augmented by a contingent of Ute scouts and a company of New Mexican volunteers (called "spies and scouts") under Capt. Blas Lucero. Canby organized his campaign in three columns, one under Maj. Henry Hopkins Sibley (no relation to Henry Hastings Sibley) and a second under Capt. LaFayette McLaws; Canby himself commanded the third.

Pushing into Navajo country, the three-pronged expedition scoured the countryside. The Ute scouts managed to destroy a large number of Navajo sheep as well as fields of crops, but none of the columns were able to close with the Navajos, who did manage to harass the rear and flanks of Canby's command, however. The area through which the troops moved was suffering from a severe drought. Dwindling forage and a lack of water resulted in the loss of much stock, finally causing Canby to call off the campaign and return to Fort Defiance.

Tactically, the campaign would have to be considered a failure, if success is measured by battles won and lost. Canby's casualties were few in number. The Navajos suffered 35 to 40 casualties, but the loss of more than 1,000 horses and thousands of sheep worked an immense hardship on the Navajos, prompting many leaders to ask for peace. Canby rejected these overtures, however, stipulating that all Navajos must agree to surrender. Canby followed this ultimatum by ordering a winter campaign in January 1861. His strategy was to establish a series of posts across Navajo territory from which to maintain pressure on the tribe.

By spring the strategy seemed to be working, but the program was interrupted by the outbreak of the Civil War, causing Canby to direct his attention to the threat of Confederate invasion of New Mexico from the south.

See also: Barbancito; Canby, Gen. Edward Richard Sprigg; Canyon de Chelly, Arizona; Carson, Christopher Houston (Kit); Manuelito; Navajos
Further Reading: Heyman, *Prudent Soldier;* McNitt, *Navajo Wars;* Utley, *Frontiersmen in Blue*

Cannibalism

Ritual cannibalism was a widespread practice among many Indian tribes throughout what is today the eastern and southern United States. The practice was predicated on the belief that by consuming the flesh of a foe, particularly that of a strong foe, the victor would inherit his enemy's strength. The practice does not seem to have been as widespread among western tribes.

Further Reading: Leach, *Arms for Empire*

Canonchet (Nanunteeno)
?–1676

A Narragansett sachem (sachem typically is used to refer to a chief of one of the Algonquian tribes), Canonchet was the son of Miantonomo. Tall and powerfully built, Canonchet was a man of courage and ability. His skills as a military leader were said to rival those of King Philip, his ally in King Philip's War. Like Philip, he weaved a path of destruction through southern New England during that war, burning Rehoboth, Delaware, and Providence, Rhode Island.

Canonchet was surprised by an English force in April 1676 and captured by a Mohegan ally of the attackers. After execution his head was delivered to the authorities at Hartford.

See also: King Philip's War; Miantonomo (Miantonomi)
Further Reading: Bourne, *The Red King's Rebellion;* Hodge, *Handbook of American Indians*

Canyon de Chelly, Arizona

Located in northeast Arizona, Canyon de Chelly (pronounced "de shay") is a sprawling canyon complex that reaches 1,000 foreboding feet high in places. A literal translation of the name means "where it flows from the canyon." For decades, Canyon de Chelly was a Navajo stronghold, a fortress from which the tribe defended itself against incursions from the Spanish, Americans, and other Indians.

The natural stronghold was penetrated by military columns on several occasions. Kit Carson's 1863–1864 campaigns destroyed so much Navajo livestock and crops that Canyon de Chelly was effectively neutralized as a stronghold.

See also: Barbancito; Canby's Campaign; Carson, Christopher Houston (Kit); Manuelito
Further Reading: Heyman, *Prudent Soldier;* Kelly, *Navajo Roundup;* McNitt, *Navajo Wars*

Captain Jack (Kintpuash)
ca. 1839–1873

A Modoc Indian leader, Captain Jack reportedly was so named by California miners because he was fond of wearing a jacket with brass buttons given him by the army. During the 1870s disagreements developed over an 1864 treaty requiring the Modocs to surrender their traditional homeland around the Lost River near the California-Oregon border and to relocate on the Klamath Reservation.

After due if grudging compliance with the stipulations of the treaty, Jack and his followers bolted from the reservation and headed into the lava beds country, a harsh and broken land fashioned by ancient lava flows. Although Jack was thoroughly opposed to returning to the reservation, he was something of a moderate and proved willing to negotiate with a peace commission set up by Gen. E.R.S. Canby. However, he was persuaded by a militant faction among the Modocs to murder the commissioners. Accordingly, when the commission assembled in January 1873 Jack produced a hidden revolver and killed General Canby while other Modocs stabbed the two remaining commissioners.

For the next five months, the Modocs were subjected to increasing pressure by army forces, which they nevertheless managed to embarrass in several encounters be-fore the conflict was finally brought to an end with Jack's capture at the end of May 1873. Captain Jack was one of four Modocs subsequently tried by a military commission and hanged at Fort Klamath in October 1873.

See also: Canby, Gen. Edward Richard Sprigg; Modoc War
Further Reading: Heyman, *Prudent Soldier;* Murray, *The Modocs and Their War*

Carleton, Gen. James Henry
1814–1873

Born in Maine, James Henry Carleton once had literary aspirations but eventually turned to a military career. In 1839 he was appointed an officer in the dragoons and spent the next nine years on the western frontier, mainly in expeditions of exploration and service in the Mexican War.

Upon the outbreak of the Civil War he was named brigadier general of California Volunteers and, after organizing a substantial force, marched east to help defend the Southwest (Arizona and New Mexico) against Confederates and Indians. After the Confederate invasion of New Mexico was repulsed Carleton was named to command the Department of New Mexico, replacing Gen. E.R.S. Canby, who had been transferred east. With the Confederate threat in the Southwest essentially eliminated, Carleton focused his entire attention on Indian conflicts, launching campaigns against the Navajos and the Apaches.

Col. Christopher (Kit) Carson's relentless campaign against the Navajos resulted in the brutal overland march of the tribe from their homeland to eastern New Mexico, where they were held captive at the infamous Bosque Redondo until a treaty in 1868 allowed them to return home. It had been Carleton's intent to convert the Navajos to Christianity, a plan that he was later forced to admit did not work.

By the end of the Civil War Carleton had been brevetted through all grades, in both the regular and volunteer army, to the rank of major general. In 1865 he was appointed lieutenant colonel of the Fourth Cavalry. He

Schenchin and Captain Jack (in leg irons)

died of pneumonia in Texas in 1873. An able commander, Carleton proved a harsh and unyielding foe to Indians.

See also: Apache Pass, Battle of; Bosque Redondo; Navajo War

Further Reading: Hunt, *Major General James Henry Carleton*; Kelly, *Navajo Roundup*

Carleton's Campaign
1862–1864

After assuming command of the Department of New Mexico in September 1862, Gen. James Henry Carleton laid plans to deal with Indian conflicts, which had received less than full attention during the Confederate invasion of the territory. The defeat and withdrawal of the Confederates from the region, however, meant that Carleton was free to concentrate on fighting Indians, specifically Navajos and Mescalero Apaches.

Free of supervision when the army abandoned Fort Stanton (near Lincoln, New Mexico) in 1861, the Mescaleros took to raiding. Carleton dealt with the matter by organizing a three-pronged campaign. Col. Christopher (Kit) Carson, commanding the First New Mexico Volunteers, was ordered to reopen Fort Stanton and operate against the Mescaleros out of that base. A second column of troops under Col. William McLeave was directed to move east from Mesilla; a third force under Capt. Thomas Roberts was to move northeast from El Paso. Carleton's orders were simple: No peace parleys were permitted. All male Indians were to be killed where found. Only women and children were to be taken prisoner.

The Mescaleros, as it turned out, were not inclined to offer much resistance. One group attempted to enter into peace talks with the troops, but, pursuant to Carleton's directives, two chiefs and several warriors were promptly shot. At a late November parley in Santa Fe with three chiefs, Carleton offered them the option of moving to a new reservation on the Pecos River near Fort Sumner, called the Bosque Redondo. There, they would be fed and protected. The other op-

tion was to face relentless pursuit by the soldiers. Most of the Mescaleros agreed to accept the offer, and by spring 1863 several hundred were at Bosque Redondo, where Carleton made arrangements with the bishop in Santa Fe to see about Christianizing them. Some Mescaleros refused to submit and continued to resist, but for the most part the Mescalero conflict had been largely resolved.

The second phase of Carleton's campaign focused on the Navajos. After a December 1862 meeting with some of the Navajo leaders proved unproductive, Carleton turned again to his most able subordinate, Kit Carson, whom he had largely credited with the successful prosecution of the Mescalero campaign. In the spring of 1863 Carleton advised Delgadito and Barbancito, two prominent voices for peace among the Navajos, that the only acceptable terms would be relocation to the Bosque Redondo. When this approach failed Carson was ordered to take the field in June with his entire regiment of about 1,000 men. Establishing a base camp near old Fort Defiance, Carson swept through Navajo country, destroying villages and crops and confiscating livestock. These efforts were reinforced by Utes and Zunis, traditional enemies of the Navajos, who launched raids of their own.

While Carson was moving through Navajo country, patrols from the newly established Fort Wingate (near present-day Grants, New Mexico) were also ranging out in search of Navajos. On 12 January 1864, Carson penetrated the remote fastness of Canyon de Chelly. Moving through the canyon, Carson's troops destroyed crops and dwellings they came across, occasionally skirmishing with Navajo war parties.

Carson's relentless drive through Navajo country produced results for the federal government. Convinced that the penetration of Canyon de Chelly had neutralized it as a sanctuary, Navajos surrendered in large numbers and began the infamous Long Walk to the Bosque Redondo, where they would remain until an 1868 treaty allowed them to return to their homeland. Carleton's treatment had been harsh if not brutal, but it effectively ended Navajo conflicts.

See also: Bosque Redondo; Carleton, Gen. James Henry; Carson, Christopher Houston (Kit); Navajos
Further Reading: Kelly, *Navajo Roundup;* McNitt, *Navajo Wars;* Trafzer, *The Kit Carson Campaign;* Utley, *Frontiersmen in Blue*

Carr, Gen. Eugene Asa
1830–1910

Born in New York, Eugene A. Carr graduated from West Point in 1850, following which he was assigned to the cavalry and served at various posts on the western frontier. He was wounded in a skirmish with Apaches in 1854, and the following year he participated in operations against the Sioux under Gen. William S. Harney.

During the Civil War Carr served mainly west of the Mississippi, emerging from the war as brevet major general of volunteers. A major in the regular army, he was assigned to the Fifth Cavalry, a regiment he led in a number of battles and campaigns on the Central and Southern Plains during the late 1860s. His most notable achievement during this period was the victory at Summit Springs, Colorado, in July 1869, when he destroyed Tall Bull's Cheyenne village and eliminated the Dog Soldiers as a military threat.

During much of the 1870s Carr was in Arizona. He was in command of the troops at Cibecue Creek, an incident in which a number of Apache scouts suddenly turned on the troops, killing several of them. Carr himself was later censured for failing to take appropriate precautions. Carr was transferred to the Sixth Cavalry in 1879. In 1883 Carr's regiment was sent to New Mexico, and in 1890 it was at Pine Ridge Agency, South Dakota, during the Wounded Knee Massacre.

Promoted to brigadier general, Carr retired in 1893 and died in Washington, D.C. He is generally regarded as one of the better officers to have served in the West during the post–Civil War period.

See also: Cibecue Creek, Incident at; Cody, William Frederick (Buffalo Bill); Summit Springs, Battle of
Further Reading: King, *War Eagle;* Thrapp, *The Conquest of Apacheria*

Carrington, Col. Henry Beebee
1824–1912

An 1845 graduate of Yale University, Henry B. Carrington served as a Union officer in the Civil War. This service—involving administrative and legal work—did not prepare him for his postwar assignment: building and garrisoning three forts along the Bozeman Trail and defending those posts against Indians who resented the army's presence in the Powder River country of northern Wyoming.

It is this one brief period in Carrington's life, which included his role in the tragic and controversial Fetterman Disaster of 21 December 1866, that causes him to be remembered in the literature of the Indian wars. Although a military board subsequently absolved Carrington of any culpability in the Fetterman affair, he was never thereafter free of the stigma. Following the Fetterman investigation he resigned from active duty and spent the remaining 46 years of his life teaching, writing history, and being ever-ready to defend his actions at Fort Phil Kearny.

Carrington was married twice. His first wife, Margaret, served with him at Fort Phil Kearny and died of tuberculosis in 1870; she may have acquired the disease from Henry, a carrier himself. Carrington's second wife, Frances, was also at Fort Phil Kearny; she lost her first husband, George Grummond, in the Fetterman fight and later married widower Carrington. Both Margaret and Frances wrote books describing their experiences at Fort Kearny.

Further Reading: Brown, *The Fetterman Massacre;* Carrington, F., *My Army Life;* Carrington, M., *Absaraka;* Hebard and Brininstool, *The Bozeman Trail;* Vaughn, *Indian Fights*

Carson, Christopher Houston (Kit)
1809–1868

A legendary figure of the Old West, Kit Carson ranks with Daniel Boone, Buffalo Bill, and Jim Bridger as one of the best-known scouts and Indian fighters. He was born in

FRANK STARR'S
NEW YORK LIBRARY

Price, Ten Cents.   Copyrighted 1877, by FRANK STARR & Co. Published on the 5th and 20th of every month. $2.25 a Year.

Vol. I.   FRANK STARR & CO., PUBLISHERS,   No. 3.
                    PLATT AND WILLIAM STS., NEW YORK.

Kit Carson, Jr., the Crack Shot of the West.

A WILD LIFE ROMANCE, BY "BUCKSKIN SAM."

Kit Carson, the crack shot of the West

38

Kentucky, but the family moved to Missouri when he was a small boy. At age 14 Carson ran away from a saddlemaker's apprenticeship to join a wagon train bound for New Mexico.

Possessing an adventurous nature, Carson soon fell in with the mountain men who headquartered in Taos, New Mexico, and readily adapted to their way of life. In time he became a skilled hunter and trapper. A chance meeting with John C. Frémont eventually resulted in Carson being commissioned to guide Frémont's three famous expeditions across the Rockies to California. Following the third expedition, Carson became involved in California's Bear Flag Revolt. He was a guide for Gen. Stephen Watts Kearny on his trek across the Southwest during the Mexican War.

Returning to New Mexico, Carson took up ranching, but upon the outbreak of the Civil War he was appointed colonel of the First New Mexico Volunteers and saw action at Valverde during the Confederate invasion of New Mexico. In 1862–1863, under orders from Gen. James H. Carleton, Carson led a campaign against the Mescalero Apaches then led a campaign through Navajo land that subsequently resulted in the capitulation of the Navajos and the infamous Long Walk to the Bosque Redondo reservation in eastern New Mexico.

In the fall of 1864 Carson led yet another column, this time against Kiowas and Comanches in the Texas Panhandle. Although Carson's force was a strong one, it was greatly outnumbered by the Indians. After a hard fight near Adobe Walls Carson was able to withdraw safely, mainly because of the advantage provided by two mountain howitzers in his command. After the Civil War Carson and his family settled near Las Animas, Colorado, where he died on 23 May 1868, barely a year after his beloved wife, Josefa, passed away.

See also: Adobe Walls, First Battle of; Bosque Redondo; Carleton's Campaign
Further Reading: Carter, *"Dear Old Kit"*; Gordon-McCutchan, *Kit Carson: Indian Fighter or Indian Killer?*; Kelly, *Navajo Roundup*

Chain of Friendship
See Covenant Chain

Cherokee Campaign
1776

In response to Cherokee raids along the southern frontier, militia from Virginia, North Carolina, South Carolina, and Georgia launched three separate strikes during the summer and fall of 1776. The Cherokees, who had been persuaded by Shawnees to go on the warpath, soon found themselves pressured on all fronts; they had been led to believe they would be supported in their efforts by Indian allies and the British. However, when the promised support failed to materialize the Cherokees finally asked for peace, eventually ceding large tracts of land east of the Blue Ridge Mountains.

Further Reading: Starr, *History of the Cherokee Indians;* Woodward, *The Cherokees*

Cherokee War, First
1759–1761

Until the early 1750s, the British enjoyed a relatively amicable relationship with the Cherokees. Indeed, Cherokee warriors supported British efforts in operations against the French and Spanish. The relationship began to deteriorate, however, when the British built two forts in Indian country in the early years of the decade.

The first of these outposts, Fort Prince George, was located some 65 miles northwest of a settlement called Ninety-six, near present-day Greenwood, South Carolina. Fort Loudoun, the second post, was located at the junction of the Tellico and Little Tennessee Rivers, southwest of Knoxville, Tennessee. Although the forts were ostensibly built to protect the Cherokees from Indian enemies and French incursions, the Cherokees came to regard them as an intrusion.

Trouble erupted in 1758, when a group of Cherokees returning from the Forbes Expedition stole horses from some settlers. Angered, the settlers struck back, killing Cherokees, who in turn retaliated with a series of raids that carried into 1759. Tensions increased as Cherokees interdicted the supply routes to Forts Loudoun and Prince George. Meanwhile, the French, not wishing to pass up a golden opportunity, worked behind the scenes trying to exacerbate the tension between the Cherokees and the British. French efforts to encourage other tribes to join the Cherokees proved unsuccessful. The Catawbas remained loyal to the British, and the powerful Creeks chose neutrality.

In the fall of 1759 South Carolina Gov. William Henry Lyttleton led a relief column to Fort Loudoun. Confronting Cherokee leaders, Lyttleton demanded that Cherokee warriors be handed over for punishment in numbers equal to white settlers who had died in raids. For leverage, the governor held the Cherokee leaders in the fort until his demands were met. Lyttleton's action resulted in a peace of sorts, but it was short-lived. In January 1760 Cherokee raids resumed with more intensity. Many settlers were killed; others were taken prisoner. The war quickly took on the aspects of brutality and duplicity that characterized frontier conflicts elsewhere.

The settlement of Ninety-six was attacked, and at Fort Prince George, where some negotiations were being conducted, the commanding officer was lured outside by Cherokees and killed. Enraged, the garrison killed the Cherokee hostages being held inside the post. In response to the growing conflict Gen. Jeffrey Amherst sent 1,300 British regulars under Col. Archibald Montgomery to punish the Cherokees. Montgomery's force was augmented by a detachment of rangers and a party of Catawbas.

In early June 1760 Montgomery destroyed several Cherokee villages, then bivouacked under the protection of Fort Prince George's guns, where he attempted, unsuccessfully, to negotiate with the Cherokees. Resuming the offensive later that month, Montgomery marched toward Fort Loudoun. Near the Cherokee village called Etchoe, the British column encountered heavy resistance. In the battle that followed, which consumed several hours, the Cherokees were finally driven back. Montgomery found the village abandoned by the time he arrived; Montgomery retired to Charleston. He had many wounded that required attention, and General Amherst needed his troops for a summer campaign in the north against the French.

Fort Loudoun, meanwhile, was in need of relief. Virginia sent a relief column, but it did not arrive in time to prevent the surrender of the post to the Cherokees, who were ecstatic over a singular victory. In a generous mood, the Cherokee leaders allowed the British garrison to march to Fort Prince George. However, in a scenario reminiscent of what had happened at Fort William Henry in 1757, young militant Cherokee warriors, unhappy with the arrangement, ambushed the column, killing many of the British soldiers and taking others captive.

In June 1761 General Amherst sent a second column to chastise the Cherokees and reestablish control over the area. This second force, nearly 2,500 strong and composed of British regulars, rangers, and Indian friendlies, was commanded by Lt. Col. James Grant. A veteran Indian fighter, Grant had been Montgomery's second-in-command the year before. Grant's column was attacked en route but reached Etchoe with only light casualties. From there Grant cut a devastating swath through Cherokee country, destroying many villages before returning to Fort Prince George early in July.

The net effect of the two British columns in successive years, particularly that of Grant's, convinced the majority of Cherokees that further resistance was futile. They had, moreover, been unsuccessful in gaining support from other tribes. In the negotiations that followed, Little Carpenter, the principal spokesman for the Cherokees, agreed to turn over Fort Loudoun together with all prisoners.

See also: England; Forts, William Henry; France; French and Indian War
Further Reading: Leach, *Arms for Empire;* Steele, *Warpaths*

Cherokees

A member of the Iroquoian tribal family, the Cherokees are said to be the largest tribe in the United States. One of the so-called Five Civilized Tribes (Cherokees, Choctaws, Chickasaws, Seminoles, Creeks), the Cherokees once occupied parts of eight states in the South and Southeast.

During the Revolutionary War the Cherokees, along with a number of other tribes, sided with the British, whom they perceived to be a lesser threat to their way of life than the American colonists. In support of the British, Cherokee war parties frequently raided outlying colonial settlements.

Following the Revolution, however, the Cherokees elected to adopt many white customs and standards. In 1827, for example, chief John Ross drafted a tribal constitution modeled after the U.S. Constitution. An alphabet was also created. Perhaps more than any other tribe, the Cherokees successfully managed the process of acculturation. Notwithstanding, strong factions among the colonies, led by Georgia, argued for Indian removal. Pressure built until the 1830s when the Cherokees, whose land holdings had been greatly reduced by virtue of various treaties and agreements, agreed to accept land in the Indian Territory of Oklahoma in exchange for what they still held east of the Mississippi River.

See also: Cherokee Campaign; Cherokee War, First; Trail of Tears
Further Reading: King, *The Cherokee Indian Nation;* Woodward, *The Cherokees*

Cheyenne Campaign
1857

During the spring of 1856 clashes between Cheyennes and whites increased. The army, attempting to chastise those it suspected of raiding and attacking wagon trains, often wound up punishing the wrong band. Angered, the Cheyennes would then retaliate with more raids on wagon trains.

Throughout the spring and summer of 1856 such raids increased along the great overland migration routes in Kansas and Nebraska. Col. William S. Harney, who had punished the Sioux at Blue Water, Nebraska, believed the same sort of punishment should be meted out to the Cheyennes. With the onset of fall, however, conditions on the Central and Southern Plains began to stabilize somewhat, and the Indians began preparing winter camps, with many bands coming together near the junction of the Solomon and Smoky Hill Rivers.

Nevertheless, during the fall and winter of 1856–1857, a punitive campaign was authorized by Secretary of War Jefferson Davis. Overall command of the expedition was assigned to Col. Edwin V. "Bull" Sumner, whose main, or north, column was to consist of two squadrons of the First Cavalry, one of the Second Dragoons, and four companies of the Sixth Infantry.

The second, or southern, column under the command of Maj. John Sedgwick, would have two squadrons of the First Cavalry; Lt. Col. Joseph E. Johnston, with the remainder of the First Cavalry, would command the third column. Each column also carried a pair of "prairie" howitzers, which differed from mountain howitzers in that they had smaller wheels to allow for faster travel over flat terrain.

The grand strategy of the expedition called for Sumner's main column to proceed from Fort Leavenworth along the Overland Trail to Fort Laramie, thence south into Colorado and a union with Sedgwick's column at Fort St. Vrain on the South Platte River. The union was set for July 4. Sedgwick, meanwhile, was to march west along the Santa Fe Trail to the present-day site of Pueblo, Colorado, then north toward the anticipated union with Sumner. While Sumner and Sedgwick between them were covering a large chunk of the Central Plains, Johnston was to survey the southern boundary of Kansas and, if possible, cooperate with the overall campaign. However, finding no opportunity to involve his command, Johnston effectively played no role in the campaign.

Early on, Sumner lost the squadron of dragoons originally scheduled for his column, as they had been assigned to Colonel Harney's expedition that was then en route to Utah to deal with the Mormons, who refused to submit to U.S. authority. The dragoons would be replaced by three additional companies of the Sixth Infantry out of Fort Laramie.

The early part of the campaign developed little contact with the Cheyennes. By July Sumner and Sedgwick had joined forces and, leaving their wagons behind, set off in search of the Cheyennes. On 29 July scouts reported Indians ahead. Alerted to the presence of the troops, the Indians had prepared for battle by washing their hands in a small lake whose waters, the medicine men assured, would render the weapons of the soldiers harmless.

Having thus prepared themselves, an estimated 300 to 350 warriors waited in line along the Solomon River. Presently the troops arrived, and Sumner ordered the charge sounded and sabers drawn. As the soldiers thundered toward them, the Cheyennes, apparently disconcerted by this tactic and perhaps believing their magic did not apply to sabers, suddenly wheeled about and fled. Some warriors were cut down by troopers, but others fought back, killing or wounding ten soldiers; a young officer named J.E.B. Stuart was hurt. However, considering the numbers involved, casualties on both sides were light due to the Indians' precipitate withdrawal.

Two days later, Sumner located the now abandoned Cheyenne village, which he promptly destroyed. Sumner's intention to continue the campaign was interrupted, however, by orders directing him to send most of his remaining troops on to Utah to join Harney's expedition. The Cheyenne Campaign of 1857 subdued the Cheyennes for a time, until increased pressures from traffic and settlers across Kansas produced a new round of raids and warfare.

See also: Blue Water, Battle of; Cheyennes; Harney, Gen. William Selby
Further Reading: Chalfant, *Cheyennes and Horse Soldiers*

Cheyennes

A member of the Algonquian family, the Cheyennes were at one time composed of northern and southern divisions. Once a woodland tribe of the upper Mississippi River valley, the Cheyennes migrated west to the Great Plains sometime during the first half of the eighteenth century, probably under pressure from the more numerous Sioux. With the acquisition of the horse they evolved into a nomadic buffalo-hunting people.

Early in the nineteenth century the tribe split, probably for reasons of trade. (There does not appear to have been a political division within the tribe.) In any case, one faction moved south, onto the Central and Southern Plains; the northern branch remained in Montana, Wyoming, and western South Dakota.

Tribal struggles with the Sioux in the north and the Comanches, Apaches, and Kiowas in the south were eventually resolved so that by the time Americans began pushing across the Plains in great numbers, they encountered fierce resistance from these Plains tribes, who soon recognized the whites as a common enemy. Of all the Plains tribes, the Southern Cheyennes may have suffered the heaviest casualties during the Indian wars of the 1860s and 1870s, particularly at Sand Creek and the Washita. They were also participants in the Fetterman Disaster (1866) and the Battle of the Little Bighorn (1876).

In 1878 Cheyennes under Dull Knife and Little Wolf left their reservation in Oklahoma and headed north to their tribal homeland on an epic journey that is sometimes referred to as the Cheyenne Trail of Tears.

See also: Cheyenne Campaign; Dull Knife; Dull Knife Outbreak; Fetterman Disaster; Julesburg, Battles of; Little Bighorn, Battle of the (Custer's Last Stand); Little Wolf; Sand Creek Massacre; Washita, Battle of the
Further Reading: Berthrong, *The Southern Cheyennes*; Grinnell, *Fighting Cheyennes*; Powell, *Sweet Medicine*; Sandoz, *Cheyenne Autumn*

Chickamaugas

A militant branch of the Cherokees whose home territory was the neighborhood of present-day Chattanooga, Tennessee, the Chickamaugas, like factions of other tribes

Massacre of the Cheyennes near Fort Robinson in Nebraska, 1879

in the Ohio River country and the Southeast, opposed neutrality with the United States and instead supported a pan-Indian movement that sought to expunge the advancing Americans from their homelands. For all intents and purposes, the 1794 Battle of Fallen Timbers marked the end of militant nativism among these tribes, and as such the Chickamauga tribal entity ceased to exist.

See also: Cherokee War, First; Nativism, Indian; Revolutionary War; Tecumseh
Further Reading: Dowd, *A Spirited Resistance*

Chickasaws

One of the Five Civilized Tribes (Cherokees, Creeks, Choctaws, Seminole, and Chickasaws), the Chickasaws are a member of the Muskogean tribal family. They were in contact with European arrivals early on. Like other native inhabitants of what is today the southern and southeastern United States, they clashed with de Soto's expedition.

Over the years, Chickasaws came to ally themselves with the British but became pawns in an imperial power struggle. The French sought to weaken the Chickasaws and undermine British influence in the area by fostering an Indian tribal war. Additionally, attacks on Chickasaw villages would further aid and abet French objectives and bring the Chickasaws into the French fold. However, the failure of French campaigns in 1736 and 1739 brought an end to French plans for dominating the region. During the Revolutionary War the British employed Chickasaws mainly against the Spanish in Florida but on occasion sent them to raid outlying American settlements in the south.

As a result of the Indian Removal Act of the 1830s, the Chickasaws, along with other members of the Five Civilized Tribes, were relocated to the Indian Territory in Oklahoma.

See also: Cherokees; Choctaws; Creeks; Indian Removal Act; Revolutionary War

Further Reading: Debo, *Road to Disappearance;* Foreman, *Five Civilized Tribes*

Chillicothe, Ohio: Battles on the Little Miami (Mad) River

Chillicothe had long been one of the vital and important centers of Shawnee life. Daniel Boone had been held prisoner there in 1778. On 10 July 1779, Col. John Bowman attacked Chillicothe with a force of about 250 men. The bulk of the warrior force, however, was out on a raid of its own, leaving the town only lightly defended. Bowman's men quickly put the few defenders and noncombatants to flight, then proceeded to loot the village before putting it to the torch. Later, as warriors returned, snipers began to inflict heavy casualties on the attackers, compelling Bowman to withdraw.

In August 1780 Chillicothe was again the objective when the village was attacked by George Rogers Clark with a force of 1,000. Again the village was empty, and what had not been destroyed by Bowman's troops was now put to the torch. From his scouts Clark learned that a force of warriors was waiting for them at Piqua Town, a dozen miles away. Anxious to strike the warrior force a hard blow, Clark advanced to Piqua and there engaged Indians in a savage fight.

See also: Clark, George Rogers; Piqua Town, Battle of
Further Reading: Bakeless, *Background to Glory;* Hurt, *The Ohio Frontier*

Chippewas
See Ojibwas (Chippewas)

Chivington, Col. John M.
1821–1894

Known as the "Fighting Parson," John Chivington was born in Ohio. After becoming a minister he preached the Gospel in the Midwest, Missouri, Kansas, Nebraska, and finally Colorado, where he was to achieve notoriety.

During the Civil War he was appointed colonel of the First Colorado Volunteers, which he led during the 1862 Confederate invasion of New Mexico, playing a key role in the Union victory at Glorietta Pass. On 29 November 1864, he led a force of Colorado Volunteers in a surprise attack on a peaceful Cheyenne village at Sand Creek, Colorado, killing half of the camp's inhabitants, mainly women and children. The incident plunged Chivington into a maelstrom of controversy from which he never escaped. Chivington spent the remainder of his life defending his actions at Sand Creek.

See also: Black Kettle; Evans, Gov. John; Sand Creek Massacre
Further Reading: Craig, *The Fighting Parson;* Dunn, *I Stand by Sand Creek;* Hoig, *The Sand Creek Massacre*

Choctaws

A tribe of Muskogean stock, the Choctaws were once part of a larger tribe that included the Creeks and Seminoles and are considered one of the Five Civilized Tribes (Cherokees, Creeks, Choctaws, Seminole, and Chickasaws). At one time Choctaw territory extended from Mississippi to Georgia, but by the time Europeans began to arrive in North America they were primarily in Mississippi and parts of Louisiana.

Although principally an agricultural people, the Choctaws were nevertheless continuously at war with Creeks and Chickasaws. They were friendly with the French and allied with them during the intercolonial wars between France and England. The Choctaws were favorably disposed toward Americans and resisted Tecumseh's pleas to organize a powerful Indian coalition, believing it futile to resist. Some Choctaws fought with Jackson at New Orleans against the British.

By 1830, having ceded most of their lands to the United States, the Choctaws began a migration to the Indian Territory.

See also: Cherokees; Chickasaws; Creeks
Further Reading: Debo, *A History of the Indians of the United States;* Hodge, *Handbook of American Indians;* Leach, *Arms for Empire*

Church, Capt. Benjamin
See King Philip's War

Cibecue Creek, Incident at
30 August 1881

In July 1881 Nocadelklinny, a Coyotero Apache medicine man and former army scout, requested and was given permission to conduct dances near Cibecue Creek. Nocadelklinny claimed that the dances would bring back spirits of departed warriors. He also proclaimed that the shirt he wore had special power that would repel bullets.

Nocadelklinny's reputation had grown considerably during the past half-dozen years, and his almost hypnotic power attracted many followers, including some of the Apache scouts who were still in army service. When the dead spirits failed to materialize as promised, Nocadelklinny claimed that his prophecy could not be fulfilled until the white man had been driven from the country.

During the next few weeks the situation deteriorated as army and territorial officials grew increasingly concerned over the likelihood of trouble. Indian agent J. C. Tiffany thought Nocadelklinny should be arrested or killed. However, Col. Eugene A. Carr, commanding Fort Apache, demurred, believing that such action might provoke trouble. Nevertheless, Carr referred the matter to his superior department commander, Gen. Orlando Willcox, who issued orders for the medicine man's arrest.

On 30 August Carr arrived at Nocadelklinny's camp with a force of 113 men, including a contingent of Apache scouts. After explaining his orders to the medicine man Carr directed that he be taken into custody. Carr then established camp some distance away, followed by the escort, which suddenly found itself nearly surrounded by Apaches, many of whom were stripped to the waist and painted as though for a fight.

When the escort reached Carr's bivouac, Nocadelklinny was placed in the center of the camp. When some of the Apaches attempted to enter the camp they were turned away. Several then opened fire on the troops, including some of the Apache scouts who, caught up in the emotion of the moment, mutinied. The fight quickly became general and lasted until darkness. Nocadelklinny himself was wounded several times and reportedly was finally killed by an ax blow from a soldier as he tried to crawl away. After a burial service for the four soldiers killed in the fight, Carr started back to Fort Apache, reaching it on the afternoon of 31 August.

After the fear of an uprising had subsided there was an official investigation of the incident and a shakeup in the Department of Arizona. In November a court-martial at Fort Grant tried five of the Apache scouts for mutiny. Three were hanged in March 1882; the remaining two were sentenced to eight years in Alcatraz and were paroled in 1884.

See also: Apache Wars; Carr, Gen. Eugene Asa; Indian Scouts and Auxiliaries
Further Reading: King, *War Eagle;* Worcester, *The Apaches*

Clark, George Rogers
1752–1818

One of the historic figures of colonial America, George Rogers Clark was the second son of Virginians John Clark and Ann Rogers Clark and the older brother of William Clark (who would gain fame by exploring the western territory with Meriwether Lewis). A surveyor by early training and profession, Clark spent most of his adult life on the frontier fighting Indians and the British, sometimes at the same time.

Clark's most notable accomplishment was the capture of Kaskaskia and Cahokia in June 1778, followed by a daring midwinter attack and capture of the British post Fort Sackville at Vincennes the following February. In 1780, 1782, and 1783 he conducted campaigns against British strongholds in the western lands—then between the Appalachian Mountains and the Mississippi River—and against the Indian villages at Chillicothe and Piqua in Ohio. Appointed Indian commissioner after the Revolutionary War, he was later relieved of that position, quite possibly as a result of the intrigues of the devious Gen. James Wilkinson.

In later years Clark was involved in colonization schemes in the Mississippi Valley. Sadly, financial commitments he had made to western merchants on behalf of Virginia during his Revolutionary War campaigns were never honored. His last years were spent in ill-health, to which excessive drinking is said to have played a part. He died at his home in Kentucky, near Louisville, in 1818.

See also: Blue Licks, Battle of; Chillicothe, Ohio: Battles on the Little Miami (Mad) River; Clark's Ohio Campaign of 1782; Clark's Ohio Campaign of 1786; Piqua Town, Battle of
Further Reading: Bakeless, *Background to Glory*

Clark, William
1770–1838

The youngest of six sons of the famous Virginia Clarks, William was the brother of the famous George Rogers Clark, Revolutionary War hero. As a small boy, William's family moved to what is now the Louisville, Kentucky, area; at age 19 William served in the Kentucky militia, fighting Indians in the Ohio River country. In 1792 he was commissioned a lieutenant in the U.S. Army, and he fought under Gen. Anthony Wayne at the Battle of Fallen Timbers in August 1794. In 1796 Clark resigned from the army in order to devote his time to running the family plantation.

In 1803 he was invited by friend Meriwether Lewis to assume the role of co-commander of the Corps of Discovery, which took on the exploration of the Louisiana Purchase, the event that cements his position in American history. In the years following his epic adventure across the newly acquired western territory, Clark was mainly involved in Indian affairs, being appointed agent for the western tribes. In June 1813 he was named governor of the Missouri Territory (formerly the Louisiana Purchase). A capable and energetic soldier, William Clark became one of the nation's ablest Indian agents.

See also: Clark, George Rogers; Fallen Timbers, Battle of

Further Reading: Ambrose, *Undaunted Courage;* Lavender, *Way to the Western Sea;* Thom, *From Sea to Shining Sea* (an excellent historical novel based on the Clark family)

Clark's Garrison, Battle of
12 March 1676

Located on the Eel River just north of Plymouth, Massachusetts, Clark's Garrison was considered an impregnable outpost. Notwithstanding, on Sunday, 12 March 1676, the Wampanoag sachem, Totoson, attacked, killing most of the inhabitants and destroying it. The raid was regarded as one of the most successful in early New England history.

See also: King Philip's War
Further Reading: Bourne, *The Red King's Rebellion*

Clark's Ohio Campaign of 1782

Although peace talks had begun in the fall of 1782 and there was a general cease-fire in the east, the British continued to encourage and support Indian raids in the West, hoping thereby to hang on to the lucrative fur trade. In the last campaign of the Revolutionary War, George Rogers Clark organized a 1,000-man force to attack the Shawnees. The disaster at Blue Licks, Kentucky, had unfairly sullied Clark's reputation—despite the fact he was not even present at the fight. He had been in overall command of the forces engaged, however, and some, including Daniel Boone, held him accountable.

With Indian raids on the rise action was needed, and Clark determined to strike the Shawnee village at Piqua Town and Chillicothe, toward which he advanced early in 1782. Proceeding cautiously with scouts in advance, the column surprised and destroyed one village at Willstown and nearly succeeded in surprising Piqua Town as well but were discovered at the last moment. Not wishing to give battle, the warriors fled, allowing Clark to destroy the village's winter food supply. The column remained in the area for several days, attempting unsuccessfully to lure the Indians into a fight. Instead, small parties sniped at the Americans and tried to draw individuals into an ambush. Mostly, however, Clark's men were not tempted.

When it became clear that there was little likelihood of dealing the Shawnee warrior force a serious blow, Clark returned to Kentucky with the knowledge he had destroyed the Shawnees' winter food supply.

See also: Blue Licks, Battle of; Chillicothe, Ohio: Battles on the Little Miami (Mad) River; Clark's Ohio Campaign of 1786; Piqua Town, Battle of; Revolutionary War
Further Reading: Bakeless, *Background to Glory*

Clark's Ohio Campaign of 1786

The treaty signed at Fort Finney, Kentucky (on the north bank of the Ohio River, near the mouth of the Miami River), on 1 February 1786, was, like its predecessors and successors, unsuccessful and short-lived. As white settlers continued to flock to the Ohio country, Indian raids, which had subsided somewhat, increased again, especially in the Illinois country. How to deal with the conflicts was a tricky matter.

In signing the Articles of Confederation, Virginia had ceded all claims to lands north of the Ohio River. All of this territory, accordingly, fell under the jurisdiction of the federal government, which refused to authorize military action. Feeling compelled to do something, Virginia elected to mobilize its militia.

Although he was no longer on active duty and had no real authority from the state of Virginia, George Rogers Clark, acting on the urgings of some of the militia colonels, reluctantly accepted command of the expedition. The expedition proceeded with its organization and assembly through the summer of 1786. By late September scouts reported that the Indians were massing along upper Wabash River. The strategy called for one column of some 800 men (mostly leftover militia who had not responded to the earlier call) under Col. Benjamin Logan to move against the Shawnees; Clark, with the main body of 1,200 men, would move against the Wabash villages.

Logan's strike was successful, mainly because most of the warriors, having learned of Clark's column anyway, had joined the villages along the Wabash. Clark's column was a mess from the start. There was dissension among the colonels, the men were unruly, and discipline was virtually nonexistent. Clark wanted to move directly against the Wabash communities but was overruled by his men, who wanted to march first to Vincennes, where supplies could reach them by boat. With no real authority to back up decisions, there was little Clark could do but acquiesce.

The column finally reached Vincennes (in present-day Indiana) only to encounter supply problems. Due to low water the boats were late, and when they finally arrived some of the provisions had been spoiled by water. Notwithstanding, the expedition eventually left for the Indian villages in upper Wabash country, near present-day Lafayette, Indiana. Forty-eight hours out of Vincennes, however, half the column, disgusted with conditions and the lack of supplies, mutinied and left. Faced suddenly with the loss of half his force, Clark made the disappointing but prudent decision to turn back with the remainder; in so doing he may have avoided a disaster. The Indians, having known of Clark's advance, were prepared to greet his arrival with an ambush.

The expedition was a failure, or at least Clark's half of it was. Rumors began to circulate that it was all due to Clark's drinking, although this is completely discounted by one of his biographers, who suggests the rumors may have been spread by the duplicitous Gen. James Wilkinson.

See also: Clark's Ohio Campaign of 1782; Revolutionary War; Shawnees
Further Reading: Bakeless, *Background to Glory*

Clinch, Col. Duncan Lamont
?–1849

Born in North Carolina, Duncan Lamont Clinch was a career army officer who saw active service, mainly against the Seminoles in Florida. Clinch's most notable role occurred while he was commander of South Georgia in 1816, when he was directed by Gen. Andrew Jackson to attack a place known as Negro Fort on the Apalachicola River. Abandoned by the British the year before, the fort had become a haven for runaway slaves and Seminoles. Clinch's objective was to recover as many slaves as possible.

Gunboats provided support for Clinch's attack. Shells from their heavy guns struck the fort's powder magazine, resulting in a gigantic explosion that killed hundreds of slaves and Seminoles. The act probably played a major role in igniting the First Seminole War.

See also: Jackson, Andrew; Seminole War, First; Seminole War, Second; Seminole War, Third
Further Reading: Covington, *The Seminoles of Florida*

Cochise
ca. 1810–1874

One of the great Indian leaders of the nineteenth century, Cochise was a Chiricahua Apache of the Chokonen band. He was born about 1810 in northern Mexico, what is today southeastern Arizona.

Two incidents had a dramatic impact on Cochise's life: His father was killed by Mexicans; his brother was executed by Americans during the tragic Bascom Affair. Both events forged Cochise into a leader whose name was feared throughout the Southwest. Cochise became the implacable foe of Mexicans and Americans.

By the early 1850s Cochise had begun to emerge as a leader of renown, and by 1858 he had become the principal chief of the Chokonen. Cochise's first contact with Americans was apparently around this time. Although there were some skirmishes with the newly arriving white men, it was not until after his brother's execution in the Bascom Affair (1861) that Cochise became the terrible enemy of the Americans. In 1872, primarily through the intercession of agent Tom Jeffords, Gen. O. O. Howard was able to negotiate the first peace in southeastern Arizona in more than a decade.

Nevertheless, continued raids by Apache bands south into Mexico resulted in military intervention. Both Cochise and Jeffords had worked to put an end to the raids, but Cochise had only minimal influence on Apaches outside the pale of his own band. His health declined, and he died in 1874. He was buried in an undisclosed location somewhere in the Dragoon Mountains of southeastern Arizona. His friend and confidante, Tom Jeffords, is said to have been the only white man who knew the location of Cochise's burial site; he never revealed it. The unusual story of the relationship between Cochise and Jeffords is poignantly told in the movie *Broken Arrow*.

See also: Apache Wars; Bascom Affair
Further Reading: Clum, *Apache Agent*; Sweeney, *Cochise*; Thrapp, *The Conquest of Apacheria*; Worcester, *The Apaches*

Cody, William Frederick (Buffalo Bill)
1846–1917

Perhaps the most recognizable name in all of western Americana, William F. Cody was born in Scott County, Iowa, but his family moved to the Fort Leavenworth area when he was only eight. After his father's death young William was employed by the firm of Majors and Russell as a courier and, later, as a pony express rider. During the Civil War he was first affiliated with militia units, later enlisting as a private in the Seventh Kansas Volunteers.

Following the Civil War, Cody headed west, hiring out as a hunter and guide. In 1867–1868 he was hired by the Kansas-Pacific Railroad to supply buffalo meat for its construction crews. It was during this period that he earned the sobriquet "Buffalo Bill," having killed more than 4,000 of the shaggy beasts. Impressed with Cody's knowledge of the country as well as his daring, Gen. Philip H. Sheridan hired him as chief of scouts for the Fifth Cavalry, a position he held for four years. During his tenure as chief of scouts Cody participated in a number of Indian battles, including that of Summit Springs, Colorado, in July 1869.

Buffalo Bill Cody and his Indian chiefs

Cody also served as a hunting guide for some of the European nobility who came to the United States on grand hunting expeditions. His reputation was growing and was further promoted by dime novelist Ned Buntline (E.Z.C. Judson), who used Cody as the hero of one of his novels. As his reputation spread, Cody began to appear increasingly on the live stage, an experience for which he quickly developed a taste; it become a normal winter activity for nearly a dozen years. During the summer months he would return to the West, there to resume his duties as an army scout.

In the aftermath of the Battle of the Little Big Horn, the Fifth Cavalry, with Cody as chief scout, was en route to join the command of Gen. George Crook. Alerted to a movement of Cheyennes to join the victorious hostile bands then in the field, the Fifth Cavalry intercepted the Indians; in the fight that followed Cody personally killed chief Yellow Hair (a Cheyenne sometimes called Yellow Hand), thereby claiming the first scalp in revenge for Custer's death.

In 1883 Cody organized Buffalo Bill's Wild West Show, which later toured Europe several times. Although often in financial trouble, the show managed to remain alive and popular for three decades. Perhaps more than any other single figure, Buffalo Bill Cody, through the medium of his Wild West Show, immortalized the American West he had known and experienced. Cody died in Denver, Colorado, in 1917 and is buried on Lookout Mountain, west of the Mile High City.

See also: Summit Springs, Battle of
Further Reading: Russell, *Lives and Legends of Buffalo Bill*

Coeur d'Alene War of 1858

In May 1858 an army column numbering 150 men commanded by Lt. Col. Edward J. Steptoe left Fort Walla Walla for Colville, Idaho, to investigate reports of Indian conflicts in the area and to satisfy miners' demands for army protection. Steptoe anticipated this would be an exercise in simply impressing the enemy, and so he failed to equip his column for serious trouble. He was apparently unaware of Indian anger at the development of the Missouri-Columbia Road, over which his command was now marching.

Near present-day Rosalia, Washington, Steptoe was confronted by a mixed body of Coeur d'Alenes, Palouses, and Spokanes, numbering about 1,000. Angrily, the Indians demanded that the army turn about and go home. Confronted by a force nearly ten times the size of his own, Steptoe agreed to do as they demanded. However, on the return march the Indians suddenly attacked the column, forcing Steptoe to take up a defensive position on a hill. The column was equipped with howitzers, which Steptoe used to hold off the Indians. After nightfall Steptoe was persuaded that the wisest course was to try an escape, which he managed to do successfully, finally returning to Fort Walla Walla.

The department commander, Brig. Gen. Newman Clarke, furious over this humiliating incident, promptly directed Col. George Wright to launch a hard campaign against the tribes involved. "You will make their punishment severe," Clarke instructed Wright. With a mixed force of troops augmented by friendly Nez Perce scouts, Wright's command confronted the Indians in two pitched battles: Spokane Plain on 1 September 1858, and Four Lakes on 5 September. With superior numbers, and able to fight the kind of traditional battle the army seldom had an opportunity to conduct in Indian warfare, Wright decisively defeated the Indians.

In the aftermath 15 of the warriors who had participated in the Steptoe incident were hanged. Their will to resist broken, the Indians agreed to move to their appointed reservations.

See also: Steptoe, Col. Edward Jenner; Wright, Gen. George

Further Reading: Burns, *Jesuits in the Indian Wars of the Northwest;* Manring, *Conquest of the Coeur d'Alenes*

Colorow
ca. 1810–1888

A Moache Ute chief, Colorow was a large man weighing more than 300 pounds. While a small boy, he was captured by Utes from Comanches during a raid. One historian has suggested that he was part Comanche and part Apache. As white presence in Ute country increased, Colorow gradually broke away from Ouray's peace policy, taking a hard-line stance against the whites. This was exacerbated when agent Nathan Meeker unilaterally replaced Colorow with hated rival Sanovick as chief, a move that quickly produced hostilities.

When Meeker, concerned about the growing tension, requested troops as a precaution, Colorow and his followers attacked a relief column under Maj. Thomas Thornburg at Milk Creek while others attacked the agency, killing Nathan Meeker and several others. The women at the agency were taken captive. After the uprising was quelled Colorow and his band were relocated to the Uintah Reservation in Utah, although they continued to hunt in western Colorado. Colorow himself died on the White River in 1888.

See also: Meeker Massacre; Ouray

Further Reading: Sprague, *Massacre;* Urquhart, *Colorow: The Angry Chieftain*

Comanches

A Southern Plains tribe of the Shosnonean linguistic family, the Comanches seem to have been inhabitants of the northern Plains perhaps as recently as the seventeenth century. Sometime in the early eighteenth century they drifted south, perhaps forced by stronger tribes such as the Lakotas. In the Southwest they established contact with the Apaches and Spaniards.

Contact with the Spanish proved to be a pivotal moment in Comanche history, as the Spanish introduced them to the horse. Thus, Comanches were among the earliest of the Plains tribes to acquire the horse and quickly became extraordinarily proficient horsemen. Possession of the horse gave them tremendous mobility to hunt buffalo, upon which their economy depended.

Feared as raiders throughout their territory, Comanches challenged Spanish, French, and Americans for more than a century. White settlers in West Texas, Oklahoma, and part of New Mexico lived a precarious existence until Comanche power was effectively broken in the Buffalo, or Red River, War of 1874.

See also: Parker, Quanah; Red River War
Further Reading: Fehrenbach, *Comanches;* Wallace, *Commanches: Lords of the Plains*

Connor, Gen. Patrick Edward
1820–1891

Something of an Irish soldier of fortune and adventurer, Patrick Connor was reportedly born in Ireland and came to the United States as a boy. At age 19 he enlisted in the army, saw action against the Seminoles in Florida, then went west to Texas. After being wounded during the Mexican War he left the army and went to California, where he engaged in prospecting and surveying. Upon the outbreak of the Civil War he was appointed colonel of the Third California Volunteer Infantry. In October 1862 he was named commander of the District of Nevada and Utah and established Fort Douglas, near Salt Lake City.

In response to raids by hostile Bannocks, Shoshones, and Utes, Connor launched a winter campaign early in 1863 that resulted in a decisive victory at Bear River near Preston, Idaho. In 1865 Connor was in overall command of a three-pronged expedition against the Sioux and Cheyennes. However, owing to a lack of coordination, inadequate supply system, and treacherous weather, the campaign fell far short of achieving its goal of punishing the northern Plains tribes, al-though Connor's column did score a victory of sorts over Black Bear's Arapahos on Tongue River. Notwithstanding, Connor was relieved of command.

Although anti-Mormon to the core, Connor later settled in Salt Lake City, where he launched a daily newspaper and was active in various mining enterprises. Despite the fact that the 1865 campaign was an overall failure, Connor was probably a better fighter than he has been given credit for.

See also: Bear River, Battle of; Connor's Powder River Expedition
Further Reading: Hafen, *Powder River Campaign;* Madsen, *Glory Hunter;* ———, *The Shoshoni Frontier*

Connor's Powder River Expedition
1865

In July 1865 a three-pronged expedition under the overall command of Gen. Patrick E. Connor moved into the Black Hills and Powder River regions for the purpose of chastising the Indian bands that had grown increasingly hostile. The first column, under Col. Nelson Cole, consisted of a mixed force of 1,400 from the Twelfth Missouri Cavalry and Second Missouri Light Artillery, supported by a large wagon train. It left Omaha and marched up the Platte River, aiming to eventually strike Indian camps in the vicinity of Bear Butte, South Dakota. The second or "Center Column" was commanded by Lt. Col. Samuel Walker. Walker's command, some 600 strong and composed of the Fifteenth and Sixteenth Kansas Volunteer Cavalry regiments plus artillery and wagons, marched out of Fort Laramie for the Black Hills.

Connor himself commanded the third column, a 500-man force comprising the Seventh Iowa, Eleventh Ohio, Second California, and Sixth Michigan Regiments plus the battalion of 179 Pawnee scouts led by Maj. Frank North, departed from Fort Laramie, marching north up the Bozeman Trail. Like the other two columns, Connor's was also encumbered by a large wagon train. Overall, the expedition was one of the largest to be assembled on the Plains up to that time. The strategy called for the three columns to rendezvous about 1 September on Rosebud Creek in southeastern Montana.

In addition to the three columns, a fourth, numbering some 50 men (civilians) and wagons, under James A. Sawyers, left the Niobrara River in western Nebraska in mid-June, heading northwest. It was guarded by a 140-man army escort, graciously furnished by the department commander, Gen. John Pope. Sawyers's train was euphemistically dubbed a road-building expedition when in fact its real purpose was to promote a route between Iowa and Bozeman, Montana. Although not officially a part of the expedition, the Sawyers group would play a role in its affairs before the campaign concluded.

By mid-August Connor had reached the Upper Powder River, having clashed three times with hostile war parties, and began construction of a post to be named Fort Connor, which would be rebuilt and renamed Fort Reno the following year. After establishing Fort Connor and leaving a garrison Connor continued northwest, and on 29 August he struck the Arapaho village of Black Bear on the Tongue River, north of present-day Sheridan, Wyoming. The fight turned out to be a rather brisk affair when the Indians counterattacked, but they were finally driven back by Connor's artillery.

Early, winterlike storms now struck the region, creating perfectly miserable conditions for campaigning. Connor, having heard nothing from either of the other two columns, sent out Indian scouts to locate them, without success. As a result, the planned rendezvous failed to materialize. Meanwhile, even as Connor was looking for Cole and Walker, the Sawyers group had been attacked in rough country near the Powder River. After surviving that episode, and after a dispute between Sawyers and the commander of the army escort, the train pushed on to the site of Fort Connor. From there Sawyers sent a party to locate Connor but found instead a large body of Arapahos, who threatened to attack for three days be-

fore finally moving off, allowing the Sawyers group to return to Fort Connor.

On 11 September Connor's scouts reported finding several hundred dead cavalry horses, along with various pieces of equipment, which subsequently turned out to be from the columns of Cole and Walker. Cole, it seemed, had made a ponderous march to Bear Butte (just north of the Black Hills); finding no Indians he headed up the Belle Fourche River, where he encountered Walker, who had departed Fort Laramie two weeks earlier. The two columns pushed on—separately but close enough to be in supporting distance of one another. Supplies, however, were beginning to run low, especially forage for the horses. There was no actual sign of the Indians, nor of Connor.

In view of what seemed to be a deteriorating situation, Colonel Cole decided to return to Fort Laramie, only to be attacked by a large Cheyenne war party, which he managed to repel. The attack changed his mind, however, and Cole now elected to head down the Powder River in search of Connor. On the night of 2 September the blistering heat through which the column had been moving suddenly gave way to the unseasonable storms and bitter-cold temperatures encountered by Connor's command. Overnight, more than 200 of Cole's horses and mules, weakened by hunger, perished on the picket lines from exposure and exhaustion.

On the morning of 5 September Cole and Walker found a large village of Sioux, Cheyennes, and Arapahos near the mouth of the Little Powder River. The village, containing more than 1,000 warriors, was essentially the same body that had been involved in the Platte Bridge fight. Swarming over the ridges and hills, the Indians attacked, and for three hours an intense fight raged. The Indians would probably have overwhelmed the troops had it not been for the artillery, which managed to keep them dispersed. Eventually, the Indians called off the fight, and after regrouping, Cole and Walker continued.

On 8 September the two columns, quite by accident, ran into another village, and yet another fight ensued. Once again, it was the artillery that made the difference. That night another winterlike storm struck, resulting in the deaths of hundreds more animals. As the columns resumed the march, Indians harassed them, but artillery continued to keep the attackers at bay. By mid-September Cole and Walker had managed to reach Fort Connor, where they were finally joined by Connor on 24 September.

At this juncture it was Connor's intention to reorganize and take the field again. However, under a recent reorganization of army departments, he was ordered to the District of Utah and was thus compelled to close out his campaign, which had largely been a failed proposition due to logistical problems and poor communications.

See also: Bozeman Trail; Connor, Gen. Patrick Edward; Platte Bridge, Battle of
Further Reading: Hafen, *Powder River Campaigns;* Madsen, *Glory Hunter;* Vaughn, *Battle of the Platte Bridge*

Conquistadores

The Spanish military who came to the New World were known as *conquistadores,* literally, "the victorious conquerors." Although the term is often used to embrace all of the Spanish adventurers, particularly those who operated in Mexico and the Southwest during the sixteenth and seventeenth centuries, it more properly refers to the military.

See also: Coronado, Francisco Vasquez de; Spain

Cooke, Col. Philip St. George
1809–1895

Born in Virginia, Philip St. George Cooke graduated from West Point in 1827. He served in the Sixth Infantry during the Black Hawk War, then transferred to the mounted arm. During the Mexican War he served as commander of the Mormon Battalion in Stephen Watts Kearny's Army of the West.

In 1854 he led a campaign against the Jicarilla Apaches. Promoted to colonel in 1858, he saw action in the Mormon War of 1857–1858 and served with Gen. William S. Harney in his campaign against the Sioux at the Battle of Ash Hollow. He commanded the Department of the Platte during Red Cloud's War (1866–1868) and the struggle for the Bozeman Trail. Cooke was noted for the system of cavalry tactics he developed for the U.S. Army. He was the father-in-law of the famous Confederate cavalry leader J.E.B. Stuart.

See also: Blue Water, Battle of; Harney, Gen. William Selby; Red Cloud's War
Further Reading: Long, *Saints and the Union;* Madsen, *Glory Hunter;* Utley, *Frontiersmen in Blue*

Córdoba (Córdova), Francisco Fernandez (Hernandez) de
?–1518

A Spanish soldier who served in Cuba and later discovered the Yucatan Peninsula, de Córdoba was also the first of his countrymen to discover evidence of the Mayan civilization. In 1517 de Córdoba was sent by Diego Velásquez, governor of Cuba, to procure Indian slaves. He first sought a source of supply in the Yucatan but encountered stiff resistance from the natives of that area, sustaining numerous wounds himself (one source claims a dozen arrow wounds).

Thus thwarted, de Córdoba turned his eye toward Florida (*La Florida*), landing at San Carlos Bay, where he was accorded another warm reception, this time by fierce Calusa warriors, who drove off the Spaniards with powerful bows that launched arrows capable of penetrating breastplate armor. De Córdoba later died from wounds sustained on this expedition.

See also: Ponce de León, Juan; Spain
Further Reading: Morison, *European Discovery of North America: The Southern Voyages;* Steele, *Warpaths*

Cornplanter
ca. 1732 [1740?]–1836

A Seneca chief known to the whites as Captain O'Beel, or John O'Bail, Cornplanter was the son of a Seneca woman and a white trader—either Dutch or English. Cornplanter took part in the treaties negotiated at

Fort Stanwix in 1784 and at Fort Harmar in 1789, although he did not actually sign either document. He was, however, a signatory to treaties in 1797 and 1802, incurring the dislike of his tribe for doing so. Cornplanter amassed considerable land holdings in Pennsylvania after the Revolutionary War but reportedly renounced all white affiliations in his declining years.

See also: Iroquois Confederacy; Treaties and Agreements, Fort Stanwix, Treaty of
Further Reading: Graymont, *The Iroquois in the American Revolution;* Hodge, *Handbook of American Indians*

Cornstalk
1720–1777

A prominent Shawnee chief, Cornstalk first achieved notice at the Battle of Point Pleasant, October 10, 1774, where his conduct of the battle drew admiration from the whites who fought against him. Cornstalk signed a treaty with Lord Dunmore in November 1774. The treaty was opposed by some of his tribe, but he nevertheless adhered to the terms of the agreement until 1777, when persistent treaty violations on the part of whites caused Cornstalk to warn settlers at Point Pleasant that he might be forced to resume warfare if the violations did not cease. Held as a hostage, he was later murdered by angry soldiers. Cornstalk's death ushered in two decades of savage raids by the Shawnees.

See also: Lord Dunmore's War; Shawnees
Further Reading: Dowd, *A Spirited Resistance*

Coronado, Francisco Vasquez de
1510–1554

One of the most recognizable names of the early Spanish presence in North America, Coronado and his two-year search for the legendary "Seven Cities of Cibola" have become one of the epic stories of the American West. As governor of the Province of New Galicia in northwest Mexico, Coronado set out from Compostela in April 1540 at the head of an expedition numbering some 300 Spaniards and 800 Indians. In addition, the column was accompanied by some wives and children as well as missionaries and black slaves. The expedition's objective was the vast wealth to be found in rumored cities of gold, the existence of which had been reported by Cabeza de Vaca and Fray Marcos, among others.

Directed by the Spanish Crown to deal more humanely with indigenous peoples, Coronado apparently sought to conduct his expedition without the harsh treatment of Indians that had characterized other Spanish forays. However, despite a more conciliatory attitude, at least at the outset, Coronado's relationship with Indians was no less violent than that of his predecessors. In July 1540 the expedition entered the Zuni pueblo of Hawikuh (near present Zuni, New Mexico), where Coronado demanded the community's surrender; the inhabitants responded by hurling stones at the Spanish, one of which knocked Coronado unconscious. Quickly recovering from this unexpected greeting, however, the Spanish soon overpowered the defenders and took control of the pueblo.

From there Coronado launched smaller probes that succeeded in capturing other Zuni and Hopi pueblos in what is today Arizona and New Mexico. One such probe may have been the first to discover the Grand Canyon; during another a Spanish column became the first to reach California. Meanwhile, Coronado's main column moved northeast to other pueblo communities on the upper Rio Grande River. There, the Spanish found the pueblos of Taos and Picuris, composing the province Tiguex, where they were received in friendship by the Tigua inhabitants. Amicable relations quickly deteriorated, however, when Coronado, having elected to spend the winter of 1540–1541 there, demanded that the Indians supply his men with clothing. When the order was refused the Spanish forcibly took what they needed. The angered Indians retaliated by driving off a portion of the Spanish horse herd and then fortifying themselves in their pueblos.

A peace was subsequently negotiated but proved short-lived. Whether deception was involved or whether there was a legitimate misunderstanding on the part of the Spanish is unclear. In any event, the situation quickly deteriorated, and many of the inhabitants were taken captive by the Spanish and either burned at the stake or killed attempting to escape. In desperation, the survivors abandoned all but two of their pueblos, where they fortified themselves and prepared for a siege. Surrounding one of the pueblos, the Spanish attacked, using ladders, but were repulsed time and again, suffering some 50 casualties in the process. The siege lasted 50 days, during which time the Indians had 200 killed and were finally compelled to surrender when their water supply was exhausted. The second pueblo suffered a shorter siege.

In the spring of 1541, motivated by Indian stories of rich cities to the northeast in the province of Quivara, Coronado pointed his column in that direction. Crossing the panhandles of Texas and Oklahoma, the Spanish penetrated as far as present-day Kansas, where Coronado finally felt compelled to return to Mexico. He found no trace of the wealth that had been anticipated at the outset of the journey. His failure to locate the riches of Cibola subjected Coronado to much official scrutiny.

See also: Llano Estacado (Staked Plains); Pueblo Indians; Spain
Further Reading: Bolton, *Coronado on the Turquoise Trail;* Hodge, *Handbook of American Indians;* John, *Storms Brewed in Other Men's Worlds;* Milanich and Milbrath, *First Encounters*

Council on the Auglaize River
1792

In 1792 tribal representatives from the Six Nations—Sauks and Foxes, Shawnees, Cherokees, Creeks, Ottawas—and others gathered at the confluence of the Auglaize and Maumee Rivers in northwestern Ohio. The location, favored by the tribes for such gatherings, was known simply as the "Glaize." Although representatives of the tribes began assembling in the summer, it was not until October that all were present and the council was actually convened. The central issue facing the council was the possibility of forming a unified Indian confederacy to confront advancing white settlements. Rivalries and bickering among the leaders, however, made it impossible for any real accord to take place; the council disbanded without having achieved any significant plan of cooperation.

See also: "Glaize," the; *specific tribes*
Further Reading: Dowd, *A Spirited Resistance;* Sword, *President Washington's Indian War*

Covenant Chain

The Covenant Chain was an early colonial task force designed to coordinate relations between Indians and British colonies. Under this arrangement, New York served as the umbrella, overseeing colonial administrators who dealt with the tribes; the Iroquois Confederacy acted in the same capacity for the Indians.

See also: Iroquois Confederacy
Further Reading: Jennings, *The Invasion of America*

Crawford, Lt. Emmet
1844–1886

Born in Pennsylvania, Emmet Crawford enlisted in the army as a private during the Civil War and was commissioned lieutenant in 1864. Crawford served in the infantry until 1870, when he transferred to the Third Cavalry stationed in Arizona. Early in 1872 the Third Cavalry was sent north to the Great Plains, where Crawford saw action against the Sioux, notably in the Battle of the Rosebud, fought on 17 June 1876.

Returning to Arizona in 1882 Crawford was placed in charge of the army unit at San Carlos Apache Reservation and directed to organize and train a contingent of Apache scouts. The undertaking proved immensely successful. Crawford led his scouts deep into Mexico in pursuit of hostile Apaches. He was transferred to Texas briefly but returned to Arizona when troubles with Geronimo developed. Once again, Crawford assumed leadership of the Apache scouts, pursuing Geronimo's band deep into Mexico's Sierra Madres Mountains.

On 11 January 1886, Crawford's command was unexpectedly attacked by Mexican troops, with Crawford sustaining a mortal wound in the fight. Although the attack seemed clearly intentional, no official action was taken against the Mexican government. Crawford was an able and courageous soldier, one whose contribution during the Apache wars has not been fully appreciated.

See also: Apache Wars; Geronimo; Rosebud, Battle of the
Further Reading: Mangum, *The Battle of the Rosebud;* Thrapp, *General Crook and the Sierra Madre Adventure*

Crazy Horse
(Tashunca Utico, Tashunka Witko)
ca. 1841–1877

An Oglala Sioux war leader, the name Crazy Horse is one of the most recognizable of all North American Indian names. A literal translation of his name is "His horse is crazy." Aloof and often regarded as mysterious by his own people, Crazy Horse was an outstanding warrior and brilliant natural tactician who steadfastly opposed white encroachment.

Crazy Horse first came into prominence during Red Cloud's War (1865–1868), when he is thought to have played a leading role in designing the ambush of Capt. William J. Fetterman's command near Fort Phil Kearny, Wyoming, on 21 December 1866. On 17 June 1876, Crazy Horse led a large war party against Gen. George Crook's Big Horn and Yellowstone Expedition in the Battle of the Rosebud in Montana. Eight days later, Crazy Horse played a prominent role in the destruction of Custer's battalion on the Little Bighorn River.

In the aftermath of the Little Bighorn, Crazy Horse did not take his band to Canada, as did Sitting Bull, Gall, and others, but instead remained in Montana to continue fighting the army forces under the

command of Col. Nelson A. Miles. Persuaded, finally, that further resistance was futile, Crazy Horse surrendered to Miles in May 1877. Later that summer, he left the agency to which he had been assigned without permission. There were rumors he was planning an outbreak, though it was never proven. In any case, he was apprehended and taken to Fort Robinson, Nebraska, as a prisoner, where he was killed by a bayonet thrust during a scuffle with a group of soldiers and Indian police. Exactly whose bayonet ended the life of the Sioux leader is unknown.

See also: Fetterman Disaster; Little Bighorn, Battle of the (Custer's Last Stand); Red Cloud's War
Further Reading: Sandoz, *Crazy Horse*

Creek Campaigns
1813–1814

During the War of 1812 the United States was concerned with British actions not only in the northern regions but also in the South (Louisiana, Mississippi, and Alabama). The United States also feared a British movement into Spanish Florida, which would place them in a position to move against New Orleans.

Within this general region dwelled the Creeks, who had strong ties to the Spanish. A faction of the Creeks known as the Red Sticks were also pro-British; the White Stick Creeks were generally partial toward the United States. Desiring to secure Florida before the British had a chance to establish a presence there, Pres. James Madison directed the army to prepare for a movement into Florida. Andrew Jackson, major general of the Tennessee militia, accordingly began to organize in Nashville in February 1813. However, the campaign was canceled when the American movement against Canada failed.

The Creeks, especially the Red Sticks, who had been influenced by Tecumseh's cry for Indian unification, nonetheless remained a concern. A small party of Red Sticks under William Weatherford (Red Eagle) journeyed to Canada to support Tecumseh and participated in the River Raisin massacre.

Another group, under leader Peter Mc-Queen, of mixed race heritage, was attacked by settlers at Burnt Corn, near Pensacola. In the aftermath of this attack white settlers, including many who had participated in the Burnt Corn affair, withdrew into the safety of Fort Mims, near Mobile; in August 1813 they were again attacked by McQueen's Red Sticks. The fort was poorly defended, and as a result most of the 700 inhabitants were killed. The Fort Mims Massacre, as it quickly came to be known, led to a full-scale campaign against the Creeks. A 1,000-man column under Brig. Gen. John Floyd moved west from Georgia while a second column of roughly equal strength, under Gen. F. L. Claiborne, moved east from Mississippi. The third and largest of the three columns, under Andrew Jackson, marched south from Tennessee. The idea was for the three columns to converge on the Creek heartland in west-central Alabama.

Floyd located and attacked one Creek village in late November 1814. After inflicting substantial casualties he was forced to withdraw due to lack of supplies. Lack of supplies and expiring enlistments also compelled Claiborne to retire after some success. Andrew Jackson, meanwhile, moved south from Fayetteville, Tennessee. In the first of two actions Jackson's cavalry inflicted heavy losses on the Red Sticks before Jackson, like Floyd and Claiborne, had to deal with low supplies and expiring enlistments among his militia. Reinforced, however, by substantial contingents of regulars and new militia, Jackson was able to resume his campaign, decisively defeating the Creeks at the Battle of Horseshoe Bend on 27 March 1814. Jackson's subsequent treaty with the Creeks secured the Southwest for the United States.

See also: Creeks; Horseshoe Bend, Battle of; Jackson, Andrew
Further Reading: Heidler, *Old Hickory's War*; Prucha, *The Sword of the Republic*

Creeks

One of the so-called Five Civilized Tribes (Creeks, Cherokees, Choctaws, Chickasaws, and Seminole), the Creeks belong to the Muskogean Nation. Creeks were essentially divided into "lower" and "upper" towns, the former occupying part of Georgia, the latter between the Alabama and Savannah Rivers.

During the seventeenth century the Lower Town Creeks were greatly influenced by the British, whereas Upper Town Creeks tended to ally with the French and Spanish. During the American Revolution, however, Lower Town Creeks took a neutral stance; Upper Town Creeks sided with the British.

During the War of 1812 differences between the two factions resulted in a civil war. Lower Town Creeks, aligning themselves with the United States, fought against Upper Town brothers, known as Red Sticks. On 27 March 1814, an American army led by Maj. Gen. Andrew Jackson soundly defeated the Red Stick Creeks at the Battle of Horseshoe Bend, Alabama. Eventually the Creeks, like most of the other Five Civilized Tribes, relocated to the Indian Territory of Oklahoma.

See also: Creek Campaigns; Horseshoe Bend, Battle of; Jackson, Andrew; Red Sticks
Further Reading: Debo, *Road to Disappearance*; Heidler, *Old Hickory*

Croatans (Croatoans)

A people of mixed race heritage from the coastal region of North Carolina, the Croatans are thought by some to have merged with Sir Walter Raleigh's famous lost colony. As a result of a long-standing claim on their part, they were given legal designation by the state of North Carolina during the 1890s, having rejected a previous classification as negro.

See also: Jamestown, Virginia
Further Reading: Hodge, *Handbook of American Indians*

Croghan, George
?–1782

An Irish immigrant, George Croghan first appeared on the North American scene about 1740. His life was largely spent on the far-flung frontier of western Pennsylvania and in the Ohio country, and he came to be recognized as an authority on both the region and its Indian tribes. He established an important trading post at Logstown, Pennsylvania, later the setting for the Logstown Treaty and Pickawillany Massacre.

An adept trader and sometimes devious speculator in western lands, Croghan was not above an occasional shady deal. Together with Robert Rogers, he negotiated a treaty with the Delawares, Shawnees, and Senecas at Fort Pitt in 1765. He also negotiated with Pontiac over control of the western outposts. Colorful and at times a crook, Croghan rendered valuable service to Indians and whites. He died, bankrupt, near Philadelphia in 1782.

See also: Forts, Camps, Cantonments, Outposts, Pitt (Pittsburgh); Pickawillany Massacre; Rogers, Maj. Robert; *specific tribes;* Treaties and Agreements, Logstown Treaty
Further Reading: Wainright, *George Croghan: Wilderness Diplomat*

Crook, Gen. George
1828–1890

Born in Ohio, George Crook graduated from West Point in 1852. Although he did not excel academically and finished near the bottom of his class, no less than William Tecumseh Sherman once described Crook as the army's best Indian fighter. Following graduation from West Point, Crook was assigned to California and the Pacific Northwest, where he served for eight years, gaining much experience with Indians, including participation in the Rogue River and Yakima Wars.

Following a distinguished Civil War career, marred only by an embarrassing capture by Confederate troops late in 1864, he returned to the far-western frontier, where he saw service against the Paiutes. In 1871 Crook was reassigned to Arizona Territory, where he employed his now considerable experience against Apaches. He became es-

The Grand Council held at General Crook's headquarters on Goose Creek, 15 June 1876

pecially noted for his use of friendly Apaches as scouts against hostile bands.

In 1875 Crook was named to command the Department of the Platte, with headquarters in Omaha. During the Great Sioux War of 1876 he operated out of Fort Fetterman, Wyoming, near present-day Douglas. On 17 March 1876, a column of Crook's troops under the tactical command of Col. J. J. Reynolds was roughly handled in a fight on the Powder River in southeastern Montana, after first scoring a resounding victory. Three months later, on 17 June, Crook was bested, or at least stymied, by Crazy Horse in the Battle of the Rosebud River in Montana. Crook was finally able to salvage something out of the summer's campaign with a marginal victory over the Sioux at Slim Buttes, South Dakota, in September.

Following his service in the Department of the Platte, Crook was sent back to Arizona to deal with resurgent Apaches. He was replaced by Gen. Nelson A. Miles in 1882 when his methods were perceived to not be working. In 1888 Crook was promoted to major general and named to head the Department of the Missouri. He died unexpectedly of a heart attack in 1890.

A tireless campaigner against Indians, he also worked hard on their behalf once hostilities had ended. He was regarded as one of the most humane military leaders during the post–Civil War Indian conflicts. Crook's failure to resume his campaign following the standoff at the Battle of the Rosebud has never been satisfactorily explained. Critics contend that his dilatory action played a significant role in Custer's defeat eight days later.

See also: Rosebud, Battle of the; Sioux War
Further Reading: Bourke, *On the Border with Crook;* Schmitt, *General George Crook*

Crows

A member of the Hidatsa tribal family, the Crows comprise two divisions: Mountain Crows and River Crows. The Mountain branch is the larger of the two, and during the eighteenth and nineteenth centuries it occupied territory in the Big Horn Mountains in northern Wyoming. The smaller branch was generally found in the Yellowstone River drainage system in south-central Montana.

Although there were instances of Crow raids on whites, the tribe tended to ally with the U.S. Army against their traditional enemies, the Sioux, furnishing scouts for various army campaigns. Possibly the Crow best known to history is Curly, believed by some to have been the only one to witness Custer's Last Stand (or most of it) and escape. The Battle of the Little Bighorn was actually fought on the Crow Reservation.

See also: Curly; Little Bighorn, Battle of the (Custer's Last Stand); Sioux War
Further Reading: Denig, *Five Indian Tribes of the Upper Missouri;* Hoxie, *Parading through History*

Curly
ca. 1859–1923

One of the most recognizable names in the field of Custeriana, Curly, a young Crow Indian scout, is believed by many to have been the last person to see Custer alive. Because of this his name is forever enshrined in the annals of western Americana.

Born in Montana, Curly had participated in several fights with the Sioux before signing on as a 17-year-old scout with Col. John Gibbon's Montana Column in the spring of 1876. When Custer marched up the Rosebud River on 22 June 1876, he took with him a detachment of six Crow Indian scouts, one of whom was Curly. The Crows, who had been a part of Colonel Gibbon's force, accompanied Custer because of their knowledge of the terrain. They were not expected to participate in any fighting that might take place.

During the Battle of the Little Bighorn Curly, who never claimed to have actually been in the fight, later said that he had observed parts of the battle and managed to escape the scene of Custer's Last Stand unscathed. He reached the confluence of the Little Bighorn and Big Horn Rivers, where on 26 June he reported to Colonel Gibbon's column of the disaster that had befallen Custer.

Almost immediately he became the subject of questioning about the battle and remained so until the end of his life in 1923. He is buried at Custer Battlefield National Cemetery.

See also: Custer, Lt. Col. George Armstrong; Gibbon, Col. John; Little Bighorn, Battle of the (Custer's Last Stand) *Further Reading:* Gray, *Custer's Last Campaign;* Marquis, *Curly the Crow*

Custer, Lt. Col. George Armstrong
1839–1876

Born in New Rumley, Ohio, on 5 December 1839, Custer's early years were divided between the family farm in New Rumley and the home of his older half-sister, Lydia Ann Kirkpatrick Reed, in Monroe, Michigan. As a consequence, Monroe became a second home to the young man, and Michigan became his adopted state.

Early on, Custer demonstrated the kind of brash, devil-may-care behavior that was to become his trademark in later life. In 1857 he managed to secure an appointment to the U.S. Military Academy at West Point, where his mischievous, undisciplined behavior nearly resulted in dismissal and his academic performance proved barely adequate. When his class graduated in June 1861, George Armstrong Custer ranked last, a standing that certainly did not hint at what the future held.

Custer's Civil War career was marked by conspicuous gallantry in action, and his flamboyant behavior made it impossible not to notice. His fair, handsome features with long, reddish-gold hair and colorful uniform made him one of the war's most striking figures. His skill and boldness as a natural leader of mounted men won the respect of friend and foe alike. By war's end he was a brevet major-general of volunteers.

Like many others in the aftermath of the Civil War, Custer found himself reduced in rank in the shrunken peacetime army. After a brief hiatus he was appointed lieutenant colonel of the newly formed Seventh Cav-

Custer's death struggle in 1876

alry. As such, Custer was technically second in command of the regiment. However, since the commander was generally absent on detached duty, Custer became the regiment's de facto commanding officer. So indelibly did he imprint his personality on the unit that it became, for all intents and purposes, Custer's regiment.

Custer's post–Civil War duty took him first to Texas on reconstruction duty, then to the frontier, where he and his regiment operated against Southern Cheyennes, Arapahos, Comanches, and Kiowas—who were then resisting the steady advance of white civilization across the Central and Southern Plains.

In November 1868 Custer, executing Gen. Philip H. Sheridan's directive to carry out a winter campaign, launched a successful surprise attack on Black Kettle's Cheyenne village along the Washita River in extreme western Oklahoma. The death of Maj. Joel Elliott and 19 troopers—some believed Custer had abandoned them during the battle—created a rift in the regiment never to heal. The Washita incident added to the Custer story in another way as well: Although it was never proven, many believe that Custer fathered a child by a young Cheyenne woman named Monaseetah, one of several taken captive at the Washita. Custer's reputation as an Indian fighter grew out of the action at Washita.

Following a brief tour of duty in Kentucky, the Seventh Cavalry was transferred to Fort Abraham Lincoln, Dakota Territory, early in 1873. That summer the regiment provided escort duty for a Northern Pacific Railroad survey, clashing with the Sioux along the Yellowstone River on three occasions.

In 1874 Custer led a large expedition to explore the interior of the Black Hills of South Dakota, despite the fact that whites' entry was prohibited by the terms of the Laramie Treaty (1868). However, gold was rumored to exist in the area in great quantities, and so the expedition was then justified in the name of science. Perhaps more importantly, Custer was confidentially directed to report on likely sites for a new military post.

General Sheridan believed that a fort located there would be better situated to help control the movement of the Indians, although had it come to pass such action would have represented an even more flagrant violation of the 1868 treaty. Custer's invasion of the Black Hills became a notorious episode and a prominent factor in the 1876 Sioux War.

In the campaign against the Sioux and their allies that got under way early in 1876, Custer was scheduled to command one of three columns ordered to take the field. However, when Custer's testimony before a congressional committee implicated Pres. Ulysses Grant's brother, Orville, in a profiteering scheme with army post traderships, Grant relieved him of command. When Custer's immediate superior, Gen. Alfred Terry, interceded on his behalf, the president relented and allowed Custer to participate in the campaign—but only as commander of the Seventh Cavalry. General Terry himself would be the overall column commander.

In June 1876 pursuant to orders from General Terry, Custer, at the head of his regiment, departed from the column's base camp on the Yellowstone River and marched up the Rosebud River in search of Indians, who were known to be in the general area. Terry's strategy was to locate the Indian village; it was hoped that between Custer's cavalry and a second column under Col. John Gibbon the Indians could be caught, rounded up, and returned to the agencies.

On June 25 Custer discovered the village along the Little Bighorn River in southeastern Montana. Dividing the regiment into three sections, he launched an attack that subsequently resulted in the destruction of five companies under his immediate command and heavy casualties among the remaining companies commanded by Maj. Marcus Reno and Capt. Frederick Benteen.

Given the sensational nature of the event and the attention it received, it is not surprising that the Custer legend began to take shape almost immediately. But more than anything else, it was Custer's widow, Elizabeth Bacon Custer, whom he had married in

1863, who devoted the remainder of her considerable life to glorifying her husband's image, beginning with the interment of his remains at West Point. When she died in 1933 the Custer legend was firmly rooted.

Brash, outspoken, and flamboyant, George Armstrong Custer was not an individual who produced a mild reaction in anyone he met. Undisciplined himself, he could nevertheless be a brutal disciplinarian to

Lt. Col. George Armstrong Custer

those serving under him. Standing just under six feet in height, with a lithe, willowy body, he was a fine physical specimen. A superb horseman, Custer could spend hours in the saddle and required little sleep to restore his depleted energy level. Contrary to much popular opinion, his judgment as a field commander, especially at the Little Bighorn, does not merit the censure earlier accorded him, as recent studies have shown.

See also: Benteen, Capt. Frederick William; Little Bighorn, Battle of the (Custer's Last Stand); Reno, Maj. Marcus Albert (Alfred); Sheridan, Gen. Philip Henry; Terry, Gen. Alfred Howe; Washita, Battle of the
Further Reading: Custer, *My Life on the Plains;* Urwin, *Custer Victorious;* Utley, *Cavalier in Buckskin*

D

Dade's Massacre
28 December 1835

In December 1835 a detachment of 108 troops under the command of Maj. Francis L. Dade left Fort Brooke near Tampa, Florida, en route to Fort King. On 28 December they were attacked by a strong war party of Seminole Indians near present-day Bushnell. Taken by surprise, the command was all but wiped out. Of the three survivors, two managed to eventually return to Fort Brooke by walking and crawling. The third died en route. As with a number of other such fights between Indians and white soldiers—where all or nearly all of the troops were killed—this one, too, has been incorrectly labeled a massacre.

Further Reading: Covington, *The Seminoles of Florida;* Laumer, *Dade's Massacre*

Deerfield, Massachusetts, Battles of

During the colonial wars few if any communities were exposed to as many Indian raids

Indians in canoe with white men captured during the Deerfield massacre

as was Deerfield, Massachusetts. On at least four occasions—1675, 1692, 1704, and again in 1746—the town was struck by savage Indian raids.

See also: King Philip's War
Further Reading: Bourne, *The Red King's Rebellion;* Jennings, *The Invasion of America;* Steele, *Warpaths*

Delgadito
ca. 1815–ca. 1855 [1864?]

A Mimbres Apache chief and member of the *Chihennes,* or Warm Springs, band, Delgadito was closely associated with Mangas Coloradas and may have assumed leadership of Cuchillo Negro's band when the latter was killed.

Like other Apache leaders, Delgadito raided often into Sonora and Chihuahua—but reportedly made an effort to remain at peace with the Americans. When his camp was attacked for no apparent reason in 1856, he accepted the recommendation of agent Michael Steck and did not retaliate. Dan Thrapp (in his *Conquest of Apacheria*) has suggested that Delgadito would have been an influential peace chief had he lived. Circumstances surrounding his death are confusing. One source says 1855, another 1856, and yet a third 1864.

See also: Apache Wars; Mangas Coloradas; Victorio
Further Reading: Thrapp, *The Conquest of Apacheria;* ———, *Victorio*

Devil's Hole Road, Battle of
14 September 1763

During Pontiac's uprising a wagon train from Fort Schlosser carrying supplies for Fort Niagara passed through a place known as Devil's Hole, so called because of the difficult and foreboding terrain. At one point a narrow trail with thick woods on the right and a deep ravine on the left provided excellent cover for a surprise attack. Here, probably 300–500 Indians ambushed the train. Frightened animals stampeded, some plunging into the ravine, dragging drivers entangled in harnesses with them. The escort had little chance to defend itself because of the suddenness of the attack, and the close quarters made it difficult to use muskets. A few managed to escape, but most were tomahawked to death.

A detachment of the British Eightieth Regiment, camped nearby, heard the sounds of battle and rushed to the rescue, but they too were attacked and routed, also suffering many casualties. The incident is sometimes referred to as the Devil's Hole Massacre.

See also: Pontiac; Pontiac's War/Rebellion/Uprising
Further Reading: Peckham, *Pontiac and the Indian Uprising*

"Digger" Indians

Western Shoshones were often called "Digger" Indians by whites because they lived on small game, which was supplemented by nuts as well as roots dug from the ground. Although related linguistically, western Shoshones had little else in common with northern Shoshones, who were primarily a seminomadic horseback people that relied on the buffalo as a source of food supply. Whites also referred to both tribes as Snakes.

Further Reading: Trenholm and Carley, *Shoshonis: Sentinels of the Rockies*

Dodge, Col. Henry
1782–1867

A politician and soldier, Henry Dodge was born in historic Vincennes (in present-day Indiana) and moved to what is now Missouri as a child. His first military service was as a major general in the Missouri militia during the War of 1812. In 1827 he moved to what is now southwest Wisconsin (then Michigan Territory), where he was active in opening up and operating lead mines.

Together with Gen. Henry Atkinson, he cowed the Winnebagos into submission by means of a strong military demonstration. And during the Black Hawk War (1832), Dodge commanded a militia force at the Battle of Wisconsin Heights, then pursued the Indians down the Wisconsin River to the final confrontation at the Battle of Bad Axe. In 1833–1834 Dodge led the First U.S. Dragoons—he had been appointed colonel by Pres. Andrew Jackson—across the Great Plains, visiting the Pawnees and proceeding as far as the Colorado Rockies.

In 1836 Dodge was named governor of Wisconsin Territory and Superintendent of Indian Affairs for the region. When Wisconsin was admitted to the Union, Dodge served first as a delegate to Congress then as governor of the state.

See also: Atkinson, Gen. Henry; Black Hawk; Black Hawk War

Further Reading: Pelzer, *Henry Dodge*; Prucha, *Sword of the Republic*

Dog Soldiers

Originally a warrior or soldier society within the Cheyenne tribe, the Dog Soldiers emerged as a separate entity by 1840. Increasingly, warriors left other societies to join the Dog Soldiers, whose growing prestige as a military group held much appeal. The group also blossomed into a haven for many who had become outcasts for one reason or another. Many traditional Cheyennes thus viewed the Dog Soldiers as outlaws.

In time, however, tribal attitudes moderated, and Dog Soldiers came to be respected for their bravery and fighting skills, which had become increasingly important as conflict with the whites escalated. Dog Soldiers had developed strong ties with the Lakota Sioux and by the late 1860s had grown into a force to be reckoned with throughout the Southern and Central Plains. Their power as a military force is considered to have been effectively ended at the Battle of Summit Springs, Colorado, in July 1869.

See also: Beecher Island, Battle of; Cheyennes; Roman Nose; Summit Springs, Battle of

Further Reading: Afton, *Cheyenne Dog Soldiers*; Grinnell, *Fighting Cheyennes*; Monnett, *The Battle of Beecher Island*

Dudley, Gov. Joseph
1647–1720

As governor of Massachusetts Colony during Queen Anne's War, Joseph Dudley was much criticized for his failure to punish the Abnakis, whose fierce raids terrorized settlements, particularly Deerfield, Massachusetts, which was the focus of several devastating raids throughout the Indian Wars period. Like many colonial authorities, Dudley was highly contemptuous of Indians, an attitude for which he and the settlers he governed paid a heavy price.

See also: Abnakis (Abenakis); King Philip's War; King William's War

Further Reading: Bourne, *The Red King's Rebellion*; Leach, *Arms for Empire*

Dull Knife
1810–1883

A noted chief of the northern Cheyennes, Dull Knife (Tash-me-la-pash-me) was born near the Rosebud River in what is now Montana. He was not especially noticed by the whites until the aftermath of the Sand Creek Massacre (November 1864), when he participated in a number of retaliatory raids on white settlements.

During the next several years Dull Knife chose to walk the road of peace, signing the Laramie Treaty of 1868 as a representative of his people. However, in 1876, a number of his followers allied themselves with the hostile, nontreaty Sioux and fought in the Battles of the Rosebud and the Little Bighorn. Dull Knife himself did not participate in these actions.

In November 1876 a command under Col. Ranald S. Mackenzie, in a surprise dawn attack, destroyed Dull Knife's village on the Red Fork of the Powder River, west of present-day Kaycee, Wyoming. Indian losses were heavy, with many survivors having to trudge through snow and cold to find succor in other villages. The following spring, Dull Knife's people were relocated to Oklahoma, an area they found unsuitable and totally unlike their Montana homeland. With illness and disillusionment rampant, Dull Knife and fellow chief Little Wolf led several hundred of their people in an epic Trail of Tears march to Montana.

After finally surrendering to military authorities at Fort Robinson, Nebraska, in the belief they would be allowed to return to Montana, Dull Knife and his people (Little Wolf and his band having separated earlier) were forced to break out a second time. Although the escape cost many lives, it also drew attention to their plight, and as a consequence the Cheyennes were eventually granted a reservation in Montana.

Despite having achieved this objective, Dull Knife grew dispirited over the plight of his people. He died in 1883 along the Rosebud River, where he had been born.

See also: Dull Knife Outbreak; Mackenzie, Col. Ranald Slidell
Further Reading: Grinnell, *Fighting Cheyennes;* Sandoz, *Cheyenne Autumn*

Dull Knife Outbreak
1878

After the Sioux War of 1876 northern Cheyennes were removed to the Indian Territory in Oklahoma during the summer of 1877. The change was drastic. In the winter that followed many of the Cheyennes fell ill and died. Desperate, chiefs Dull Knife and Little Wolf led a band of 300 northward toward their old home in Yellowstone country. The exodus is sometimes referred to as the Cheyenne Trail of Tears.

The Cheyennes had several minor skirmishes with pursuing troops, and young warriors, in direct violation of the chiefs' directive to avoid confrontations, killed several settlers and, in so doing, caused a wave of fear to spread across western Kansas and Nebraska. Near the Platte River, Little Wolf and Dull Knife came to a parting of the ways. The latter, feeling the pressure of pursuit by the army, believed the time had come to give up and negotiate a settlement. Accordingly, Dull Knife and his followers surrendered to the military at Camp Robinson, Nebraska, in October 1878. Little Wolf, however, continued north with his band toward the Yellowstone country.

Dull Knife had hoped to have his people assigned to the same reservation as the Sioux. In any case, he had made a firm decision not to return to Oklahoma, which, the

army insisted, must be the case. When the Cheyennes refused to budge, the military authorities cut off water and food for a week. In January 1879, hungry and frustrated by the stalemate, the Cheyennes broke out of their confinement, using a few weapons the women had managed to secrete under their dresses at the time of surrender. Caught off-guard, the troops nevertheless reacted quickly, shooting down many Cheyennes as they tried to escape, putting an end to their effort.

News of the incident soon spread, arousing much public sympathy for the plight of the Cheyennes. Faced with such a groundswell of public opinion, the army finally relented and agreed to let the Cheyennes remain at Pine Ridge Agency. Little Wolf, meanwhile, reached Montana, where he surrendered to the army in March 1879. Eventually, these Cheyennes were signed on as army scouts and were later joined by some of Dull Knife's people. In 1884 Little Wolf's Cheyennes were permanently assigned to the new Lame Deer Agency in southeastern Montana.

The experience had been harsh and costly for the Cheyennes, but by perseverance they won the right to remain in their homeland.

See also: Dull Knife; Little Wolf; Sioux War
Further Reading: Sandoz, *Cheyenne Autumn*

Dunmore, Lord
See Lord Dunmore's War

Dustin, Hannah
1659–?

One of the best-known captives of the colonial wars, Hannah Dustin was captured by Abnakis during a raid on Haverhill, Massachusetts, on 15 March 1697. Mrs. Dustin was carried off to the Indian camp, along with her new baby and a nurse. One of her captors later killed the infant by dashing it against a tree.

On the night of 29 March Hannah and her nurse awoke quietly, picked up hatchets, and killed all but two of the sleeping Indians; an old woman and a boy managed to escape the vengeful mother. Aware that Massachusetts offered a bounty for Indian scalps, Mrs. Dustin then scalped her captors, after which she and her nurse escaped and returned to Haverhill, where she was reportedly paid 25 pounds.

Hannah Dustin's story was later related by Cotton Mather in *Humiliations Followed with Deliverances* (published in 1697). Like that of Mary Rowlandson, the Dustin story became a colonial best-seller.

See also: Rowlandson, Mary White
Further Reading: Vaughan, *New England Frontier*

Dutch

The Dutch presence in the New World was brief compared to that of the other European powers, lasting little more than half a century, from 1609–1664. Probably the earliest Dutch effort in the New World was actually undertaken by an Englishman, Henry Hudson, who had been hired by the Dutch to locate the fabled Northwest Passage. Like others before and after him, Hudson found no mythical route to the Orient, but he did discover the mighty river that today bears his name. Later, the Dutch West India Company, granted a charter by the Netherlands in 1621, established trading posts along the river at Fort Orange (Albany) and Wiltwyck (Kingston), New York, and another in present-day Connecticut—The House of Hope (Hartford). New Amsterdam (New York City), reportedly purchased from the Indians for $24 in 1624, was the principal community and seat of government.

Initially, the Dutch approached the New World as commercial opportunists rather than colonizers. As such, they soon developed a lucrative fur trade with Indian tribes of the area, particularly Mohawks, who, as a result, were among the earliest of the tribes to acquire firearms. The Dutch also developed a brisk trade with Mahicans and Raritans. As trade flourished, demand for beaver pelts grew until by the mid-seventeenth century the area's supply had been largely exhausted.

Dutch envoys discussing a treaty with the Indians at Fort Amsterdam

The decline of fur supply led the Dutch to look increasingly toward the acquisition of Indian lands.

Dutch relations with the Indians were ambivalent at best and often harsh, leading to on-again off-again warfare with the tribes for more than two decades. Unlike English colonies in New England and Virginia, Dutch settlements were never much more than trading outposts. The ruling body was composed primarily of businessmen, among whom there was considerable dissension and bickering. As a consequence, the infrastructures of Dutch communities in the New World were not designed for permanency. The Dutch were supplanted by the English, who seized New Amsterdam in 1664 and renamed it New York.

See also: England; France; Mahicans; Mohawks; Raritans
Further Reading: Jennings, *The Invasion of America;* Steele, *Warpaths*

Dutch-Indian Wars
1641–1664

Although not continuous, the Dutch-Indian Wars were closely linked and were essentially an outgrowth of harsh and often brutal treatment of Indians by the Dutch. In the 15 years that followed Henry Hudson's discovery of the river that now bears his name, the Dutch built several trading posts in the area and began a brisk trade with Indians.

In 1621 the Dutch West India Company was formed and three years later established a trading post at the site of what is today Albany, naming it Fort Orange. By 1626 a flourishing trade with Mahicans and Raritans had expanded to include the Mohawks, who had warred with the Mahicans for a share in the Dutch trade. But Dutch relations with Indians were anything but cordial, their policy vacillating between harsh and brutal. Nevertheless, Indians' acquisition of firearms and iron implements made the fur trade a profitable arrangement for them as well.

By the third decade of the seventeenth century the area's beaver population had been largely depleted. As a result, the Dutch began

thinking in terms of land acquisition to offset the loss in trade. The appointment of Willem Kieft as governor of New Netherlands (the formal title was actually director-general) was to have a profound impact on Dutch-Indian relations during the next few years. In 1641 Kieft offered a bounty on Raritan Indian scalps because they retaliated when Dutch livestock trampled their cornfields. Two later killings—one Indian, one white—gave Governor Kieft an excuse to lead a punitive column through the countryside in a show of force. The column found few Indians, however, and accomplished little.

Determined, nevertheless, to punish the Indians, Kieft next asked for a war vote from the patroons (ruling landowners), who rejected the idea, believing they lacked the strength to wage war successfully. Their recommendation, however, did not move Kieft from his position on the issue. Then, in February 1643, Mohawks moved down the Hudson River valley to exact tribute from the Wappingers, who fled to Kieft seeking protection. The governor, however, permitted the Mohawks to attack the Wappinger village at Pavonia (present-day Jersey City). Some 70 Wappingers were killed, and a large number were taken into slavery by the Mohawks. Kieft then ordered his own troops to kill the remaining Wappingers, most of whom were women and children. The act revolted the Mohawks, who had stopped short of killing noncombatants. The incident became known as the Slaughter of the Innocents.

Kieft's brutal treatment of the Wappingers plunged the Dutch into all-out war with some 11 small tribes in the area, who went on a rampage, slaughtering Dutch settlers and burning farms. Terror-stricken settlers fled to New Amsterdam for protection. Kieft, recognizing that the situation had gotten out of hand, tried to negotiate with the Indians, who were in no mood to parley. Pressing their attack, they laid siege to New Amsterdam. Because of their strong economic ties to the Dutch, the Mohawks did not involve themselves in what is sometimes referred to as Kieft's War.

In an effort to seize the initiative from the Indians, the Dutch hired an Englishman, Capt. John Underhill, to retaliate. Underhill, who had acquired a reputation as a ruthless but successful Indian fighter during the Pequot War, launched a forceful campaign against the Indians, employing the same tactics there that he had used at Mystic Harbor: surrounding and attacking an Indian village, then setting it afire, killing those who tried to escape. Underhill's tactics compelled the Indians to lift their year-long siege of New Amsterdam and agree, finally, to peace in 1644.

The peace lasted until 1655, when a Dutch farmer killed a Delaware woman for stealing peaches. The incident triggered further hostilities in what became known as the Peach War. The Dutch farmer was killed in retaliation, which in turn produced additional killings. Gov. Peter Stuyvesant, who had replaced Willem Kieft as governor, activated the militia. The next three years witnessed a period of unsettled conditions, with sporadic fighting. The Dutch maintained their economic friendship with some tribes while continuing to clash with others.

In 1658 the Dutch asked the Susquehannocks to intervene in their continuing war with the Esopus Indians, a tribe that dwelled along the Hudson River. Motivated by their own desire to establish a trade link with the Dutch, the Susquehannocks agreed to act as intermediaries. Despite the efforts of the Susquehannocks, the Esopus and their allies, the Minisinks, attacked Wiltwyck (Kingston) in September 1659. Governor Stuyvesant called a peace parley, which the Indians agreed to participate in. However, the first night after the talks had begun, Dutch soldiers murdered the Indians while they slept. The angered Indians retaliated, and the fighting continued until 1660, when Stuyvesant, adopting a new tactic, took Indian children as hostages in an effort to force the Indians to comply. When the Esopus refused to be coerced, Stuyvesant sold the children into West Indian slavery.

In 1664 Stuyvesant enlisted the support of the Mohawks, who proved better intermediaries than the Susquehannocks, eventually persuading the Esopus to end their five-year opposition to the Dutch. The conclusion of the war with the Esopus ended two decades of fighting between indigenous tribes and Dutch traders. Sixteen sixty-four also marked the end of Dutch reign in the New World, highlighted by English seizure of New Amsterdam, which was renamed New York.

See also: Dutch; Kieft, Willem; Mahicans; Mohawks; Pequot War; Raritans; Wappingers
Further Reading: Jennings, *The Invasion of America;* Steele, *Warpaths*

E

Encomienda

The *encomienda* (a lawful charge or authorization) was a system introduced by the Spanish on their northern colonial frontier. Essentially, it was designed to reward colonists who had worked on behalf of the Spanish Crown with the personal services of Indian families. The number of families or individual Indians included in the grant depended on the value and importance of the colonist's own service to the Crown. The designated Indians were expected to provide the colonist with labor and/or tribute. Although slavery, per se, was not permitted in the Spanish empire, the encomienda system amounted to the same thing. In principle it was intended not only as a means of rewarding valued service to the Crown but also to promote the growth of a strong colony, one that made a contribution to the Crown, while improving the overall well-being of the community, particularly with regard to spreading the word of Christianity among the natives.

In practice, however, the encomienda resulted in the creation of a feudal-like system under which the Indians suffered much abuse at the hands of ruthless lords. Although there were loud protests decrying the practice, with much discussion pro and con, the system would survive more or less intact until it was finally abandoned following the Pueblo Revolt of 1680. Not surprisingly, encomienda was a root cause of the revolts and uprisings that the Spanish would be forced to contend with at a later date (Popé's Pueblo revolt and the Pima uprising led by Luis Oacpicagigua).

See also: Popé (El Popé); Pueblo Indians; Spain

Further Reading: John, *Storms Brewed in Other Men's Worlds*

England

Of the five major European powers (England, France, Spain, Sweden, and the Netherlands) whose presence affected the development of North America, England's was perhaps the most far-reaching. Unlike France and Spain, England approached the New World with a philosophy of settlement—establishing colonies whose presence would contribute to the empire's growth and development.

Although France is generally acknowledged to have had the best rapport with Native American peoples, England also forged strong ties, thanks notably to the work of men such as Sir William Johnson. Largely as a result of the efforts of Johnson and his son, most of the Iroquois Confederacy supported Great Britain during the American Revolution.

Between the Revolutionary War and the War of 1812, England actively promoted hostilities between the Indian tribes of the Ohio River country and the fledgling United States. Desirous of maintaining economic ties to a profitable fur trade, England took advantage of Indian fears over the mounting flow of American settlers into the region to strengthen their own position by supporting Indian attacks on American settlements.

Save for boundary disputes in the Pacific Northwest, which were essentially resolved by the mid-nineteenth century, British power in the United States effectively ended with the Peace of Ghent, which was signed

William Penn's treaty for England with the Indians

in 1815 and officially concluded the War of 1812.

See also: France; French and Indian War; Spain
Further Reading: Dowd, *A Spirited Resistance;* Mahon, *The War of 1812;* Wright, *The Cultural Life of the Colonies*

Esopus

A division of the Munsee tribe, the Esopus lived along the west bank of the Hudson River in what is today Greene and Ulster Counties, in the vicinity of Kingston, New York. The Esopus were one of five tribes occupying the general region, the others being the Catskills, Mamekotings, Waoranex, Warranawonkongs, and Warasinks. For reasons not entirely clear, though it was probably a territorial dispute, the Esopus waged an ongoing war with the Dutch during the 1650s and early 1660s.

Despite brutal tactics by the Dutch, which included selling Esopus children into West Indian slavery, Esopus refused to surrender, stoutly resisting all Dutch efforts to dominate them. At first the Dutch employed one of their Indian trading partners, the Susquehannocks, to persuade the Esopus to concede. When this failed the Dutch turned to another of their allies, the Mohawks. Using raids and reprisal tactics, the powerful Mohawk nation finally applied enough pressure to force the Esopus to capitulate.

The fate of the Esopus, like that of a number of tribes after subjugation, was to find strength by merging with others. Esopus merged with Moravians, Munsees, and Mahicans in what is now Pennsylvania.

See also: Dutch-Indian Wars; Mahicans; Mohawks; Susquehannocks (Susquehannas)
Further Reading: Hodge, *Handbook of American Indians;* Steele, *Warpaths*

Evans, Gov. John
1814–1897

Born in Ohio, John Evans earned a medical degree, and after practicing in Ohio, Illinois, and Indiana he moved to the Chicago area, where he began investing in real estate and eventually compiled a fortune. Entering politics, Evans was defeated for a congressional seat in 1854. However, in 1862 he was appointed governor of Colorado Territory by Pres. Abraham Lincoln; he served simultaneously as Superintendent of Indian Affairs.

In June 1864 Evans issued a proclamation of safety to all Indians who agreed to place themselves under army protection. In the meantime, however, public pressure for punitive action against the Indians caused the governor to turn the matter over to the immediate military authority in the area, represented by Col. John M. Chivington. He did this despite the fact that some Indian bands, notably Black Kettle's band, had surrendered and considered themselves to be under government protection. The result was the tragic massacre at Sand Creek on 29 November 1864.

John Evans's role in the Sand Creek affair is and was controversial, and opponents of his administration were quick to use it against him. Confronted with the opprobrium of Sand Creek and the accusations brought against him, Evans resigned as territorial governor. He remained in Denver, however, and became a successful railroad entrepreneur, founding the Colorado Seminary, which later became the University of Denver.

See also: Black Kettle; Chivington, Col. John M.; Sand Creek Massacre
Further Reading: Kelsey, *Frontier Capitalist*

F

Fallen Timbers, Battle of
20 August 1794

Fallen Timbers was the end result of U.S. efforts to resolve a crisis in the region north of the Ohio River that had been building with the increasing flow of settlers into the area following the end of the Revolutionary War and was exacerbated by the Indians' defeat of Gen. Josiah Harmar in 1790 and his successor, Gen. Arthur St. Clair, the following year.

The continued British presence in the region and their general support of the Indian position added to the volatile situation. After more than two years of military preparation and an unsuccessful last-minute political effort designed to resolve matters peaceably, a U.S. force commanded by Gen. Anthony (Mad Anthony) Wayne finally got under way in late July 1794.

Marching north from his staging area at Fort Greenville, near what is present-day Greenville, Ohio, Wayne's objective was a concentration of Indian villages located at the confluence of the Maumee and Auglaize Rivers, an area known as the Grand Glaize. Wayne's command (it was now officially the Legion of the United States, not the U.S. Army), estimated between 3,000 and 4,000 men, comprised regular infantry and Kentucky mounted militia. Opposing the Legion was an allied Indian force of some 1,500 Shawnee, Miami, Ottawa, Potawatomi, Wyandot, and Delaware warriors under Blue Jacket, Little Turtle, Turkey Foot, Egushawa, and Little Otter.

From Fort Greenville the Legion moved steadily but cautiously northeast. By mid-August Wayne had reached the abandoned village site on the Grand Glaize, and after destroying the extensive fields of corn and other vegetables—in effect, the Indian commissary—he crossed the Maumee River and pushed on toward the British post of Fort Miamis, where his scouts reported the Indians were concentrating. Some 5 miles southwest of Fort Miamis was an area, about a mile long and 200 to 400 yards wide, filled with trees that had been toppled by a tornado years before. Known as Fallen Timbers, it was a nightmarish place of dense brush, swampy patches, and second-growth trees. As the Legion moved through on the hot and humid morning of 20 August, the advance unit of Kentucky militia suddenly found itself under attack by Ottawas under Little Otter and Egushawa. Despite Wayne's precautions to avoid surprise, the attack caught the Legion off-guard, routing the advance units and driving them back on the main body, which Wayne had divided into two wings. The Second and Fourth Sub Legions under Col. John Hamtramck were on the left; Gen. James Wilkinson's First and Third Sub Legions occupied the right flank.

Two junior officers at the battle who would later achieve renown were Wayne's aide, Lt. William Henry Harrison, and Lt. William Clark, who would explore the Louisiana Territory with Meriwether Lewis. Among the Indians was a rising young Shawnee warrior named Tecumseh. The Indian army had positioned itself to ambush the Americans as they moved through Fallen Timbers. However, the impulsive Ottawas, who attacked from the center, had sprung the trap prematurely. Moreover, in pursuing the temporarily disorganized lead elements of the Legion the Ottawas penetrated too far to be supported when Wayne's main body responded.

As a result, the initiative gradually swung to the Legionaires, who now pressed forward, pushing the Ottawas back. In the belief that an empty stomach sharpened their fighting skills, Indian warriors often fasted the night before a battle. In this case, however, they had already been fasting for two to three days, expecting the Americans to arrive earlier, and many had left their positions to search for food. Thus, the premature attack cost the Indians the element of surprise, and their main line was weakened by the absence of hungry warriors. As the Legion advanced behind out-thrust bayonets, the Indian line collapsed, and the Indian forces fled toward the safety of Fort Miamis. Expecting help from the British, they arrived only to find the gates of the fort closed to them.

The Indians discovered the British were not prepared to extend their support to the battlefield. Wayne pursued almost to the gates of the British post, and for a time it appeared there might be a confrontation. The Battle of Fallen Timbers was one of the decisive battles in the long history of America's Indian wars. It resulted in the Greenville Treaty, which effectively ended the crisis in the region.

See also: Harmar, Gen. Josiah; Little Turtle (Me-she-kin-no-quah); St. Clair, Arthur; Treaties and Agreements, Greenville, Treaty of; Wayne, Gen. Anthony (Mad Anthony)
Further Reading: Gilbert, *God Gave Us This Country;* Sword, *President Washington's Indian War*

"Far" Indians

Sometimes written as "Farr," the term was used by early English writers to refer to Indians who lived beyond the pale of English settlements, particularly in the regions of the Ohio River and Great Lakes.

Further Reading: Hodge, *Handbook of American Indians*

Fetterman, Capt. William Judd
1833–1866

Born in Connecticut, William Judd Fetterman was commissioned first lieutenant in the Eighteenth Infantry upon the outbreak of the Civil War. His war career was marked by gallant and meritorious service, for which he was awarded a brevet rank of colonel. Following the Civil War, he was appointed captain in the Eighteenth Infantry and assigned to Fort Phil Kearny, Wyoming, near present-day Sheridan.

Although a popular officer among the garrison at Fort Kearny, Fetterman soon found himself at odds with the post commander, Col. Henry B. Carrington. Although Fetterman had no experience in Indian warfare, he was of the opinion that Carrington was too cautious in responding to Indian raiding parties. On 21 December 1866, under orders to proceed to the relief of a wood train then under attack, Fetterman brashly pursued the Indians over Lodge Trail Ridge, a high land mass east of the fort, despite Carrington's specific orders not to do so.

Once beyond Lodge Trail Ridge, Fetterman's mixed force of cavalry and infantry, numbering 81 men, was caught in a cleverly laid ambush, in which a young warrior named Crazy Horse may have played a key role. In the bitter struggle that followed, Fetterman's entire command was wiped out to a man. Ironically, Fetterman had earlier boasted that given a company of soldiers (roughly 80–100 men) he would ride through the entire Sioux nation.

See also: Carrington, Col. Henry Beebee; Fetterman Disaster; Forts, Camps, Cantonments, Outposts, Phil Kearny
Further Reading: Brown, *The Fetterman Massacre;* Carrington, F., *My Army Life;* Carrington, M., *Absaraka*

Fetterman Disaster
21 December 1866

On 21 December 1866, Capt. William J. Fetterman led a mixed force of cavalry and infantry, totaling 81 men, out of Fort Phil Kearny, Wyoming, near present-day Sheridan, in relief of a wood train that was under attack by Sioux and Cheyenne warriors.

Fetterman had been specifically ordered by his commanding officer, Col. Henry B. Carrington, not to pursue the Indians beyond Lodge Trail Ridge, a high land mass 3 miles northeast of Fort Kearny. Although controversy surrounds Fetterman's decision, most agree that he chose to disregard Carrington's directive, seeing in the moment an opportunity to properly chastise the Indians. Ironically, he had boasted earlier that with a company of soldiers—about 80 men—he could ride through the entire Sioux nation.

Exactly what happened once Fetterman's command crossed Lodge Trail Ridge is still debated, but the evidence, particularly recent archaeological finds, suggests that the pursuing soldiers, led by the mounted detachment, were lured by a decoy party and then suddenly attacked by a large war party lying in ambush on both sides of the ridge along which the troops were advancing.

Overwhelmed, the soldiers fought desperately. Many were killed early on. Others died attempting to withdraw back along the ridge. A small group, including Fetterman and Capt. Fred Brown, fought a last stand at the site of the present-day marker along U.S. Highway 87. It is generally believed that Brown and Fetterman both took their own lives rather than risk falling into the hands of the Indians.

Sometimes incorrectly referred to as a massacre, the Fetterman Disaster was a significant event in the Indian wars. It was the worst defeat the U.S. Army had suffered in the Trans-Mississippi West up to that time and was eclipsed only by the Battle of the Little Bighorn a decade later. Thereafter, the Indians referred to the Fetterman Disaster as "The Battle of the Hundred in the Hands." As with the Custer fight, no soldiers survived.

See also: Carrington, Col. Henry Beebee; Crazy Horse (Tashunca Utico, Tashunka Witko); Fetterman, Capt. William Judd; Sioux
Further Reading: Brown, *The Fetterman Massacre;* Hebard and Brininstool, *The Bozeman Trail;* Utley, *Frontier Regulars;* Vaughn, *Indian Fights*

Firearms
Breechloader (as Opposed to Muzzleloader)
This was a type of firearm designed to be loaded by inserting a fixed cartridge into the breech of the weapon, rather than through the muzzle. A hinged plate or gate on the top of the breech lifts up to allow the cartridge to be inserted into the chamber. The gate is then closed, the hammer is cocked, and the piece is ready to fire.

Available as a carbine or a rifle, the breechloader was introduced during the last half of the nineteenth century and remained a standard army weapon until the turn of the century. A variety of manufacturers produced breech-loading weapons in calibers ranging from .42 to .50. By far, the most widely used by the U.S. Army during the post–Civil War Indian conflicts in the West was the .45-70 Springfield. The carbine version was used by the cavalry, with the infantry using the longer-barreled rifle model, known as the "Long Tom."

Carbine
This was a short-barreled shoulder weapon usually employed by mounted troops. In the immediate post–Civil War period, some cavalry regiments on the western frontier were armed with the Spencer and other breech-loading carbines, but by the mid-1870s the standard shoulder arm was the .45-70 Springfield breechloader, sometimes called the "trap door" Springfield. Although less effective at longer distances than the rifle, the shorter barrel made the carbine easier for the mounted soldier to manage. The weapon was housed in a scabbard attached to the saddle when not in use.

Handgun (Revolver, Pistol)
The earliest handguns were matchlocks and flintlocks. The invention of the percussion cap in 1835 made possible the creation of the first modern handgun system, which eventually employed a revolving cylinder containing loads or bullets. In a single-action system the hammer is cocked prior to each shot. The cocking mechanism simultaneously causes the cylinder to revolve to the next chamber. In the later double-action system, pulling the trigger automatically cocks and fires the weapon in one movement.

Early revolvers were large and cumbersome, barely qualifying for the name handgun. One early model produced by the Colt Patent Firearms Manufacturing Co. was dubbed the "Dragoon" and was carried in holsters attached to the pommel of the Dragoon's (a mounted soldier) saddle. During the late Indian wars of the nineteenth century cavalrymen were armed with the Model 1873 Colt Revolver.

Rifle

This was a long-barreled shoulder weapon usually employed by infantry. Up to and throughout the Civil War, the standard-issue infantry weapon was the muzzle-loading rifle. By the end of the Civil War the development of breech-loading technology had made the muzzleloader obsolete. The Springfield-Allin breechloader (a Civil War weapon converted from the muzzle-loading principle) was introduced in the immediate aftermath of the Civil War and was the standard infantry issue weapon until replaced by the Springfield "trap door" model in the mid-1870s. The rifle version of the "trap door" Springfield was known as the "Long Tom."

The Plains Indians feared the infantry's "Long Toms" more than the cavalry carbines, as it was more accurate over a greater distance than the carbine version with which the cavalry was armed.

Snaphance (Musket)

The most commonly used firearm during the Jamestown (Virginia) colonial period, the Snaphance employed a wheel-lock system of ignition, in which the priming powder was ignited from sparks created by a rotating metal wheel striking a piece of flint.

Harquebus

The principal military firearm of the sixteenth century, it was introduced to the New World by the Spanish and later used by both the British and French. The harquebus was a muzzle-loading, smooth-bore musket, meaning that the projectile, usually a round lead ball (though it might actually be anything that could be discharged through the barrel) was inserted or loaded from the muzzle. Not until the middle of the nineteenth century would muzzleloaders be supplanted by firearms that were loaded through the breech.

The harquebus was fired by means of a matchlock system in which a length of treated flaxen rope, like a wick, is first ignited. Glowing like an ember, this wick in turn ignites the priming powder that has been placed in a "pan," thereby discharging the weapon. Typically, harquebuses were about four feet long and up to .70 caliber, weighing 11 to 13 pounds. Because it was slow and cumbersome, the harquebus was less effective in warfare against the native peoples of the New World than were edged weapons, lances, and the crossbow. Probably the weapon's biggest asset was the noise and smoke it produced.

Further Reading: McChristian, *The U.S. Army in the West;* Moller, *American Military Shoulder Arms,* vol. 1

Forsyth, Maj. George Alexander (Sandy)
1837–1915

Born in Pennsylvania, George Alexander Forsyth enlisted as a private when the Civil War began. Quickly promoted to first lieutenant of cavalry, he served with distinction throughout the war, ending up with the permanent rank of major and brevet rank of brigadier general of volunteers.

During the summer of 1868, as a member of Gen. Philip H. Sheridan's staff, Forsyth received authorization to enlist a company of frontier scouts to fight Indians. In September 1868 Forsyth's Scouts, as they came to be known, were attacked by a large force of Cheyenne Dog Soldiers on the Arickaree Fork of the Republican River in extreme northeastern Colorado. In the Battle of Beecher Island the scouts managed to survive a nine-day siege; Forsyth himself was wounded three times.

In 1873 Forsyth conducted a military reconnaissance of the Yellowstone River as far as the mouth of the Powder River. The following summer he was Sheridan's personal representative on Custer's expedition to explore the Black Hills of South Dakota, unknown at the time and under treaty off-limits to whites. Forsyth also served in the Southwest against the Apaches.

During his military career Forsyth participated in more than 70 engagements and was wounded four times. He later wrote two books detailing his military experiences. He was not related to James W. Forsyth, an officer who also served on Sheridan's staff and on the western frontier and who is sometimes confused with George Forsyth.

See also: Beecher Island, Battle of
Further Reading: Dixon, *Hero of Beecher Island;* Monnett, *The Battle of Beecher Island*

Forsyth, Col. James William
1834–1906

Born in Ohio, James William Forsyth graduated from West Point in 1856. His first active-duty assignment was in the Pacific Northwest, followed by service in the Civil War, from which he emerged with the brevet rank of brigadier general. From 1869 to 1878 he served first as aide then military secretary to Gen. Philip H. Sheridan. During this period he conducted a military reconnaissance of the Yellowstone River. In 1878 he saw action against Bannocks during the Bannock uprising.

In 1886 he was promoted to colonel and named commander of the Seventh Cavalry. Forsyth was the senior officer present at the Wounded Knee Massacre and so figured importantly in that disaster. Forsyth's handling of the affair caused Gen. Nelson A. Miles to relieve Forsyth of command and bring charges against him. The charges were subsequently dropped, however, and Forsyth resumed his career. He was promoted to major general in 1897 and retired shortly thereafter.

A capable officer, Forsyth was liked and respected by his men. He is often mistakenly referred to as the brother of George Alexander (Sandy) Forsyth, an unrelated army officer with whom he served.

See also: Beecher Island, Battle of; Wounded Knee Massacre

Further Reading: Dixon, *Hero of Beecher Island;* Utley, *Indian Frontier of the American West;* ———, *Last Days of the Sioux Nation*

Forts, Camps, Cantonments, Outposts

During the 400 years between Columbus and Wounded Knee, literally hundreds of forts, camps, outposts, and supply depots were established. Some were erected by communities as havens of safety to which settlers from the surrounding countryside could flee during hostilities. Others were established by the military to protect a segment of the frontier and to act as locations from which campaigns could be launched.

A word about nomenclature: The terms *fort, camp, cantonment,* and *outpost* are often used interchangeably. Generally speaking, however, a fort was regarded as a permanent establishment, even though many actual forts were short-lived. Camps or cantonments were usually temporary in nature. Sometimes a permanent establishment might follow, with the cantonment or camp then reclassified as a fort. Fort Keogh, Montana (the site of Miles City), for example, was originally Cantonment Keogh.

Generally, forts east of the Mississippi tended to be pallisaded enclosures. From the early colonial period through, roughly, the War of 1812, forts were frequently subjected to attack by French or British troops and their Indian allies, depending on the particular war in question. The siege of Fort William Henry during the French and Indian War is a striking illustration of this type of warfare. Thus, forts and outposts needed to be enclosed in order to be defended. In contrast, forts west of the Mississippi were seldom stockaded, Fort Phil Kearny in Wyoming being a singular exception to that rule. In part this was due to the terrain, which, owing to its openness, was not as conducive to direct attack as forts in the heavily timbered East and Midwest. Then, too, technological advances in weaponry, especially field artillery, increasingly tended to render a walled outpost obsolete. Finally, many western military posts tended to be little more than a group of wooden or adobe structures that were barely hovels.

The forts listed here played a role in one or more of the many Indian wars and campaigns. They are offered solely as a reference for the reader and provide the name, location, and dates of service. Unfortunately, space does not permit even a cursory history of these sites. If, however, the fort was the scene of a notable event it is described as much as possible. If the fort or post is currently a national or state historic site, that information is also included. This list is by no means comprehensive. It is intended to be representative, and readers seeking more information are referred to the bibliography, which provides titles with in-depth coverage.

An 1815 watercolor of Fort Harrison

Abraham Lincoln
Mandan, North Dakota
service, 1872–1891
Custer's last headquarters and the fort from which he marched on his last campaign; state park

Apache
San Carlos Apache Reservation, Arizona
service, 1870–

Assiniboine
Havre, Montana
service, 1879–1911

Atkinson
Fort Atkinson, Iowa
service, 1840–1849

Atkinson
Omaha, Nebraska
service, 1819–1827

Bascom
Tucumcari, New Mexico
service, 1863–1870

Belknap
near Graham, Texas
service, 1851–1867

Benton
near Great Falls, Montana
service, 1869–1881

Bliss
El Paso, Texas
service, 1848–present (active post)

Bowie
near Willcox, Arizona
service, 1862–1894
national historic site

Bridger
near Lyman, Wyoming
service, 1858–1890
state historic site

Buford
Williston, North Dakota
service, 1866–1895
state historic site

C. F. Smith
near Yellowtail Dam, Montana, on Big Horn River
service, 1866–1868

Casper
Casper, Wyoming
service, 1864–1867
state historic site

Churchill
near Virginia City, Nevada
service, 1860–1869

Clark
near Brackettville, Texas
service, 1852–1949

Clinch
near Pensacola, Florida
service, 1823–1834

Cobb
Fort Cobb, Oklahoma
service, 1859–1869

Collins
Fort Collins, Colorado
service, 1863–1867

Colville
Colville, Washington
service, 1859–1882

Concho
near San Angelo, Texas
service, 1867–1889

Craig
near Socorro, New Mexico
service, 1854–1884

Crawford
Prairie du Chien, Wisconsin
service, 1816–1856

D. A. Russell
Cheyenne, Wyoming

service, 1867–present (currently active as Warren Air Force Base)

Dalles
near Dalles, Washington, on Columbia River
service, 1850–1867

Davis
Alpine, Texas
service, 1854–1891
national historic site

Dearborn
Chicago, Illinois
service, 1803–1836
scene of Dearborn Massacre (1812)

Defiance
near Arizona–New Mexico border
service, 1851–1861

Defiance
Defiance, Ohio
service, 1794–1797

Detroit (Pontiac)
Detroit, Michigan
service, 1796–1851

Dodge
Dodge City, Kansas
service, 1865–1882

Douglas
near Salt Lake City, Utah
service, 1862–1965

Ellis
near Bozeman, Montana
service, 1867–1886

Fetterman
near Douglas, Wyoming
service, 1867–1882
state historic site

Fillmore
near Mesilla, New Mexico
service, 1851–1862

Finney
near Louisville, Kentucky
service, 1786–1793

Fred Steele
near Rawlins, Wyoming
service, 1868–1886
troops from this post under Maj. Thomas Thornburg were attacked at Milk Creek, Colorado, en route to White River Agency during hostilities with Utes in 1879

Garland
near Alamosa, Colorado
service, 1858–1883

Gibson
Muskogee, Oklahoma
service, 1824–1890

Grant
Bonita, Arizona
service, 1865–
site of Camp Grant Massacre (1871)

Greenville
Greenville, Ohio
service, 1793–1797

Griffin
near Abilene, Texas
service, 1867–1881

Hall
near Pocatello, Idaho
service, 1870–1883

Hamilton
Hamilton, Ohio
service, 1791–1797

Harker
Kanapolis, Kansas
service, 1864–1873

Harmar
near Marietta, Ohio
service, 1785–1790

Harrison
near Terre Haute, Indiana
service, 1811–1818

Hartsuff
near Burwell, Nebraska
service, 1874–1881

Hays
Fort Hays, Kansas
service, 1865–1889

Howard
Green Bay, Wisconsin
service, 1816–1852

Huachuca (Why-Choo-ka)
Sierra Vista, Arizona
service, 1877–present (active post)

Jefferson Barracks
near St. Louis, Missouri
service, 1826–1946

Kearney
Kearney, Nebraska
service, 1848–1871
state historic site

Keogh
Miles City, Montana
service, 1876–1908

Klamath
Klamath Falls, Oregon
service, 1863–1889

Lapwai
near Lewiston, Idaho
service, 1862–1885

Laramie
near Torrington, Wyoming
service, 1849–1890
national historic site

Larned
near Larned, Kansas
service, 1859–1878
national historic site

Leavenworth
Leavenworth, Kansas
service, 1827–
oldest permanent military post west of Missouri River

Logan
Denver, Colorado
service, 1887–1946

Logan
near Diamond City, Montana
service, 1869–1880

Lowell
Tucson, Arizona
service, 1862–1891

Lyon
near Lamar, Colorado
service, 1860–1889

Madison
Fort Madison, Iowa
service, 1808–1813

McDowell
Phoenix, Arizona
service, 1865–1891

McPherson
near North Platte, Nebraska
service, 1863–1880

Meade
near Deadwood, South Dakota
service, 1878–1944

Michilimackinac
between Lake Michigan and Lake Huron
service, 1796–1894

Missoula
Missoula, Montana
service, 1877–1946

Mohave
near Yuma, Arizona
service, 1859–1890

Phil Kearny
near Sheridan, Wyoming
service, 1866–1868

Pitt (Pittsburgh)
Pittsburgh, Pennsylvania
service, 1777–1811

Platte Bridge Station
near Fort Laramie, Wyoming
service, 1855–1859

Fort Union and the distribution of goods to the Assiniboines

Randall
near Fort Randall Dam, South Dakota
service, 1856–1892
state historic site

Ransom
Fort Ransom, North Dakota
service, 1867–1872
state historic site

Recovery
near Fort Recovery, Ohio
service, 1793–1796

Ridgely
near New Ulm, Minnesota
service, 1853–1867
state historic site

Riley
Junction City, Kansas
service, 1853–present (active post)

Ripley
near Brainerd, Minnesota
service, 1849–1877

Robinson
near Crawford, Nebraska
service, 1874–
Crazy Horse was killed there in 1877; state historic site

Saybrook
west bank of Connecticut River, Connecticut
service, ca. 1634–1676

Scott
Fort Scott, Kansas
service, 1842–1873
national historic site

Shaw
near Great Falls, Montana
service, 1867–1891

Sisseton
near Lake City, South Dakota
service, 1864–1889
state historic park

St. Clair
near Eaton, Ohio
service, 1791–1796

Stanton
Lincoln, New Mexico
service, 1855–1896

Sully
Pierre, South Dakota
service, 1863–1894

Union
near Watrous, New Mexico
service, 1851–1891

Union
near Williston, North Dakota
service, 1864–1865

Washakie
Lander, Wyoming
service, 1869–1909

Washington
Cincinnati, Ohio
service, 1789–1804

Wayne
Fort Wayne, Indiana
service, 1794–1819

William Henry
Lake George, New York
service, 1755–1757
scene of massacre during French and Indian War

Wingate
near Gallup, New Mexico
service, 1862–1911

Winnebago
near Portage, Wisconsin
service, 1828–1845

Yuma
Yuma, California
service, 1850–1882

Zarah
near Great Bend, Kansas
service, 1864–1869

Fox Massacre
See Fox Wars

Fox Wars
1711–1733

The Fox, or Mesquakie, Indians lived along the eastern shore of Lake Michigan. Allies of the Iroquois Confederacy, the Fox were enemies of the Ojibwas (Chippewas), with whom they were often at war. The French, who enjoyed a profitable trade with the Ojibwas, Hurons, and Ottawas, supported these tribes in their wars with the Fox, particularly the Ojibwas.

In 1711, perhaps hoping to develop a stronger working relationship with the Fox, the French persuaded them to move closer to Detroit. The effort, however, resulted in a tragedy when nearly 1,000 Fox were massacred by traditional Indian enemies while the French, unwilling to jeopardize their rela-

tionship with the other tribes, failed to intervene. The Fox retaliated with savage raids against French trading parties. As these raids began to have a noticeable effect on trade between Louisiana and the Northeast, the French provided support for a number of Ojibwa campaigns against the Fox during several succeeding years, most of which were only moderately successful.

In 1730 a mixed French-Indian army managed to corner the Fox, who were moving east in an effort to unite with their Iroquois allies. Heavily outnumbered, some 500 Fox were killed and nearly as many taken prisoner. For all intents and purposes, this destroyed the Fox as a tribal entity. The loss of the Fox component meant that the Iroquois Confederacy had lost its one western trading partner, which in turn effected the precarious intercolonial political balance. England coveted western lands already claimed by France and Spain. Because of Iroquois support for the Crown, they were considered British subjects, which in turn meant that since the Iroquois had conquered the Ohio country (in British purview) it was British territory. A strong Fox entity would have fallen under this umbrella.

See also: France; Iroquois Confederacy; Ojibwas (Chippewas); Sauks and Foxes
Further Reading: Edmunds and Peyser, *The Fox Wars;* Leach, *Arms for Empire;* Steele, *Warpaths*

France

From roughly 1500–1760, five major European powers impacted the development of North America. Of the five (England, France, Spain, Sweden, and the Netherlands), France, until its defeat by Great Britain in the French and Indian War, controlled more territory than any of its competitors. Spain's presence was largely limited to Florida and the Southwest. The Dutch and Swedes had some impact along the North Atlantic seaboard, but it was really France and England who vied for domination of North America.

From the beginning the French concentrated more on exploration and trade than on colonization. Accordingly, they were able to take advantage of Indian fears over the loss of land to establish stronger Indian alliances than the British, whose appetite for land steadily became a source of great concern for the Indians. The French also demonstrated more respect for Indian culture and were more amenable to intermarriage, both of which helped to solidify their standing with many tribes.

As troubles between France and England developed during the seventeenth and eighteenth centuries their conflicts spread to North America. Between 1689 and 1754 the two nations engaged in four North American wars. The fourth and final of these wars, known as the French and Indian War, resulted in the defeat of France and, in effect, the loss of its North American empire.

See also: Dutch; England; French and Indian War; Spain
Further Reading: Jennings, *The Invasion of America;* Steele, *Warpaths*

Free, Mickey
ca. 1847–1915

An interpreter and scout, Mickey Free was born in Mexico. His mother, Jesusa, was Mexican; his father is variously reported to have been either Apache or an Irishman named Tellez. About 1860, Jesusa moved into southeastern Arizona, where she became involved with a questionable character named John Ward. Eleven-year-old son Felix adopted the Ward name.

In 1861, Felix was captured by a raiding party of Apaches, thereby becoming a hostage in the famous Bascom Affair. Felix was later adopted by the Apaches, and in 1872 he enlisted in the Apache Scouts, serving as an interpreter and, some said, a spy. Sometime during this period he adopted the name Mickey Free, by which he is known to history. The loss of sight in one eye as a boy together with his generally rough looks gave him a sinister appearance. He was considered a valuable scout and interpreter.

See also: Bascom Affair
Further Reading: Thrapp, *Al Sieber;* ———, *The Conquest of Apacheria*

French and Indian War
1755–1763

The final intercolonial war between France and England, the French and Indian War, like the three wars before it, had European roots. Called the Seven Years War in Europe, it actually began two years earlier than its European counterpart. The three prior French-English conflicts in America were largely centered in the Northeast, but the French and Indian War shifted to the Ohio River valley, an area that had become increasingly important as European interests began to reach west beyond the Appalachians.

The French, who sought a corridor of trade to connect the Mississippi River and Louisiana with their outposts on the Great Lakes and beyond, built a series of forts in the Ohio Valley, the most important being Fort Duquesne (Pittsburgh). At the same time, the British Crown, with a continuing eye toward colonization, had offered large land grants for settlement. Under the circumstances, it was inevitable that the two powers would collide.

The opening stages of the war saw the advantage go to the French. As early as 1754, a young Virginian named George Washington distinguished himself in an unsuccessful attempt to capture Fort Duquesne. The following year saw a second, more determined effort, albeit one that was to end ignominiously. A column of British regulars under the command of Gen. Edward Braddock was ambushed and routed by the French and their Indian allies in July 1755. British casualties were heavy; Braddock himself was killed. Humiliated and devastated, the British column was forced to withdraw. The Ohio Valley Indians, concerned with the growing threat of settlements, viewed Braddock's defeat as an opportunity to strike a further blow against the English. In the following year thousands of white settlers from Virginia and Pennsylvania to South Carolina felt the fury of Indian attacks.

The British position continued to deteriorate. Increasingly, Indian tribes, some from as far west as the Great Lakes, threw their support behind the French, seeing an oppor-

Massacre of the St. Francis Indians by Rogers's Rangers in the French and Indian War

tunity to not only drive back the hated white settlers but to plunder as well. Despite the efforts of Sir William Johnson, Indian agent extraordinaire, the British, who had seen the powerful Delaware and Shawnee nations ally with the French, feared the Iroquois might also join the enemy.

In August 1756, a combined French and Indian force captured Fort Oswego on Lake Ontario and the following year took Fort William Henry, situated at the foot of New York's Lake George. Following the capture of Fort William Henry, immortalized in James Fenimore Cooper's *Last of the Mohicans*, many of the British garrison, including women and children, were massacred by Indian allies of the French as they marched out of the fort, despite customary assurances of honorable treatment as prisoners of war. The French, mortified at the slaughter, were unable to control their allies.

The 1757 appointment of the controversial William Pitt as British prime minister was perhaps the turning point in the French and Indian War. One of Pitt's first steps was to strengthen the British forces in North America and appoint able commanders to prosecute the war to a successful conclusion. He also instituted a stronger policy regarding the employment of Indian allies. No less important, particularly in this area of Indian relations, was the work of Sir William Johnson, whose tireless efforts to convince the Iroquois to remain neutral at last bore fruit. The Iroquois, in turn, persuaded the Delawares to cease warfare against the British. The tide was beginning to turn.

During the summer of 1758 a strong British force failed to take Fort Ticonderoga (Fort Carillon to the French), but that failure was offset by the capture of Louisbourg, on Cape Breton Island, and Fort Frontenanc, both located in Ontario. British fortunes were also improving in the south, where Gen. John Forbes cut a new trail through the

Pennsylvania wilderness in yet another effort to take Fort Duquesne.

Forbes's strategy produced the Treaty of Easton, in which the British managed to enlist strong Indian support for their effort to take Fort Duquesne, which many of the Indians were anxious to see abandoned—regardless of who it belonged to. In return for the Indians' support the British provided certain financial considerations and their promise to withdraw from the Ohio River country. Surrounded and unable to be supplied, the French abandoned Fort Duquesne, which Forbes promptly occupied and renamed Fort Pitt.

A year later, in 1759, a mixed force of British regulars and Iroquois allies took Fort Niagara. Sensing the vulnerability of their position, the French then abandoned Fort Carillon (Ticonderoga) and Crown Point and withdrew to Canada. In September 1759 British Gen. James Wolfe's defeat of the French army, commanded by the Marquis Louis-Joseph de Montcalm, on the Plains of Abraham resulted in the surrender of Quebec. The deaths of the two generals, Wolfe and Montcalm, has made the British victory one of the epic stories of history. For all intents and purposes, the British victory at Quebec marked the end of the French and Indian War, although some historians believe France had privately conceded victory to the British.

The Treaty of Paris, signed in 1763, officially ended the intercolonial wars between England and France. The end of the French and Indian War was a watershed event that marked the end of French power in North America. As a result of the treaty, England acquired Canada and all of Spanish Florida. For the next two decades England would be the sole, dominant power in North America.

See also: Braddock's Campaign; England; France; Johnson, Sir William; Treaties and Agreements, Easton, Treaty of
Further Reading: Hurt, *The Ohio Frontier;* Leach, *Arms for Empire;* Steele, *Warpaths*

G

Gall (Pizi)
1840–1894

A prominent Hunkpapa Sioux leader, Gall was born in what is now South Dakota. He earned a reputation as a warrior early in his career but came into prominence at the Battle of the Little Bighorn, where warriors under Gall's leadership opened the fight by contesting the charge of Maj. Marcus Reno's battalion down the valley of the Little Bighorn. In the aftermath of the Custer disaster Gall went to Canada with Sitting Bull, but in 1880 he and his followers returned to the United States and surrendered to the army. After settling on the Standing Rock Reservation Gall turned to farming and became an advocate of the federal government's plan for Indian education.

A powerful and influential warrior during the Indian wars, Gall is also said to have been a man of great courage and integrity. He died at Oak Creek, South Dakota, in 1894.

See also: Little Bighorn, Battle of the (Custer's Last Stand); Reno, Maj. Marcus Albert (Alfred); Sioux; Sioux War
Further Reading: Utley, *The Lance and the Shield*

Galvanized Confederates/Yankees

"Galvanized Confederates" was a Civil War term that applied to Confederate prisoners of war who had agreed to serve on the western frontier fighting Indians rather than spending time in a prisoner-of-war camp. During 1864 and 1865, six regiments of these "galvanized" volunteers participated in operations against hostile Indians. There were also Union prisoners of war who agreed to fight for the South and were called "Galvanized Yankees."

Further Reading: Brown, *The Galvanized Yankees*

Gatewood, Lt. Charles B.
1853–1896

Born in Virginia, Charles B. Gatewood graduated from West Point in 1877. He was assigned to the Sixth Cavalry, serving almost exclusively in Arizona against the Apaches. Indeed, he may have had more experience against the Apaches than any other army officer. Gatewood saw action in the campaigns against Victorio and was a member of Crook's 1883 expedition into the Sierra Madres of Mexico. He played a prominent role in the operations against Geronimo but has never received due credit for persuading Geronimo to surrender.

Transferred north, Gatewood was at Wounded Knee in 1890. He was injured by a dynamite blast at Fort McKinney, Wyoming, and forced to retire. He died in Denver.

See also: Apache Wars; Crook, Gen. George; Geronimo; Miles, Gen. Nelson Appleton; Victorio
Further Reading: Bourke, *An Apache Campaign in the Sierra Madre*; Thrapp, *Al Sieber*; ———, *The Conquest of Apacheria*

Geronimo
ca. 1829–1909

A member of the Bedonkohe band, a small subgroup of the Chiricahua Apaches, Geronimo was the last major recalcitrant Indian leader to surrender. Geronimo's Apache name was Goyakla, or "One Who Yawns." He was probably born near the Gila River in what is today southwestern New

Apache leader Geronimo

Mexico or southeastern Arizona. Like many Apaches of the time, Geronimo developed an intense hatred of Mexicans early in life; his mother, wife, and children had been killed by Mexican soldiers.

During the 1870s he developed a reputation as a leading guerrilla warrior, possessing skills honed under the likes of Mangas Coloradas, Cochise, and others. However, it was during the five-year period from 1881–1886 that his reputation really grew. On three occasions during these years he broke out of the hated San Carlos Reservation, raiding and terrorizing through southeastern Arizona and deep into Mexico.

Three times, Geronimo surrendered to military authorities, including twice to Gen. George Crook. Following each surrender, however, he felt compelled to break out and pursue his raiding ways. Finally, in 1886 he

surrendered to Gen. Nelson A. Miles for what proved to be the third and last time. Geronimo and the Apaches who had surrendered along with him were then shipped off to Fort Pickens, Florida, for several years before being relocated to Fort Sill, Oklahoma, where Geronimo died in 1909 after contracting pneumonia.

See also: Apache Wars; Apaches; Cochise; Crook, Gen. George; Mangas Coloradas; Miles, Gen. Nelson Appleton

Further Reading: Debo, *Geronimo;* Thrapp, *The Conquest of Apacheria;* Worcester, *The Apaches*

Ghost Dance

The so-called Ghost Dance was a late-nineteenth-century messianic movement among western Indian tribes and is perhaps the best-known example of such movements. The arrival of the last decade of the nineteenth century found most western Indian tribes discouraged and disillusioned over their status in life and the disappearance of traditional cultures. Into this climate of despondency appeared a Paiute prophet named Wovoka, believed by some to have been the son of an earlier prophet.

Wovoka preached a message of hope, one that promised a new order in which the Indians would forever be free of the white man's yoke. Indeed, Wovoka soon came to be regarded as something of a redeemer, a messiah. His followers were instructed to dance their traditional slow, shuffling, circular dance, which eventually became known as the Ghost Dance, because the movement also emphasized the return to life of dead Indians. Wovoka's word was reinforced by a total eclipse of the sun in 1889.

Although Wovoka preached a philosophy of nonviolence, some Lakota Sioux leaders departed from that philosophy, urging that the whites be driven out. They also said that anyone who wore the special ghost shirt would be safe from the bullets of the white men, a belief that would lead to awful consequences. The Ghost Dance movement culminated in the tragedy at Wounded Knee, South Dakota, in December 1890.

See also: Wounded Knee Massacre
Further Reading: Mooney, *The Ghost Dance;* Utley, *The Indian Frontier of the American West*

Gibbon, Col. John
1827–1896

Born in Pennsylvania, John Gibbon graduated from West Point in 1847. His active-duty career began too late to serve in the Mexican War; however, he did see action against the Seminoles and later served in Utah.

During the Civil War Gibbon served with great distinction, rising to the rank of brevet major general of volunteers. He was severely wounded in the hip at the Battle of Fredericksburg and thereafter walked with a noticeable limp, which later prompted the Plains Indians to call him "One Who Limps."

Following the Civil War he served on the western frontier. During the 1870s he commanded the military District of Montana; troops under his command formed the Montana Column during the Sioux War of 1876, first moving eastward along the Yellowstone River to prevent the Indians from escaping to the north. Advance elements were the first white men to discover the bodies of Custer's ill-fated battalion. In 1877 Gibbon led a battalion against the Nez Perce, and in a hard-fought battle along the Big Hole River in southwestern Montana he sustained a serious thigh wound.

During the latter part of his army career, Gibbon commanded the Department of Dakota and the Division of the Pacific. A solid, reliable, if somewhat unspectacular soldier, Gibbon was also the author of a number of magazine articles, the most notable being an account of the Sioux War of 1876.

See also: Big Hole, Battle of the; Nez Perce War; Sioux War
Further Reading: Gaff, *Adventures in the West*

Girty, Simon
1741–1818

Known as the "Great Renegade," Simon Girty was one of three Girty brothers: Simon, James, and George. Captured by Indians during the French and Indian War, Girty was eventually returned to his own people, but as a result of captivity he had become almost totally Indian in his outlook.

Girty served the British as a scout for 20 years, siding with them throughout the Revolution. An able practitioner of Indian warfare, he led many raids on Kentucky settlements, earning a reputation as the most hated man in the Ohio Valley. Girty retained his Indian ties after the Revolution and unsuccessfully attempted to discourage tribes from signing the Greenville Treaty after the Battle of Fallen Timbers. During the War of 1812 Girty moved to Canada, where he died in 1818.

See also: Boonesboro, Kentucky; Fallen Timbers, Battle of; Harrodsburg, Kentucky; Shawnees; St. Clair's Campaign
Further Reading: Bakeless, *Background to Glory;* Hurt, *The Ohio Frontier;* Sword, *President Washington's Indian War*

"Glaize," the

An area in northwestern Ohio at the junction of the Auglaize and Maumee Rivers, the "Glaize" was a favored gathering place for Indian tribes of the region. A grand council was held there in 1792.

See also: Council on the Auglaize River; Fallen Timbers, Battle of
Further Reading: Sword, *President Washington's Indian War*

Gnaddenhutten Massacre
March 1782

In March 1782 a group of 90 Delawares who had been converted to Christianity, called Moravians, were put to death by mallet blows to the head as punishment for raids and depredations committed by non-Moravian Delawares. The killings, which took place at Gnaddenhutten, Pennsylvania, came to be known as the Gnaddenhutten Massacre. Although the massacre was soundly condemned by the Pennsylvania legislature, no action was ever taken against Col. David Williamson, who had ordered the executions.

Simon Girty

See also: Iroquois Confederacy; Moravians; Revolutionary War
Further Reading: Dowd, *A Spirited Resistance*

Good Friday Massacre
See Powhatan War

Grattan Massacre
19 August 1854

On 18 August 1854, a Mormon emigrant reported to Lt. Hugh Fleming, the commanding officer at Fort Laramie, Wyoming, that a Brulé Sioux warrior from one of the many camps along the Platte River had stolen and butchered a stray cow. Second lieutenant John L. Grattan, a recent graduate of West Point and new to the ways of the West, requested permission from Fleming to be allowed to take a detachment and arrest the guilty party. Finally yielding to his subordinate's entreaties, Fleming authorized Grattan to take 27 men and two field pieces to the Indian camp where the violator was believed to be. As events would later prove, it was a foolish move on Fleming's part, as tensions were running high; the situation was not one to be entrusted to an inexperienced and impetuous young officer.

An attempt to negotiate with chief Conquering Bear for the surrender of the guilty warrior failed. Grattan, like other young officers before and after him, believed Indian behavior had gotten out of hand and was looking for an excuse to chastise them. Accordingly, when the Sioux failed to turn over the guilty warrior Grattan ordered his men to open fire. Both of the field pieces were poorly aimed and inflicted little damage to the Indian camp. However, Conquering Bear was mortally wounded. As a consequence the angry Sioux swarmed Grattan's party, killing the rash lieutenant and all but one of his men, who managed to escape and reach Fort Laramie, where he died several days later.

Although the number of U.S. troops involved in the Grattan incident was small, it emboldened the Sioux to intensify their raids along the Oregon-California Trail.

See also: Forts, Camps, Cantonments, Outposts, Laramie; Sioux
Further Reading: McCann, "The Grattan Massacre"

Great Law of Peace of the Longhouse

The Great Law refers to a philosophy among the Iroquois Confederacy that promoted the concept of a "great peace" among the tribes outside the Confederacy. A nation's failure to accept this peace invited war against that nation by the combined power of the Confederacy.

See also: Iroquois Confederacy
Further Reading: Jennings, *The Invasion of America*

Great Platte River Road
See Overland Trail

Great Sioux Reservation

The Great Sioux Reservation was created by the Treaty of Fort Laramie (1868), which essentially set aside all of the present-day state of South Dakota west of the Missouri River. Owing to its substantial size, the area was known as the Great Sioux Reservation.

See also: Treaties and Agreements, Fort Laramie, Treaty of
Further Reading: Prucha, *American Indian Treaties*

Great Swamp Fortress

The Great Swamp fortress, as it was called, was a Narragansett stronghold located in the middle of a huge swamp, believed to have been near present-day South Kingston, Rhode Island. Intended as a place of refuge from the expanding pressures of the English colonists, the fort was located and burned in December 1675 by a colonial force guided by friendly Indians.

See also: King Philip's War
Further Reading: Bourne, *The Red King's Rebellion*

Grierson, Col. Benjamin Henry
1826–1911

Born in Pennsylvania, Benjamin Grierson was a music teacher in the Midwest prior to the Civil War. When war broke out Grierson enlisted in the army and was assigned to the cavalry, despite the fact that he did not like horses, having been kicked by one as a boy. Notwithstanding, he was soon appointed an officer and by 1863 had been promoted to brigadier general of volunteers. In the spring of 1863 Grierson led what was probably the most celebrated of all Union cavalry raids, from LaGrange, Tennessee, to Baton Rouge, Louisiana, in support of Grant's Vicksburg campaign.

After the war Grierson was appointed colonel of the Tenth Cavalry, one of two all-black cavalry regiments in the army. Grierson took great pride in his regiment, which compiled an outstanding record on the frontier, building Fort Sill, Oklahoma, and participating in numerous actions against Comanches, Kiowas, and Apaches. He retired in 1890 as a general in the regular army. Grierson had proved himself an able and efficient soldier.

See also: Buffalo Soldiers; Mackenzie, Col. Ranald Slidell; Red River War
Further Reading: Haley, *The Buffalo War*; Leckie, *Unlikely Warriors*; Pierce, *The Most Promising Young Officer*

Grouard, Frank
1850–1905

A valuable army scout on the northern Plains during the Sioux wars of the 1870s, Frank Grouard was born in the Society Islands of the South Pacific, the son of a Mormon missionary and a native woman. In 1852 Frank's father returned to America and settled in California, where he joined a spiritualist group. For reasons that are unclear, Frank was adopted at this time and moved to Utah with his new family.

At age 15 Grouard ran away to Montana, where he was hired as a mail carrier, in which capacity he was captured by the Sioux four years later. Grouard spent the next six years living with the Sioux, and after his initial treatment as a captive, he came to enjoy a certain freedom. He learned the language and customs and came to know many of the prominent leaders of the day, including Sitting Bull and a rising young warrior named Crazy Horse.

In 1874 he broke away from the Sioux and returned to the white way of life. Two years later, in 1876, he was hired as a scout by Gen. George Crook and played a major role in two campaigns that Crook led during the Great Sioux War. He participated in the Battles of the Powder River (17 March), the Rosebud (17 June), and Slim Buttes (9 September). Grouard continued in government service as an interpreter after the Indian conflicts had ended. He was at Fort Robinson, Nebraska, when Crazy Horse surrendered in 1877 and was also at Wounded Knee in 1890. Grouard is also said to have been prominently involved in suppressing road agent activity in the Black Hills and western Nebraska.

Tall and powerfully built, Grouard had a swarthy appearance, with features that suggested a mixed race heritage. As for his skill as a guide, General Crook is once reported to have remarked that he would rather lose one-third of his command than to be deprived of Grouard's services.

See also: Crazy Horse (Tashunca Utico, Tashunka Wikto); Crook, Gen. George; Sioux War; Rosebud, Battle of the; Sioux; Sitting Bull
Further Reading: DeBarthe, *Life and Adventures of Frank Grouard;* Vaughn, *With Crook at the Rosebud*

H

Harmar, Gen. Josiah
1753–1813

Born in Pennsylvania and a veteran of the Revolutionary War, Josiah Harmar was later stationed in the Northwest frontier, where he was involved in treaty negotiations with the Indians. He also attempted to create a military force capable of providing security for the Northwest and fought a number of battles with Indians.

In 1790 he assembled a force of 1,500 poorly equipped and undisciplined troops and moved out from his base at Fort Washington (Cincinnati) with the objective of driving the Indians out of the Ohio country. He was defeated by the Miami war chief Little Turtle in several engagements and forced to fall back to Fort Washington. He was relieved of his command as a result of the failed expedition but was later absolved of wrongdoing by a court of inquiry. Harmar died in Philadelphia in 1813.

See also: Little Turtle (Me-she-kin-no-quah); St. Clair, Arthur

Further Reading: Gilbert, *God Gave Us This Country*; Hurt, *The Ohio Frontier*; Sword, *President Washington's Indian War*

Harney, Gen. William Selby
1800–1889

Born in either Tennessee or Louisiana, William S. Harney preferred a naval career but accepted a lieutenant's commission in the army; by the end of his career he had served in the three major branches—infantry, cavalry, and artillery.

Harney saw service in the Black Hawk War and in the Second Seminole War. During the course of the Seminole conflict he executed a surprise attack on the Seminoles by dressing his men as Indians, despite specific orders to the contrary. Although he distinguished himself in the Mexican War, Harney was also court-martialed by Gen. Winfield Scott for disobedience. The ruling was later overturned, and Harney finished the war as a brevet brigadier general.

As a result of the Grattan Massacre (1853), Harney was called back from leave in France to deal with Indian conflicts. In August 1855 he led a retaliatory campaign against Brulé Sioux at Blue Water Creek, Nebraska. The attack resulted in substantial loss to the Sioux, who were chastened for some time to come. Following his success at Blue Water, Harney returned to Florida for more service against the Seminoles. In 1858 he was promoted to brigadier general in the regulars and given command of the Department of Oregon.

As a result of what later proved to be unfounded suspicions of Confederate sympathies, Harney was retired from the army in 1863. In 1868, however, he was a member of the commission that negotiated the Treaty of Fort Laramie, perhaps the most significant between western tribes and the United States. Harney died in Orlando, Florida.

See also: Blue Water, Battle of; Grattan Massacre; Seminole War, First, Seminole War, Second; Seminole War, Third

Further Reading: Mahon, *History of the Second Seminole War*; Utley, *Frontiersmen in Blue*

Harrison, William Henry
1773–1841

One of the best-known figures in American history and perhaps second only to Andrew Jackson for his impact on Indian-white relations during the early nineteenth

The death of Tecumseh during the Battle of Thames, in which U.S. forces were commanded by William Henry Harrison, in 1813

century, Harrison was born in Virginia on 22 February 1773, the son of a prominent politician. After spending 1787–1790 in two different colleges, including the Physicians and Surgeons College in Philadelphia, he abandoned academia to enter the army.

Harrison served as aide-de-camp to Gen. Anthony Wayne at the Battle of Fallen Timbers. Following promotion to captain he resigned his commission to accept an appointment as secretary of the Northwest Territory in 1798. Appointed governor of the Indiana Territory, Harrison negotiated a number of treaties with Indians in the region, acquiring much land in the process. These land acquisitions particularly inspired resistance by unhappy Indian factions led by Tecumseh and his brother, Tenskwatawa, known as Prophet. Harrison's concern that Indian agitation over lost land and other issues would eventually mean trouble led him to seize the initiative and move against the Indians at the Shawnee village of Prophet's Town on Tippecanoe Creek in November 1811. Although the battle was considered a victory, it was by the narrowest of margins.

During the War of 1812 Harrison defeated a combined British and Indian force at the Battle of Thames on 5 October 1813, in which Tecumseh was killed. In later years, Harrison served in Congress and was the first U.S. minister to Colombia. After an unsuccessful 1836 presidential bid he ran again in 1840, with John Tyler as his vice-presidential candidate. The slogan "Tippecanoe and Tyler, too" carried Harrison into the White House, where he fell ill soon after. He was the first U.S. president to die while in office.

See also: Fallen Timbers, Battle of; Tecumseh; Tippecanoe, Battle of; Wayne, Gen. Anthony (Mad Anthony)
Further Reading: Berton, *Flames Across the Border;* Gilbert, *God Gave Us This Country;* Sword, *President Washington's Indian War*

Harrodsburg, Kentucky

Located southwest of Lexington, Harrodsburg was the first white settlement in what is now Kentucky. Founded in 1775 by two brothers, William and James Harrod, it was established as a palisaded settlement due to the frequency of Indian raids. Indeed, Harrodsburg and Boonesboro, founded two years later, were the only two settlements in Kentucky strong enough to withstand the fierce raids, especially by Shawnees.

See also: Boone, Daniel; Boonesboro, Kentucky; Shawnees
Further Reading: Bakeless, *Background to Glory;* Hurt, *The Ohio Frontier*

Hatch, Col. Edward
1832–1889

Born in Maine, Edward Hatch spent time at sea as a young man before moving to Iowa, where he became a lumberman. He was commissioned captain in the Second Iowa Cavalry upon the outbreak of the Civil War, eventually rising to colonel of the regiment. He was with Grierson on the famous raid through Mississippi in 1863 and later fought in the Battles of Franklin and Nashville. By the end of the war he was a brevet major general of volunteers.

After the war he was appointed lieutenant colonel of the Ninth Cavalry, serving first in Texas, where he had to deal with a conflict arising out of race riots. In 1876 he was named commander of the Department of New Mexico, where he was soon involved in pursuing the Apache war chief Victorio. In 1879 he was ordered to send troops to Colorado to deal with new Ute uprisings, which seriously affected his ability to counter the raids of Victorio. Hatch was one of three individuals named to a commission charged with deciding which Utes were responsible for killing a dozen whites during the Meeker Massacre, and in 1881 he was succeeded as district commander by Col. Ranald S. Mackenzie.

In 1889, while on duty at Fort Robinson, Nebraska, Hatch fractured a hip when he was thrown from the buggy he was driving.

He died unexpectedly from complications while recovering.

See also: Colorow; Mackenzie, Col. Ranald Slidell; Meeker Massacre; Ouray; Victorio
Further Reading: Brown, *Grierson's Raid;* Sprague, *Massacre;* Thrapp, *The Conquest of Apacheria;* ———, *Victorio;* Wilson, *Under the Old Flag*

Hayfield Fight, the
1 August 1867

On 1 August 1867, a Cheyenne war party, augmented by a contingent of Sioux warriors, attacked a small group of haycutters near Fort C. F. Smith in southern Montana near present-day Yellowtail Dam. The attack was one of a two-pronged effort by the Indians to expel the army from the Powder River country and close the Bozeman Trail, which ran from near Casper, Wyoming, to the gold camps around Virginia City, Montana. The second part of the effort took place the following day, when another war party attacked the woodcutters near Fort Phil Kearny, Wyoming, 20 miles south of present-day Sheridan.

The haycutters had erected a makeshift corral out of rough logs and brush as a defensive position if needed, which it was. While a dozen haycutters worked they were guarded by a detachment of 19 soldiers from Fort Smith. When the Indians attacked on the morning of 1 August, the haycutters and their escort withdrew into the corral, where they withstood several attacks throughout the course of the day, due largely to the presence of the defenders' recently acquired breech-loading rifles. The Indians finally dispersed when a relief column from the fort arrived on the scene.

The Hayfield and Wagon Box fights, which these two events came to be known, were nearly identical in all aspects and are notable because they were among the first occasions in which attacking Indians were confronted by breech-loading technology. Both fights also demonstrated that a small group of determined and well-armed defenders, strongly positioned, were capable of withstanding attacks from large Indian war parties.

See also: Bozeman Trail; Forts, Camps, Cantonments, Outposts, C. F. Smith; Forts, Camps, Cantonments, Outposts, Phil Kearny; Wagon Box Fight
Further Reading: Keenan, *The Wagon Box Fight;* Potomac Corral of Westerners, *Great Western Indian Fights;* Utley, *Frontier Regulars*

Horseshoe Bend, Battle of
27 March 1814

In an effort to remove the threat of a Creek-British alliance in the Southwest (Alabama, Mississippi, and Louisiana at that time) during the War of 1812, and especially in the wake of the Creek massacre at Fort Mims, a strong military force was organized to move into the region and destroy the military capability of the Creeks.

The strategy, one that was often employed during the Indian wars, was to send three converging columns. One column was to advance west from Georgia, and a second was to approach from the southeast; the third (and largest), under Andrew Jackson, major general of the Tennessee militia, was to strike south from Tennessee. The first two columns enjoyed some success but were forced to withdraw from the field due to low supplies and the expiration of volunteer enlistments. Thus it was left to Andrew Jackson to deliver what was hoped would be the coup de grace.

After assembling his command at Fayetteville, Tennessee, Jackson moved south across the Tennessee River, established a supply depot he called Fort Deposit, then pushed on and established Fort Strother on the Coosa River. In early November 1813 Jackson's cavalry, under Gen. John Coffee, attacked and killed nearly 200 Creeks in a fierce fight near Tullushatchee. This was followed by another fierce fight on 9 November when Jackson's main body killed an estimated 300 Creeks.

Although the campaign had been considered a success thus far, Jackson found himself having to deal with the same problems

1845 engraving of the massacre at Fort Mims, which led to the Battle of Horseshoe Bend

encountered by the other two columns, that is, low supplies and expiring enlistments. However, the arrival in early 1814 of a regiment of regulars, together with new militia from Tennessee, swelled the ranks of Jackson's army to nearly 5,000. Thus reinforced, Jackson resumed his campaign. The main body of Creeks was located on a peninsula in a sharp bend of the Tallapoosa River in eastern Alabama near the present-day town of Dadeville. Here the Creeks were positioned behind a log stockade designed to utilize crossing fields of fire. Although the position was a strong one, the Creeks had provided for an escape by secreting a flotilla of canoes along the river bank.

Jackson initiated his attack on 27 March. While Coffee's cavalry cut off the line of retreat, Cherokee scouts stole the Creek canoes. Following an artillery barrage against the stockade, Jackson sent his infantry forward. Although the Creeks resisted with a stubborn defense, Jackson's force was too strong to turn back, and eventually the Creeks were compelled to yield. Jackson's casualties numbered about 200 while the Creeks lost 500 killed and many others wounded. The few surviving Creeks fled to the safety of Florida.

The victory gave Jackson a national image. He was promoted to major general in the regular army for his triumph at Horseshoe Bend, which had effectively eliminated the Creeks as a military threat, enabling Jackson to gain large land cessions at the Treaty of Fort Jackson on 9 August. The victory at Horseshoe Bend also made it possible for Jackson to capture Pensacola and thereby ensure the virtual impregnability of New Orleans.

See also: Creek Campaigns; Creeks; Jackson, Andrew; Red Sticks

Further Reading: Heidler, *Old Hickory's War;* Prucha, *Sword of the Republic*

Howard, Gen. Oliver Otis
1830–1909

Born in Maine, Oliver Otis Howard graduated from West Point in 1854. He saw service against the Seminoles in 1857 and generally enjoyed a successful Civil War career, during which he lost an arm at the Battle of Fair Oaks. He ended the war as a brigadier general in the regular army. After the war he was appointed commissioner of the Freedmen's Bureau, a controversial post because the agency became noted for corruption and dishonest practices; Howard himself seems not to have been involved.

In 1872 Pres. Ulysses S. Grant sent him to Arizona to negotiate a peace with the Apaches, and with the help of agent Thomas Jeffords, Howard was able to achieve the first peace with Cochise in many years. In 1874 he was appointed commander of the Department of Columbia, a position he held until 1880. His tenure in this position included responsibility for the Nez Perce War of 1877. Howard's campaign against the Nez Perce has generally been considered good to adequate if not quite brilliant. He has, however, been criticized for the unreasonable demands he imposed on the Nez Perce, which later led to their bolting from the reservation. His campaign against the Bannocks a year later is considered by some to have been more effectively conducted than that against the Nez Perce.

Following his retirement from the army in 1894 Howard wrote several books detailing his experiences with Indians.

See also: Bannock War; Joseph; Nez Perce War
Further Reading: Carpenter, *Sword and Olive Branch,* Howard, *My Life Experiences*

I

Indian Creek Massacre
20 May 1832

During the Black Hawk War, in the aftermath of the Battle of Stillman's Run, a band of Potawatomis attacked the farm of William Davis on Indian Creek, north of present-day Ottawa, Illinois. The Indians reportedly were angry with Davis for constructing a dam across the creek. In the attack, some 15 settlers were killed; two young women were taken captive but later released.

See also: Black Hawk; Black Hawk War
Further Reading: Jackson, *Black Hawk*

Indian Removal Act
1830

First proposed by Thomas Jefferson in 1803, the concept was predicated on persuading or compelling, if necessary, the Indians to relinquish their lands east of the Mississippi River in exchange for lands west. No official action was taken on the idea, however, until 1825 when Pres. James Madison formally presented it to Congress, which debated the proposal for another five years before enacting legislation in 1830. Proponents of the concept believed that removing tribes was the only way to keep them from being obliterated by the spread of white civilization. The idea, however, faced strong opposition, especially from the religious sector.

The concept was strongly supported by Andrew Jackson, and it was during his presidency that the legislation was enacted. A veteran Indian campaigner, Jackson believed that tribes should not be treated as sovereign nations but should be subject to the laws of the federal government. Jackson, accordingly, negotiated removal treaties with the so-called Five Civilized Tribes, but some segments resisted the move. Many Cherokees, for example, had to be forced by the army to relocate west of the Mississippi River, and fierce Seminole resistance led to the Second Seminole War (1835–1842). In Illinois-Wisconsin country resistance on the part of the Sauks and Foxes preceded the Black Hawk War.

The Indian Removal Act ultimately created the Indian Territory, in present-day Oklahoma. The relocation journey to the Indian Territory became known as the Trail of Tears. Thirteen groups made the westward migration, which lasted about six months. The route was named for the suffering and deaths endured by the Cherokees.

See also: Cherokees; Chickasaws; Choctaws; Creeks; Jackson, Andrew; Seminoles; Trail of Tears
Further Reading: Debo, *History of the Indians of the United States*; Foreman, *Indian Removal*

Indian Scouts and Auxiliaries

Some Indian tribes allied themselves with white forces as scouts and guides or, if present in sufficient numbers, as soldiers to supplement the fighting strength of the army. Nearly always the European powers (and later the United States) offered a tribe economic gain and military assistance against their traditional enemies. The promise of plunder also offered a powerful inducement. But if the Indians derived a benefit, so, too, did the white forces who took advantage of their allies' knowledge of the country and of the opposing tribe or tribes.

Notable instances of Indian-white alliances included the Mohawks in King Philip's War. Later the Mohawks allied with the British against the French and the Americans. Choctaws and Chickasaws were with Anthony Wayne at Fallen Timbers, and Andrew Jackson had Cherokee allies in the Creek War. In the West Crows, Shoshones, and Pawnees augmented army columns in the Sioux campaigns, and Crook used Apache scouts to great advantage in the Apache wars.

See also: Apache Wars; Horseshoe Bend, Battle of; King Philip's War; North Brothers; Rosebud, Battle of the
Further Reading: Dunlay, *Wolves for the Blue Soldiers;* Grinnell, *Two Great Scouts*

Indian War
1864

During the spring of 1864 Colorado Gov. John Evans, along with other territorial officials, believed the Plains tribes were readying for war. And there were just enough incidents of raids and stock depredations to support that fear. In June, the murder of the Hungate family south of Denver fueled the apprehension of Colorado citizens. In response, columns under Col. John M. Chivington and Gen. Samuel Curtis moved east from Fort Lyon, Colorado, and west from Fort Riley, Kansas, respectively, but were unable to locate any Indians.

Farther north along the Platte River in Nebraska, Gen. Robert Mitchell found plenty of evidence of Indian activity between Forts Kearny and Laramie but was unsuccessful in catching let alone punishing the raiders. With Cheyenne activity rampant in the area, a powerful striking force under the department commander, General Curtis, was assembled at Fort Kearny in August. However, a 13-day sweep across the Plains again yielded no results. Meanwhile, the summer of 1864 also found Governor Evans issuing his proclamation of safety to all Indians who demonstrated their peaceable intentions by placing themselves in the custody of the army. The proclamation would have tragic consequences before the year was out.

As Curtis, Mitchell, and others searched in vain for hostiles, a third expedition under a Kansan, Gen. James Blunt, probed west from Fort Larned in September and at first was no more successful than the others. However, on 25 September his advance struck a large body of Cheyennes and soon found itself in desperate straits. Blunt arrived with the main body and drove off the attackers. Following this clash, Blunt returned to Fort Larned.

Through October and most of November there was little further military activity. However, on 29 November Chivington's Colorado Volunteers struck Black Kettle's ostensibly peaceful Cheyenne village at Sand Creek, perpetrating the Sand Creek Massacre. At about the same time that Chivington's command was in motion toward Sand Creek, Col. Christopher (Kit) Carson was marching out of Fort Bascom, New Mexico, at the head of some 350 New Mexican volunteer cavalry in response to Comanche and Kiowa depredations along the Santa Fe Trail.

On 25 November Carson's command attacked Little Mountain's village, which was unexpectedly reinforced by a large war party of Comanches whose presence had been unsuspected by Carson. In a hard fight, the first of two at what was called Adobe Walls, the troops managed to drive off the Indians, thanks mainly to its artillery. Kit Carson's expedition perhaps notwithstanding, the Indian War of 1864 would have been remembered for the ineffectiveness of its campaigns had it not been for Sand Creek. In the Indian wars of the West, Sand Creek was a watershed event that produced a terrible backlash, beginning with attacks on Julesburg, Colorado, in January 1865. The reverberations of Chivington's act would carry to Wounded Knee and beyond.

See also: Adobe Walls, First Battle of; Carson, Christopher Houston (Kit); Cheyennes; Dog Soldiers; Evans, Gov. John; Julesburg, Battles of; Sand Creek Massacre

Further Reading: Hoig, *The Sand Creek Massacre;* Kelsey, *Frontier Capitalist;* Leckie, *Military Conquest of the Southern Plains;* Ware, *The Indian War of 1864*

Indian War
1867–1869

In the years immediately following the Civil War, westward expansion across the Great Plains, especially Kansas, was encouraged by railroad construction and the lure of free land promised by the Homestead Act. This westward movement exacerbated tensions between the Plains tribes and white settlers. Already angry over the 1864 Sand Creek Massacre, the Cheyennes attacked and burned the Julesburg, Colorado, stage station in 1865.

Faced with defending the nation's westward advance, the U.S. Army found itself caught between the public outcry over Sand Creek on the one hand and those who demanded retribution for the 1866 Fetterman Massacre on the other. During the summer of 1867 Maj. Gen. Winfield Scott Hancock, the Union hero of Gettysburg who now commanded the Department of Missouri, led a large column of troops across Kansas. Intended mainly to impress the Indians, the campaign served more to rile tribes. Hancock, however, did personally meet with some of the principal Indian leaders, and this in turn produced the notable Treaty of Medicine Lodge later that year. By virtue of the Medicine Lodge agreement and promised annuities, Arapahos and Cheyennes, including the militant Dog Soldiers, agreed not to attack the railroad and stage routes and to generally keep the peace. Congress, however, was slow to ratify the agreement, and

Maj. Gen. Winfield Scott Hancock

when the annuities failed to arrive the impatient warriors resumed their raiding ways.

Following this campaign Hancock was transferred to the Department of the East and was replaced by Gen. Philip H. Sheridan. As he had done throughout the Civil War, Sheridan brought a driving determination, this time to punish recalcitrant Indian bands, and employed unorthodox methods when necessary. Recognizing the need for mobility when retaliating against the swift strikes of the Indian raiders, Sheridan authorized the formation of a company of civilian frontiersmen under one of his staff officers, Maj. George A. (Sandy) Forsyth. On 21 September 1868, Forsyth's Scouts engaged a large Indian war party in the Battle of Beecher Island along the Arickaree Fork of the Republican River in northeastern Colorado, managing to survive repeated attacks for nine days before a relief column arrived.

Active operations did not cease with the departure of summer weather. Sheridan had also decided that a winter campaign against the Indians held great potential. Accordingly, in November 1868 Lt. Col. George Armstrong Custer's Seventh Cavalry attacked and destroyed a large Cheyenne village along the Washita River in western Oklahoma. But Sheridan did not stop with Custer's triumph on the Washita. In December a fresh column followed the Indian trail south from the Washita. At this juncture, however, the campaign encountered a snag when the troops were unable to distinguish between hostile and nonhostile Indians. In addition to Cheyennes and Arapahos, several thousand Comanches and Kiowas had become part of the equation. Many of them had surrendered to Gen. William B. Hazen at Fort Cobb and now enjoyed army protection.

Forced to honor Hazen's agreement, Sheridan could do no more than order any Comanches or Kiowas who had not surrendered to present themselves at Fort Cobb. To ensure compliance, Sheridan took two prominent chiefs as hostages and threatened to hang them if his directive was not obeyed.

The threat worked and most, though not all, came in. On Christmas Day Maj. Andrew Evans attacked and destroyed a Comanche village on Soldier Springs along the North Fork of the Red River, marking the second time in as many months that the army had seriously crippled Indians' capacity for winter survival.

Both the Cheyennes and Arapahos, meanwhile, had remained elusive. Early in 1869 Custer, with a company-sized force, managed to force some Arapahos into Fort Sill, a new post then under construction in southwestern Oklahoma. In March Custer located another Cheyenne village on the extreme eastern edge of the Texas Panhandle. Like Sheridan, Custer managed to take three chiefs as hostages, using them as a bargaining tool to secure the release of two white women captives and to ensure the surrender of the band, which he did.

This largely concluded Sheridan's winter campaign, which could be considered a success in the sense that it demonstrated the army's ability to conduct a campaign in the winter months when the tribes were largely confined to villages. Yet there had really been little resolution of the Indian problem itself.

Meanwhile, farther north on the Central Plains, army columns had been equally active, though with little contact until the arrival of warmer weather. On 11 July, Col. Eugene A. Carr of the Fifth Cavalry, including scout Buffalo Bill Cody and the North Brothers (Frank and Luther) at the head of their famed Pawnee Battalion, struck Tall Bull's Cheyenne Dog Soldier camp at Summit Springs, Colorado, near present-day Sterling. Taken completely by surprise, the Dog Soldiers were quickly routed, with Tall Bull himself killed in the fighting (by Buffalo Bill, some said). Of the two white women captives in the camp at the time, Susanna Alderdice was killed outright by her captors, but Maria Weichell, though wounded, survived.

From the army's point of view, the Indian War of 1867–1869 could be viewed as successful, even if in a narrow context. There were victories at Washita, Soldier Spring, and Summit Springs, of which the latter was particularly notable because it effectively eliminated the Dog Soldiers as a serious military threat on the Central and Southern Plains. The army had also demonstrated its ability to conduct winter campaigns. Despite this, however, the conflicts with the Indians remained largely unresolved. Matters on the Southern Plains would not be settled until the Red River War of 1874–1875; it would take the Great Sioux War of 1876 to resolve matters on the northern Plains.

See also: Beecher Island, Battle of; Carr, Gen. Eugene Asa; Dog Soldiers; Forsyth, Maj. George Alexander (Sandy); Red River War; Summit Springs, Battle of; Washita, Battle of the
Further Reading: Leckie, *Military Conquest of the Southern Plains;* Monnett, *The Battle of Beecher Island;* Utley, *Frontier Regulars*

Inkpaduta (Scarlet Point)
ca. 1815–ca. 1879

A Wahpekute Sioux leader, Inkpaduta, or Scarlet Point, was born in what is present-day South Dakota. A tall man with a face pitted from smallpox, physical appearance may have matched a reputation as renegade. Reportedly, Inkpaduta's attitude toward whites stemmed from an incident in which a brother and his family were murdered by a whiskey peddler and horse thief. Inkpaduta's personal anger and bitterness would affect his relationship with whites for the remainder of his life. He became a militant, and along with a small band of followers he refused to sign the Treaty of Traverse des Sioux (1851).

The winter of 1856–1857 was a desperate one for the Sioux, who had been disarmed for killing a settler's dog and thus were unable to provide food for families by hunting. Angered, Inkpaduta and his band of renegades perpetrated the infamous Spirit Lake Massacre at Lake Okoboji in northwestern Iowa, murdering some 50 settlers. Two weeks later Inkpaduta's band killed more settlers in Minnesota. Following these rampages the band fled west into Dakota Territory. There are unconfirmed rumors that Inkpaduta played a role in the 1862 Minnesota uprising and that he and his followers left a trail of murder and

theft from North Dakota to Nebraska. Inkpaduta reportedly was an active participant in all of the major engagements on the northern Plains during the next two decades, including Whitestone Hill, Killdeer Mountain, and Little Bighorn. He reportedly died in Canada sometime around 1879.

See also: Killdeer Mountain, Battle of; Little Bighorn, Battle of the (Custer's Last Stand); Little Crow, Minnesota Sioux Uprising; Sully, Gen. Alfred; Whitestone Hill, Battle of
Further Reading: Robinson, *History of the Dakota or Sioux Indians;* Sharp, *History of the Spirit Lake Massacre;* Utley, *Frontiersmen in Blue*

Innocents, Slaughter of
See Slaughter of the Innocents

Iroquois Confederacy

The Iroquois Confederacy was probably the best example of an intertribal alliance in North America. Forged sometime during the fifteenth or sixteenth century, the alliance was thought to have been the creation of a Huron mystic named Deganawida. The Confederacy, or Five Nations, as it was also known, initially consisted of five tribes: Mohawks, Oneidas, Onondagas, Cayugas, and Senecas. The Confederacy became Six Nations when the Tuscaroras became part of the alliance following their defeat early in the eighteenth century.

The territory of the Confederacy and, accordingly, its sphere of influence was considerable, reaching from the Hudson River in the east to Lake Ontario in the west. Internally, the Confederacy was perceived as a "longhouse." The easternmost member, the Mohawks, were appropriately enough dubbed "Keepers of the Eastern Door," whereas the western-based Senecas were "Keepers of the Western Door." The Confederacy's guiding principle was the "Great Law of Peace of the Longhouse People," although "peace" by their definition did not exclude war as a means of obtaining that objective.

See also: Great Law of Peace of the Longhouse; Mohawks; Revolutionary War
Further Reading: Hodge, *Handbook of American Indians;* Jennings, *The Invasion of America;* Steele, *Warpaths*

J

Jackson, Andrew
1767–1845

Andrew Jackson was born in South Carolina and emigrated to Tennessee, opening a law office in Nashville at the age of 21; he became the seventh president of the United States in 1829. Earning the nickname "Old Hickory" for his toughness, Jackson served as a member of the U.S. House of Representatives and the U.S. Senate and was judge of the Tennessee Superior Court. One of the most effective Indian fighters of his time, Jackson defeated the Creeks at the important Battle of Horseshoe Bend, Alabama, in 1814 and conducted a harsh campaign against the Seminoles in the First Seminole War. His stunning defeat of the British at the Battle of New Orleans made him a national hero.

Although a tough and relentless campaigner against the Indians, he was not duplicitous in his dealings with them. He was a strong advocate of Indian removal from lands east of the Mississippi River, a policy that was enacted during his presidential administration. He died at his estate, the Hermitage, near Nashville in 1845.

See also: Creek Campaigns; Creeks; Horseshoe Bend, Battle of
Further Reading: Covington, *The Seminoles of Florida;* Heidler, *Old Hickory's War;* Remini, *Andrew Jackson and the Course of American Empire*

Jamestown, Virginia

The first permanent English colony in North America, Jamestown was founded in 1607 and named for England's King James I. Many of the original colonists were indentured servants, sent by the Virginia Company of London, which had been granted a charter to develop a colony in the New World. Additionally, the Virginia Company had a mandate to exploit the area's mineral resources and to locate the elusive Northwest Passage.

The chosen site was a peninsula well upstream on the James River, where it would be hidden from any venturesome Spaniards, who had previously visited the area in 1561. Unfortunately, the site was located on swampy ground and proved unhealthy for inhabitants, who had to contend with dysentery, malaria, and a host of other maladies in addition to hostile Indians, whose bellicose attitude was often, though not always, the result of abuse and misunderstanding by the colonists themselves.

Located in the heart of the Powhatan Confederacy, Jamestown was the focus of Indian attention during the Powhatan, or First Virginia, War. Jamestown was twice burned—in 1676 and again in 1698—and knew little peace during the nearly 100 years of its existence. In 1699, a year after the second fire, the capital of colonial Virginia was moved to Middle Plantation (present-day Williamsburg), and Jamestown gradually fell into disuse. Eventually, the course of the James River created an island of the original site, which is today preserved as part of the Colonial National Historic Park system administered by the National Park Service. In addition to being the first permanent English colony, Jamestown is notable for two other "firsts": the introduction of slavery and the cultivation of the tobacco crop.

See also: England; Treaties and Agreements, Middle Plantation, Treaty of; Powhatan Confederacy; Powhatan War
Further Reading: Jennings, *The Founders of America;* Steele, *Warpaths*

This 1622 engraving demonstrates the violence of the Jamestown massacre.

Jenkins's Ear, War of
1740–1743

In 1739 conflict arose between Britain and Spain over violations of the treaty that followed the War of the Spanish Succession. A British merchant captain, Robert Jenkins, accused the Spanish of cutting off his ear while interrogating him about trade violations, thereby giving the conflict that followed its unique name.

In January 1740, Gov. James Edward Oglethorpe, founder of the Georgia colony, invaded Spanish Florida with a mixed force of Creeks, Cherokees, and Chickasaws. Although Oglethorpe enjoyed some success, he finally withdrew to Georgia after twice failing to capture St. Augustine, the primary objective. The short-lived war ended in 1743, though further changes in Europe's political structure led to a new conflict in 1744.

See also: Chickasaws; Creeks; Oglethorpe, James Edward
Further Reading: Leach, *Arms for Empire*; Steele, *Warpaths*

Johnson, Sir William
1715–1774

A diplomat, trader, and soldier, Sir William Johnson was one of the most extraordinary individuals in Great Britain's North American colonies. Born in Ireland, Johnson came to North America as a young man and took charge of a large family estate in the Mohawk Valley. He quickly demonstrated a willingness to accept Indian manners and customs, establishing a rapport with the tribes that few white men were able to equal. As a result, he became the number-one trader of furs in the colony and acquired much land in the process. Indeed, by the time of his death, in 1774, he was the largest landowner in the colonies.

Johnson was especially successful in gaining the confidence of the Iroquois Confederacy, particularly the Mohawks, becoming an adopted member of that tribe. He married Molly Brant, who was the elder sister of Joseph Brant. Joseph became John-

Sir William Johnson

son's protégé and one of the most influential and important Indian warrior chiefs in North America. It was largely through the efforts of Johnson that the Iroquois tribes allied themselves with the British rather than the French during the intercolonial struggles between the two powers, a relationship that remained steadfast during the American Revolution.

In 1746 Johnson was appointed Superintendent of Indian Affairs, the first time that such authority had been vested in a single individual. He served in that capacity for five years, resigning in 1751, but remained active in an informal capacity. His skill in dealing with Indian tribes has seldom been equaled. He believed firmly in the idea of separating Indian hunting lands from white settlements, a philosophy that was the basis for the Treaty of Fort Stanwix (1768).

In 1755 Johnson led an expedition against the French at Crown Point, and though he failed to take that objective he did inflict a defeat on the French at Lake George that proved significant in that it kept the French from advancing any farther south. Four years later, in 1759, he led a mixed British and Indian force that captured Fort Niagara and participated in the attack on Montreal. Johnson's son John and a supposed nephew named Guy Johnson were also effective as diplomats, leading mixed forces of Tories and Indians against the colonists during the Revolution.

See also: Brant, Joseph (Thayendanega); French and Indian War; Iroquois Confederacy
Further Reading: Axelrod, *Chronicle of the Indian Wars;* Flexner, *Mohawk Baronet;* Steele, *Warpaths*

Johnson's Campaign
1780

This campaign is more accurately described as a combined effort on the part of Sir John

Johnson, son of Sir William Johnson, and Mohawk chief Joseph Brant. In May 1780 Johnson, with a force numbering some 400 Tories and 200 Indians, launched an intense campaign against colonial outposts and settlements in New York's Mohawk Valley.

While Johnson was burning Johnstown Joseph Brant attacked Caughnawaga then moved down the Ohio River and ambushed a militia force moving out of Pennsylvania. Brant turned north, uniting with Johnson and a large party of Senecas under chief Cornplanter. With this unified force Johnson devastated the Schoharie Valley in October 1780. He was finally turned back by a militia force under Gen. Robert Van Rensselaer that had been augmented by a band of Oneidas, one of two tribes of the Iroquois Confederacy to ally with the colonists.

See also: Brant, Joseph; Cornplanter; Iroquois Confederacy; Johnson, Sir William; Mohawks; Revolutionary War
Further Reading: Jennings, *Empire of Fortune;* Wood, *Battles of the Revolutionary War*

Nez Perce chief Joseph

Joseph
ca. 1840–1904

A legendary leader of the Nez Perce Indians, Joseph (Hin-mah-too-yah-lat-kekt, or Thunder Rolling in the Mountains) is believed to have been born in Oregon's Wallowa Valley. Joseph became chief of his band upon the death of his father, Old Joseph, in 1871. Joseph's band was one of five nontreaty bands of Nez Perce who had refused to leave their Wallowa Valley homeland and remove to Idaho in accordance with treaty provisions. In 1877 Gen. O. O. Howard, attempting to enforce the terms of the treaty, directed these nontreaty bands to move to the Idaho reservation or be subject to forcible removal. Refusing to comply with Howard's order, the nontreaty bands began their epic flight for freedom and the sanctuary of Canada.

Joseph has sometimes been called a Red Napoleon, which he was not. Indeed, he was not even a warrior chief, and he was not the head of all the nontreaty bands, as is often implied. He was brave, courageous, and a leader of considerable diplomatic skill who subsequently came to be regarded as the spokesman for the united bands of Nez Perce.

By the time of the Nez Perce surrender at the Battle of Bear Paw Mountains in October 1877, his legend had already begun to grow, probably because of his profound and eloquent address at the time of his surrender, when he declared, "From where the sun now stands, I will fight no more forever." Following the Nez Perce War, Joseph and his people were first sent to Oklahoma and later to the Colville, Washington, reservation, where Joseph died in 1904.

See also: Howard, Gen. Oliver Otis; Miles, Gen. Nelson Appleton; Nez Perce War
Further Reading: Hampton, *Children of Grace;* Lavender, *Let Me Be Free;* McWhorter, *Hear Me My Chiefs*

Julesburg, Battles of
7 January and 2 February 1865

In the aftermath of the Sand Creek Massacre (November 1864), Cheyennes, Sioux, and

Arapahos vowed to retaliate. Accordingly, by early 1865 an encampment that included perhaps as many as 1,500 warriors had formed in eastern Colorado. Their first strike fell on Julesburg, in northeastern Colorado. An important stagecoach stop, Julesburg was a small community with store and storage facilities. Nearby was a small army post, Fort Rankin, garrisoned by a company of the Seventh Iowa Cavalry.

On the morning of 7 January 1865, about 1,000 Sioux and Cheyennes waited in ambush just outside the little settlement, using a small decoy party to entice the soldiers to come out in pursuit. As hoped, the troops responded, but anxious young warriors revealed the trap too soon, allowing the soldiers to fight their way back to the fort, where they were quickly joined by members of the settlement and the occupants of a recently arrived westbound stagecoach. Un-

able to do much else, the occupants of the fort watched helplessly while Indians spent the day plundering the settlement before finally departing as evening arrived. Learning of the attack, an army column under Gen. Robert Mitchell, department commander, led an unsuccessful pursuit of the Indians, who in the weeks that followed raided up and down the Platte Valley.

On 2 February, the Indians returned to attack Julesburg a second time, and once again the inhabitants of the settlement watched the raiders burn and plunder before moving on. The attacks on Julesburg were significant because they sent a clear message that there would be atonement for the tragedy perpetrated by Col. John M. Chivington at Sand Creek.

See also: Cheyennes; Sand Creek Massacre
Further Reading: Grinnell, *Fighting Cheyennes;* Utley, *Frontiersmen in Blue;* Ware, *The Indian War of 1864*

K

Kamiakin
ca. 1800–ca. 1877

A principal chief of the Yakimas, Kamiakin was born in what is present-day Washington. The discovery of gold in the 1850s led to a number of treaties with Indian tribes of the Pacific Northwest, with a view toward providing miners greater access to the ore country. An outspoken opponent of this encroachment, Kamiakin was the leading figure of resistance when war erupted in 1855, vowing to keep whites out of his country.

Although the Indians were subsequently subjugated, Kamiakin himself never acquiesced and died in relative obscurity. Tall and an eloquent speaker, Kamiakin has been largely overlooked by history.

See also: Steptoe, Col. Edward Jenner; Yakima-Rogue War
Further Reading: Burns, *Jesuits in the Indian Wars of the Northwest;* Utley, *Frontiersmen in Blue*

Keepers of the Eastern and Western Doors

In the political structure of the Iroquois Confederacy, the westernmost tribe, the Senecas, protected the Confederacy's western flank, hence they were the guardian, or keeper, of the "western door." The Mohawks were the guardian of the eastern door. The Senecas were the most isolated of the Confederacy, whereas the Mohawks controlled access to and from the European colonies.

See also: Great Law of Peace of the Longhouse; Iroquois Confederacy
Further Reading: Jennings, *The Invasion of America;* Steele, *Warpaths*

Kelly, Luther S. (Yellowstone)
1849–1928

A noted Indian scout and frontiersman of the 1870s and 1880s, Yellowstone Kelly is said to have known the valleys of the Yellowstone and upper Missouri Rivers as well as or better than any white man of the period. Born in Geneva, New York, Kelly enlisted in the Union Army at the close of the Civil War and spent the next three years in Minnesota and the Dakotas. Following his discharge from the army, he headed west to live as a hunter and trapper.

During the 1870s Kelly served as chief scout for the District of the Yellowstone under Col. Nelson A. Miles and participated in the closing campaigns against the Sioux and Nez Perce. After his Montana experience, Kelly spent time in western Colorado and participated in two Alaskan expeditions. In 1900 he was appointed an officer in the Fortieth U.S. Volunteers and saw service in the Philippines. Returning to the United States he became Indian agent at the San Carlos Apache Reservation in Arizona. From 1908 to 1915 he was involved in mining activities in Nevada. In 1915 he and his wife retired to Paradise, California, where he died in 1928. He is buried on the rimrock above Billings, Montana.

Further Reading: Keenan, *From New York to Paradise;* L. Kelly, *Yellowstone Kelly*

Keokuk
ca. 1780–1848

Keokuk (He Who Has Been Everywhere) was a Sauk born near what is present-day Rock Island, Illinois, and is reported to have been French on his mother's side. Although not a chief in the hereditary sense, Keokuk was ambitious and a gifted speaker, traits that helped propel him into a position of leadership among his people.

Keokuk led the peace faction of his people during the Black Hawk War although he vacillated at times, and this tentativeness allowed Black Hawk to become the more dominant figure of that period. After Black Hawk's defeat at Bad Axe, Gen. Winfield Scott arbitrarily appointed Keokuk chief. However, he continued to be opposed by Black Hawk, who remained the de facto leader of the Sauk and Fox peoples. Keokuk died in Kansas in 1848. The city of Keokuk, Iowa, is named in his honor.

See also: Bad Axe, Battle of; Black Hawk; Black Hawk War
Further Reading: Jackson, *Black Hawk*

Kieft, Willem

Willem Kieft was governor-general of New Netherlands from 1639 to 1646, and his heavy-handed tactics were primarily responsible for the first of the so-called Dutch-Indian wars. He imposed heavy taxes on local tribes in an effort to offset losses from a diminishing fur trade. Later, Wappingers sought his protection from the Mohawks, but he refused them sanctuary. After the Mohawks had wreaked havoc among the Wappingers, Kieft sent Dutch troops against the survivors, many of whom were women and children. The affair is known as the Slaughter of the Innocents. In 1646 Kieft was replaced as governor-general by Peter Stuyvesant.

See also: Dutch; Dutch-Indian Wars; Mohawks, Slaughter of the Innocents; Wappingers
Further Reading: Jennings, *Empire of Fortune;* ———, *The Invasion of America;* Steele, *Warpaths*

Killdeer Mountain, Battle of
28 July 1864

During the two years following the 1862 Minnesota Sioux uprising, army columns pursued the militant Eastern Sioux, who had fled west to the Dakotas and Montana to seek refuge among their Lakota, or Western Sioux, cousins. On 28 July 1864, Brig. Gen. Alfred Sully, with a mixed force of more than 2,000 infantry and cavalry, followed a large Indian trail that led to the heavily wooded slopes of Killdeer Mountain (also called Tahkahokuty Mountain) in northwestern North Dakota, near the present-day town of Killdeer. The Indians, aware of Sully's approach, were prepared to offer opposition with a force estimated at 1,600 to 6,000, the former being Sully's assessment, the latter being that of the Indians themselves, which seems more realistic.

Forming his command in a British-style square, Sully advanced in ponderous fashion, repelling several attacks by the Sioux, who were unable to penetrate Sully's formation. In the late afternoon the mounted battalion under Maj. Alfred Brackett launched a saber charge against the Sioux, driving them back. Sully followed up this success with an artillery bombardment, forcing the Indians to abandon their supplies and flee. Sully then proceeded to destroy the abandoned supplies and equipage. Sully's casualties amounted to five killed and ten wounded. The Indians were estimated to have lost 100 or more.

See also: Minnesota Sioux Uprising; Pope, Gen. John; Sibley, Gen. Henry Hastings; Sully, Gen. Alfred; Whitestone Hill, Battle of
Further Reading: Pfaller, "The Sully Expedition of 1864"; Sully, *No Tears for the General*

King George's War
1744–1748

King George's War was the third intercolonial conflict in North America between England and France. In Europe it was referred to as the War of Austrian Succession. Fighting had been ongoing in Europe for several years before hostilities in North America were officially recognized as war. King George's War was typical of intercolonial conflicts in that it consisted mainly of raids and counterraids between the French and their Micmac and Abnaki allies, who were pitted against the English and their Mohawk allies.

Probably the most notable event was the British capture of Louisbourg on Cape Breton Island, Nova Scotia, in 1745 following a six-week siege. Other than this, however, it was mainly a war of savage frontier raids, which intensified late in 1745. The Mohawks attacked French supply lines with considerable success, but the French retaliated with swift and deadly strikes of their own. Notable were attacks on Fort Saratoga; Great Meadows, Connecticut; Deerfield, Massachusetts; and the fight at Barr's Meadow on 25 August 1746.

In 1747 a British plan conceived by Sir William Johnson to attack Montreal failed due to organizational breakdowns and a lack of support from other colonial forces. Although the influential Johnson was successful in recruiting the Mohawks, he was unable to persuade the remaining members of the Iroquois Confederacy to support the effort. Another reason for the failure of the Montreal campaign was that a raid on Fort St. Frederic (Crown Point, New York) had

yielded little while costing the Mohawks heavy casualties.

Although the Treaty of Aix-la-Chapelle (1748) formally ended the war on both sides of the ocean, it did not resolve differences between France and England in North America, which would not occur until the conclusion of the French and Indian War. The treaty also did not put an end to Indian raids. The Abnakis still considered themselves at war with the English and pursued raids relentlessly.

See also: Abnakis (Abenakis); England; France; French and Indian War; Johnson, Sir William; Mohawks
Further Reading: Leach, *Arms for Empire;* Steele, *Warpaths*

King Philip's War
1675–1676

The years following the end of the Pequot War in 1638 were marked by an uneasy peace in New England. The period had witnessed a deterioration in the relationship

General Geoffe repulsing the Indians at Hadley Mountain during King Philip's War

between Indians and colonists. Many colonial elders who had established a working relationship with the tribes had died, as had the Wampanoag sachem Massasoit. As a result, policymaking devolved to a new generation, perhaps less inclined to be as accommodating as predecessors.

The relationships among Indian tribes had also changed, as they sought to effect arrangements with the white colonies that would improve their own positions. These conditions, coupled with a diminution of both the fur and wampum trades—and the insatiable thirst for more land on the part of the growing New England colonies—led eventually to the conflict known as King Philip's War. With the death of Massasoit in 1661, the sachemship of the Wampanoag passed to his son, Wamsutta, who had taken the Christian name Alexander. Wamsutta sold parcels of tribal land to Rhode Island, a move that proved politically unwise, since Plymouth Colony coveted the same lands.

Wamsutta was arrested and brought before the Plymouth authorities to answer charges of conspiracy. He became ill, and he died while journeying homeward after being released. Many, including his brother, Metacom (or Metacomet—called Philip by the English), believed Wamsutta had been poisoned during his interrogation. Thus, when he succeeded to the sachemship upon his brother's death Philip did so with an increasingly hardened attitude toward the colonists.

A further point of aggravation occurred when Plymouth established a new settlement at Swansea (near Fall River) in 1667. The site was not only practically on Philip's doorstep but also on land not owned by the colony. An angry Philip protested and threatened reprisal but was subsequently persuaded to back down and even to surrender his firearms. His appeal was heard by the United Colonies, who rejected his claim and levied such a heavy fine that Philip was forced to sell the land. The resulting sale, however, produced enough revenue for Philip to purchase additional firearms after paying the fine.

There is evidence to suggest that Philip was planning war against the colonies and was then in the process of enlisting the support of other tribes. In any case, a Christian Indian named John Sassamon, who had studied at Harvard and had at one time acted as an aide to Philip, was persuaded by the English to serve as an ambassador of sorts to Philip. Sassamon reported back that Philip was preparing for war. Shortly thereafter Sassamon was murdered, for which three Wampanoags were tried, convicted, and executed, thereby triggering the war that followed. In the wake of the execution Swansea was evacuated, and the settlement was looted by angry Wampanoags.

If Philip had been carefully preparing for war, this incident undoubtedly set things in motion sooner than planned. The colonists were divided over whether their response ought to be offensive or defensive. Massachusetts Bay Colony, which itself had been coveting nearby Narragansett land, elected to mobilize its forces along with Plymouth. Despite the competitive relationship between the two colonies, there may have been a covert arrangement regarding a division of Indian lands once hostilities ended. Indeed, the basis for the United Colonies—Plymouth, Massachusetts Bay, Rhode Island, and Connecticut—was to provide a unanimity of spirit and action when threatened by a common foe.

Thus far Philip had been largely unsuccessful in persuading the Narragansetts to ally with him; a few did, but most agreed to support the English. Faced with conducting a war he was probably not ready to wage, Philip nevertheless launched a series of raids that virtually paralyzed the English settlements. Following this he moved into the Pocasset territory ruled by a sachem named Weetamo, who was his sister-in-law and the widow of Wamsutta. Operating from deep within the Pocasset swamp, Philip completely frustrated a combined Plymouth–Massachusetts Bay campaign. Eventually moving northwest out of the swamp, he was pursued by the English with a contingent of Mohegan allies but continued to elude and frustrate his pursuers.

Yet the English strategy was primarily defensive, though a few individuals, such as 35-year-old Benjamin Church out of Rhode Island, believed a more aggressive policy should be pursued. Church, who argued that militia units needed to adopt Indian tactics, was eventually granted the freedom to put his theories into practice and did so with considerable success. After the war Church and his son published a history of King Philip's War based on his field notes.

Having been at least temporarily stymied in their quest to defeat Philip, the United Colonies chose to attack the Narragansetts during the winter of 1675–1676. The attacking force, nearly 1,000 strong, was led by Gov. Josiah Winslow. Plymouth-born, Winslow, like Philip, was the son of a former leader (in his case, the first governor). Suspicious that an attack might be forthcoming, the Narragansetts had constructed a strong, pallisaded fortress in a large swampy area. The colonists, having learned the location of the village through a captured Narragansett, attacked twice. Losses on both sides were heavy before the English managed to burn the stockade, driving the inhabitants out. Although the attack was a tactical success, it forced the Narragansetts into an alliance with Philip.

A formidable foe in their own right, the Narragansetts were led by Canonchet, son of Minatonomo and a powerful warrior regarded by some as more able than Philip himself. Indeed, Canonchet's contribution to the war effort included the burning of Rehoboth and Providence, Rhode Island, in the early spring of 1676.

In February 1676 Philip attacked and burned Lancaster, Massachusetts, killing many of the inhabitants and capturing a number of others, including Mary Rowlandson, who was to become perhaps the most famous Indian captive in colonial history. After being ransomed she wrote an account of her experiences, which later became a best-seller. The raids continued: Medfield, Weymouth, Groton, Plymouth, and Rhode Island all felt the wrath of Philip's warriors. But the raids and reprisals were not limited to Philip and the English settlements. In May 1676 a large body of Sokoki Abenaki gathered to fish along the Connecticut River near what is present-day Turners Falls, Massachusetts. The Indian village, called Peskeompskut, was something of a base camp and rest area.

Frustrated by the colonies' seeming inability to deal with the raids, Capt. William J. Turner, like Benjamin Church, argued that the war had to be taken to the Indians. He learned from a former captive that the village was only lightly guarded. Moving in, Turner launched a surprise attack, slaughtering anywhere from 100 to 300, mostly noncombatants. Presently, however, the warriors returned, and the attackers suddenly found themselves in desperate straits. The attacking English column survived but suffered heavy casualties; Turner himself was killed. Despite the turnabout the raid was not without military significance, as the attackers destroyed forges used to repair muskets as well as a large inventory of lead and other supplies, all of which were extremely difficult for the Indians to replace.

During the summer of 1676 the English launched a number of small, privately funded expeditions against Philip without great success. Then, in mid-August, Philip's army was surprised in the great Assowamset Swamp near Mount Hope (present-day Bristol, Massachusetts). Philip himself was shot and killed—ironically, by an Indian ally. Philip's head was displayed for many years atop a pole at Plymouth's Fort Hill. But Philip's death did not bring an immediate end to the fighting. By the summer of 1677 the war had reached New Hampshire and Maine. The reestablishment of a fort at Pemaquid (in Maine) provided a strong enough presence to encourage treaty discussions, leading ultimately to the Peace of Casco (1678), which officially marked the end of the conflict.

King Philip's War was the costliest in New England history. An estimated 3,000 Indians were killed, perhaps one-third being Wampanoag. Philip's wife and nine-year-old child were sold into West Indian slavery.

The colonists, too, suffered heavy casualties, including an estimated 1,300 soldiers and 1,000 civilians. Additionally, some 90 towns were attacked during the course of the war; many were burned, and 12 were completely destroyed. The effects of the war were far-reaching in other ways as well. The Indian capacity for resistance in New England was largely crushed, and the political structure of the colonies changed.

See also: Canonchet (Nanunteeno); Treaties and Agreements, Casco, Peace of; Massasoit; Pequot War; Peskeompskut Massacre; Philip (King Philip, Metacom, Metacomet); Wamsutta (Alexander)
Further Reading: Bourne, *The Red King's Rebellion;* Jennings, *The Invasion of America;* Steele, *Warpaths*

King William's War
1689–1697

The first of the intercolonial wars between France and England in North America, King William's War is sometimes referred to as the Abnaki War because it pitted the English and their Iroquois allies against the French and their Abnaki allies. The European component of the conflict was known as the War of the League of Augsburg. A deteriorating situation in northern New England set the stage for the North American phase of the European war.

In the years following the Dutch departure from New York, the Iroquois Confederacy established new economic ties with the English, an alliance that was to largely remain steadfast during the next century. Despite the reassurance of their relationship with the Iroquois, however, the British were concerned over an alliance between France and the Abnakis, a powerful Algonquian tribe from Maine, who in turn were allied with Pennacooks, Penobscots, Micmacs, and others. In large part the concern was based simply on the increasing rivalry between France and England for control of North America. In addition, there was also a fear that Catholicism (perhaps epitomized by Louis XIV of France) was on the rise and was seen to have targeted Protestantism. In North America there was a disturbing rumor to the effect that French Catholics were preparing a savage alliance with the Indians to take over the colonies and install Catholicism.

In Massachusetts, British colonists upset an uneasy peace by taking Abnaki prisoners in response to the killing of English cattle. Abnaki raids followed, and in April 1688 Sir Edmund Andros, recently appointed governor of all the northern colonies now called the Dominion of New England, launched a retaliatory strike, capturing a French outpost on Penobscot Bay on the pretext that it was British property. Aside from this, Andros concentrated on building forts and employing a largely defensive strategy to deal with the Abnaki raids. His tenure as governor was short-lived, however, and he was deposed as a result of the Protestant Revolt in England in the spring of 1689, which saw James II replaced by William of Orange.

With the war in Europe officially under way, Louis XIV chose the aging Comte de Frontenanc to govern New France. A 70-year-old curmudgeon, Frontenanc decided to move south from Canada and invade British New York, an unwise move since Frontenanc lacked the necessary resources to execute his strategy. In the first real strike of the war a large contingent of Iroquois attacked Lachine, a French settlement near Montreal, in July 1689, virtually destroying the settlement and killing many of its inhabitants. As a result of the Lachine Massacre Frontenanc decided to adopt guerrilla tactics. No quarter was asked and none was given. As the Iroquois terrorized the French, the Abnakis and their allies retaliated in like form against the English.

During the winter of 1689–1690, Frontenanc led a force from Montreal down into New England, striking Schenectady and slaughtering many in retaliation for Iroquois raids. This was followed in March with a similar attack on Salmon Falls, New Hampshire. In an effort to gain the initiative, a British squadron under the command of Maine-born frontiersman Sir William Phips captured the lightly defended Port Royal, Maine, in the spring of 1690. Buoyed by this success, the British decided to launch an invasion of Canada in August 1689 with Phips in command. However, beset by a number of military and logistical problems and with the ranks devastated by smallpox, the offensive came to naught. Although Frontenanc's guerrilla tactics spread terror through the northern colonies, they had accomplished little of real substance for the French cause.

In 1691 an aging and barely mobile Capt. Benjamin Church, hero of earlier troubles, was called on to help counter the Abnaki raids. Church's efforts produced some success, but the raids continued. In 1692 Wells, Maine, and Deerfield, Massachusetts were victims of raids that continued for the next several years.

In a March 1697 raid on Haverhill, Massachusetts, Abnakis captured Hannah Dustin, mother of eight and one of the most famous of New England's Indian captives. After capture, Hannah and a companion attacked their captors, killing all but two as they slept, and made their escape.

In September 1697 the Treaty of Ryswick ended the European war, which in turn brought an end to the conflict in North America, though New England continued to see sporadic fighting for some time. As a postscript to King William's War, the Iroquois Confederacy and western tribes allied with the French continued their struggle. Near the end of the century, most likely in 1698 or 1699, a major battle took place between these factions on the shores of Lake Erie, resulting in an Iroquois defeat.

See also: Abnakis (Abenakis); Dustin, Hannah; England; France; Iroquois Confederacy
Further Reading: Jennings, *Empire of Fortune;* Leach, *Arms for Empire;* Steele, *Warpaths*

Kiowas

From the mid-eighteenth century on, the Kiowas were a tribe of the Southern Plains. Prior to that time they seem to have dwelled in what is today southern Montana and now consider themselves closely related to the Crows, who still live in that region. During the last half of the eighteenth century the Kiowas were forced south by Sioux and Cheyennes. On the Southern Plains they eventually established ties with Comanches and by the mid-nineteenth century were regarded as skilled buffalo hunters and warriors. Like the Comanches, they fiercely resisted white encroachment while continuing to raid villages of their traditional enemies, the Navajos and Utes.

See also: Comanches; Navajos; Red River War; Utes
Further Reading: Haley, *The Buffalo War;* Leckie, *Conquest of the Southern Plains;* Nye, *Bad Medicine and Good*

L

Land Cessions, Northwest Ordinance

The Greenville Treaty (1795) left boundary questions unresolved. Concerned for future U.S. hopes after Spain ceded Spanish Louisiana to France, Thomas Jefferson urged the acquisition of all possible lands along the eastern border of the Mississippi River. Accordingly, between 1803 and 1809 William Henry Harrison, newly appointed governor of Indiana Territory, concluded no less than 13 separate treaties with the Indians, thereby acquiring for the United States large tracts of land in the old Northwest Territory as far north as Wisconsin.

Further Reading: Prucha, *American Indian Treaties*

Langlade, Charles Michel de

See Pickawillany Massacre

Lawton, Lt. Henry Ware
1843–1899

Born in Ohio, Henry Ware Lawton joined the Ninth Indiana Infantry upon the outbreak of the Civil War and was later commissioned lieutenant in the Thirtieth Indiana Infantry. He was later awarded the Medal of Honor for his conduct during the fighting around Atlanta. After the Civil War he remained in the army as a lieutenant, serving in the Forty-First and the Twenty-Fourth Infantry regiments. In 1871 he transferred to the Fourth Cavalry, where he rapidly developed a reputation as an absolutely dependable quartermaster.

After the Battle of Palo Duro Canyon in September 1874, Lawton was given the job of slaughtering more than 1,000 Indian horses. Later transferred to Arizona, Lawton served under Gen. Nelson A. Miles in the last Apache campaigns, leading a detachment of scouts deep into the remote Sierra Madre Mountains of Mexico in search of Geronimo. During the Spanish-American War Lawton served in Cuba and then in the Philippines, where he was killed in the fighting around Manila.

See also: Apache Wars; Geronimo; Miles, Gen. Nelson Appleton; Palo Duro Canyon, Battle of; Red River War
Further Reading: Carter, *On the Border with Mackenzie;* Pierce, *Most Promising Young Officer;* Wooster, *Nelson Miles*

Little Bighorn, Battle of the (Custer's Last Stand)
25–27 June 1876

Early in 1876 the War Department initiated military action to compel recalcitrant bands of northern Plains Indians to return to their assigned agencies. As part of the Dakota Column commanded by Brig. Gen. Alfred H. Terry, the Seventh Cavalry, commanded by Lt. Col. George Armstrong Custer, headed up the Rosebud River from its confluence with the Yellowstone River on 22 June 1876, under orders to locate and follow the hostile Indian trail.

General Terry's strategy was to place the Indians between Custer and a mixed force of infantry and cavalry commanded by Col. John Gibbon. Gibbon's force, known as the Montana Column because it consisted of troops taken from duty stations in western Montana, had recently united with Terry's command. The plan

A lithograph portraying one of the most famous battles of the time, the Little Bighorn

called for the Montana Column to move west along the Yellowstone River to its confluence with the Big Horn River. At that point Gibbon, with Terry accompanying, was to turn south to be in position to cooperate with Custer's cavalry, which (it was hoped) would be driving the Indians from the east. Terry's orders to Custer, however, were discretionary and allowed Custer ample latitude in which to exercise tactical judgment.

Discovering a large Indian trail, Custer followed it to the west, reaching the valley of the Little Bighorn River in southeastern Montana very early on 25 June. From the Crows Nest, a high point on the divide separating the valleys of the Rosebud and the Little Bighorn, Custer's Crow scouts detected the Sioux pony herd some 15 miles distant. Initially planning to rest his regiment through the day and then to attack the Indian village at dawn on 26 June, Custer was forced to revise his plan when it appeared the Indians had discovered his presence. He decided to attack immediately.

Custer divided the regiment into three battalions. Three companies under Capt. Frederick Benteen were ordered to scout to the left to ensure that the Indians did not escape in that direction. Ironically, the breakup and dispersal of an Indian village before an attack could be launched was always of paramount concern to the officer in command. A second battalion of three companies together with the Indian scouts, under Maj. Marcus Reno, was directed to cross the Little Bighorn River, charge down the valley, and attack the village. Meanwhile, the third

A wooden cross marks the grave of a soldier who fell during the Battle of the Little Bighorn in Montana.

and largest of the three battalions, five companies commanded by Custer himself, would approach the Indian village on a course roughly parallel to that of Reno's but above and to the right, hidden from Reno's view by the intervening bluffs above the river.

No one really knows Custer's strategy that sultry Sunday afternoon, but most historians believe Reno's attack was intended as a diversionary movement, which would have allowed Custer, commanding the largest battalion of the regiment, to strike the village from an unexpected quarter with the main body. Although this was in keeping with the Indian-fighting tactics of the time, not much went right for the Seventh Cavalry. Encountering much stiffer resistance than he anticipated, Reno halted his charge down the valley, retreated into the timber along the river, and finally abandoned that location, retreating in panic across the Little Bighorn River to the safety of the bluffs above it.

Whether and to what extent Custer was aware of Reno's situation has been debated ever since. Also unclear is whether Custer actually attempted to cross the river and attack the village or was in fact himself attacked and driven back before he had an opportunity. Regardless, the Custer battalion was eventually forced to seek the higher ground north-northeast of the river. Still, it is arguable whether this move was in keeping with Custer's overall offensive plan or indicated a shift to the defensive. At some point, however, the five companies were forced to assume a defensive posture and were eventually overwhelmed. The final act of the drama saw Custer and a few others gathered atop Custer Hill in the famous "last stand" for which the battle is best known. Custer himself sustained two wounds, but it is not clear whether he was hit early in the fight or later, during the last stand.

Meanwhile, some 5 miles to the southeast at what is known as the Reno-Benteen defense site, the three companies of Major Reno were joined by the pack train and Captain Benteen's battalion, returning from its earlier scout to the left. Here the Reno-Benteen command, although suffering substantial casualties, managed to hold out until relieved by the Terry-Gibbon column on 27 June.

In this, the most famous of all battles fought during the American Indian wars, the Seventh Cavalry lost some 260 men, including about 210 on Custer field—nearly 40 percent of its prebattle strength. The Custer family lost five of its members in the fight in addition to George: two brothers, Capt. Tom Custer and Boston Custer; a nephew, Armstrong Reed; and a brother-in-law, Lt. James Calhoun. No real consensus seems to exist on Indian losses. The battle was at once the apex and the nadir for the Sioux and their allies.

See also: Custer, Lt. Col. George Armstrong; Rosebud, Battle of the; Sioux; Sioux War
Further Reading: Fox, *Archaeology, History, and Custer's Last Battle*; Gray, *Centennial Campaign*; ———, *Custer's Last Campaign*; Stewart, *Custer's Luck*; Utley, *Cavalier in Buckskin*

Little Crow
ca. 1803–1863

A Mdewakanton Santee Sioux chief, Little Crow was born around 1803 in what is today Minnesota. Little Crow was a reluctant signer to the Treaty of Traverse des Sioux (1851), the agreement that more than any other shaped Indian-white relations in the upper valley of the Mississippi River.

Twice during the 1850s Little Crow traveled to Washington, seeking to improve conditions for his people. In the aftermath of the 1857 Spirit Lake Massacre, when U.S. officials declared that annuities would not be distributed until Inkpaduta and his band were caught, Little Crow conducted an unsuccessful pursuit.

When Minnesota Sioux rose up against whites in August 1862, Little Crow was reluctant to become involved. Although his people had not been treated fairly, he recognized the futility of resistance. But he eventually yielded to pressure and led the Sioux during the fighting that bloody summer, becoming wounded in the fighting at Fort Ridgely. When the uprising was quelled Little Crow escaped to Dakota but later returned to Minnesota, where he was killed by settler Nathan Lampson and his son near Hutchinson.

See also: Inkpaduta (Scarlet Point); Minnesota Sioux Uprising; Spirit Lake Massacre
Further Reading: Anderson, *Little Crow*; Carley, *The Sioux Uprising*

Little Turtle
(Me-she-kin-no-quah)
1752–1812

The son of a Miami father and Mahican mother, Little Turtle became head chief of the Miami at an early age and came to be highly regarded by the members of both tribes. Like many Indian leaders, Little Turtle believed there was more to be feared from the American colonists than the British and, accordingly, threw his support behind the latter during the Revolution. In the post-Revolution years, Little Turtle continued his militant opposition to the influx of settlers in the Ohio country in what is sometimes referred to as Little Turtle's War. Little Turtle did not resign to the futility of further opposition until after Anthony Wayne's victory at Fallen Timbers in 1794. When the Greenville Treaty was signed Little Turtle declared that he was the last to sign it and would be the last to break it. True to his word, he was thereafter loyal to the United States and spent his last years promoting the cause of temperance among his people.

An outstanding warrior and leader of his people, Little Turtle died on 14 July 1812.

See also: Little Turtle's War; Treaties and Agreements, Greenville, Treaty of; Wayne, Gen. Anthony (Mad Anthony)

Further Reading: Gilbert, *God Gave Us This Country;* Hurt, *The Ohio Frontier;* Sword, *President Washington's Indian War;* Young, *Little Turtle*

Little Turtle's War
1786–1795

The conflict often called Little Turtle's War represented a continuation of the struggle for the Ohio River country, which began with the first migration of white settlers into this rich and fertile region and increased sharply in the years after the Revolution as veterans, awarded land grants in the military reserve in lieu of payment, swelled the ranks of immigrants. Although England had agreed to surrender its claim to all lands in the Old Northwest Territory as a result of the Treaty of Paris in 1783, the British were able to retain a strong de facto presence in the area by refusing to relinquish key outposts, and the United States lacked the resources to enforce the treaty. Motivated by the lucrative economics of their trade with the Indians, the British, represented by agent Alexander McKee, continued to encourage and support Indian resistance to American settlements.

In January 1786, in response to increasing Indian raids, the United States assembled a conference at Fort Finney, near the confluence of the Ohio and Miami Rivers. Shawnees argued that the lands in question belonged to them; Indian commissioners Richard Butler and George Rogers Clark threatened war if the Indians did not acquiesce. Although the threat caused some of the Shawnee chiefs to back down, others such as Little Turtle and Blue Jacket maintained their militant stand.

In the fall of 1786 Clark launched an abortive campaign against tribal strongholds in the Wabash country. Logistical

American troops fighting Indians during the Battle of Fallen Timbers on the Maumee River, 1794.

problems, desertions, and, apparently, Clark's drinking all contributed to the failure of the expedition. At the same time, a second column under the command of Benjamin Logan, mostly mounted and including Daniel Boone and Simon Kenton, attacked Shawnee villages along the Mad River. Although Logan's effort resulted in the destruction of several villages and much of the Indian's corn supply, it inflicted no damage on the warriors who were away raiding. Perhaps more important, Logan's raid served to bring together disparate factions among the Shawnees.

The passage of the Northwest Ordinance in 1787 created the Northwest Territory, comprising what would eventually become the states of Ohio, Indiana, Michigan, Illinois, Wisconsin, and part of Minnesota. Arthur St. Clair (pronounced Sinclair), a veteran of the Revolutionary War, was appointed governor of the new territory. Officially, the federal government was now obliged to defend this country and to turn back illegal squatters. Yet the enactment of the Northwest Ordinance also provided a source of needed revenue for the hard-pressed U.S. government, which sold land to speculators such as the Ohio Company.

In the decade following the Revolution, dealing with the tribes of the Northwest (and elsewhere, for that matter) was a thorny issue for the United States. There was no clear-cut policy and, until the ratification of the U.S. Constitution (which took place over a three-year period, 1787–1790), no real central authority for addressing questions relating to land boundaries, recompense, and so on.

Between 1784 and 1794, the year of Gen. Anthony Wayne's deciding victory at Fallen Timbers, a number of treaties were entered, but none did much to resolve the fundamental sticking point, namely, that Americans wanted the Ohio country, which Indians did not wish to give up. By 1790, in response to public demands for protection against Indian raids, a punitive expedition under the command of Gen. Josiah Harmar, a Revolu-

tionary War veteran but lacking experience in fighting Indians, was soundly whipped by Shawnees under the able warrior Blue Jacket.

Emboldened by their success against Harmar, the Indians increased their raids throughout the Ohio country settlements. Meanwhile, the British, who up to now had been supportive of the Indians, took on a more conciliatory role. Fearing that the increased Indian raids might result in a strong reaction from the United States that would affect Britain's presence in the region, they offered to negotiate a peace between the tribes and the United States. The proposal was rejected, however, and in the fall of 1791 a second expedition was launched, this one under the command of General St. Clair himself, who was still territorial governor. St. Clair proved even less adept as a field commander than Harmar. On 4 November 1791, a powerful force of Shawnees and Miamis under Little Turtle and Blue Jacket launched a surprise attack against St. Clair's camp near present-day Fort Wayne, Indiana, killing and wounding more than 1,000. The defeat was staggering, the worst ever suffered by the U.S. Army up to that time in terms of the numbers engaged. Disgraced, St. Clair resigned his commission, though he remained governor of the territory. The defeat moved Congress to consider a larger army, which was finally authorized in 1792.

President Washington chose Gen. Anthony Wayne to organize the army and conduct a successful campaign against the Ohio Indians. A Pennsylvania veteran of the Revolution, "Mad Anthony" Wayne, as he was known, had a solid reputation as a soldier and fighter. During the next 12 months Wayne went about the business of recruiting and training his army while the Indians, including a young Shawnee warrior named Tecumseh, continued to raid and terrorize the Ohio country settlements and inflict defeats on several columns sent against them.

By the spring of 1793 Wayne was able to get under way, moving his army, known as Wayne's Legion, to Fort Washington, near present-day Cincinnati. The campaign was put on hold, however, when the government, attempting to resolve the crisis without military action, agreed to meet with tribes during the summer of 1793. For its part, the United States agreed to relinquish all claims north of the Ohio River except for the immediate area around Cincinnati. The Indians, however, rejected the offer, demanding the departure of all settlers from the region. By the fall of 1793 talks had broken off, and Wayne prepared to resume his campaign, although supply problems and the traitorous behavior of his second in command, Gen. James Wilkinson, resulted in postponement till the next spring.

In August 1794 allied Indians under Blue Jacket and Tecumseh prepared to attack Wayne and destroy him, much the same as they had to St. Clair. Little Turtle, who by this time had come to believe that the only way for the Indians to truly defeat the Americans was with massive British aid (which he correctly suspected was never to be forthcoming), counseled against the attack, but the strident voices of Blue Jacket, his arch rival Tecumseh, and others were not to be denied.

Moving toward the suspected site of the Indian villages, Wayne's command was struck in a surprise attack along the Maumee River in an area of dense undergrowth and downed trees known as Fallen Timbers. Although momentarily stunned, Wayne recovered, and in one of the most decisive battles between Indians and whites he inflicted a stunning defeat, which led to the signing of the Greenville Treaty and a decade of peace in the Ohio River country.

See also: Harmar, Gen. Josiah; Little Turtle (Me-she-kin-no-quah); Ohio Company (of Virginia); St. Clair, Arthur; Tecumseh; Wayne, Gen. Anthony (Mad Anthony)
Further Reading: Gilbert, *God Gave Us This Country;* Hurt, *The Ohio Frontier;* Sword, *President Washington's Indian War*

Little Wolf
ca. 1820–1904

Little Wolf was born in Montana and became a northern Cheyenne chief. By the mid-nineteenth century, when the white presence was beginning to be felt in the Trans-Mississippi West, Little Wolf was a recognized war leader. He may have been present at the Fetterman Massacre and at the Battle of the Little Bighorn.

Following Col. Ranald S. Mackenzie's victory over Dull Knife's Cheyenne village in November 1876, Little Wolf, along with other Cheyennes, was sent to a new reservation in Oklahoma's Indian Territory. In 1878, angry and dissatisfied with conditions in Oklahoma, Little Wolf and Dull Knife led a breakout from the reservation and headed north to their home territory in Montana. In Nebraska the two groups divided. Dull Knife surrendered his band to the army at Fort Robinson, Nebraska; Little Wolf and his followers continued to Montana, where they were eventually allowed to remain. Little Wolf later served for a time as an army scout under Gen. Nelson A. Miles.

See also: Cheyennes; Dull Knife; Dull Knife Outbreak
Further Reading: Grinnell, *The Fighting Cheyennes;* Sandoz, *Cheyenne Autumn*

Llano Estacado (Staked Plains)

A vast expanse of high plains some 30,000 square miles in size, the Llano Estacado lies mostly in the Texas Panhandle; about one-third of it is located in eastern New Mexico. In Spanish, *estacada* means "fence" or "spike." One legend has Spaniards, perhaps Coronado's expedition, driving stakes into the ground to mark a trail; another theory suggests that the sharp, pointed tips of the profuse Yucca plant resemble spikes sticking up.

The Staked Plains figured prominently in the Indian wars of the Southwest. Comanches crossed this area frequently on raids into New Mexico. It was also here that a group of unscrupulous traders and brigands known to history as the Comancheros developed a brisk trade with Indians of the area.

See also Adobe Walls, First Battle of; Comanches; Palo Duro Canyon, Battle of
Further Reading: Haley, *The Buffalo War;* Pierce, *The Most Promising Young Officer*

John Logan finds his murdered family.

Logan, John
ca. 1725–1780

Born in Pennsylvania, John Logan took his name from a former governor of Pennsylvania with whom he had been friendly. Logan, whose Indian name was Tah-gah-jute, was a Mingo, the name given members of the Iroquois Confederacy who lived beyond the pale of Iroquois territory. Although one source has his father as French, John Logan remained neutral during the French and Indian War. About 1770 he and his family moved to the Ohio frontier, where they lived an isolated life.

In the spring of 1774 a dozen members of his family were murdered on Yellow Creek by a group of angry Virginians in retaliation for Indian depredations. The incident provoked Lord Dunmore's War. Furious, John Logan struck back with a war party he assembled and wrought havoc along the Ohio frontier and into Pennsylvania. In response, Lord Dunmore, governor of Virginia, launched a campaign against the Shawnees. The strategy was not only to retaliate for

Logan's raids but also to clear Indians out of the beckoning Ohio country, thereby raising land values.

Dunmore's army was successful in defeating a large Shawnee war party at the Battle of Point Pleasant in October 1774. The Virginians also destroyed a number of Shawnee villages, thus compelling the Shawnees to agree to peace terms. John Logan was killed by relatives near Detroit in 1780.

See also: Lord Dunmore's War; Ohio Company (of Virginia)
Further Reading: Bakeless, *Background to Glory;* Hurt, *The Ohio Frontier*

Longhouse

A communal dwelling used by members of the Iroquois Confederacy, longhouses featured a wooden framework covered with bark. Longhouses ranged in size from 150 to 200 feet in length and somewhat resembled a World War II Quonset hut. A single longhouse might house several families who functioned as a clan. The inhabitants slept on the floor, storing food and other items on overhead racks.

See also: Iroquois Confederacy
Further Reading: Debo, *History of the Indians of the United States*; Jennings, *The Invasion of America*

Looking Glass
ca. 1823–1877

A Nez Perce war chief, Looking Glass was born in the Wallowa Valley of northeastern Oregon and figured prominently in the Nez Perce conflict of 1877. Although Joseph has come to be thought of as the leader of the Nez Perce on their epic flight for freedom, it was Looking Glass who directed their actions against the pursuing soldiers. Looking Glass lost credibility after the Battle of the Big Hole, however, when the Nez Perce were surprised by an army force under Col. John Gibbon after Looking Glass had counseled a rest, saying the soldiers were too far behind to catch them. As a consequence, he was replaced by other war leaders.

When the Nez Perce reached the Bear Paw Mountains, Looking Glass was again called on to lead the people, and once again he counseled a rest because the soldiers were far behind. As at the Big Hole, however, Looking Glass did not realize that other army columns were in the field and far closer than he realized. Thus, the Nez Perce were surprised a second time and finally forced to surrender to troops under Col. Nelson A. Miles. Looking Glass himself was killed in the first day's fighting.

See also: Bear Paw Mountains, Battle of; Howard, Gen. Oliver Otis; Joseph; Miles, Gen. Nelson Appleton; Nez Perce War
Further Reading: Brown, *The Flight of the Nez Perce*; Hampton, *Children of Grace*

Lord Dunmore's War
1773

White dissatisfaction with treaty boundaries established during the 1760s created an increasingly volatile situation in Kentucky and Ohio, which eventually led to what is known as Lord Dunmore's War. In 1773 John Murray Dunmore, colonial governor of Virginia, commissioned a survey of parts of Kentucky and Ohio lands that had been guaranteed to the Shawnees by virtue of the Treaty of Fort Stanwix (1768). Angry Shawnees threatened to kill any whites who crossed the Ohio River into Kentucky. Accordingly, when the survey party moved into the off-limits area in May 1773, it was attacked. All in the party were killed except one member, who was sent back as a reminder that the Shawnees' warning was not an idle threat.

The following year, 1774, Dunmore unilaterally took possession of western Pennsylvania and Kentucky for Virginia, using the original charter as justification. Settlers began to migrate into the area, staking claims and establishing settlements such as Harrodsburg. Inevitably, there were isolated attacks by both settlers and Indians, and tensions rose.

At the invitation of trader George Croghan a group of Shawnee chiefs, including Cornstalk, traveled to Pittsburgh in an effort to negotiate a peace. Dunmore, however, seized the opportunity to hold the chiefs hostage. After their release the chiefs were attacked by angry whites, who killed Cornstalk's brother, Silverheels. In retaliation the Shawnees struck back, massacring a dozen white settlers in the Baker's Cabin Massacre.

This in turn brought about the murder of Mingo chief John Logan's family by a group of white banditti. At this juncture Dunmore, fearing a general Indian war, mobilized the militia and set out to seize the initiative by attacking the Shawnees first. Meanwhile, efforts to persuade Iroquois, Delawares, and Cherokees to remain neutral were successful due to the negotiating skills of Sir William Johnson, George Croghan, and James Robertson (one of the founders of Nashville). The Shawnees were thus deprived of allies.

Dunmore's strategy was to send two columns against the Shawnees. The first, consisting of some 1,500 men and commanded by Dunmore himself, would move down the Ohio River toward the Shawnee villages in central Ohio; a second force under Col. Andrew Lewis approached from the south. The two columns were to rendezvous at the confluence of the Kanawha and Ohio Rivers. The presence of both columns was known to the Indians. Apparently feeling insecure on the river, Dunmore changed his plan and instead marched overland toward the Shawnee villages. On 10 October a war party under Cornstalk surprised Lewis near the mouth of the Kanawha River. After a fierce, day-long fight that caused heavy casualties on both sides, the Indians withdrew.

Dunmore's conduct of the campaign came under harsh criticism. At one point the governor had called a halt, but a near-mutiny in Lewis's command seems to have persuaded him to resume. Caught, finally, between the two advancing columns, the Shawnees asked for peace, and a truce was effected on 26 October 1774. The upshot was the Treaty of Camp Charlotte, under which Dunmore coerced the Shawnees into relinquishing their claims to Kentucky. The treaty thus opened the Ohio country, although it did not end Indian resistance, and much blood would yet be shed before the struggle for the Ohio River valley had ended.

See also: Johnson, Sir William; Logan, John; Treaties and Agreements, Logstown Treaty
Further Reading: Dowd, *A Spirited Resistance;* Hurt, *The Ohio Frontier*

❧ M ❧

Mabila (Mobile), Battle of
18 October 1540

In May 1539 an expedition commanded by Hernando de Soto (ca. 1500–1542) landed near what is present-day Tampa, Florida. A wealthy Spanish hidalgo, de Soto had served under Pizarro in South America, amassing a fortune in the process. As a result of his generous support of Emperor Charles V, de Soto was awarded the governorship of Cuba and the right to exploit a huge tract in La Florida of his choosing.

De Soto's expedition was a formidable one, numbering some 600 conquistadores about equally divided between cavalry and infantry. Many of the officers and men had served under de Soto in Central America and South America, thus providing him with a veteran nucleus. As an added bonus, de Soto had Juan Ortiz, a survivor of the disastrous Narváez expedition four years earlier. Ortiz had managed to survive among local Indians and as such would be a knowledgeable guide for the expedition.

Armament included lances, swords, crossbows, and a few harquebuses. The traditional breastplate armor, which had worked well enough in Europe, was found to be easily penetrated by the powerful longbows of Native Americans, and so armor was eventually discarded for a type of heavy quilted shirt or jacket that provided far better protection from the fearsome Indian arrows. Although de Soto had arranged for his command to be amply provisioned before setting out, it was clearly evident that the expedition would need to rely on foodstuffs furnished by native villages. As it turned out, this would be an early version of Sherman's March to the Sea during the Civil War, albeit with a significantly different finish.

Indian villages that were unfortunate enough to encounter this expedition were the poorer for it. De Soto's strategy was to capture the chief, or *cacique* (pronounced kah-seek—a Haitian term for lord or prince), and hold him or her captive until the expedition's needs were satisfied, after which it was on to the next village, where the prisoner was released and the process repeated. In addition to stripping these villages of their food supplies and leaving them destitute, the expedition treated many of the inhabitants inhumanely. Women were raped and men were often put to work as baggage bearers for the expedition; many were killed.

Not surprisingly, the expedition found itself constantly skirmishing with angry Indians throughout the course of its travel, which ranged northward through Georgia and the Carolinas as far as the Tennessee River, where de Soto turned south. Approaching a pallisaded Choctaw village called Mabila, near present-day Selma, Alabama, the expedition was greeted by Tascaloosa, a tall, handsome chief with a dignified mien. De Soto held the chief for ransom. After first refusing de Soto's demands for food and women, the chief relented when threatened with use of force, then offered to guide the expedition to the village, sending messengers ahead to make necessary preparations. Upon reaching Mabila, the Spaniards were treated to a community dance, during which Tascaloosa slipped away. The chief's departure proved to be a signal for the warriors to attack. Surprised, the Spanish were driven from the village.

As they pursued the invaders into the open area beyond the pale of their village, the warriors suddenly found themselves confronted by the Spanish cavalry. Despite fierce resistance on the part of the warriors, the cavalry, which was now able to maneuver, gained the upper hand and finally drove the Indians back into the village compound. As momentum swung to the Spanish, de Soto's infantry was able to regroup and eventually breach the walls of the town, which they proceeded to put to the torch. Although they continued to resist with a stubborn fury, the inhabitants suffered frightful casualties. Many died in the fire and others committed suicide when it became evident that their cause was lost.

Indian casualties in this fight (which historian Hubert Howe Bancroft calls "probably the greatest Indian battle ever fought within the United States") were estimated at 2,500. Spanish casualties numbered 20 killed and 150 wounded, including de Soto himself; his nephew was among those killed. Although stung by the fight at Mabila, de Soto's expedition regrouped and continued its journey, eventually penetrating as far as present-day Arkansas and Texas and discovering the Mississippi River in the process; it clashed with Indians along the way. De Soto died of a fever in 1542. The expedition managed to remain intact for nearly a year, at which time the survivors made their way to Mexico.

See also: Spain
Further Reading: Hodge, *Handbook of American Indians*, vol. 2; Milanich and Milbrath, *First Encounters*; Steele, *Warpaths*

Mackenzie, Col. Ranald Slidell
1840–1889

Born in New York City, Ranald Slidell Mackenzie graduated from West Point in 1862 first in his class. During a distinguished Civil War career he was wounded twice and was a brevet major general of volunteers by the end of the war. After the war Mackenzie served briefly in the infantry and in 1871 was appointed colonel of the Fourth U.S. Cavalry, the regiment with which he was thereafter associated.

From 1871 to 1876 Mackenzie and the Fourth Cavalry were active on the Southern Plains, campaigning against Comanches, Kiowas and Kickapoos. In 1873 Mackenzie led a successful "unofficial" strike deep into Mexico in pursuit of Kickapoo raiders. This effort was followed by a significant victory against a large band of Comanches and Kiowas at Palo Duro Canyon, Texas, in September 1874.

Transferred to the north in 1876, Mackenzie again scored a major victory, this time against Dull Knife's band of northern Cheyennes on the Red Fork of Wyoming's Powder River. In 1881 Mackenzie was involved in the Ute removal from Colorado and then assigned to the command of the District of New Mexico. Although still young, Mackenzie began to fall into ill health by this time, possibly due to the effects of syphilis and possibly due to a hereditary, degenerative disease. In any case, because of "mental instability" he was forcibly retired from the army in 1884 and died five years later.

Once referred to by Ulysses S. Grant as the "most promising young officer in the army," Mackenzie is regarded by some as the most effective of all the fighting soldiers on the western frontier.

See also: Palo Duro Canyon, Battle of; Red River War
Further Reading: Pierce, *The Most Promising Young Officer*

Mahicans

The Mahicans were a large tribe of Algonquian-speaking Indians who originally inhabited the region along the Hudson River as far north as Lake Champlain. By the mid-nineteenth century the powerful Mohawks had driven them east into what is now Massachusetts. Mahican tribal unity was effectively destroyed during the so-called Dutch-Indian wars, when Dutch traders supplied Mahican enemies with firearms. A tribal name that is often used confusingly in histories, *Mahican* is often interchanged with *Mohegan,* and both have been called *Mohican.*

Ranald Slidell Mackenzie

See also: Dutch-Indian Wars
Further Reading: Hodge, *Handbook of American Indians;*
Jennings, *The Invasion of America;* Steele, *Warpaths*

Mangas Coloradas
ca. 1795–1863

A noted Apache leader of the mid-nineteenth century, Mangas Coloradas—Red Sleeves, or Blood-Splattered Shirt—was born around 1795, probably in what is today southwestern New Mexico. He was a member of the Coppermine band of the Eastern Chiricahuas, whose home territory was near the headwaters of the Gila River. A giant of a man, Mangas reportedly stood six feet, six inches tall and weighed perhaps 250 pounds, which means he towered above typical Apache warriors by nearly a foot. Mangas Coloradas was a giant of a man in other respects as well, being a consummate warrior and the dominant Apache of his era; his name was feared throughout northern Mexico into southwestern New Mexico and southern Arizona.

In 1858 the discovery of gold brought prospectors into the area occupied by his people. In an effort to discourage gold hunters from prospecting in Coppermine territory, Mangas advised them of other areas where gold was more plentiful. Suspecting treachery, however, a group of miners captured the unsuspecting Mangas, tied him to a tree, and whipped him. The act had far-reaching consequences, as Mangas thereafter vented his wrath on Anglos as well as Mexicans, with whom the Apaches had long been at war.

In July 1862 he joined forces with his son-in-law Cochise (another daughter was married to another rising young warrior named Victorio) to attack a column of eastbound California volunteers at the Battle of Apache Pass, east of present-day Willcox, Arizona. Wounded in this fight, Mangas was taken to Janos, Chihuahua, for medical treatment. Early in 1863, back in New Mexico and apparently seeking a truce with the whites, he was tricked and taken into custody by American troops. Official reports state that he was shot and killed while attempting to escape, but the evidence seems clear that Mangas was in fact forced to resist the taunting of his guards, who repeatedly probed his legs and feet with the heated tips of their bayonets.

Mangas Coloradas is considered by some to be the greatest of all Apache leaders.

See also: Apache Pass, Battle of; Apache Wars; Apaches
Further Reading: Conner, *Joseph Reddeford Walker and the Arizona Adventure;* Sweeney, *Cochise;* Thrapp, *The Conquest of Apacheria*

Manifest Destiny

This is a controversial term that originated during the 1840s and embodied the belief that Anglo-Americans had a God-given duty and responsibility to settle and colonize North America. As such, the concept was often used as justification for subjugating any of the indigenous peoples who resisted the advance of civilization or merely happened to be in the way.

Further Reading: Billington, *Westward Expansion;* Turner, *The Significance of the Frontier in American History;* Utley, *Frontiersmen in Blue*

Manuelito
1819–1893

Born in what is now Utah, Manuelito was one of the most accomplished Navajo war leaders. He seems to have been recognized as head chief of the Navajos from 1870 to 1884.

In 1846 Manuelito signed what proved to be a largely ineffectual treaty with Alexander Doniphan. He also took part in confer-

ences with Gov. David Meriwether in 1855 and Col. Henry Dodge the following year. The earlier conference erroneously recognized Manuelito as principal leader of the Navajos. Although he accepted treaties that were constricting to his people in what he believed was the best interest of the Navajos, he later came to oppose these agreements and gradually found himself in conflict with U.S. authorities as a consequence. Disputes over grazing lands eventually led to a breakdown in Navajo-American relations.

Between 1858 and 1861 Manuelito was allegedly involved in a number of confrontations with U.S. troops, including an attack on Fort Defiance in 1860. In 1861 Manuelito signed a treaty with Col. E.R.S. Canby. Despite this, however, Navajo raids escalated with the outbreak of the Civil War and resulted in Kit Carson's campaigns into Navajo land in 1863 and 1864 and the subjugation of the tribe. Manuelito at first refused to be sent to the Bosque Redondo Reservation in eastern New Mexico but finally surrendered to U.S. authorities at Fort Wingate, New Mexico.

See also: Canby, Gen. Edward Richard Sprigg; Canby's Campaign; Carleton, Gen. James Henry; Carleton's Campaign; Carson, Christopher Houston (Kit); Navajo War; Navajos
Further Reading: Kelly, *Navajo Roundup;* McNitt, *Navajo Wars*

Marias, Massacre on
See Baker's Attack on the Piegans

Mariposa War
1851

The Mariposa War was a brief conflict involving the Mariposa Indians living in central California, who raided trading posts in the San Joaquin Valley as an expression of their anger and frustration over increasing pressure from white prospectors. A successful retaliatory campaign against these Indians by the so-called Mariposa Battalion brought a quick end to the conflict.

Further Reading: Crampton, *The Mariposa Indian War*

Massacre

By strict definition, *massacre* refers to wanton, indiscriminate killing or slaughtering of unarmed individuals, usually noncombatants. The term has, however, often been applied indiscriminately to any victory in battle where there were no survivors on one side. The "Custer Massacre" (1876) and the "Fetterman Massacre" (1866) are examples of such misuse of the term. Proper usage is limited to situations where those on one side are mostly unarmed and noncombatants. The Camp Grant Massacre (1871) and the Massacre at Fort William Henry (1757) are thus illustrations of correct usage.

Further Reading: Steele, *Betrayals;* Utley, *Frontiersmen in Blue;* ———, *Frontier Regulars;* Worcester, *The Apaches*

Massasoit
?–1662

Massasoit means, literally, great chief. The principal chief of the Wampanoag tribe, Massasoit reigned in the region near what is present-day Bristol, Rhode Island. Introduced to colonists by Sachem, Massasoit first encountered the Puritans at Plymouth in 1621. Historian Samuel Drake has praised him as "a chief renowned more in peace than war." Although the English often took advantage of him—taking land and otherwise mistreating him—Massasoit remained friendly to the new colonists until his death in 1662. Massasoit's son, Metacomet (King Philip), fought King Philip's War (1675–1678) against the English.

See also: King Philip's War
Further Reading: Bourne, *The Red King's Rebellion;* Hodge, *Handbook of American Indians*

Matowaka (Matoaka)

See Pocahontas (Matowaka, Matoaka)

Meeker, Nathan Cook
1817–1879

Born in Ohio, Nathan Meeker earned a living as newsman, teacher, and businessman in early adulthood. In 1865 he was an agricultural writer for Horace Greeley's paper.

His compelling belief that agriculture held the key to the future led him to dream of a utopian colony, which he established in Colorado in 1870, calling it Greeley. In 1878 he was appointed agent at the White River, Colorado, Ute agency, where he wasted no time attempting to force his agricultural practices on the Utes without regard or concern for their cultural traditions. Of these, none infuriated the Utes more than his insistence on plowing an area they used as a pasture for their horses. This eventually led to an incident in which Meeker and nine of his agency personnel were killed by angry Utes, who also took the Meeker women hostage but later released them.

See also: Colorow; Meeker Massacre; Milk Creek, Battle of; Ouray
Further Reading: Sprague, *Massacre: The Tragedy at White River*

Meeker Massacre
29 September 1879

During the 1870s silver strikes in Colorado brought many whites into the western part of the state. As a result, the Utes were persuaded to sell large tracts of their land to accommodate the growing population. By the end of the decade tension between Indians and whites had reached a dangerous level. The Utes harbored much anger over their treatment, and whites were quick to blame the Utes for any crime that occurred.

In the spring of 1878 Nathan C. Meeker was appointed agent at White River in northwestern Colorado. Meeker proved a poor choice, especially for White River, where tensions were running particularly high. Meeker operated under the philosophy that the Utes could and should be transformed, literally overnight, into an agricultural society. He insisted, for example, on plowing up meadows where Ute ponies grazed. Acts such as this provoked the Utes to a point that even Meeker feared a violent reaction and asked the army for help.

When Maj. Thomas Thornburg arrived in the area with a column of troops from Fort Fred Steele, Wyoming, the Utes became angry, as they thought the troops had come to arrest them. In a meeting with Ute leaders, Thornburg assured them that the soldiers had not come for that purpose. However, when Thornburg moved his command forward so as to be closer to the agency, the Utes interpreted this as a hostile action and attacked the soldiers. In the fight that followed at Milk Creek Canyon, Thornburg was killed and his besieged command was rendered helpless. The Utes, their anger now unleashed, attacked the agency. Meeker and nine of his employees were quickly slaughtered; Mrs. Meeker and her daughter Josephine, together with another woman and two children, were taken captive.

As news of the event spread, troops were rushed to the area from various stations in the West. A full-scale military reprisal was avoided, however, largely through the efforts of Ouray and former Ute agent Charles Adams, who managed to negotiate with the White River band for the release of the women.

See also: Meeker, Nathan Cook; Milk Creek, Battle of
Further Reading: Emmitt, *The Last War Trail*; Sprague, *Massacre: The Tragedy at White River*

Memeskia
See Old Briton (Memeskia)

Merritt, Gen. Wesley
1834–1910
Born in New York City, Wesley Merritt graduated from West Point in 1860. In the year prior to the outbreak of the Civil War he served in Utah with the Second Dragoons. He compiled an enviable record during the Civil War as both a staff and field officer, and by the end of the conflict he had been promoted to major general of volunteers. After the war Merritt was named lieutenant colonel of the Ninth Cavalry, serving in Texas for eight years. In 1876 he was promoted to full colonel and appointed to head the Fifth Cavalry. During the Great Sioux War he was placed in command of all of the cavalry in Brig. Gen. George Crook's Big

Horn and Yellowstone Expedition and saw action at the battles of War Bonnet Creek and Slim Buttes.

In 1877 and 1878 Merritt was involved in campaigns against the Nez Perce and the Bannocks. In 1879 he led a column to relieve the besieged Thornburgh command on Milk River during the Ute War. In 1895 Merritt was promoted to major general in the regular army and in 1898 was named to command the American Expeditionary force to the Philippines. He died in 1910.

See also: Sioux War; Slim Buttes, Battle of
Further Reading: Alberts, *Brandy Station to Manilla Bay*

Mesquakie
See Sauks and Foxes

Metacomet (Metacom)
See Philip (King Philip, Metacom, Metacomet)

Miantonomo (Miantonomi)
?–1643
A prominent chief of the Narragansett tribe, Miantonomo had an uncertain relationship with the English despite the fact that he aided them in the Pequot War. The flimsy relationship was probably due more to the colonists' general mistrust of all Indians than to anything specific on the part of Miantonomo. Captured during the Narragansett War with the Mohegans, Miantonomo was taken prisoner by Uncas and turned over to the English. Tried by the newly formed Commissioners of the United Colonies of New England, Miantonomo was found guilty of violating the Treaty of Hartford and sentenced to death. However, since the commissioners were actually acting outside their jurisdiction, Uncas agreed to act as executioner, a role he soon fulfilled. According to one source, Miantonomo was executed in "barbarous fashion." In 1841 a monument was erected to the slain Narragansett leader on the spot where he was executed. The site is known today as Sachem's Plain.

See also: Pequot War
Further Reading: Hodge, *Handbook of American Indians;* Jennings, *The Invasion of America;* Steele, *Warpaths*

Micmac Raids on Nova Scotia

Ceded to Britain as a result of the Treaty of Utrecht, the area known as Acadia (present-day Nova Scotia) was geographically important to France and England. When France built Fort Beausejour adjacent to Acadia, England countered by building Fort Lawrence as a deterrent. Although officially the treaty had removed French control in the area, they sought to retain their hold by inciting Micmac raids on British settlements, using French missionary Abbe Le Loutre as their unofficial instrument. Like most of the differences between the two nations in North America, the problem was not fully resolved until after the French and Indian War.

See also: French and Indian War
Further Reading: Axelrod, *Chronicle of the Indian Wars;* Leach, *Arms for Empire*

Miles, Gen. Nelson Appleton
1839–1925

Massachusetts-born, Nelson A. Miles was commissioned a first lieutenant in the Second Massachusetts Infantry upon the outbreak of the Civil War. Wounded four times during the conflict, he was awarded the Medal of Honor; he became a brevet major general of volunteers by the end of the war.

In 1866 he was appointed colonel of the Fortieth Infantry, and in 1869 he became colonel of the Fifth Infantry. During the 1870s and 1880s he was an active and aggressive field commander in campaigns against Kiowas and Comanches on the Southern Plains and against Sioux, Cheyennes, and Nez Perce on the northern Plains. In 1886–1887 he conducted a successful campaign against the Apaches in the Southwest, which resulted in the final surrender of Geronimo and the last of the hostile Apache bands. In 1890 he was promoted to major general, and in 1895 he was named general of the army. He led operations against Puerto

According to Gen. Nelson Appleton Miles, the Indians were forced to rebel because they were starving while the Indian agents got fat on "Profits."

Rico during the Spanish-American War and was promoted to lieutenant general in 1900.

Miles died in 1925 while attending a Ringling Brothers Circus performance in Washington, D.C. Vain, arrogant, and ambitious to a fault, Miles is nevertheless regarded by many today as one of the most effective Indian fighters in the western frontier army.

See also: Apache Wars; Geronimo; Nez Perce War; Red River War; Wolf Mountains, Battle of
Further Reading: Johnson, *The Unregimented General;* Miles, *Personal Recollections and Observations;* Pohanka, *N. A. Miles;* Wooster, *Twilight of the Frontier Army*

Military Units, White

Along with weapons, uniforms, and accouterments, white military units underwent noticeable changes between the earliest colonial conflicts and the end of the nineteenth century. Accordingly, not all of the units listed below were applicable for every Indian war or campaign.

Artillery
The branch of the army that supports infantry and cavalry through the use of various calibers of cannons, howitzers, and rifled field pieces.

Battalion
Usually three companies or troops of infantry/cavalry, although the number could and did vary from two to five depending on circumstances. Nominally, a battalion was commanded by a major, but it was not uncommon to find a captain or lieutenant colonel functioning as a battalion commander. In 1889 cavalry battalions were officially known as squadrons, although unofficially the term had been in use for some time.

Brigade
Two to three regiments of infantry/cavalry, usually commanded by a brigadier general.

Cavalry
Soldiers on horseback. Traditionally, cavalry traveled and fought on horseback.

Their primary role was to strike swiftly and breech the enemy lines, then pursue a demoralized foe. In North America, cavalry tactics changed dramatically because of the terrain and, by the mid-nineteenth century, the introduction of rifled and breech-loading firearms. Additionally, fighting Indians, especially the horseback tribes of the West, called for a new approach to cavalry tactics. Accordingly, during the Indian wars cavalry operated almost entirely as mounted infantry, using the horse as a means of transportation.

Company-Troop-Battery
A tactical-size military unit; on paper numbering 100 to 150 men, in practice it was often fewer. Nominally commanded by a captain, units were actually often led by lieutenants. Infantry units were called companies, as were the cavalry until 1883, when they officially became troops. Artillery units of this size were called batteries.

Division
Two to three brigades, usually commanded by a major general.

Dragoons, Mounted Infantry, and Mounted Rangers
Whether referred to as dragoons, mounted infantry, or mounted rangers, these were the soldiers who rode to war and fought on foot.

Infantry
Soldiers who marched into battle on foot, thus the name "foot soldiers." The infantry was and is considered the backbone of any army. In the American West, the U.S. infantry was called "walk-a-heaps" by the Sioux because of the ability to march great distances.

Legion
Legion has roots in Roman history. Briefly revived by the United States in the last decade of the eighteenth century, a legion was intended to be a mixed force of infantry and cavalry. Anthony Wayne's army that

fought at Fallen Timbers was known as Wayne's Legion. Although the idea did not survive in the early American army, the concept of mixing cavalry (today's armor) with foot soldiers remains valid.

Militia
Citizen soldiers who are called upon to provide military service to a state in times of emergency.

Regiment
Tactical-size unit usually consisting of 12 companies or troops of infantry/cavalry or batteries of artillery. A regiment's paper strength was about 1,000, and it was nominally commanded by a colonel or lieutenant colonel.

Regular
A soldier who enlists in the U.S. Army, as distinct from "volunteer" or "militia."

Squadron. *See* Battalion.

Volunteers
Citizen soldiers furnished by the states for service as federal troops. The majority of Civil War soldiers were volunteers from the various states. Some served on the western frontier against Indians.

Further Reading: Rickey, *Forty Miles a Day;* Utley, *Frontier Regulars;* ———, *Frontiersmen in Blue;* Weigley, *History of the U.S. Army*

Milk Creek, Battle of
29 September 1879
In the fall of 1879 agent Nathan Meeker, concerned over what he perceived as growing hostility on the part of the Utes served by his agency, requested military support. Responding to Meeker's request, Maj. Thomas Thornburg left Fort Fred Steele, Wyoming, near present-day Rawlins and reached the vicinity of the White River Agency near present-day Meeker, Colorado, on 26 September 1879, with a force of some 150 soldiers augmented by a few civilians and a wagon train.

The Utes, already thoroughly disenchanted with Meeker and his insistence that they immediately forsake their traditional way of life to become farmers, viewed the arrival of the soldiers as an act of betrayal. The Utes were temporarily pacified, however, when it was agreed at a meeting between the parties that the soldiers would not move up to the agency itself. However, on the morning of 29 September Thornburg decided to move his mounted detachment closer to the agency in order to be readily available in the event of an emergency.

After crossing Milk Creek, the agency's northern boundary, Thornburg was suddenly attacked by a Ute war party. Thornburg himself was killed early on and his command soon found itself in a desperate situation as the Utes, positioned on the surrounding bluffs, could easily fire down on the trapped soldiers. The army column that had come to provide support for Meeker was soon under siege and itself in need of assistance.

While Thornburg's beleaguered command responded as best it could other Utes swooped down on the agency, killing Meeker and a number of others. In addition, Meeker's wife and daughter, together with another woman and two children, were captured and taken hostage. By nightfall Capt. J. Scott Payne, now in command of the Thornburg column, sent couriers to report his situation. During the next several days Payne's men were subjected to deadly sniping fire from the well-placed Utes but managed to hold their position. On 5 October a relief column under Col. Wesley Merritt arrived to break the siege.

In this, the only real battle of the Ute War, the army had suffered losses of ten killed and 23 wounded.

See also: Colorow; Meeker, Nathan Cook; Meeker Massacre; Ouray; Utes
Further Reading: Sprague, *Massacre*

Minnesota Sioux Uprising
August 1862
One of the bloodiest and costliest Indian wars in U.S. history, the 1862 Sioux uprising

in Minnesota was the culmination of problems and conflicts that had accrued over a number of years. The 1851 Treaty of Traverse des Sioux resulted in the eastern branch of the Sioux nation signing away some 24 million acres of rich land in southeastern Minnesota. Then, in 1858, several chiefs, greedy for higher annuity payments, arranged for the sale of an additional one million acres. Unfortunately, the actual cash return to the Indians was minimal after the claims of various traders were satisfied.

In addition to annuity payments, the 1851 treaty also provided encouragement and inducements to the Indians for making the transition from a hunting to an agricultural society, a difficult change under the best of circumstances. Moreover, many Lower Sioux (there were two Sioux reservations in Minnesota—Lower and Upper) were unhappy with being relocated to a prairie reservation far from the woodlands they loved.

Yet another factor was Inkpaduta (Scarlet Point), a rogue Wahpekute Sioux and perpetrator of the 1857 Spirit Lake Massacre who eluded troops sent to apprehend him. Frustrated, the government declared that no rations or annuities would be forthcoming until Inkpaduta was caught, thus holding all of the Eastern Sioux responsible for one man's renegade behavior. Nevertheless, Little Crow, chief of the Mdewakanton band, led an unsuccessful search for Inkpaduta, who had escaped to the vastness of western Dakota.

With the outbreak of the Civil War, troops from all over the frontier were sent east to fight Confederates, and many young men joined volunteer regiments from their respective states and marched off to join their counterparts in the regular army. The absence of soldiers and young men of fighting age did not go unnoticed by the Indians.

By summer 1862 the southern Minnesota countryside was on the verge of a major Indian outbreak. A general crop failure the previous fall had created a serious food shortage for those Indians trying to convert to an agri-

Execution of the 38 Sioux Indians at Mankato in December 1862

cultural base. This—coupled with the late arrival of annuity payments, which had not been forthcoming due to a congressional debate over whether to pay in paper currency or in gold—meant that many Indians had no way to provide subsistence for themselves. By mid-July the presence of some 5,000 starving Indians at the Upper Agency forced agent Thomas Galbraith to issue emergency food rations. However, when provisions failed to arrive at the Lower Agency, trader Andrew Myrick declared that if the Indians were hungry "they should eat grass," a statement he was to regret.

The stage was thus set for 17 August 1862, the day four young Wahpeton braves, on a boast and dare, murdered five white settlers. The incident, though spontaneous, nevertheless expressed the accumulated Indian dissatisfaction of the past few years. The killings quickly stirred the Indians to further action. Pressured to take the warpath, Little Crow finally did so, albeit reluctantly, and within 24 hours the uprising was under way in earnest. Terror spread throughout the country around the Lower Agency, located on the Minnesota River near Redwood Falls. By sunset on 18 August more than 400 settlers had been brutalized, burned, and hacked to death. Survivors fled to nearby Fort Ridgely.

Learning of the unfolding disaster, Capt. John March led a detachment of 78 men out of Fort Ridgely, but nearly half of his command was killed when the Sioux attacked the column as it attempted to cross the river. Marsh himself drowned. Meanwhile, Fort Ridgely, reinforced somewhat by a few scattered outlying detachments, now mustered about 175 men plus some 300 settlers who had managed to escape the wrath of the angry Sioux. On 20 August Little Crow attacked the fort with a war party estimated to be as many as 800. Two days of desperate fighting ensued, during which a regular artilleryman, Sgt. John Jones, used Fort Ridgely's three old howitzers to break up every Indian assault.

To the west of Fort Ridgely another fierce battle was waged at the town of New Ulm, where defenders finally managed to repel the Indian attackers, though casualties were heavy and, for a time, the issue was in doubt. By the end of this week of terror a reported 800 settlers had perished. But Fort Ridgely and New Ulm proved to be the high-water mark for the uprising. Little Crow, who had counted on reinforcements from other Sioux bands, now discovered that he and his followers stood alone.

Meanwhile, Col. Henry Hastings Sibley of the Minnesota militia had been directed by the governor to march to the aid of the stricken settlers in the area. Accordingly, within a week Sibley was on the move with a force of 1,500. His advance was cautious and slow, however, and it was nearly September before he reached the area. Sibley's first chore was to dispatch a burial detachment, which was attacked by a strong war party at Birch Coulee on 2 September. Although suffering heavy casualties, the troops managed to hold out until a relief column arrived on the afternoon of 3 September (Sibley had heard the heavy firing at Birch Coulee) and drove off the attackers.

Reinforcements continued to pour into the area, and in mid-September Sibley headed upriver in search of the hostiles. The Sioux, meanwhile, argued over whether to flee or to stand and fight. Finally, learning that Sibley was near Wood Lake, the consensus favored an attack. However, a detachment of soldiers on a foraging expedition encountered the Indians and prematurely sprang the planned surprise attack, thus enabling Sibley to score a decisive victory.

During the next three days many of the hostiles began defecting from Little Crow's band, surrendering themselves and releasing captives at what came to be called Camp Release near present-day Montevideo, Minnesota. The Battle of Wood Lake effectively ended the uprising, though some of the hostiles, including Little Crow himself, remained at large. By the end of November 1862 a military commission had sentenced 303 Indians to death, a figure that was later reduced to 38 by Pres. Abraham Lincoln. The 38 were hanged in Mankato in December in what remains the largest public execution in U.S. history.

Like Inkpaduta, Little Crow and his followers fled west to Dakota. Sibley, lacking the necessary supplies, was unable to pursue. However, campaigns in 1863 and 1864 by Sibley and Gen. Alfred Sully produced decisive victories for the army in the Battles of Whitestone Hill and Killdeer Mountain. As a result of these victories, Sioux chances of mounting any further resistance east of the Missouri River were effectively destroyed.

Little Crow and his son returned to Minnesota; while picking berries they were shot and killed by two farmers in the summer of 1863.

See also: Killdeer Mountain, Battle of; Little Crow; Sully, Gen. Alfred; Whitestone Mountain, Battle of; Wood Lake, Battle of
Further Reading: Carley, *The Sioux Uprising of 1862;* Clayton, *Little Crow;* Josephy, *The Civil War in the American West*

Modoc War
1872–1873

In the years following an 1864 U.S.-Modoc treaty, settlers along the California-Oregon border grew increasingly unhappy with the Modoc presence in the area. In 1872 the Indian Bureau requested army assistance in removing the Modocs from their home territory, in the Lost River country in northern California, to the Klamath reservation in Oregon. Accordingly, in November 1872 a 40-man detachment under the command of Capt. James Jackson was dispatched to execute agent Thomas Odeneal's directive.

Upon arriving at the Indian camp the Modocs were ordered to surrender all firearms, but fighting suddenly broke out and continued for a half-hour before the Modocs finally fled. Casualties on both sides in this initial clash had been light. Following the skirmish, Captain Jack's band escaped across Tule Lake in boats while those led by

Modoc Indians in the lava beds awaiting the attack

Hooker Jim moved around the lake, killing more than a dozen settlers before the two bands united in an area known as the stronghold, a huge natural rock fortress created centuries before by lava flows. Henceforth, it would be war in the lava beds.

With news of the uprising army reinforcements soon began moving into the area. The second confrontation occurred when a force under the command of Col. Frank Wheaton attacked the Modoc stronghold at dawn on 17 January 1873. Dense fog aided the defenders, bringing the advance to a temporary halt. When the fog lifted, however, the troops were subjected to heavy fire from the Modoc positions and forced to withdraw. A stalemate quickly developed. Government officials reasoned that the Modocs might be induced to come out and discuss peace terms. The Modoc conflicts had not helped President Grant's peace policy, and his administration was anxious to resolve the difficulties without further bloodshed if at all possible.

Although history has remembered Captain Jack as the Indian villain, he seems to have been genuinely interested in negotiating a settlement. However, the hard-liners among the Modocs, egged on by a medicine man known as Curly Headed Doctor, took a militant stand. While details for a meeting with the Modocs were being worked out the department commander, Gen. E.R.S. Canby, increased the number of troops around the stronghold. In April 1873 the conference convened. The U.S. government was represented by General Canby, Indian Bureau Superintendent Alfred Meacham, and Methodist minister Eleaser Thomas. The Modoc principal was Captain Jack, who demanded a reservation in traditional Modoc lands along Lost River.

During the course of discussions it was learned that an attempt would be made on Canby's life, but the general refused to believe the Modocs would try something so foolish. But during talks on Good Friday, 11 April, Captain Jack suddenly produced a revolver from inside his coat and killed Canby. Other Modocs stabbed the two remaining members of the committee. Thomas died,

but Meacham managed to survive and make his way back to the army camp. Just as they would be three years later after the Custer disaster, the army and the nation were shocked by the news of Canby's murder. E.R.S. Canby would prove to be the only general officer of the regular army to lose his life in the Indian wars.

In the aftermath of the Canby murder, the army promptly resumed the offensive. On 15 April Col. Alvin Gillem launched what would be a three-day assault on the stronghold. During the day the two sides exchanged long-range fire while at night Gillem's artillery shelled the Modoc positions. On 17 April the troops advanced, only to discover that the Modocs had abandoned the stronghold and moved deeper into lava country. A 65-man reconnaissance sent out by Gillem was attacked and subsequently lost a third of its command, including all of the officers.

In the meantime, Canby's successor, Gen. Jefferson C. Davis (no relation to the former Confederate president) arrived on the scene. Davis had to find a way to deal not only with the Modocs but also a severe morale problem among troops badly dispirited by defeats at the hands of the Modocs. Meanwhile, the Modocs were experiencing some dissension in their own ranks. Curly Headed Doctor, Hooker Jim, and other staunch militants, who had reportedly goaded Captain Jack into murdering Canby, had now grown tired of fighting and broke off from Jack's band. A few days later they were attacked by a cavalry patrol and suffered a number of casualties.

Having lost the will to continue the fight, the survivors surrendered. No doubt hoping for lenient treatment, they agreed to contact the still hostile Modoc camp. Subsequently, a number of Captain Jack's band were persuaded to surrender, although Jack himself refused to do so. Pursued relentlessly by cavalry detachments, Captain Jack's band, now greatly reduced in size, was surprised on 29 May, but once more the Modocs eluded capture. Four days later, on 3 June, Captain Jack and a few followers were located; this time there was no option but to surrender, thus bringing to an end one of the army's most frustrating Indian campaigns.

Perhaps no other group of Indians had leaders with names as colorful as those of the Modocs—Captain Jack, Hooker Jim, Bogus Charley, Curly Headed Doctor. Best known because of his later assassination of Canby, Captain Jack is said to have been given the name by miners in the area because he was fond of wearing an army jacket with brass buttons. Though the Modoc War itself was over, the army still seethed over Canby's murder. Accordingly, in July a military commission found six Modocs guilty of murder. Of these, two were sentenced to life; four, including Captain Jack, were hanged at Fort Klamath on 3 October 1873.

See also: Canby, Gen. Edward Richard Sprigg; Captain Jack (Kintpuash); Modocs
Further Reading: Heyman, *Prudent Soldier;* Murray, *The Modocs and Their War*

Modocs

A branch of the Lutamian tribe, the Modocs inhabited the area around Lost River near the California-Oregon border. A portion of their territory included a harsh, broken area created by ancient lava flows.

During 1872–1873 the Modocs became embroiled in a war with the United States stemming from a dispute over an 1864 treaty that stipulated the Modocs would relocate to the Klamath Reservation in southern Oregon. Finding reservation life not at all to their liking, the Modocs, led by Captain Jack (Kintpuash), left and returned to their Lost River homeland, thereby setting off the Modoc War. Military efforts to force compliance with the treaty's terms produced a conflict, which was unduly long primarily as a result of difficult terrain. The war included some embarrassing setbacks for the U.S. Army before the issue was finally resolved.

The Modoc War is also notable because it marked the only time during the Indian wars that a general officer of the regular army lost his life: Gen. E.R.S. Canby was murdered by Captain Jack during the course of peace discussions.

See also: Canby, Gen. Edward Richard Sprigg; Captain Jack (Kintpuash); Modoc War
Further Reading: Murray, *The Modocs and Their War;* Stern, *The Klamath Tribe*

Mohave War
1858

The Mohave conflict of 1858 has been called a war, though it scarcely deserves to be so identified. The Mohaves were a small tribe who lived along the Colorado River just to the north of the Yumas, to whom they were closely related.

Like Yuma territory, Mohave territory included a principal crossing of the Colorado River. In the mid-nineteenth century, one of the routes to California ran west from Albuquerque and crossed the Colorado River where the present-day states of Nevada, California, and Arizona come together. Travelers could cross the river there, then turn south to pick up the California trail at Yuma Crossing.

In 1858 a Mohave war party attacked and laid siege to an immigrant wagon train, which was eventually forced to return to Albuquerque. As a result, a company of dragoons arrived from California to examine the country and build an outpost at what was known as Beale's Crossing, named for Lt. Edward Beale of the U.S. Navy, who had established the crossing several years earlier during an experiment involving the use of camels in the desert Southwest.

The Mohaves attacked the dragoons. The brief skirmish that followed produced several casualties but resolved nothing. Continued hostility on the part of the Mohaves brought an additional 700 men of the Sixth Infantry to the area, which discouraged further Mohave activity. Later, a post was built on the site and named Fort Mohave.

See also: Yuma War
Further Reading: Bandel, *Frontier Life in the Army;* Utley, *Frontiersmen in Blue*

Mohawks

A prominent name in early North American literature and history, the Mohawks were one of the original five members of the powerful Iroquois Confederacy. The Mohawks were the most easterly situated member of the Confederacy, occupying the valley of the Mohawk River near present-day Schenectady, New York, as far north as the St. Lawrence River. Their easterly location proved advantageous, introducing the Mohawks to European trade earlier than many other tribes in the region. The Mohawks were among the first to open trade with the Dutch, acquiring firearms and iron goods in exchange for beaver pelts.

The acquisition of firearms early on made the Mohawks one of the most prominent tribal forces in the wars of the seventeenth and eighteenth century. Indeed, firearms allowed the Mohawks to extend the force of their rule as far north as Hudson Bay and west to the Mississippi.

The entire Iroquois Confederacy was devastated by a smallpox epidemic in 1633, and the Mohawks in particular continued to suffer substantial losses as a result of the almost continuous warfare that was waged during the seventeenth and eighteenth centuries. During the American Revolution, the Mohawks, heavily influenced by Sir William Johnson and his brother-in-law, Joseph Brant, sided with the British. At war's conclusion most Mohawks, maintaining their loyalty to the British Crown, relocated to Canada.

See also: Brant, Joseph; Iroquois Confederacy; Johnson, Sir William
Further Reading: Debo, *A History of the Indians of the United States*; Hodge, *Handbook of American Indians*; Steele, *Warpaths*

Mohegans

The Mohegans were an Algonquian tribe—the name means wolf—whose original territory was along the Pequot (now Thames) River in Connecticut and north and east into what is now Massachusetts and Rhode Island. The Mohegans were originally a division of the Mahican group at the time of the early English settlements in New England. The Mohegans and Pequots were orig-

inally part of the same tribe, led by chief Sassacus. A division occurred when a subchief named Uncas split off with a group of followers and established a territory of their own near what is present-day Norwich, Connecticut.

The Mohegans were generally allied with the English during the Pequot War. Both Mohegans and Mahicans have been called Mohicans and along with Uncas are names made famous through the writings of James Fenimore Cooper. The Mohegans have managed to retain some tribal identity to the present day. In 1993 several hundred were reportedly living in Connecticut.

See also: Pequot War; Uncas
Further Reading: Hodge, *Handbook of American Indians*, vol. 1; Jennings, *The Invasion of America*; Steele, *Warpaths*

Mohicans
See Mahicans

Moravians

A religious sect that originated in Bohemia, the Moravian movement was established in the Bethlehem, Pennsylvania, area of the American colonies about 1740. Indians who adopted Christianity through Moravian influence and then chose to live in white Moravian communities were often referred to as Moravians, or Christian Indians. They often became the target of raids by other Indians and of retaliations by non-Moravian whites for raids and depredations they had nothing to do with. A group of Delaware Moravians were the victims of the tragic Gnaddenhutten Massacre in March 1782.

See also: Gnaddenhutten Massacre
Further Reading: Dowd, *A Spirited Resistance*; Hurt, *The Ohio Frontier*

Muscle Shoals, Grand Council on
1776

In July 1776 a large contingent of Shawnees, Delawares, Ottawas, Cherokees, and Wyandots held a council along the Tennessee River at Muscle Shoals, near present-day Florence, Alabama, to address the growing problem of white settlements in the Ohio River valley. At this council, the eminent Shawnee chief Cornstalk ended his stand on neutrality and chose to support the British cause. The choice was a practical one. The colonists were the ones moving into the area, and by supporting Britain the Indians, in effect, made it more hazardous for settlement to take place.

See also: Cornstalk; Ohio Company (of Virginia); Shawnees

Further Reading: Dowd, *A Spirited Resistance;* Hurt, *The Ohio Frontier;* Leach, *Arms for Empire*

Mystic River Massacre
See Pequot War

N

Narváez, Pánfilo de
1480–1528

Narváez was a Spanish hidalgo who led a 600-man expedition to Florida in June 1527, ostensibly to erect a *presidio* and establish a community. After landing near what is present-day Tampa–St. Petersburg, Narváez directed his ships to continue around the west coast of Florida in search of a good harbor while he marched overland with some 300 men. It was expected that they would rendezvous in the vicinity of Apalachee Bay. The decision was to have disastrous consequences for Narváez.

The overland march proved to be miserable and exhausting, with the column having to fend off repeated attacks by Apalachees near the present-day site of Tallahassee. Like the Calusas, the Apalachees were expert archers, with powerful bows that launched arrows capable of penetrating Spanish breastplate armor.

Their treatment of Indians they encountered was harsh and often brutal. In one instance, Narváez ordered the nose cut off of a Timucua *cacique* (chief) named Hirrihigua, when the chief failed to comply with Spanish demands for food and slaves. Then, as a further object lesson, Narváez directed that the chief's mother be torn apart by the big war dogs that accompanied the Spanish column. The Indians retaliated with a vengeance.

Now began the real trial for this ill-fated expedition. Reaching Apalachee Bay, Narváez found it empty of ships. Unbeknownst to him the ships had been there but, finding no trace of the overland expedition, concluded that Narváez must have arrived be-fore they did and accordingly sailed off in search of their comrades, eventually reaching Mexico.

With provisions exhausted, the overland column was compelled to subsist on their horses. They managed to construct make-shift vessels using hides and hollowed-out logs, which proved sufficiently seaworthy to get them to Pensacola Bay. Indian attacks persisted, however, especially at night. Casualties from hunger and fighting continued to deplete the Spanish ranks, but eventually they managed to reach Mobile Bay and cross the Mississippi. From there they set sail, hoping to reach Mexico, but many were lost in a storm at sea, including Narváez himself.

Only four members of the original Narváez expedition survived: Cabeza de Vaca, Alonso del Castillo, Andrés Dorantes, and Dorantes's black slave Esteban (or Estevan). De Vaca's odyssey—he eventually made his way to Mexico to relate the trials of the expedition—is one of the great sagas in North American history.

See also: Mabila (Mobile), Battle of; Spain
Further Reading: Debo, *A History of the Indians of the United States;* Milanich and Milbrath, *First Encounters;* Steele, *Warpaths*

Natchez Revolt
1729

During the eighteenth century the Natchez, an Indian tribe living in what is today the state of Mississippi, had their initial European contact with the French. The relationship was never cordial. In 1729 Jean Baptiste Le-moyne Sieur de Bienville, commandant at Fort Rosalie, ordered the Natchez to move one of their towns because it occupied land where he proposed to build a new settlement. He seems not to have cared that the town contained a holy temple housing ancestral remains and an eternal fire.

Angered, the Natchez rose in rebellion and massacred the French garrison. In retaliation, the French assembled a mighty force that included some 700 Choctaws, enemies of the Natchez. The French army assaulted the Natchez village, and in the gruesome battle that followed it wiped out much of the tribe. Most of the fewer than 500 that survived were sold into Haitian slavery; the Natchez ceased to exist as a tribal entity.

See also: Choctaws; France
Further Reading: Debo, *History of the Indians of the United States;* McDermott, *Frenchmen and French Ways in the Mississippi Valley*

Native Americans

In 1513 that part of America north of the Rio Grande contained more than 500 independent native tribal groups, each with its own linguistic structure and perhaps totaling 18 million people. The name "Indian" is generally attributed to Columbus, who mistakenly believed he had reached India and named the indigenous peoples he discovered *Los Indios,* the name later being anglicized to Indian.

Further Reading: Josephy, *500 Nations*

Nativism, Indian

Between 1750 and 1820 there flowered a movement among eastern woodland Indians that was known as nativism or pan-Indianism. Fundamentally, the movement advocated a return to the traditional way of life, that is, one in which tribes shed all connection to the white world. But the issue was far more complex than that.

Nativism is thought to have begun among Indians along the upper reaches of the Susquehanna River and gradually spread through the East and into the Deep South. Probably the most eloquent spokesman for the idea of pan-Indian unity was Tecumseh,

who traveled widely through the East and South preaching the doctrine.

The concept was adopted by other prophets—such as Tecumseh's younger brother Tenskwatawa, Neolin, and Seekaboo—who stressed the spiritual importance of purifying existence by rejecting white ideas, habits, and trappings. Others, including Tecumseh himself, were no less zealous in championing the cause of Indian unity yet were perfectly comfortable with the idea of using white weapons, equipment, and assistance to achieve that end.

Although the "word" as preached by Tecumseh and the prophets found ready acceptance among followers, some were lukewarm about the idea or rejected it altogether. Many tribal leaders and their members were far more comfortable with the idea of accommodating the white settlers and receiving the benefits a nonconfrontational relationship offered.

Nativism among the eastern tribes had largely disappeared by the 1820s if not earlier, Tecumseh having been killed in battle during the War of 1812. The concept did not sweep up the western tribes nearly to the extent it did tribes east of the Mississippi River, but there were echoes of the movement later in the nineteenth century. The prophet Wovoka, a Paiute shaman, preached the gospel of the Ghost Dance, which set the stage for the massacre at Wounded Knee in 1890.

See also: Cibecue Creek, Incident at; Ghost Dance; Tecumseh; Tenskwatawa (Prophet)
Further Reading: Dowd, *A Spirited Resistance*

Navajo War
1863–1864

The outbreak of the Civil War diverted the attention of federal military authorities in the New Mexico Territory from Indian conflicts to a possible Confederate invasion of the area. For their part, the Indians were quick to perceive that the troops who ordinarily kept them in check were now otherwise occupied. Accordingly, Navajo and Apache raids increased throughout the territory and continued largely unchecked until the Confederate threat was eliminated in the late spring of 1862.

With the Confederate threat removed, the new commander of the military district, Brig. Gen. James Henry Carleton, moved swiftly to readdress old problems. In the fall of 1862 Col. Christopher (Kit) Carson moved against the Mescalero Apaches and by spring 1863 had effectively forced them into submission.

In April 1863 Carleton turned his attention to the Navajos, ordering Barbancito and Delgadito, the two Navajo leaders most inclined toward peace, to remove their people to the Mescalero Apache Reservation at Bosque Redondo in eastern New Mexico. When the Navajos refused Carleton directed Carson to address them as he had the Mescalero: Any adult Navajo male who was found was to be considered hostile after a given date—and dealt with accordingly.

After stationing two companies of his First New Mexico Volunteers at Fort Wingate in June, Carson established a base camp at the site of old Fort Defiance. From there he struck out with a force of about 400 men, moving through Navajo country on a series of scouts. The objective was to destroy Navajo crops and villages and to capture livestock, thereby weakening the will to resist. Carson also used the opportunity to persuade the Navajos to surrender whenever the opportunity presented itself.

Carson's command was also augmented by a sizable detachment of Indian scouts from the Ute, Zuni, and Hopi tribes. For these Indian scouts, traditional enemies of the Navajos, the campaign offered an opportunity to loot and plunder. In a sense, the Navajos had more to dread from these scouts than from Carson's own New Mexican Volunteers.

Through the summer Carson's command inflicted considerable damage on the Navajo economy, although there had been little actual fighting and Navajo casualties were light. By September it was clear that the campaign was working for the government; many Navajos surrendered and continued to do so over the next several months. Yet a

great many were still at large, and so Carson continued his campaign through the fall of 1863 and into the winter of 1863–1864, pushing into the remote fastness of Canyon de Chelly in what is now northeastern Arizona, destroying fields and orchards and rounding up Navajo livestock. The penetration of Canyon de Chelly convinced most of the remaining Navajos that further resistance was futile, and in droves they began to surrender to Carson.

Eventually, those who surrendered were sent on the infamous Long Walk to the Bosque Redondo in compliance with General Carleton's directive. In 1868 a new treaty was concluded with the Navajos, allowing them to return to their ancestral homeland.

See also: Barbancito; Canby, Gen. Edward Richard Sprigg; Canby's Campaign; Carleton, Gen. James Henry; Carson, Christopher Houston (Kit); Navajos
Further Reading: Hunt, *Major General James H. Carleton;* Kelly, *Navajo Roundup;* McNitt, *Navajo Wars;* Utley, *Frontiersmen in Blue*

Navajos

A branch of the Southern Athapaskan linguistic family, the Navajos, like many Indian tribes, refer to themselves as "the people" or some variant thereof. The name itself seems to be adapted from a phrase meaning "cultivated fields," although the tribe does not appear to have been an agricultural society until its arrival in the Southwest, where it was introduced to agricultural techniques by Pueblo culture.

Traditional enemies of Utes and Comanches as well as Hopis and Zunis, the Navajos soon found themselves at war with the Spanish invaders and, later, with the Americans. Like the Apaches, to whom they are distantly related, the Navajos came to be feared as raiders. In 1863–1864, however, their military power was essentially broken by Kit Carson's sweeping campaigns that penetrated deep into Navajo territory, destroying fields and crops and compelling the tribe to yield. Subsequently, the Navajos were marched off to Bosque Redondo in eastern New Mexico on what was known as the Long Walk. In 1868 a new treaty was negotiated that allowed the Navajos to return to their traditional homeland.

See also: Bosque Redondo; Canby's Campaign; Canyon de Chelly, Arizona; Carleton, Gen. James Henry; Manuelito; Navajo War
Further Reading: Iverson, *Navajo Nation;* McNitt, *Navajo Wars*

New Ulm, Battles of
19 and 23–24 August 1862

During the 1862 Minnesota Sioux uprising New Ulm was attacked twice. The largest white settlement near the Sioux Reservation, New Ulm was located at the confluence of the Cottonwood and Minnesota Rivers. With a population of about 1,000 the community was a logical objective for the Sioux, who knew that many of New Ulm's young men were off serving in the Civil War, thus leaving the community poorly defended. In its weakened condition, the town presented an attractive target for plunder.

On 18 August 1862, word of the uprising reached New Ulm when people from outlying farms arrived with reports. As preparations for defense quickly got under way, women and children were ushered into the town's two largest buildings for safety, and messengers were dispatched to nearby communities for help. Midafternoon on 19 August about 100 Sioux attacked, firing down into the town from nearby bluffs. In response, a group of citizen soldiers counterattacked, driving the Sioux back. The New Ulm cause was aided by a heavy thunderstorm that further discouraged the Sioux and brought the day's fighting to an end.

During the next four days more groups of citizen soldiers arrived, and overall command of the defense was given to Charles Flandrau, an influential and highly respected local man. Flandrau could count on perhaps 300 volunteers at best, most poorly armed.

On the morning of Saturday, 23 August the Sioux launched a second attack, this one far larger and more determined. In a long skirmish line the Indians advanced, yelling furiously. As the attackers pressed forward the defenders fell back, allowing the Indians to slowly envelope the town and set fire to many buildings. The smoke from the burning structures provided a screen for the Sioux advance, which was finally halted by New Ulm's citizen soldiers, who fought from behind barricades and eventually compelled the Sioux to retire. On Sunday, 24 August the Sioux appeared again but did not attack.

It became clear that the Indians were not going to renew the attack, and since food and ammunition were running low it was decided to evacuate the town and head for Mankato, 30 miles distant. Accordingly, on the morning of 25 August the evacuation got under way, with nearly 2,000 people and 150 wagons reaching Mankato safely that night. New Ulm's casualties during the two attacks amounted to 34 killed and some 60 wounded. Indian losses are not known.

See also: Birch Coulee, Battle of; Little Crow; Minnesota Sioux Uprising; Sibley, Gen. Henry Hastings; Wood Lake, Battle of
Further Reading: Carley, *The Sioux Uprising of 1862*

Nez Perce

A member of the Shahaptian family, the name Nez Perce is of French derivation and means, literally, pierced nose, although in recent eras this was not a trademark of the tribe. Thus, the label is not necessarily accurate. Historically, the Nez Perce lived in what is now Idaho, northeastern Oregon, and southeastern Washington. Lewis and Clark were almost certainly the first Americans to encounter the tribe, which may have had earlier contact with French-Canadian or English explorers or traders.

Although primarily dwelling in mountains and foothills, the Nez Perce were also active buffalo hunters, venturing onto the Plains annually in pursuit of the shaggy beasts. They were also excellent horsemen and breeders of fine animals, including the Appaloosa.

Like Crows and Shoshones, the Nez Perce were traditional enemies of the Sioux and Blackfoot. Although celebrated in history books for providing horses and guidance to the Lewis and Clark expedition, they are perhaps best known for an epic flight toward Canada during the Nez Perce War of 1877. After defeating and eluding columns of U.S. troops sent to return them to their reservation, the Nez Perce were finally caught and defeated by troops under Col. Nelson A. Miles in the Battle of Bear Paw Mountains, just 40 miles from the U.S.-Canada border.

See also: Bear Paw Mountains, Battle of; Camas Meadows, Battle of; Joseph; Looking Glass; Nez Perce War; White Bird Canyon, Battle of
Further Reading: Brown, *The Flight of the Nez Perce;* Hampton, *Children of Grace;* Lavender, *Let Me Be Free*

Nez Perce War
1877

The treaty of 1863 reduced the Nez Perce landholdings, guaranteed them by virtue of an 1855 treaty, in order to provide white prospectors access to rich gold deposits. The boundary realignment divided the Nez Perce into two factions: those who agreed to abide by the treaty and those who did not. The latter group came to be known as the nontreaty Nez Perce and refused to leave their traditional homeland in Oregon and Idaho. One of the nontreaty bands was led by Old Joseph, a highly respected head man who died in 1871. His son, Young Joseph, who was destined to become one of the best-known Indians in American history, assumed the leadership role of the band upon the death of his father.

Although the nontreaty Nez Perce had been at odds with the U.S. government in the years following the 1863 treaty, the issue did not come to a head until settlers began clamoring for access to land that continued to be occupied by the nontreaty bands. At an 1876 council Gen. O. O. Howard, commanding the Department of Columbia, and four other commissioners discussed the issue with the Nez Perce, who remained determined. With no resolution forthcoming, the situation continued to deteriorate. Troops

were brought into the area, although it was understood they would be used to assist the Indian Bureau's efforts to relocate the Nez Perce should force be necessary.

A final council between Joseph and General Howard was held in May 1877, at which time Howard pointed out to Joseph that only one of two choices was open to the Nez Perce: move or fight. Howard then gave the Nez Perce 30 days in which to comply with the directive to move. In this tense climate, the spark that ignited the war came when three young Nez Perce men attacked and murdered four white settlers. The circumstances were chillingly similar to those of the 1862 Minnesota uprising.

Fearful of reprisal, the nontreaty bands headed south toward the Salmon River country, home territory of White Bird's band. Having recently arrived in the area, General Howard ordered a detachment of cavalry under Capt. David Perry to go after the Nez Perce. Along the way, Perry learned that young Nez Perce warriors had murdered another 15 settlers, making for an even uglier situation. On 18 June Perry's command was ambushed in White Bird Canyon and suffered heavy casualties—the first of several embarrassing encounters for the army in their efforts to make the Nez Perce comply with governmental directives.

Stunned, Howard took personal command and promptly launched a pursuit of the Nez Perce, marching from Fort Lapwai, Idaho, with a mixed force of 400 cavalry and infantry. He also ordered more troops into the area and requested additional reinforcements from outside his jurisdiction. At the same time, Howard sent a detachment under Capt. Stephen Whipple to bring in the village of Looking Glass. Whipple was augmented by a force of civilian volunteers whom he was unable to control and who attacked the Nez Perce village on their own volition. Whipple had intended to negotiate with Looking Glass, but when the civilians attacked the Indians fled.

By early July the nontreaty bands that had come together numbered between 800 and 1,000, including perhaps 300 warriors.

On 11 July Howard's column caught up with the Nez Perce on the Clearwater River. In the spirited action that followed the Nez Perce were able to fend off the troops and effect a safe withdrawal. At this juncture the Nez Perce strategy was to work east, possibly to find refuge among the Crows, or to seek the sanctuary of Canada. Accordingly, through the remainder of July the Nez Perce moved up the Bitterroot Valley and into Montana, where they were surprised in their camp along the Big Hole River by a column of troops under Col. John Gibbon. Gibbon, commanding the District of Montana, had marched from Missoula with a force of about 150 soldiers and a contingent of civilians.

Initially, Gibbon's attack was successful, but the Nez Perce rallied and counterattacked, eventually forcing the army into a defensive perimeter, where they suffered heavy casualties, Gibbon being among them. Howard, meanwhile, was coming hard but was unable to reach the scene in time to prevent the Nez Perce from escaping. Dismayed at the outcome of the Battle of the Big Hole, Howard nevertheless lost no time in pursuing. On 19 August he managed to get close enough to skirmish with his elusive quarry at Camas Meadows but lost a large number of mules to the Nez Perce.

And so the flight of the Nez Perce continued. On 22 August they entered Yellowstone Park, killing two tourists during their passage. Meanwhile, as the situation escalated other military units were ordered to assist Howard, whose command was frazzled and depressed. Col. Samuel D. Sturgis, with six troops of the Seventh Cavalry, was closest at hand and promptly moved to intercept the Nez Perce. After they slipped around him once, Sturgis managed to clash with the Nez Perce early in September at Canyon Creek, Montana (near present-day Billings), only to have his command bloodied in the process; the Nez Perce again effected an escape.

On 23 September the Nez Perce, having set Canada as their goal, crossed the Missouri River at Cow Island, east of Fort Benton. Thus far they had gotten the best of the U.S. forces at every encounter, but the losses in killed and wounded and the suffering of the survivors exacted a heavy toll. However, the goal was now close at hand, and the soldiers were too far behind to catch them before they reached the border.

Meanwhile, unknown to the Nez Perce, a strong column of troops under the command of Col. Nelson A. Miles was closing in on them. Miles had responded to General Howard's request for assistance and promptly marched north from his headquarters at Fort Keogh, Montana (present-day Miles City), to intercept the fleeing Nez Perce. On 30 September Miles surprised the Nez Perce camp at Bear Paw Mountain. In the initial attack Miles succeeded in capturing most of the Nez Perce pony herd, but just as they had done at the Big Hole the Nez Perce rallied and fought back, inflicting heavy casualties on their attackers.

With the Nez Perce in too strong a position to assault, Miles was forced to adopt siege tactics. For the next five days the two sides fired back and forth as targets presented themselves. Occasionally, the boom of Miles's field piece reverberated through the autumn chill. Finally, on 5 October with his people exhausted and hungry and many of his warriors dead, Joseph surrendered to Miles and Howard, who had at last caught up with the people that had so long eluded him. The Nez Perce surrender was marked by one of the most moving speeches in American history. Joseph declared, "From where the sun now stands, I will fight no more forever."

Although a handful of Nez Perce managed to slip across the border into Canada, most accepted Joseph's surrender, thereby ending the war and bringing to a close their epic flight to freedom.

See also: Big Hole, Battle of the; Camas Meadows, Battle of; Howard, Gen. Oliver Otis; Joseph; Miles, Col. Nelson Appleton; Nez Perce; White Bird Canyon, Battle of
Further Reading: Brown, *The Flight of the Nez Perce;* Hampton, *Children of Grace*

North Brothers

The North brothers—Frank Joshua (1840–1885) and Luther Heddon (1846–1935)—

were well-known figures in the Indian wars on the Central and northern Plains during the 1860s and 1870s, primarily because of their association with the Pawnee Scouts, a group originally conceived and formed by Frank North.

Born in New York, Frank moved with his father to Nebraska at age 16. As a hunter, he later had occasion to become acquainted with the Pawnees. Intrigued, he learned their culture and became fluent in their language. In 1864 he was asked by the Pawnee Indian agent to serve as an interpreter. His suggestion to organize a company of Pawnee scouts was approved by the U.S. Army, and in January 1865 the Pawnee Scouts became a reality.

Luther North was born in Ohio and, like his brother, moved to Nebraska at a young age. The boys' father, Thomas North, froze to death a year after settling in Nebraska. In 1863 Luther enlisted in the Second Nebraska Volunteer Cavalry and participated in Sully's 1863 campaign against the Sioux. When the Pawnee Scouts were formed Luther joined his brother Frank in that enterprise, being appointed captain of one company of scouts; Frank served as major in overall command of the battalion.

During the next dozen years the two brothers led the famed Pawnee Battalion in many campaigns against Sioux and Cheyennes, including Gen. Patrick Connor's Powder River Expedition in 1865 and Col. Ranald Mackenzie's attack on Dull Knife's Cheyenne village in November 1876. Possibly the most famous engagement they participated in was the Battle of Summit Springs, Colorado, on 11 July 1869, in which Frank claimed to have killed the Dog Soldier chief Tall Bull. Buffalo Bill Cody, however, also laid claim to the act.

After the Pawnee Scouts were disbanded in 1877 both brothers joined Cody's famed Wild West Show and were also involved in a ranching operation with Cody near North Platte, Nebraska. In 1884, during a show performance in the East, Frank was thrown from a horse and trampled. Although he survived the injury he died the following year of asthma, from which he had long suffered.

Although Luther lived far longer, his later life was not particularly noteworthy. He was employed for a time as a tax collector, and he devoted considerable time to preserving the memory of the Pawnee Scouts. During the 1870s he had become good friends with George Bird Grinnell, the well-known naturalist and ethnologist who later compiled the story of the Pawnee Scouts.

See also: Cody, William Frederick (Buffalo Bill); Connor's Powder River Expedition; Pawnees; Summit Springs, Battle of
Further Reading: Danker, *Man of the Plains;* Grinnell, *Two Great Scouts*

O

Oatman Family

In 1850 Royce and Mary Ann Oatman, together with their seven children (four girls and three boys, ranging in age from one to 17), left their Illinois home for California. When the wagon train they had joined in Missouri reached Tucson, the Oatmans and two other families elected to push on when the other members of the train decided to remain in the area for a time. Between Tucson and Yuma the other two families halted, and so the Oatmans continued on alone.

About 80 miles east of Yuma the family was attacked, probably by Yavapai Indians, though that is not certain. Both parents and four children were killed. Two of the girls, Olive and Mary Ann, were taken captive and later sold to the Mohaves as slaves. The oldest son, Lorenzo, was left for dead, but he recovered and managed to return to Yuma. Later he continued to California, believing that his two missing sisters had probably not survived.

Mary Ann died in 1852, but Olive survived and was eventually rescued and reunited with her brother. As her story of captivity circulated, Olive became something of a celebrity. The story of her ordeal was subsequently written and published by the Reverend Royal Stratton. Like the Mary Rowlandson saga from an earlier generation, Olive Oatman's story was widely read. Both stories were written by ministers.

In 1868 Olive married John Fairchild. The couple had three children and eventually moved to Texas, where Olive died in 1903.

See also: Rowlandson, Mary White; Dustin, Hannah
Further Reading: Conner, *Joseph Reddeford Walker and the Arizona Adventure;* Stratton, *Captivity of the Oatman Girls*

Occaneechees

A small tribe of Indians first encountered by whites during the seventeenth century in what is today southern Virginia and northern North Carolina, the Occaneechees were a branch of the Siouan language group. Until the late seventeenth century the Occaneechees, by virtue of their geographic location, made direct trade between the Virginia settlements and the Cherokees difficult, if not impossible. As a result of Bacon's Rebellion and the Indian War of 1675–1676, however, the Occaneechees were no longer a factor in the evolving relationship among natives and European colonists in the region. For all intents and purposes they ceased to exist as an identifiable people, their remnants being absorbed by other Indian tribes.

See also: Bacon's Rebellion
Further Reading: Hodge, *Handbook of American Indians*

Oglethorpe, James Edward
1696–1785

An English philanthropist, James Edward Oglethorpe received a charter to establish a colony in present-day Georgia in 1732. During his 11-year tenure Oglethorpe enjoyed, at best, modest success in attempting to secure Spanish Florida for the British Crown. Like Sir William Johnson in the north, however, Oglethorpe was successful in persuading numbers of Creeks, Choctaws, and Chickasaws to remain loyal to the British.

See also: Chickasaws; Choctaws; Creeks; Spain
Further Reading: Leach, *Arms for Empire*

Ohio Company (of Virginia)

In March 1749 King George II of England issued a 200,000-acre land grant in the Three

An 1858 portrait of Olive Oatman

Forks region of the Ohio River to a group of British traders and land speculators from Virginia. In return, the Ohio Company, as it was known, agreed to establish a settlement of 100 families, together with a protective fort, within seven years. The move incurred the enmity of the French and Indians. The French viewed this as a threat to their outposts, where they had established a lucrative fur trade with Indians. The tribes, for their part, tended to be more supportive of the French, who were less interested in promoting settlement in the region than were the British.

Further Reading: Hurt, *The Ohio Frontier;* Leach, *Arms for Empire*

Ojibwas (Chippewas)

A large tribe within the Algonquian linguistic family, the Ojibwas once occupied land that stretched from southeastern Ontario across the Great Lakes and as far west as Montana, although their central territory was the upper Great Lakes country. Traditional enemies of Iroquois, Sioux, and Mesquakie, they were largely responsible for compelling some Sioux to move west, onto the Great Plains, and the Mesquakie to move south. The Ojibwas were a strong military presence in the Old Northwest, steadily and effectively resisting white encroachment from the time of the French and Indian War through the War of 1812. The Ojibwas played an important role in Braddock's defeat and were strong supporters of Pontiac during the uprising of 1763.

See also: Braddock's Campaign; Fox Wars; Iroquois Confederacy; Pontiac's War/Rebellion/Uprising; Sioux
Further Reading: Edmunds and Peyser, *The Fox Wars;* Warren, *History of the Ojibway People*

Ojo Caliente (Warm Springs), New Mexico

In 1874 a reservation for the Eastern Chiricahua Apaches was established at Ojo Caliente, northwest of present-day Truth or Consequences, New Mexico, which was called Hot Springs until in the 1950s, when the name was changed to that of the popular radio program. The area was favored by the Apaches, who had established a homeland there before it had been assigned to them as a reservation. The band that dwelled there came to be known as the Warm Springs Apaches and was led throughout the 1870s by the great chief Victorio. Much of the conflict between Apaches and whites in this part of the Southwest might have been avoided had the Apaches been allowed to remain at Ojo Caliente.

See also: Apache Wars; Victorio
Further Reading: Thrapp, *The Conquest of Apacheria;* ——, *Victorio;* Worcester, *The Apaches*

Old Briton (Memeskia)

Memeskia was a Wyandot chief who came to be known to English settlers as Old Briton. Disenchanted by French treatment, Memeskia led his band from the Detroit area into the Ohio country, where they were welcomed by English traders working out of Pennsylvania.

While the Logstown Treaty was being negotiated, a mixed Indian force of Ottawas and Chippewas commanded by a leader of mixed race heritage named Charles Michel de Langlade attacked the main Wyandot village at Pickawillany, an important British trading post in the Ohio country operated by the influential George Croghan. Many inhabitants of the village were killed in the attack, including Old Briton, whose body was roasted and eaten by the attackers in keeping with the cannibalistic ritual practiced by many Eastern Woodland tribes.

See also: Croghan, George; Treaties and Agreements, Logstown Treaty
Further Reading: Leach, *Arms for Empire;* Steele, *Warpaths*

Oneidas

A member of the Iroquois Confederacy, the Oneidas once occupied the territory south of Oneida Lake in New York and later were also found along the upper reaches of the

Susquehanna River. Probably due to Jesuit influence, the Oneidas were friendly toward the French. The Oneidas and Tuscaroras remained neutral during the American Revolution, despite the fact that most of the Iroquois Confederacy allied themselves with the British.

See also: Iroquois Confederacy
Further Reading: Hodge, *Handbook of American Indians;* Jennings, *The Invasion of America*

Onondagas

A member of the Iroquois Confederacy, the Onondagas occupied the territory between what is present-day Onondaga County, New York, and Lake Ontario. By the mid-nineteenth century, however, it was said that nearly half the tribe was living in Canada along the Saint Lawrence River. Although they had considerable contact with French Jesuit missionaries, the Onondagas, like most of the Iroquois Confederacy, largely supported the British during the American Revolution.

See also: Iroquois Confederacy
Further Reading: Hodge, *Handbook of American Indians;* Jennings, *The Invasion of America*

Opechancanough
1545–1644

Opechancanough assumed the leadership of the Powhatan chiefdom upon half-brother Powhatan's death in 1618. Actually, another brother, Opitchapan, was the legitimate heir to the chiefdom, but he seems to have been willing to defer to the more aggressive Opechancanough, who proved far more militant toward whites than his brother. This belligerent attitude may possibly have stemmed from an incident involving John Smith, who once threatened him at gunpoint as a deterrent against aggressive behavior on the part of Opechancanough's followers.

From 1622 to 1644 Opechancanough directed the Powhatan Confederacy in a costly war against the English, including the Good Friday massacre of some 320 Jamestown colonists. Following an unstable truce in 1632, Opechancanough launched his final campaign in 1644, when he was nearly 100 years old and almost totally blind. After being taken into custody he was shot in the back and killed by white guards.

See also: Jamestown, Virginia; Pocahontas (Matowaka, Matoaka); Powhatan Confederacy
Further Reading: Steele, *Warpaths*

Oriskany, Battle of
6 August 1777

Approaching Fort Stanwix (near Rome, New York), a British column under Gen. Barry St. Leger was detected by Oneida scouts working with colonial forces. Responding to the threat, a hastily assembled militia column was sent to intercept the British. St. Leger learned of the colonial force, however, and took steps to strike first.

A force of some 400 Mohawks under Joseph Brant ambushed the oncoming colonials at a place called Battle Brook, about 6 miles from Fort Stanwix. Brant chose his ground well, striking in a narrow ravine. The action was intense, with the colonials suffering heavy casualties. The arrival of British troops to support Brant and a relief column sent from Fort Stanwix to aid the defenders intensified the fighting.

At one point the British, attempting to deceive the hard-pressed colonials, sent in a Loyalist unit known as the Royal Greens with their coats turned inside out. The ruse failed, however, when some of the Loyalists were recognized by the colonials. After nearly six hours of hard fighting the Mohawks decided to pull out; their withdrawal forced the Loyalists to retire as well. One authority has stated that in proportion to the numbers engaged, Oriskany was the bloodiest battle of the Revolution.

See also: Brant, Joseph (Thayendanega); Oneidas
Further Reading: Wood, *Battles of the Revolutionary War*

Osceola
ca. 1803–1838

A Seminole leader, Osceola achieved his status not as a hereditary chief but rather

Osceola

through his clearly demonstrated skills during the Second Seminole War. His black wife was a former slave, one of many who had managed to escape captors and find refuge among the Seminoles of Florida.

Osceola opposed the treaties of 1831 and 1832. In 1835 he and his followers killed five whites, including agent Wiley Thompson, in an incident that touched off the Second Seminole War. During that war Osceola demonstrated his superior ability as a guerrilla fighter, waging a brilliant two-year campaign, the capstone being the destruction of Maj. Francis Dade's column on 28 December 1835. Through trickery, Gen. Thomas Jesup managed to apprehend Osceola, who was subsequently held prisoner at Fort Moultrie, where his health rapidly declined; he died in 1838.

See also: Seminole War, First, Seminole War, Second; Seminole War, Third
Further Reading: Covington, *The Seminoles of Florida;* Laumer, *Dade's Last Command*

Ouray
1820–1880

A Ute chief of the Uncompahgre band, Ouray's father was Ute, his mother Jicarilla Apache. He became chief upon the death of his father. Unusually well educated, Ouray demonstrated a desire to maintain friendly relations with whites who moved into Ute territory in ever increasing numbers. Throughout his adult life Ouray worked for peace, traveling to Washington twice on behalf of his people.

During the 1879 incident involving northern Utes at the Meeker Massacre, Ouray, along with agent Charles Francis Adams

and Secretary of the Interior Carl Schurz, played a key role in preventing a dangerous situation from escalating into full-scale war. Ouray died of kidney failure in 1880.

See also: Meeker Massacre; Schurz, Carl; Utes
Further Reading: Smith, *Ouray;* Sprague, *Massacre*

Overland Trail
1841–1866

Often called the Oregon Trail and sometimes the California Trail (it was actually both), this historic route is best referred to as the Overland Trail, or the Great Platte River Road. During the mid-nineteenth century it was the primary corridor for westbound traffic between the Missouri River and South Pass, Wyoming. The main trail had branches running down into Colorado and north into Montana. Beyond South Pass there were several splits, which were followed depending on one's final destination and the lateness of the season.

It should be noted that the Overland Trail was really more general direction than specific trail, since the exact route varied from year to year according to conditions. Within that context, the trail emanated in Kansas and Missouri and proceeded along a westerly course that generally paralleled the Platte River, hence the name Great Platte River Road. Although there were conflicts with Indians from time to time, emigrants crossing the Plains between 1841 and 1866—the most active period for the trail—had more to fear from weather, disease, and fatigue than hostile Indian attacks.

Further Reading: Mattes, *The Great Platte River Road*

P

Palo Duro Canyon, Battle of
28 September 1874

On 20 September 1874, Col. Ranald S. Mackenzie, commanding the Fourth U.S. Cavalry, led his regiment along the eastern edge of the Llano Estacado (Staked Plains) in northwestern Texas in pursuit of hostile Comanches and Kiowas. Colonel Mackenzie's column was one of four to take the field during the Red River, or Buffalo, War of 1874. During the night of 26 September Indian raiders attempted to stampede Mackenzie's horse herd, but strong security measures and a prompt response foiled the effort and drove the raiders off.

When the pursuit resumed Mackenzie's scouts discovered a large Indian village on the floor of the Palo Duro Canyon (literally, the canyon of hard wood) south of present-day Amarillo, Texas. The canyon itself, a huge, spectacular gash cut into the caprock of the Southern Plains by the Prairie Dog Town Fork of the Red River, was a favorite campsite of Southern Plains tribes. Because of its remoteness, the area had not previously been penetrated by the U.S. military. As a result, the Indians felt relatively secure within the confines of the deep canyon, which remains one of the most impressive in the nation, second only to Arizona's Grand Canyon.

The scouts had discovered a narrow, winding animal trail descending into the depths of the canyon, and in the predawn darkness Mackenzie's troopers began the descent, leading their horses down the slim passageway, which barely qualified as a trail. Incredibly, the soldiers reached the floor of the canyon undetected. In the attack that followed the surprised Indians, a mixed village of Comanches, Kiowas, and Cheyennes, offered little resistance, with most fleeing down the canyon. After destroying the village and its contents, Mackenzie's men slaughtered more than 1,000 ponies, a severe blow to the tribes, who depended on the horse for mobility.

As battles go, Palo Duro Canyon did not amount to much. Although later some Indians returned and opened fire on the troops, casualties on both sides were light: two soldiers and a reported three Indians. The engagement was, however, significant in that the loss of the horse herd rendered a large body of Indians immobile and signaled the beginning of the end of the Red River War.

See also: Mackenzie, Col. Ranald Slidell; Red River War
Further Reading: Haley, *The Buffalo War;* Pierce, *The Most Promising Young Officer*

Pamunkeys

The largest tribal entity within the Powhatan empire, the Pamunkeys occupied an area near the confluence of the Pamunkey and Mattapony Rivers in what is today King William County, Virginia. The tribe is believed to have numbered about 1,000 during the early seventeenth century, including 300 warriors.

See also: Powhatan Confederacy
Further Reading: Hodge, *Handbook of American Indians*

Parker, Quanah
ca. 1845–1911

A noted leader of the Kwahadi band of Comanches, Quanah Parker was the son of a white woman, Cynthia Ann Parker, and Co-manche chief Peta Nocona, who married Cynthia Ann after her capture in a Co-manche raid. While a young man Quanah became a noted war chief in his own right, leading his tribesmen in fierce opposition to white settlers, the buffalo hunters in particular. He was one of the principal war chiefs at the second Battle of Adobe Walls, among others.

Forced to surrender in 1875 following the U.S. Army's prosecution of the Red River War, or Buffalo War, Quanah settled on the reservation assigned to him. Accepting the fact that the whites had won, Quanah encouraged his people to pursue the ways of peace. He died near Fort Sill, Oklahoma, in 1911.

See also: Adobe Walls, Second Battle of; Comanches; Palo Duro Canyon, Battle of; Red River War
Further Reading: Haley, *The Buffalo War;* Neely, *The Last Comanche Chief*

Pawnees

A member of the Caddoan family, the Pawnees are among the oldest of the Great Plains tribes. Pawnees tended to side with the European power that seemed to exercise the most influence over Pawnee destiny at the time. Eventually, as the American presence in the Transmississippi West increased, the Pawnees came to ally themselves with the United States, becoming one of the first western Indian tribes to serve as scouts for the U.S. Army. The famous Pawnee Battalion, led by brothers Frank and Luther North, participated in a number of campaigns and battles against their traditional enemies, the Sioux and Cheyennes, during the 1860s and 1870s.

See also: Connor's Powder River Expedition; North Brothers; Summit Springs, Battle of
Further Reading: Danker, *Man of the Plains;* Dunlay, *Wolves for the Blue Soldiers;* Grinnell, *Two Great Scouts;* Hyde, *Pawnee Indians*

Paxton Riots
December 1763

In retaliation for the killing of settlers by Indians, an Irish immigrant vigilante group calling itself the Paxton Boys (they were from Paxton, County Donegal) attacked and murdered six peaceful Conestoga Indians in Lancaster County, Pennsylvania, in December 1763. Although Gov. John Penn issued a warrant for their arrest, it was largely ignored. Fearing for the safety of other peaceful Conestogas in the area, authorities confined them to the local jail for protection. This, however, proved no deterrent to the Paxton Boys, who attacked the jail, killing and mutilating all 14 Conestogas.

Fueled by the Paxton Boys, some 500 vengeful rioters marched on Philadelphia, intending to kill some 140 Indians converted to Christianity known to be quartered there. The mob was finally dispersed by a militia force. Although many regarded the killings with outrage, nobody was punished. Ironically, 56 Indians later died of smallpox contacted in the army barracks where they had been quartered.

See also: Moravians
Further Reading: Steele, *Warpaths*

Peace Policy, President Grant's

Shortly after taking office in 1869, Pres. Ulysses S. Grant introduced his "peace policy" as a means of dealing with Indian conflicts in the West. The policy itself was a response to the outcries of humanitarians over the killing and bloodshed that had taken place on the Central and Southern Plains during 1867 and 1868.

A key figure in Grant's new policy was Ely Parker, a Seneca Indian from New York. A former member of Grant's Civil War family, Parker was named Commissioner of Indian Affairs. Probably the strongest voices urging the president to adopt an attitude of peace and understanding came from the Quaker community. With Civil War casualty lists still fresh in the nation's mind, the climate was receptive for voices that urged a peaceful rather than a military solution.

The military had long believed that management of the Indians should be in the hands of the War Department rather than the Department of the Interior. The army, they argued, was in a better position to monitor Indian activities and promptly punish those who misbehaved. Additionally, the army pointed out that the current Indian Bureau was an ineffective bureaucracy with many corrupt agents. With Grant's election to the presidency, most army men believed he would support their position. Thus, Grant's introduction of his peace policy came as something of a shock.

Despite the disappointment, there was some reason for optimism within the military. The policy directed that army officers be appointed to serve as Indian agents and that any Indians not residing on their reservation would be considered hostile. Almost immediately, however, the new policy ran into difficulty. The destruction of a Piegan village by Maj. Eugene Baker on Montana's Marias River in 1870 and Arizona's infamous Camp Grant Massacre in 1871 reawakened the public horror created several years earlier by Col. John M. Chivington and the Sand Creek Massacre. This, coupled with the murder of Gen. E.R.S. Canby by Captain Jack while negotiating a peaceful settlement of the Modoc crisis, demanded revisions in the policy. The one bright spot during this period was Gen. O. O. Howard's peace treaty with Apache leader Cochise.

Though well intentioned, Grant's peace policy was not at all designed to address the crux of the conflict: increased white presence and the loss of tribal lands. The eruption of the Red River War on the Southern Plains in 1874 marked the end to the peace policy just five years after its introduction.

Further Reading: Utley, *Frontier Regulars;* Wooster, *The Military and U.S. Indian Policy*

Pequot War
1636–1638

The issues surrounding the Pequot War are among the more complex in the history of the confrontations between Indian peoples and European colonists. It was the first such conflict in New England, rooted in land ownership (as was true in virtually all Indian-white clashes). In this instance, how-

ever, the problem was exacerbated by a power struggle between rival and rapidly expanding English settlements in southern New England; there was also an ongoing struggle for dominance among various Indian tribes. The combination produced a volatile situation.

Although the Pequot War is generally said to have begun in 1636, it actually had its genesis two years earlier, when a nefarious English trader named John Stone was killed by Indians for his kidnapping and otherwise brutal treatment of them. Although those responsible for Stone's death were later proved to be Western Niantics, who were neighbors of the Pequots who occupied the territory on the west side of the Pequot (now the Thames) River, the Pequots bore the onus of an act they had not committed. As a result of their continuing clash with the Narragansetts, the Pequots found themselves cut off from further trade with the Dutch and, accordingly, sought to recoup their economic loss by opening a channel of trade with the Massachusetts Bay settlement.

The Pequots, whose number had been reduced perhaps as much as 75 percent by a devastating smallpox epidemic in 1633, were feeling the pressure of neighboring tribes, of which the Narragansetts were the most powerful. Further recognizing the threat posed by the rapidly developing English colony, the Pequots also sought to use the English as mediators in settling their differences with the Narragansetts. The ensuing arrangement came to be known as the Massachusetts Bay–Pequot Treaty of 1634.

The killing of the nefarious Stone, which seems not to have troubled his countrymen, suddenly took on importance when the Massachusetts Bay authorities figured the incident might be used to political advantage in their negotiations with the Pequots. Accordingly, the English demanded the surrender of Stone's killers and further demanded a large wampum payment, to which the Pequots agreed. Subsequently, however, only a portion of the tribute was paid, and the Pequots explained that only two of the killers were still alive, where-abouts unknown.

For whatever reason, the English chose not to press the matter, thereby maintaining a reasonably peaceful status quo for the next two years. However, in 1636 a Mohegan chief named Uncas reported the Pequots were preparing for war, ending the peaceful coexistence. Whether Uncas was attempting to achieve his own political end (the Mohegans were rivals of the Pequots) is questionable, but in any case his report proved to be the trigger for war.

The English again demanded Stone's killers, but once again the Pequots explained why they were unable to comply. In the meantime, the situation worsened, with the killing of a second trader, probably by Narragansetts, on Block Island. Whether the Pequots were at all involved in this second murder apparently seemed irrelevant to the English; the time for action was at hand. It has also been suggested that whoever subjugated the Pequots would control a large portion of the Connecticut Valley, territory coveted by Plymouth, Massachusetts Bay, and some smaller Connecticut settlements already in the area.

At any rate, Massachusetts Bay organized a strike force to find the guilty Indians on Block Island, then proceed to the mainland and there punish the Pequots. The strike force, 90 strong, was led by three captains—John Endecott, John Underhill, and William Turner. Quite aside from the political motives, it was a highly charged climate, ruled more by emotion than reason. The settlers, convinced of the Indians' hostile intent, dwelled on the killings of Stone and Oldham and feared the worst. Captain Endecott reportedly wanted to kill all Indian men and capture the women and children for the West Indian slave trade.

The Indians on Block Island had meanwhile melted into the woods; the strike force, unable to locate the Indians, pushed on to Fort Saybrook at the mouth of the Connecticut River. There, the settlers met with Pequot sachems and demanded a confrontation on the field of battle. When the Pequots,

who likely did not understand the demand, failed to show, the strike force vented its wrath on their villages and crops before finally departing. Thus provoked, the Pequots laid siege to Fort Saybrook, which was garrisoned by only a handful of men. The siege itself was an on-again off-again affair that lasted nearly a year. There were feeble efforts to reinforce the fort, which somehow managed to survive.

Meanwhile, the Pequots, not unlike the English, also attempted to forge an alliance, in this case with the Narragansetts. That undertaking subsequently failed, due mainly to the efforts of intermediary Roger Williams, who was sent out by Massachusetts Bay to persuade the Narragansetts to honor their neutral position. (The famous Williams, regarded as an expert in dealing with Indians, had originally been expelled by the Bay settlement because of his heretical beliefs; Williams put his personal feelings aside to serve what he regarded as a higher purpose, in which he was successful.)

In April 1637 Pequots raided the settlement at Wethersfield (near present-day Hartford), killing several and taking two female captives. That spring proved especially costly, with some 30 settlers losing their lives. As a consequence, the English settlements decided to pool their forces against the Pequots, a decision that proved difficult to implement due to political and religious differences among the colonies. Notwithstanding these internal squabbles, a mixed force of colonists and Mohegans under the command of Uncas moved against the Pequots, with minimal success. Reinforced by more colonists and the addition of some 500 Narragansett and Niantic allies, the expedition moved a second time.

The second strike made its objective the stronghold of the Pequot sachem Sassacus, near present-day Groton, Connecticut. Subsequently, however, it was decided to attack the Pequot village on Mystic River instead. The reason for the change in objectives is not entirely clear; it may have been a case of choosing the lightly defended village over Sassacus's strongly defended camp. It has also been suggested that the colonists set out with the avowed purpose of perpetrating a massacre. Whether that was the intended end or whether it just worked out that way will never be known with certainty. In any case, what followed was indeed a massacre.

On 26 May 1637, the strike force reached the new objective on Mystic River. Deploying in two circles around the village (it was actually a fort), the attackers then set it afire, slaughtering Pequots as they attempted to escape. It was gruesome business. The Narragansett allies reportedly expressed their disapproval of the English brutality by departing from the field. Meanwhile, warriors from the main Pequot stronghold had learned of the attack and hastened to the relief of their brethren, but they arrived too late to assist. In all, an estimated 300 to 700 Pequots died at Mystic River, compared to some 20 to 40 English colonists.

The Mystic River Massacre was an ugly climax to an ugly war, but it was not quite the end. Pequots who survived were hunted through the summer by the English and the Narragansetts, who found the stomach to again unite with the colonists. The toll of Pequots killed continued to rise. Captured women and children were given over to the Narragansetts as spoils of war.

The war's final chapter was written in July 1637, when a surviving band of Pequots was finally surrounded in a large swampy area near present-day New Haven, once again suffering heavy casualties. For all practical purposes the episode in the great swamp marked an end to the war. The power of the Pequots had been decidedly broken. The Treaty of Hartford (September 1638) would delineate the terms of the English-Narragansett victory. Pequots who had managed to escape the wrath of the English sought refuge with other tribes. Ironically, surviving Pequots would ally with the English during King Philip's War nearly four decades later.

See also: Mohegans; Treaties and Agreements, Massachusetts Bay–Pequot Treaty; Treaties and Agreements, Hartford, Treaty of; Uncas; Williams, Roger

Further Reading: Jennings, *The Invasion of America;* Steele, *Warpaths*

Peskeompskut Massacre
19 May 1676

On 19 May 1676, an English strike force numbering some 150 men under the command of Capt. William J. Turner attacked an Abnaki village on the Connecticut River near what is present-day Montague, Massachusetts. With most of the warriors absent, Turner's force swept through the camp, killing the few warriors who rose to its defense and slaughtering many noncombatants. The main body of warriors, however, returned before the English had departed and, in turn, inflicted heavy casualties on the attackers, including Captain Turner, who was killed.

See also: King Philip's War
Further Reading: Bourne, *The Red King's Rebellion*

Petite Guerre, La

In the late seventeenth century Count Louis Frontenanc, governor of New France, relied on *la petite guerre,* or guerrilla warfare, to defeat the British. Usually a mixed force of French regulars and Indian allies would strike a settlement or outpost without warning. After burning and looting the settlement, perhaps killing many inhabitants, the attackers would disappear as quickly and as silently as they had arrived. The tactic struck a reign of terror throughout the northeastern colonies. Eventually, this form of waging war was adopted more and more by England and France, particularly during the French and Indian War.

See also: French and Indian War
Further Reading: Steele, *Warpaths*

Philip (King Philip, Metacom, Metacomet)
1640–1676

Son of the Wampanoag chief Massasoit, Metacom (or Metacomet) assumed the sachemship of his tribe upon the death of his brother Wamsutta, who had become chief following the death of their father in 1661. Wamsutta had taken the Christian name Alexander while Metacom adopted Philip. Exactly why he took the appellation "King" is not clear, but perhaps it was because of his leadership and regal bearing. He is said to have been tall, handsome, and physically imposing. One authority has called him the "most remarkable of all New England's Indians." At any rate, to the English colonists of that era he was known as King Philip of Pokanoket (Pokanoket being the principal village of the Wampanoag).

The death of Massasoit in 1661 followed soon thereafter by that of Wamsutta elevated Philip to the sachemship of the Wampanoag under unfortunate circumstances. Bitterness over the death of his brother, whom he believed had been poisoned by the English, and his mounting resentment over the increasingly heavy-handed treatment of the Indians eventually led to what has come to be known as King Philip's War. It is thought that when war erupted in 1676 Philip was in the process of creating an Indian confederacy that would have united all the tribes of New England against the English. The war, which began with a killing and reprisal, probably triggered events sooner than Philip wished.

Before it ended in August 1677 the war proved the costliest of any Indian-white conflict in New England. In a surprise raid in 1676, colonial forces attacked the Wampanoag village, burning it and killing many of the inhabitants including Philip, who was killed by an Indian ally of the English. He was subsequently beheaded, with his head being placed atop a pole in Plymouth. The remainder of his body was quartered in the fashion of the day, and the pieces hung in trees, a gruesome end for one who was regarded as a traitor and not deserving the dignity of a proper burial.

Though his rein was brief, Philip must be regarded as one of the most influential Indians of North American history, ranking alongside Tecumseh, Pontiac, and others.

See also: King Philip's War; Wamsutta (Alexander)

Further Reading: Bourne, *The Red King's Rebellion;* Steele, *Warpaths*

Pickawillany Massacre
21 June 1752

While negotiations for the Logstown Treaty were under way near Ambridge, Pennsylvania, a French trader named Charles Michel de Langlade, of mixed race heritage, led a mixed force of some 250 Ojibwas, Potawatomis, and Ottawas in an attack on the Miami (Twightwee) village at Pickawillany (Piqua), Ohio. The effort was perceived by the French as a means of undermining British influence among the western Indian tribes. Langlade's Indians, being traditional enemies of the Miami, needed little encouragement.

The attack took the village by complete surprise, resulting in the deaths of a dozen or more, including a British trader and the Miami chief, Memeskia, known to the English as Old Briton. The attackers, gloating over their great success, roasted the corpse of Old Briton and consumed it in a ritualistic feast. The attack on Pickawillany aided the French cause, at least temporarily, in that it caused the Miami, who were thoroughly cowed, to move to a location where they would be assured of French protection.

See also: France; Old Briton (Memeskia); Treaties and Agreements, Logstown Treaty
Further Reading: Leach, *Arms for Empire*

Pima Revolts

Although the great Revolt of 1680 was by far the strongest Indian reaction to Spanish treatment, it was not the only such example. In 1695 the Pimas of Lower Pimeria Alta (Sonora, Mexico, and southern Arizona) rebelled briefly; the Pimas of Upper Pimeria Alta offered more formidable resistance to Spanish treatment in 1751.

As with the Revolt of 1680, one individual was the catalyst for the uprising of 1751. On 20 November 1751, the Pimas, led by Luis Oacpicagigua, burned churches and killed 18 Spaniards. However, when promised support from the Papago and Apache tribes failed to materialize, it assured the demise of the uprising, which was eventually suppressed by Gov. Diego Parrilla.

Imprisoned, Luis Oacpicagigua was later released on his own recognizance and escaped execution by promising to rebuild the churches he had destroyed, promises that were never honored. The failure of the 1751 uprising did not mark the end of Piman resistance, however. For 150 years thereafter, they successfully employed guerrilla tactics against the Spanish, Mexicans, and Americans.

See also: Popé (El Popé); Spain
Further Reading: Axelrod, *Chronicle of the Indian Wars*

Pine Ridge Reservation

Located in what is present-day southwestern South Dakota, the Pine Ridge Reservation was created out of the Great Sioux Reservation established by the Laramie Treaty (1868), which, in the years following that treaty, was gradually reduced in size and eventually carved into four separate reservations. Pine Ridge was the site of the tragic Wounded Knee Massacre in 1890.

See also: Sioux; Treaties and Agreements, Fort Laramie, Treaty of; Wounded Knee Massacre
Further Reading: Utley, *Indian Frontier of the American West*

Piqua Town, Battle of
August 1780

In August 1780 George Rogers Clark led a 1,000-man expedition supported by cannons to attack the Indian village at Chillicothe, Ohio. The expedition was born out of a continuing need to respond to Indian raids that plagued the Kentucky settlements.

Clark reached Chillicothe only to discover that it had been abandoned. Scouts reported that the warrior force, having learned of Clark's advance, had chosen to assemble and receive Clark's attack at Piqua Town. After burning the empty village, Clark's column advanced toward Piqua.

Crossing the Miami River, Clark attempted to flank the Indians on the left. As the attackers moved across an open prairie toward the town, they were fired upon from behind by a group of Indians positioned behind a fence; the main body of defenders fired from positions along a ridge, causing the attack to falter.

Reorganizing, Clark pushed his line forward a second time. Gradually, the Indians were compelled to give ground and were forced into a defensive structure of logs. Clark proposed to assault the log structure with his cannon when the Indians suddenly emerged, forming a line like European troops. The advancing front puzzled Clark's troops, and another group of Indians began firing into their rear.

Issuing orders to fire carefully, Clark's men began to inflict casualties that presently forced the Indians to withdraw. During this part of the fighting, Joseph Rogers—a cousin of George Rogers Clark who had been captured and taken into the tribe quite some time before—bolted across the field toward the Kentuckians, who were unable to distinguish him from the Indians they were fighting. Rogers was shot (actually by both sides) and died shortly thereafter.

Having taken enough casualties, the Indians withdrew. Believing that the great renegade Simon Girty was approaching with reinforcements, Clark elected not to pursue. After burning the village and destroying the fields of corn Clark headed back to Kentucky.

See also: Clark, George Rogers; Girty, Simon; Shawnees
Further Reading: Bakeless, *Background to Glory*

Piscataway, Siege of
See Bacon's Rebellion

Pitt, William
1708–1778

As British secretary of state, William Pitt was responsible for American colonial affairs during the crucial years of the French and

Indian War. A highly popular but controversial statesman, Pitt was first appointed in 1756; he encountered strong opposition from within his own government. Despite this, he proved a dynamic and forceful leader, upgrading the level of British forces in the colonies, including the appointment of qualified leaders. Dismissed in 1757, he was reappointed almost immediately.

Probably more than any other single individual, William Pitt was responsible for Britain's victory in the French and Indian War. Known as the Elder Pitt and the Great Commoner, he collapsed and died in Parliament while protesting the English government's failure to pursue total victory in the Revolutionary War.

See also: Braddock's Campaign; French and Indian War
Further Reading: Leach, *Arms for Empire*

Platte Bridge, Battle of
26 July 1865

During the summer of 1865, as a result of threatening moves by bands of Sioux and Cheyennes in the area, the commanding officer at Platte Bridge Station (near present-day Casper, Wyoming) sent a detachment of troops under Lt. Caspar Collins to reinforce a wagon train arriving from the west. The garrison at Platte Bridge Station consisted of Civil War volunteers from Kansas and Ohio, most of whom would soon be released from service now that the war had ended. Lieutenant Collins, whose father was colonel of the Eleventh Ohio Volunteers, was en route to Platte Bridge Station for another assignment at the time.

As Collins and his detachment crossed the Platte River bridge, they were observed by an estimated 1,000 to 3,000 warriors, mostly Cheyennes with some Sioux. A short distance beyond the bridge the Indians swarmed to the attack. Collins ordered a retreat back across the bridge, but his small detachment was quickly surrounded. The fighting was desperate. Collins, though wounded in the hip, stopped to aid a stricken soldier; both were killed. Despite the intensity of the fighting, however, all but

five of the detachment managed to make it across the bridge to the safety of the Platte Bridge stockade, aided by fire from the post's howitzer.

Meanwhile, the wagon train continued its approach from the west. Sgt. Amos Custard, commanding the train's escort, heard the howitzer fire and sent a detachment ahead to investigate. This detachment, too, was attacked but also managed to fight its way to the safety of the stockade. Custard and the remainder of his escort quickly corralled the wagons and repulsed several attacks before finally being overwhelmed and killed. Indian casualties in the fight were estimated at nearly 200, compared to about 30 soldiers.

The fight at Platte Bridge was a harbinger of things to come on the northern Plains during the next three decades. Casper, Wyoming, is named for the young lieutenant who lost his life in this action (interestingly, the names are not spelled the same).

See also: Bozeman Trail; Forts, Camps, Cantonments, Outposts, Fort Casper; Sioux War
Further Reading: Vaughn, *The Battle of Platte Bridge*

Pocahontas
(Matowaka, Matoaka)
1596–1617

One of the enduring Indian figures in U.S. history, Pocahontas has come to symbolize the transcendence of love over ethnic and cultural differences. The daughter of Powhatan, principal ruler of the Powhatan Confederacy, Pocahontas, whose real name was Matowaka or Matoaka, is reputed to have saved Capt. John Smith from a cruel death by interceding with her father on his behalf. In so doing she may have saved other English colonists as well, thereby ensuring her place in history.

The name Pocahontas means playful or frolicsome and as such provides insight into this rather remarkable young woman's personality. She is said to have been her father's "dearest daughter" and very much a free spirit. Although romantics have long associated Pocahontas and John Smith as lovers, they were not. However, in 1613

Pocahontas rescuing Captain Smith

A rare view of Pocahontas as painted by an unknown British artist

Pocahontas did fall in love with and marry Englishman John Rolfe, that story being a romance in itself.

Following John Smith's departure for England in 1609, relations between colonists and Indians began to deteriorate. With the help of a disaffected minor leader in the Powhatan chiefdom, Pocahontas was decoyed aboard an English ship and later taken to Jamestown as a hostage. With her as leverage, the colonists were able to effect a shaky peace with chief Powhatan. While prisoner of the English Pocahontas met and eventually married Rolfe, who later pioneered the tobacco industry in Virginia. The union proved to be a stabilizing but temporary influence between Powhatan's people and the English colonists.

Pocahontas eventually accompanied her husband to England, where she was converted to Christianity, taking the name Lady Rebecca. In 1617, preparing to return to the New World, Pocahontas contracted smallpox and died at age 21. She was buried in the cemetery at Gravesend Church.

See also: Jamestown, Virginia; Powhatan Confederacy
Further Reading: Hodge, *Handbook of American Indians*

Ponce de León, Juan
ca. 1460–1521

One of the better-known Spanish explorers because of his quest for the fabled Fountain of Youth, Ponce de León accompanied Columbus on his second expedition in 1493. In 1509 he was appointed governor of Puerto Rico, and during his tenure he amassed a considerable fortune, extracting gold from native subjects. The Crown, after replacing him with a new governor in 1512, rewarded Ponce de León with a grant to seek out new lands. Armed with this authority, and apparently captivated by the lure of those fabled restorative waters, Ponce de León elected to search for the fountain in the land he was eventually to christen La Florida on Easter Sunday 1513.

Landing at the site of present-day St. Augustine, Ponce de León encountered immediate opposition on the part of Timucuas, who drove the Spanish off. Undeterred, Ponce de León followed the Florida coastline to the west, landing at San Carlos Bay, where he was attacked by Calusa warriors while his force was repairing the ships. Finally withdrawing, Ponce de León returned to Puerto Rico, thence to Spain, where the Crown provided him with a royal grant to colonize La Florida. Returning to the Caribbean, he was engaged in various enterprises during the next several years before his second and final expedition to Florida in 1521.

Landing at San Carlos Bay again, this time with a force of more than 200 men together with missionaries and livestock, Ponce de León intended to establish a settlement, but once more he was driven off by the numerically superior Calusas, who demonstrated their considerable skills as bowmen. Discouraged, the expedition returned to Cuba, where Ponce de León died of wounds sustained in the fighting at San Carlos Bay.

See also: Spain
Further Reading: Morison, *The European Discovery of America: The Southern Voyages;* Steele, *Warpaths*

Pontiac
ca. 1720–1769

A renowned Ottawa chief, Pontiac was born near Detroit about 1720, possibly on the Canadian side of the Detroit River. He may have been part Miami or Ojibwa on his mother's side. By the middle of the eighteenth century Pontiac was an established warrior who fought on the French side during the French and Indian War; he may have been among those who inflicted the disastrous defeat on Gen. Edward Braddock in 1755.

In 1757 Pontiac and his followers—he had acquired a substantial number by this time—played a key role in the siege of Fort William Henry. Most likely Pontiac was also involved in other important battles during this period, including those at Forts Duquesne and Niagara. Along with Detroit's French garrison Pontiac accepted British occupation by Maj. Robert Rogers in 1760 as the balance of power in the area changed from France to Britain. Following Gen. Jeffrey Amherst's decree prohibiting the distribution of amenities to the Indians, however, Pontiac assumed a position of leadership in opposing English rule, which for him became increasingly disenchanting. In all probability his opposition was aided and abetted by clandestine French efforts.

Although Pontiac's role as the overall leader of what came to be known as Pontiac's War has been challenged if not refuted by his biographer, it does seem clear that he played a pivotal role, at least in the unsuccessful attack on Fort Detroit in 1763.

The meeting of Pontiac and his embassy with Major Rogers and his troops

Despite some success elsewhere, however, the Indian coalition that was forged during this period proved unable to remain a viable force and gradually weakened as the summer of 1763 waned. The following spring, Pontiac unsuccessfully attempted to rally Indian support from among the tribes in the Illinois country. In 1765, after long consultation with agent-trader George Croghan, Pontiac finally agreed to British terms, finding them more acceptable at that point than those of the French.

During his earlier efforts to enlist support from the Illinois tribes Pontiac also made enemies, who now decided that the Ottawa leader must be assassinated. Accordingly, in the spring of 1769 Pontiac was killed by a warrior at Cahokia under circumstances that remain unclear. The place of his burial is also unknown. Regarded as one of the outstanding Indian leaders in American history, Pontiac, like other leaders before and after him, saw the value of pan-Indian union but was unable to achieve it.

See also: Amherst's Decree; Braddock's Campaign; Croghan, George; Pontiac's War/Rebellion/Uprising
Further Reading: Peckham, *Pontiac and the Indian Uprising*

Pontiac's War/ Rebellion/Uprising
1763–1769

Although he was not an overall leader of the conflict that bears his name, Pontiac was certainly an important figure in its events, at least those in the greater Detroit area. The image of Pontiac as the central leader was probably the creation of historian Francis Parkman, who labeled him the "great conspirator." Pontiac's war (or rebellion or uprising; it's known by each variant), as it is sometimes called, covered an unusually large sweep of country—from the northern Great Lakes to Ohio and Pennsylvania—and was one of the earliest examples of militant Indian nativism at work.

In the fall of 1760 British Gen. Jeffrey Amherst, over the protests of Sir William Johnson and others, eliminated the long-standing (French) practice of supplying Indians with ammunition. Ever since the European nations had established colonies in North America two centuries earlier, Indians had become increasingly dependent on firearms for hunting as well as for waging war. Unlike the Europeans, however, Indians lacked the resources to produce quantities of ammunition. As a consequence, Amherst's decision worked a real hardship on the tribes, who were increasingly dependent on the English as the French presence in North America declined.

In this climate there appeared a Delaware prophet named Neolin, who preached a policy advocating a return to the pure Indian way of life. He was probably not the first such spokesman for Indian nativism, nor would he be the last. In any case, many, including Pontiac, embraced his teachings.

In the summer of 1761 the British commandant at Fort Detroit discovered an Indian plot to attack it and Forts Niagara and Pitt. Amherst sent reinforcements to Detroit, but the expected attack did not materialize then or the following summer, when rumors surfaced again. The end of the French and Indian War in 1763 provided the Indians another reason to be disenchanted, as France ceded most of its North American holdings to England without consulting the tribes. In response, Pontiac called a grand council in April 1763 and urged the Potawatomis and Hurons to join his own Ottawas in rising up against the British.

Pontiac devised a strategy to capture Fort Detroit by a ruse. He and a party would enter the post under peaceful pretenses but carry concealed weapons. Once inside, they would be able to surprise the garrison and signal Indians outside the fort to attack. The attack was scheduled for 7 May but had to be called off. An Indian woman known only by her English name, Catherine, was supposedly in love with the fort's commander, Maj. Henry Gladwin; she informed her lover of the plan, forcing Pontiac to call off the attack. Egged on by angry warriors, Pontiac tried again the following day, but Gladwin would allow only Pontiac himself to enter the fort.

His strategy foiled, Pontiac turned to raiding the surrounding area. A war party also fired on the fort for several hours; the effort produced few casualties on either side. In council, some of the French who were still in the area urged Pontiac to seek a truce, which he did. However, in the parley that followed Pontiac took the British officer sent out to negotiate as his hostage. Now boasting a force of some 1,500 Pontiac, believing he was in a strong bargaining position, demanded the surrender of Fort Detroit, which Major Gladwin promptly refused. Pontiac's warriors thereupon laid siege for several hours, with Gladwin still refusing to surrender until the hostage had been returned safely. His demand was rejected, and the officer, Capt. Donald Campbell, was subsequently murdered by an Ojibwa warrior.

The Indians, meanwhile, continued to raid throughout the area. In the spring of 1763 Fort Sandusky was captured and its garrison killed. The Indians added Forts St. Joseph and Miami, and so Indian successes continued to mount. In June a 100-man supply column en route to Fort Detroit was attacked near the west end of Lake Erie, with most of the men being killed or captured. Later that month, Fort Ouiatenon (Lafayette, Indiana) fell to Pontiac's warriors. Farther north, at Fort Michilimackinac, the garrison was lured outside to watch a game of lacrosse. When the ball was thrown into the fort, according to a prearranged stratagem, the Indians rushed inside to take control of the post.

Indian attacks were occurring as far east as Pennsylvania. Desperate to deal with an escalating situation, General Amherst ordered Col. Henry Bouquet, commanding at Fort Pitt, to use germ warfare by exposing Indians to blankets infected with smallpox when they arrived to negotiate the fort's surrender, which they had previously demanded. Bouquet, temporarily away from the post, directed his second-in-command to execute Amherst's order. At a parley the Indians were exposed to the disease, the British refused to surrender, and the Indians (Delawares) withdrew to rethink their strategy, only to discover that many had been stricken with smallpox. Between May and September 1763 the Senecas laid siege to Forts Niagara and Detroit. The latter post, however, was still able to receive supplies by boat via Lake Erie and the Detroit River.

Despite the epidemic of smallpox that plagued the Delawares, the Indians were able to maintain pressure on Fort Pitt. In August Colonel Bouquet, leading a strong relief column to the fort, was ambushed at a place called Edge Hill. Despite the surprise attack, Bouquet was able to achieve tactical advantage by using the high ground and launching a surprise counterattack that carried the day, though it resulted in heavy casualties for the British as well as the Indians. The battle itself was called Bushy Run, after the stream where the British camped.

The siege against Fort Detroit ended in the fall, and in October Pontiac agreed to peace terms. Yet Indian raids continued elsewhere, reflecting how the war had grown beyond Pontiac's influence. Amherst's conduct of the war came under sharp criticism and he was ordered back to England, replaced by Gen. Thomas Gage, who wasted no time sending a pair of strong columns to sweep areas known to harbor Indian raiders.

On 7 September 1764, Col. John Bradstreet executed a treaty with the tribes at Fort Detroit. The treaty required the Indians to recognize the King of England as their sovereign and reasserted the terms of the earlier Treaty of Easton. Pontiac himself was not present at the signing of this treaty, and it was another two months before the last Indian recalcitrants surrendered at the Muskingham River. In July 1766 Pontiac and several other leaders finally came to terms with Sir William Johnson at Fort Oswego, New York.

The war had been costly for the white settlements that were affected. An estimated 2,000 civilians and some 400 soldiers died during the conflict. Although exact Indian casualties are unknown, they were also high.

See also: French and Indian War; Johnson, Sir William; Pontiac; Treaties and Agreements, Easton, Treaty of
Further Reading: Jennings, *The Invasion of America;* Leach, *Arms for Empire;* Peckham, *Pontiac and the Indian Uprising*

Popé (El Popé)
?–1688

Although his origins are somewhat shrouded in obscurity, Popé was a mystic and medicine man believed to have been from the Tewa Pueblos who successfully organized and launched the Pueblo Revolt of 1680. Embittered by Spanish oppression, Popé had earlier been imprisoned by the Spanish for his efforts to forge an alliance between the Apache and Pueblo nations for the purpose of retaliating against the harsh Spanish treatment. Following imprisonment Popé planned and launched the brutally successful Revolt of 1680, which saw him assume a dictatorship as brutal as the Spanish he overthrew. He seems to have been an individual totally consumed by the anger and bitterness he felt toward the Spanish. His reign lasted eight years; he died in 1688.

See also: Pueblo Revolt of 1680; Spain
Further Reading: Hodge, *Handbook of American Indians;* Knaut, *The Pueblo Revolt of 1680*

Pope, Gen. John
1822–1892

Born in Kentucky, John Pope graduated from West Point in 1842. After initial duty with the Topographical Engineers he served in the Mexican War, after which he returned to the engineers and worked in the upper Mississippi River valley and Arizona. Upon the outbreak of the Civil War he was commissioned a brigadier general of volunteers and enjoyed some success early on; he was then defeated at Second Manassas.

In the fall of 1862 he was reassigned to the new Department of the Northwest, where his principal assignment was to quell the Sioux uprising that had devastated southern Minnesota in August. During the summers of 1863 and 1864 he sent strong columns of troops into the Dakotas in pursuit of Sioux who had fled Minnesota after the uprising. Pope's field commanders, Gen. Alfred Sully and Col. Henry Hastings Sibley, each enjoyed some success with their respective campaigns.

In 1864 Pope was assigned to the new Division of the Missouri, where he again found himself facing an Indian conflict, in this instance the massacre at Sand Creek, Colorado. Following this duty he spent time in the South before returning to the Midwest, where he commanded the Department of the Lakes. After terms as head of the Department of California and the Division of the Pacific, he retired as a major general; he died in 1892.

See also: Indian War (1867–1869); Minnesota Sioux Uprising; Sand Creek Massacre; Sibley, Gen. Henry Hastings; Sully, Gen. Alfred
Further Reading: Carley, *Sioux Uprising of 1862;* Ellis, *General Pope and U.S. Indian Policy;* Hoig, *The Sand Creek Massacre*

Powhatan (Wahunsonacock, Wahunsenacawh)
1547?–1618

Wahunsonacock, better known to the early Virginia colonists as Powhatan, was the principal chief (mamanatowick) of what is usually (and incorrectly) referred to as the Powhatan Confederacy. However, he may be better known as the father of Pocahontas (Matowaka). The name Powhatan, or falling waters, was taken from one of his favorite dwelling places, the falls of the James River near present-day Richmond.

John Smith described Powhatan as a man of dignified bearing, and certainly he was effective at ruling the estimated 30 tribal groups of the Powhatan Confederacy. About 60 years of age when Jamestown was founded, Powhatan apparently greeted the English colonists with a degree of cordiality at first, but he developed a harsher attitude toward the newcomers as relations between the two peoples deteriorated.

See also: Jamestown, Virginia; Pocahontas (Matawaka, Matoaka); Powhatan Confederacy
Further Reading: Hodge, *Handbook of American Indians;* Rountree, *The Powhatan Indians*

Powhatan Confederacy

The Powhatan Confederacy (the local pronunciation today being POW-a-tan) was a grouping of several tribes belonging to the Algonquian linguistic family who inhabited the coastal plain or tidewater area of eastern Virginia. "Confederacy" is a misnomer; the political structure was a chiefdom ruled by one principal leader (the mamanatowick) supported by a number of lesser chiefs (weroances). At its zenith the Powhatan empire reportedly comprised some 30 tribes and 14,000 individuals, including an estimated 3,000 warriors. The largest tribal entity within the empire was the Pamunkeys, with an estimated population of 1,000, including 300 warriors.

As in any society governed by an absolute ruler or overlord, the effectiveness of the ruler is in direct proportion to the ability to maintain absolute control. At the time of the founding of Jamestown in 1607, the Powhatan empire was ruled by Powhatan, the father of Pocahontas. When Powhatan died in 1618 he was succeeded by his half-brother Opechancanough, who proved far more militant in dealing with English colonists. Opechancanough's death in 1644 signaled the beginning of the end for the Confederacy.

See also: Jamestown, Virginia; Opechancanough; Pamunkeys; Pocahontas (Matawaka, Matoaka); Powhatan (Wahunsonacock, Wahunsenacawh); Powhatan War
Source: Hodge, *Handbook of American Indians;* Rountree, *The Powhatan Indians of Virginia*

Powhatan War
1607–1646

The Powhatan War was a conflict between English colonists in the Tidewater country of

Detail of a map of Virginia in 1612 showing Powhatan in the royal wigwam

eastern Virginia and the tribes of the Powhatan Confederacy. The war was a two-stage conflict, the first beginning with the arrival of the Jamestown colonists in 1607 and lasting until about 1613. The second stage, which embraced the peak years of the conflict and was by far the more costly in terms of human life, lasted nearly three decades, from 1619 to 1646. Like most of the conflicts between Indians and European colonists, this was essentially a struggle for control of land. Shortly after the founding of Jamestown, chief Powhatan, principal leader of the Powhatan Confederacy, launched a raid against the new settlement, thus initiating a series of on-again off-again attacks and reprisals by both sides.

At the outset, the military advantage belonged completely to the Indians, but by 1609 the arrival at Jamestown of trained soldiers wearing armor capable of deflecting Powhatan arrows, combined with a new and tougher discipline among the surviving members of the colony, led to a gradual shift in the balance of power. Eleven years of confrontations notwithstanding, Powhatan proved generally more conciliatory toward the English colonists than his successor. The marriage of his daughter Pocahontas to the Englishman John Rolfe around 1613 established a more or less peaceful climate that was short-lived.

Following Powhatan's death in 1618, leadership of the Confederacy was assumed by his half-brother Opechancanough, who soon demonstrated that his policy toward the colonists would be far more militant. In 1621 an English trader named Morgan was killed by Indians, which prompted the execution of a well-known Powhatan warrior suspected by some as being the killer. This eye-for-an-eye justice was to produce enormous and far-reaching consequences. In retaliation, on Good Friday, 22 March 1622, Opechancanough carefully and craftily launched a surprise attack along the line of the colony. By day's end nearly 350 colonists had been slaughtered.

If Opechancanough expected that the Good Friday slaughter would weaken the colonists' resolve, he was badly mistaken. Instead, the colonists struck back with renewed vigor. In April 1623 the English managed to poison some 200 Powhatan who had been invited to attend a phony peace conference. Opechancanough, however, managed to escape. In November the English followed this up by attacking and burning a Powhatan village.

In 1632 both sides agreed to a truce, and though it was violated many times it held up for the next dozen years. During the life of the truce the English colony continued to grow. Tobacco rapidly increased in importance, meaning colonists needed more land. This demand, in turn, resulted in the Powhatan tribes being squeezed into an ever smaller part of their territory.

In April 1644, now nearly 100 years old and practically blind, Opechancanough rose up to make one last effort to drive out the English. He again attacked the settlements on the James River. This time the toll was even higher than it had been on Good Friday 1622, with almost 500 colonists killed. The English retaliation was predictably swift, thorough, and deadly. Gov. William Berkeley authorized a massive campaign that swept through the colony, burning and otherwise destroying any Indian village within reach.

In 1646 Opechancanough, who had been captured by a force of militia, was taken to a Jamestown prison, where he was later assassinated by one of the guards. Opechancanough's death ended the Powhatan War and signaled the end to the once powerful Powhatan chiefdom.

See also: Jamestown, Virginia; Opechancanough; Powhatan Confederacy
Further Reading: Rountree, *The Powhatan Indians;* Steele, *Warpaths*

Praying Towns/ Praying Indians

The concept of the praying town was the creation of a missionary named John Eliot, who founded the first praying town in 1651. By 1675 there were 14 located throughout the

An 1856 engraving of John Eliot preaching to the Indians

Massachusetts Bay–Plymouth–Connecticut colonies.

The concept was an outgrowth of the belief that Indians were heathens and needed to be converted to the true faith—to become praying Indians, as it were. Once this had been accomplished, it was thought, new converts next needed to distance themselves from all tribal customs and ways. They were also to become thoroughly "English" in their style of life, adopting Christian names, manners, and modes of dress.

Indians were supposedly induced to adopt Christianity by the lure of great spiritual rewards in the hereafter. The present was not overlooked, however, since praying Indi-

ans received special consideration in trade agreements with the colonists, thereby creating disunity among the tribes. In war situations, Indians who had been converted to Christianity often fought on the side of the colonists. Sometimes, however, the new mantle of Christianity was not enough to protect them from ill treatment during wartime.

See also: Moravians
Further Reading: Jennings, *The Invasion of America;*
Steele, *Warpaths*

Proclamation of 1763
On 7 October 1763, King George III of England created four new provinces from territo-

rial acquisitions in Quebec, Florida, and Grenada. The Proclamation of 1763 closed to white settlement a large area bordered by the Appalachians on the east, the Mississippi River on the west, the Great Lakes on the north, and Florida on the south. It was not well received by the English colonists, who increasingly looked on the Ohio River valley as a natural choice for expansion. Within five years, however, the plan was modified to allow controlled expansion by colonists. From the perspective of the American Indian, the Proclamation of 1763 was probably the first to recognize and set aside specific tracts of land exclusively for Indian use. As such, it was a forerunner of the reservation system.

See also: England
Further Reading: Leach, *Arms for Empire*; Prucha, *American Indian Treaties*; Steele, *Warpaths*

Prophet's Town

Located on Tippecanoe Creek near what is present-day Lafayette, Indiana, Prophet's Town was a Shawnee village and the headquarters for Tecumseh's pan-Indian movement of the early nineteenth century. Built by Tecumseh and his brother Tenskwatawa, known as the "Prophet," the site was partially destroyed by William Henry Harrison following the Battle of Tippecanoe on 8 November 1811.

See also: Tecumseh; Tenskwatawa (Prophet); Tippecanoe, Battle of
Further Reading: Debo, *History of the Indians of the United States*

Pueblo Indians

Pueblo, which means town or village, refers to Indians who lived in dwellings that were primarily constructed of stone or adobe. Although they hunted some, the Pueblos were essentially an agricultural people who lived in more or less permanent communities, in contrast to the nomadic and seminomadic tribes whose lifestyles were tied to the migratory patterns of the animals they hunted. In ancient times the Pueblo population extended from western Arizona to the Texas

Panhandle and from central Utah and southern Colorado into Mexico. In historic times Pueblo communities ranged from northeastern Arizona to present-day Kansas and, roughly, from Taos, New Mexico, to El Paso, Texas.

Zunis were the first of the Pueblo peoples to have contact with European civilization. As a result of Spanish oppression, there were several revolts or uprisings among the Pueblos in what is present-day New Mexico. Mainly, these occurred in the seventeenth century, the most prominent being the Revolt of 1680, though another revolt occurred as late as 1751.

See also: Pima Revolts; Popé (El Popé); Pueblo Revolt of 1680
Further Reading: Hodge, *Handbook of American Indians*; Knaut, *The Pueblo Revolt of 1680*

Pueblo Revolt of 1680

The most widespread and violent of the several uprisings among the Pueblo communities during the Spanish colonial period, the Revolt of 1680 was largely fomented by El Popé, a Tewa Pueblo medicine man and mystic. Popé had earlier been imprisoned by the Spanish for his role in creating a mutual alliance between Pueblos and Apaches that resulted in two years of guerrilla warfare against the Spanish.

Following his release from prison, Popé began to formulate plans for a major rebellion. By working through the various tribal councils he was successful in gaining the support of the principal Pueblo communities. However, because the various communities were widely separated, the logistics of coordinating the revolt was enormous—a challenge to which Popé nevertheless proved more than equal. Runners were sent to each community to prepare for the appointed day, which was eventually set for 13 August 1680. Popé had ingeniously devised a knotted rope calendar, on which the last knot would be untied on the day of the revolt.

Popé was ruthless about maintaining secrecy, even to the extent of having his brother-in-law executed because of suspected treachery. Despite his efforts to cloak the movement, however, word leaked out, and Popé was forced to launch the uprising three days early, on 10 August 1680. The revolt struck like a thunderclap. The Spanish missions at Taos, Pecos, and Acoma were burned and the priests there murdered. On 15 August Popé marched on Santa Fe with an army of 500, killing an estimated 400 along the way, including 20 missionaries.

Although the Spanish garrison at Santa Fe numbered only 50, it had a cannon that held off Popé's army for four days. Eventually, some 2,500 survivors of the siege fled down the Rio Grande to El Paso. Entering Santa Fe, Popé immediately occupied the governor's palace and established himself as dictator. All vestiges of Christianity were purged. Churches were burned, vestments and icons desecrated, and those who exhibited the least sympathy for anything Spanish were summarily dealt with.

The control achieved by the revolt lasted eight years, being sustained by the force of Popé's reign, which proved as harsh and oppressive as that of the Spanish whom he had expunged. Following Popé's death in 1688 the Spanish, taking advantage of the unrest among the Pueblos, gradually resumed control of the lost territory. In 1689 they captured Zia Pueblo and by 1692 had reoccupied Santa Fe.

See also: Popé (El Popé); Pueblo Indians; Spain
Further Reading: Kessell, *Kiva, Cross, and Crown;* Knaut, *The Pueblo Revolt of 1680*

Queen Anne's War
1702–1713

The second of the four major intercolonial wars between France and England, Queen Anne's War (after Queen Anne of England) was known in Europe as the War of the Spanish Succession, so called because of a controversy surrounding the legitimate heir to the Spanish throne, which some feared would result in a French-Spanish alliance.

By 1699 France had established a colony in Louisiana and built a fort at what is now Detroit. A strong French presence in the West was of growing concern both to the British and to the Iroquois Confederacy. Notwithstanding this concern, military action was confined to the east and south. In 1702 a British naval expedition attacked and looted Spanish-held St. Augustine, Florida. Following that effort, a mixed force of South Carolina colonists and Chickasaws burned the town and then marched through western Florida, destroying Indian resistance as they went. The objective was to provide the British with a corridor into the Gulf settlements.

As they had done in the north, the French made a major effort to gain Indian support and were moderately successful. Creeks and Choctaws allied themselves with the French, but Chickasaws remained loyal to the British, and Cherokees stayed neutral.

In New England, Deerfield, Massachusetts, which had been hard-hit during King Philip's War and King William's War, was struck again. In February 1704 a mixed force of French and Abnakis attacked the town, killing many of the inhabitants as they slept. Raids and counterraids continued. There were British raids on French Acadia in 1704 and Port Royal, Nova Scotia, in 1706. The French attacked the English settlement of Bonavista, Newfoundland, and captured St. Johns, Newfoundland, in 1708. They were unsuccessful, however, in their effort to capture Charleston, South Carolina. British plans to invade Quebec twice went awry, but in 1710 the British did capture Acadia, Nova Scotia.

Philip of Anjou's succession to the Spanish throne, coupled with a general weariness of the war itself, brought an end to the conflict. The Treaty of Utrecht, signed on 13 July 1713, ceded Nova Scotia and Hudson's Bay to the English.

See also: Deerfield, Massachusetts, Battles of; England; France; King Philip's War; King William's War; Spain
Further Reading: Leach, *Arms for Empire;* Weeks, *The American Indian Experience*

R

Rangers

Historically, rangers were military units composed of irregular soldiers organized to carry out military operations in an informal and nontraditional style. Usually rangers were exclusively volunteers who were chosen because of their superior marksmanship and frontier survival skills.

The first such unit with official status was probably that created by Robert Rogers in 1756, known as Rogers's Rangers. Although sometimes highly effective in launching retaliatory strikes against hostile tribes during the prerevolutionary colonial frontier wars, these rangers were also undisciplined and difficult to control. As a result, traditional military leaders never entirely warmed to the idea, despite the fact rangers provided a tough, highly mobile force capable of fighting Indians on their own terms. As the frontier moved west, variations on the ranger theme continued to surface. A volunteer unit of frontiersmen who served under a regular army officer won fame in the Battle of Beecher Island in 1868. The U.S. Army Rangers of World War II and today's special forces are modern versions of the ranger concept.

See also: Beecher Island, Battle of; Rogers, Maj. Robert; Rogers's Raid on St. Francis
Further Reading: Weigley, *History of the U.S. Army*

Raritans

The Raritans were a division of the Delaware nation, occupying the valley of the Raritan River in what is present-day New Jersey. *Raritan* is a corruption of a name that means, loosely, overflowing stream. The name seems to have been assigned by early Dutch traders, probably because much of their territory happened to be along a stream or waterway located in a flood plain.

A small tribe, Raritans found themselves caught between the Dutch and stronger neighboring tribes. As tribal numbers diminished as a result of these pressures, remnants merged with other similarly affected bands and relocated to a reservation in New York and, eventually, west to Wisconsin.

Further Reading: Hodge, *Handbook of American Indians;* Steele, *Warpaths*

Red Cloud (Makhpiya-Luta)
1822–1909

An influential Oglala Sioux chief, Red Cloud was born near the Platte River in what is today Nebraska. He established himself as a warrior while still a youth. In a raid on the Pawnees he killed the guard of the horse herd, capturing several of the animals in the process. In the years that followed the counting of his first coup, Red Cloud developed a reputation for harsh treatment of opponents among his own people as well as his enemies. He was also renowned for his fierceness in battle, and by 1860 he had emerged as a leading Lakota warrior.

Red Cloud was present at the Grattan Massacre (1854) and the Platte Bridge fight (1865), two significant clashes that heralded the troubled times on the northern Plains that were to prevail during the next two decades. In 1866 Red Cloud vehemently opposed U.S. government efforts to build forts along the Bozeman Trail, which ran approximately from the site of present-day Casper,

American Horse and Red Cloud (right)

Wyoming, to the burgeoning Montana gold camps. His opposition led eventually to what was called Red Cloud's War, its most noted event being the tragic Fetterman Disaster of 21 December 1866. Some believe Red Cloud was present at the Fetterman Disaster and the Wagon Box Fight in August 1867, but this has never been established.

The Indians' determined opposition to U.S. military presence in the Powder River region led to the Laramie Treaty (1868), which, among other things, closed the three Bozeman Trail forts and thus was a victory for Red Cloud, even if a temporary one. In the years following Red Cloud's War he became more moderate and seemed ready to accept reservation life. With other Indian leaders he made several journeys to Washington as part of the government's effort to demonstrate the extent and power of the white man's world.

Red Cloud's last years were marked by feuds with agents, military authorities, and those of his own people who opposed his leadership. He died in 1909, remembered in history as one of the prominent Indian leaders of the nineteenth century.

See also: Bozeman Trail; Fetterman Disaster; Forts, Camps, Cantonments, Outposts, Phil Kearny; Red Cloud's War; Wagon Box Fight
Further Reading: Hyde, *Red Cloud's Folk;* Larson, *Red Cloud;* Olson, *Red Cloud and the Sioux Problem*

Red Cloud's War
1866–1868

Red Cloud's War was a two-year conflict between the Lakota Sioux, led by Oglala chief Red Cloud, and the U.S. Army. To support the mission of protecting travelers along the Bozeman Trail from what is present-day Casper, Wyoming, to the Montana gold camps, the army constructed Fort Reno near Kaycee, Wyoming, Fort Phil Kearny south of Sheridan, Wyoming, and Fort C. F. Smith on the Big Horn River in Montana.

Angered by the white presence in Wyoming's Powder River country, the Sioux raided and harassed wagon trains, army patrols, and civilian employees who operated out of the forts. The high point of resistance occurred on 21 December 1866, when the Sioux wiped out Capt. William J. Fetterman and his entire command of 80 men. This disaster was partially offset by U.S. victories at the Wagon Box and Hayfield fights the following year. Red Cloud's War ended with the signing of the Laramie Treaty in 1868, which resulted in the closure of the Bozeman Trail and the abandonment of the three forts.

See also: Bozeman Trail; Fetterman Disaster; Red Cloud (Makhpiya-Luta); Wagon Box Fight
Further Reading: Hebard and Brininstool, *The Bozeman Trail;* Olson, *Red Cloud and the Sioux Problem;* Utley, *Frontier Regulars*

Red Jacket (Sagoyewatha)
1756–1830

A noted orator and chief of the Seneca tribe, Red Jacket was generally supportive of the British during the Revolution, as were the majority of tribes in the Iroquois Confederacy. He is said to have acquired his name from a red jacket received as a gift from a British officer; it was replaced each time it wore out.

Unlike most of his contemporaries, Red Jacket seems not to have been much of a fighter. Indeed, he was upbraided by Cornplanter for failing to offer significant resistance during Gen. John Sullivan's devastating sweep through Iroquois territory in 1779. He was also censured by Mohawk chief Joseph Brant. Notwithstanding, he expressed strong opposition to the second

Seneca war chief Red Jacket

Treaty of Fort Stanwix (1784) and remained a staunch traditionalist and opposed the introduction of white ways into Indian customs.

See also: Brant, Joseph (Thayendanega); Iroquois Confederacy; Johnson, Sir William; Treaties and Agreements, Fort Stanwix, Treaty of
Further Reading: Hodge, *Handbook of American Indians;* Josephy, *500 Nations*

Red River War
1874–1875

The general failure of Pres. Ulysses S. Grant's so-called peace policy caused the government to adopt more aggressive tactics in addressing issues in the Trans-Mississippi West. On the Southern Plains some Indians, having failed to receive treaty-guaranteed annuities, were further angered by white hide-hunters who slaughtered thousands of buffalo. In the spring of 1874 Kiowas, Comanches, and Cheyennes launched raids throughout the Texas Panhandle, culminating that June in the fierce attack on a small trading center for the hide-hunters known as Adobe Walls.

In response, Gen. Philip H. Sheridan, commanding the Military Division of the Missouri, decided to send four columns of troops into the Llano Estacado (Staked Plains) in western Texas. Col. Nelson A. Miles commanded an 800-man column of the Sixth Cavalry and Fifth Infantry and moved south into Indian country. On 30 August Miles encountered a body of Indians nearly the size of his own command. In a five-hour running battle in which he used Gatling guns and field pieces to good advantage, Miles had the upper hand, but he was finally forced to call off pursuit due to lack of supplies. In late September a large force of Kiowas and Comanches attacked Miles's supply train, putting it under siege for three days before relief arrived.

Meanwhile, a second column of the Fourth Cavalry under Col. Ranald S. Mackenzie, moving in from the south, was attacked on the night of 26 September by a force of Comanches estimated at 250. Attempts to run off the cavalry horses, however, were unsuccessful due to Mackenzie's strict security; the

raiders were driven off. Launching an immediate pursuit the following morning, Mackenzie's scouts reported a large Comanche, Kiowa, and Cheyenne village in Palo Duro Canyon (literally, canyon of hard wood) on the Prairie Dog Town Fork of the Red River.

This huge chasm in the Staked Plains was a favorite home for the tribes of the area, who felt a certain sense of security within its confines. Descending into the canyon along a narrow, winding animal trail, Mackenzie's troops surprised the village in a dawn attack and captured the large horse herd. After destroying most of the village, Mackenzie's troopers slaughtered the bulk of the Indian ponies, retaining some for their own use. By destroying the horses Mackenzie severely limited the Indians' ability to conduct raids.

That autumn a third column of troops under Col. George P. Buell continued a sweep through the countryside, burning any village that was found. In late October Miles took the field again. A detachment under the command of Lt. Frank D. Baldwin attacked Gray Beard's Cheyenne village on 8 November, rescuing two Kansas girls who had been captured in September. Although Baldwin destroyed the village, Gray Beard and most of his band escaped. From the west yet another column of troops, this one under Maj. William Price, encountered Gray Beard and his band on the escape. For some reason, however, Price failed to attack Gray Beard, for which Miles later preferred charges. The area now became a focal point for troops. Lt. Col. John (Blackjack) Davidson moved south from Fort Sill in pursuit of Gray Beard, and though he got close he wasn't quite able to catch the Cheyennes. Miles sent another column in pursuit but lost the Indians in the vastness of Palo Duro Canyon.

The arrival of winter curtailed offensive operations and the cold, combined with military pressure, proved too much for the Indians. Some had begun to surrender during the fall, and by the following June most others had surrendered, including Gray Beard, Stone Calf, and the powerful Quanah Parker. But that April a misunderstanding between a group of Cheyennes and some

Fort Sill soldiers led to a skirmish; the Indians escaped but were caught by troops of the Sixth Cavalry on Sappa Creek in western Kansas. The fight at Sappa Creek was the last battle of the war.

See also: Adobe Walls, First Battle of; Adobe Walls, Second Battle of; Mackenzie, Col. Ranald Slidell; Palo Duro Canyon, Battle of; Parker, Quanah
Further Reading: Haley, *The Buffalo War;* Utley, *Frontier Regulars*

Red Sticks

"Red Sticks" referred to militant members of the Creeks who waged war, particularly against white settlers. Red was the color of blood and thus symbolized war; the color white symbolized peace. Within a tribe, clans that carried out warlike functions or activities were identified by red markings; a declaration of war was marked by the erection of a red pole in the center of the village. During the period when pan-Indianism was flourishing, Tecumseh, during a legendary journey to recruit support for an Indian coalition, is said to have encouraged Creek warriors to carry their "red sticks" into battle, which would give rise to a special power that would enable the warriors to locate and destroy their enemies.

See also: Creek Campaigns; Creeks; Horseshoe Bend, Battle of
Further Reading: Dowd, *A Spirited Resistance;* Gilbert, *God Gave Us This Country;* Heidler, *Old Hickory's War;* Hodge, *Handbook of American Indians*

Reno, Maj. Marcus Albert (Alfred)
1834–1889

Born in Illinois, Marcus Reno graduated from West Point in 1857 and was assigned to the First Dragoons. The first four years of the young officer's career were spent in the Pacific Northwest. Upon the outbreak of the Civil War he was transferred east and enjoyed a solid if unspectacular career, ending the war as a brevet brigadier general of volunteers.

In 1868 Reno was appointed major in the Seventh Cavalry, the regiment with which he was thereafter to be inextricably linked.

In command of three companies and the regiment's contingent of Indian scouts, Reno opened the Battle of the Little Bighorn (June 1876) by charging down the valley to attack the lower end of the huge Indian village. The subsequent rout of his command to the bluffs above the river, coupled with his conduct during the next two days, came under severe censure by many. In 1879 Reno requested an official hearing to settle the matter, and although the court of inquiry found nothing improper in his conduct it did nothing to erase the stigma from his name. To this day he continues to be vilified by many.

In the years immediately following the Little Bighorn his conduct as an officer came under fire, and in 1880 he was charged with drunkenness and with striking a junior officer. To make matters worse, he was also charged with peeping at his commanding officer's daughter through a window at the family home. As a result, he was court-martialed and dismissed from the army. He died of cancer nine years later. In the 1960s, at the request of a descendant, the charges were reviewed and subsequently dropped. Marcus Reno was restored to rank and reburied in Custer Battlefield National Cemetery.

See also: Benteen, Capt. Frederick William; Custer, Lt. Col. George Armstrong; Little Bighorn, Battle of the (Custer's Last Stand)
Further Reading: Graham, *The Custer Myth;* Terrell, *Faint the Trumpet Sounds;* Utley, *Cavalier in Buckskin*

Revolutionary War
1775–1784

During the American Revolution, Great Britain and the American colonies sought Indian allies. Most tribes tended to side with the British, not because they felt any special sense of allegiance to the Crown (the Mohawk Joseph Brant excepted), but because they viewed British victory as less threatening than American westward expansion. As the Indians perceived it, a colonial victory would nullify the terms of the Proclamation of 1763, which set aside lands for exclusive Indian use.

Notwithstanding, among the northern tribes, Oneidas and Tuscaroras elected to

Indian commissioner George Rogers Clark

side with the colonists, as did the Mahicans. Southern tribes, for the most part, stayed neutral or sided with the British. Most of the Iroquois Confederacy likewise remained loyal to the British, due largely to the efforts of Sir Guy Johnson, son of Sir William Johnson. Guy Johnson was also successful in forging alliances with some of the tribes from the Great Lakes region.

At the outset of the Revolution, the British were said to have had an Indian army numbering in excess of 3,000, although that number is suspect because groups of Loyalists (also known as Tories) sometimes disguised themselves as Indians. During the Revolution, frontier settlements throughout Virginia, Pennsylvania, and New England were subjected to continuous Indian raids. The Cherry and Mohawk Valleys in New York and the Wyoming Valley in Pennsylvania were among those especially hard-hit. Militia companies, organized to protect settlements, were often away fighting the British, thereby leaving communities with little or no defensive capabilities. Exaggerating the numbers of Indians allied with the British served as a psychological weapon against the American colonists, particularly those in remote areas who lived in almost constant fear of Indian attack.

Thus, the colonies conducted a two-front war: one against British regulars, the other against the Crown's Indian allies who raided outlying regions. In the past, the colonies had enjoyed the support of the British in fighting France and its Indian allies, but now the situation was different: Mustering resources to fight a European power and Indian raiding parties was a difficult challenge indeed.

Britain's Indian allies were sometimes difficult to control. When the British captured Fort Ticonderoga during General John Burgoyne's campaign in 1777, they were unable to prevent their burning and looting. Yet Indian forces working with the British played important roles, as in the Battle of Oriskany in August 1777. (In the prelude to that fight an American militia general named Nicholas Herkimer tried unsuccess-

fully to have Mohawk leader Joseph Brant assassinated.)

In the spring of 1778 a large force of Senecas and Cayugas, the former under Gu-Cinge, augmented by some 400 rangers and Tories disguised as Indians and led by Col. John Butler, launched a series of attacks in Pennsylvania's Wyoming Valley. Against one outpost, called Wintermoot's Fort, the garrison was drawn out by a ruse and ambushed. More than 400 were killed and wounded and many bodies mutilated in what is known as the Wyoming Valley Massacre. Meanwhile, Mohawks under Joseph Brant raided through New York's Cherry Valley, burning villages. Unlike most of his colleagues, Brant chose to destroy property rather than slaughter helpless settlers.

During the autumn of 1778 colonial forces from New York and Pennsylvania campaigned independently, destroying major Indian villages, even as Brant and others were doing the same to colonial settlements elsewhere. In retaliation, a large mixed force of Indians and Tories attacked and burned the stockade at Cherry Valley. As in the Wyoming Valley Massacre, many were killed and many bodies mutilated. The horror was compounded when some of the Indians engaged in cannibalistic rites.

Concluding that the situation demanded stern measures, Gen. George Washington organized a three-column strike force. Gen. John Sullivan was ordered to march with 2,500 men through the Susquehanna Valley while Gen. James Clinton headed up the Mohawk Valley with a 1,500-man force; Col. Daniel Brodhead was directed to move from Fort Pitt up the Allegheny River with 600 men and unite with Sullivan at Tioga. Their combined column would then join Clinton's column at Genesee on the New York–Pennsylvania border.

Sullivan did not get under way until June, but in April Clinton had destroyed most of the main Iroquois villages as he moved through the Mohawk Valley. Finally under way, Sullivan burned a number of Indian villages during the summer and into the fall. While Sullivan and Clinton were destroying every Indian village they could locate, Joseph Brant was not idle, burning the town of Minisink in July.

Indian-white conflicts were not limited to the eastern theater. In 1775 Indian concerns over the increasing number of white settlements in Kentucky had led to bloodshed there. As a result, Shawnees began raiding Kentucky settlements despite chief Cornstalk's argument for neutrality. George Rogers Clark played a key role in developing a defensive strategy for the Kentucky settlements. Clark and companion John Gabriel Jones returned to Williamsburg (in Kentucky, then under Virginia's control) for aid. Clark eventually persuaded Virginia to formally adopt Kentucky as one of its counties and to authorize him to raise a body of militia in its defense.

Meanwhile, in July 1776 a large assemblage of Indians came together at Muscle Shoals on the Tennessee River to discuss their response to increasing white encroachment and whether to become involved in the war between Britain and the colonies. Many, though not all, of the gathered Delawares, Ottawas, Cherokees, and Shawnees opted to support British efforts. Cornstalk, who had been a voice of neutrality among the Shawnees and still hoped to avoid becoming embroiled, was finding it increasingly difficult to maintain neutrality.

By the spring of 1777 Indian raids in Kentucky had increased, forcing most settlers out of the region. Only the strongly fortified settlements of Harrodsburg and Boonesboro were stout enough to withstand the pressure. In April a force of Shawnees under Black Fish began a four-day siege of Boonesboro; Daniel Boone was among those wounded.

Having been authorized to raise a militia army, George Rogers Clark launched an expedition against British posts at Kaskaskia, Cahokia, and Vincennes; he also planned to move against Detroit. Clark reasoned that capturing these outposts, which served as supply points for Britain's Indian allies, would relieve much of the pressure on Kentucky.

During the summer of 1777, in response to Indian raids in what is present-day West Virginia, Congress sent a force under Gen. Edward Hand to attack the British supply depot near the site of present-day Cleveland. Upon learning of Hand's mission, Cornstalk and his son Silverheels journeyed to Fort Randolph near Point Pleasant, Ohio, to warn the Americans that Shawnees would retaliate in force if the attack was carried out. Cornstalk, his son, and another Shawnee were taken hostage and later killed by a party of frontiersmen who overpowered the guards. The killings triggered a series of massive raids throughout the region, involving perhaps as many as 3,500 vengeful warriors. Any remaining Shawnee neutrals were surely influenced by this act.

Meanwhile, despite setbacks, which included operating with a smaller force than he anticipated, Clark captured Kaskaskia, Cahokia, and Vincennes during the summer of 1778 and the following winter in one of the epic campaigns in American military history.

In July 1779 a Continental Army column under Col. John Bowman destroyed the main Shawnee village at Chillicothe, Ohio. The attack, however, had little effect on the Shawnee warrior population, most of whom were absent on raids of their own. Nevertheless, the attack further enraged the Shawnees. In the spring of 1780 a large force of Indians augmented by some British regulars launched a strike into Kentucky. Among this expedition were the notorious Simon Girty and his two brothers. Following an attack on Ruddell's Station on the South Licking River, the garrison surrendered, having been assured of protection. However, as at Fort William Henry and the Wyoming Valley, the Indians could not be restrained, and a massacre ensued. In response, George Rogers Clark mobilized a force of 1,000 and attacked the Shawnees at Piqua Town, near present-day Springfield, Ohio, destroying the village and inflicting a stinging defeat.

In the South, a large colonial column guided by friendly Catawbas devastated militant Cherokee villages. During the summer of 1777 the Cherokees sued for peace, ceding large tracts of land in northeastern

Tennessee. Elsewhere in the South, the powerful Creeks allied with the British late in 1778. However, the British seemed to be less successful at coordinating Indian activities there than they were in New England. As a consequence, Creek raids were less effective in supporting British efforts against the colonies.

In the Northeast, General Sullivan's campaign hurt the Indians badly but in turn provoked retaliatory raids. In the spring of 1780 a massive raid on Mohawk Valley settlements resulted in destruction rivaling what Sullivan had wrought. During these raids Joseph Brant was wounded, but he returned to even more vigorous action in 1781, striking Cherry Valley yet again. That fall, Brant was unsuccessful in persuading Delawares who had been converted to Christianity, called Moravians, to join his Mohawks in raiding western Pennsylvania settlements.

Moravians were in particular danger from Indian raids, and so they were directed to leave the region; harsh winter conditions prompted them to ask for permission to return temporarily. But they returned in the immediate aftermath of Brant's devastating raids and quickly became the target of a retaliatory strike by Col. David Williamson, who ordered 90 Moravian men and women executed by mallet blows to the head in an episode known as the Gnaddenhutten Massacre. Although the incident was condemned by the governor, neither Williamson nor any of his command were punished.

The Gnaddenhutten Massacre provoked retaliatory raids by angry Delawares, which, in turn, resulted in a second Moravian campaign against Indian villages in northwestern Ohio. However, the column, commanded by Col. William Crawford, was ambushed and surrounded by a mixed force of Shawnees and Delawares. Casualties in Crawford's column were heavy. Crawford himself was captured and slowly tortured to death. Simon Girty had tried to warn Crawford prior to the ambush, but the colonel refused to heed the warning of a renegade.

The near total destruction of Crawford's column produced yet another round of punitive expeditions. Kentucky continued to be the scene of much fighting. At a place called Blue Licks, the Kentucky militia suffered its worst-ever defeat, with nearly 100 casualties. Daniel Boone had counseled against the militia's attacking in this instance but was overruled.

The surrender of Lord Charles Cornwallis at Yorktown in 1781 officially ended the American Revolution, but Indian-white conflicts along the westward-expanding frontier would continue.

See also: Blue Licks, Battle of; Boone, Daniel; Brant, Joseph (Thayendanega); Clark, George Rogers; Girty, Simon; Gnaddenhutten Massacre; Johnson, Sir William; Oriskany, Battle of
Further Reading: Bakeless, *Background to Glory;* ———, *Daniel Boone;* Wood, *Battles of the Revolutionary War*

Reynolds, Charles Alexander (Lonesome Charley)
1842–1876

Born in Illinois, Charley Reynolds moved to Kansas as a boy. Like many of his generation, he was attracted to the frontier early on, and in 1860, at age 18, he headed to Colorado, where he spent the next year as a trapper. When the Civil War began, in 1861, Reynolds enlisted in the Tenth Kansas Volunteers and saw action in Missouri and Arkansas. After the war he spent time on the Santa Fe Trail as a guide and trader and, later, was a buffalo hunter.

By 1870 Reynolds had moved to Dakota, continuing the life of a sometime-guide and buffalo hunter. Two years later, thanks to his acquaintance with Gen. Philip H. Sheridan, he was invited to join a select company of army officers and frontiersmen Sheridan was organizing to provide hunting opportunities for Grand Duke Alexis of Russia. During this outing he met Lt. Col. George Armstrong Custer.

His knowledge of the country and skills as a scout were in demand. In 1873 he was hired by Custer as scout for the Northern Pacific Railroad's Yellowstone survey expedition. The following year he guided Custer's Black Hills expedition, and in 1875 he guided Capt. William Ludlow's expedition through central Montana and into Yellowstone Park.

In the Centennial summer of 1876, Reynolds was again with Custer, this time on an ill-fated expedition. Reynolds was killed with Maj. Marcus Reno's command in the opening phase of the Battle of the Little Bighorn.

See also: Custer, Lt. Col. George Armstrong; Little Bighorn, Battle of the (Custer's Last Stand); Sheridan, Gen. Philip Henry
Further Reading: Gray, "On the Trail of Lonesome Charley Reynolds"

Rogers, Maj. Robert
1732–1795

One of the most colorful and controversial figures in American colonial history, Robert Rogers was born on the Massachusetts frontier. As a young man during the French and Indian War, Rogers organized Rogers's Rangers, a military unit specially trained to travel and fight in the frontier-backwoods style. As such, the Rangers served the British cause well. The group's most noted accomplishment was its devastating 1759 raid on the Huron village of St. Francois (St. Francis).

In 1760 Rogers accepted the surrender of the French posts of Detroit and Michilimackinac. During a visit to England he published his journals and *Ponteach,* said to be one of the first dramas created by an American-born colonist. Upon returning to America he was charged with treason and embezzlement, but he was subsequently acquitted due to lack of evidence. On yet another journey to England he was thrown in prison for nonpayment of debts. Rescued from the ignominy of prison by his brother James, who paid off the creditors, Rogers was allowed to return to America.

During the Revolutionary War he was suspected by George Washington of being a British spy, which indeed he seems to have been. Escaping, he managed to reach British lines, where he proceeded to organize a second ranger battalion called the Queen's Rangers. Rogers, however, did not seem to enjoy the same success with the second unit and was defeated at Mamaroneck in 1776. Subsequently relieved of command, he returned to England in 1780.

During his last years Rogers's personal life was a shambles. Divorced and no doubt disillusioned, he died in poverty in a London boarding house in 1795, a tragic figure. His life was romanticized in Kenneth Roberts's novel *Northwest Passage,* the film version of which casts Spencer Tracy as Rogers.

See also: French and Indian War; Rangers; Rogers's Raid on St. Francis
Further Reading: Leach, *Arms for Empire;* Roberts, *Northwest Passage;* Steele, *Warpaths*

Maj. Robert Rogers

Rogers's Raid on St. Francis
October 1759

In October 1759 Maj. Robert Rogers, famous for creating Rogers's Rangers, an elite battalion of woodsmen who fought in the frontier style, led some 140 rangers in a surprise attack on the important French mission town of St. Francis, Canada. The town was put to the torch, and many Abnaki inhabitants were killed. The raid, which had been authorized by British Gen. Jeffrey Amherst, was in retaliation for Abnaki raids against colonial settlements. The story of the St. Francis raid is described in the novel *Northwest Passage,* by Kenneth Roberts; it later became a film that casts Spencer Tracy as Rogers.

See also: Abnakis (Abenakis); French and Indian War; Rogers, Maj. Robert
Further Reading: Jennings, *The Invasion of America;* Leach, *Arms for Empire;* Steele, *Warpaths*

Rogue River War
1853

The Rogue River War of 1853, the first of two American conflicts with Rogue Indians, has been called a war between territorial militia and Indians. The influx of miners to gold-rich areas of southern Oregon and northern California led eventually to conflict with Indians. Indian raids on isolated white settlements and the brutal treatment of Indians by whites—who all too often made no distinction between the guilty and the innocent—created a hostile environment.

In 1853 the Rogue Indians, who had been suppressed for depredations committed two years earlier, became the object of retaliation for raids committed by other wandering bands from northern California. As a result, the Rogues struck back in an uprising that threatened much of southwest Oregon. A detachment of regulars and a company of volunteers under Capt. Bradford Alden and Joseph Lane, the territorial delegate, pursued the Indians, killing some 200 in a hard fight on 24 August 1853. It may have been the only Indian war decided by one battle. The resulting Table Rock Treaty provided that the Rogues would surrender their land and be assigned to a permanent reservation.

Further Reading: Utley, *Frontiersmen in Blue*

Roman Nose
ca. 1830–1868

A renowned warrior of the Southern Cheyennes, Roman Nose took part in most of the major battles on the Central and Southern Plains during the 1860s. Like Tall Bull and others he took to the warpath following the Sand Creek Massacre in November 1864. He was involved in the fight at Platte Bridge in 1865 and participated in the attacks on the Cole and Walker columns the same year.

Roman Nose was especially sensitive to the observance of religious rituals and taboos prior to battle. He always went into battle wearing a special headdress that was believed to hold certain powers. Roman Nose was always careful to avoid eating anything touched by metal prior to a battle. However, just prior to the Battle of Beecher Island in September 1868 he accidentally violated this taboo. He nevertheless entered the fight, believing he would be killed—and he was.

Roman Nose was not a chief, though he has sometimes mistakenly been referred to as such. He was a highly respected warrior and during his last years was a prominent member of the Dog Soldiers.

See also: Beecher Island, Battle of; Dog Soldiers; Platte Bridge, Battle of; Sand Creek Massacre
Further Reading: Afton, *Cheyenne Dog Soldiers;* Grinnell, *Fighting Cheyennes;* Hyde, *Life of George Bent;* Monnett, *The Battle of Beecher Island*

Rosebud, Battle of the
17 June 1876

On 29 May 1876, Brig. Gen. George Crook, commanding the Military Department of the Platte, marched out of Fort Fetterman, Wyoming, near the site of present-day Douglas with a force of 1,000 cavalry and infantry. Known as the Big Horn and Yellowstone Expedition, the column also included a party of Montana miners as well as civilian guides and packers. Crook's column was one of three ordered into the field with the mission of forcing recalcitrant bands of northern Plains tribes, notably Sioux and Cheyennes, to return to their respective agencies.

Moving north along the old Bozeman Trail, Crook's force was augmented by nearly

The defeat of Roman Nose by Major Forsyth during the Battle of Beecher Island in 1868

General Crook's battle on the Rosebud River in Montana

300 Crows and Shoshone warriors. The arrival of these Indian allies, enemies of the Sioux, swelled Crook's column to more than 1,300 men; it was thus one of the largest ever to take the field against western tribes. On the morning of 17 June 1876, Crook was unexpectedly attacked along Rosebud River near the site of present-day Kirby, Montana. The war party, possibly equal to his own force or nearly so, consisted mainly of Sioux and was led by Crazy Horse and other prominent warriors.

Caught by surprise, Crook's command was separated and forced to fight a segmented battle. After several hours of hard fighting the Indians withdrew, which later caused Crook to claim victory, since the Indians had left him in possession of the field. Despite the intensity of the fighting Crook's casualties were moderate: 10 killed and 23 wounded. Indian casualties are unknown, although Crazy Horse reportedly put the number at just more than 100, regarded as high.

After the battle Crook withdrew to his base camp at Goose Creek, the site of present-day Sheridan, Wyoming, to await the arrival of reinforcements. In so doing Crook effectively removed his command from further participation in the summer campaign. It is believed by some that Crook's failure to pursue the Indians was a factor in Custer's disastrous fight on the Little Bighorn, which occurred eight days later and 30-odd miles to the north.

See also: Crook, Gen. George; Indian Scouts and Auxiliaries; Little Bighorn, Battle of the (Custer's Last Stand); Sioux War
Further Reading: Finerty, *War-Path and Bivouac;* Mangum, *The Battle of the Rosebud;* Utley, *Frontier Regulars*

Rowlandson, Mary White
1635–1678

Captured in a raid on Lancaster, Massachusetts, in February 1676 during King Philip's War, Mary White Rowlandson, wife of the community's minister, Joseph Rowlandson, became perhaps the most celebrated captive of the early colonial period. Originally the captive of an Indian named One-Eyed John, she was later sold to the Narragansett sachem Quinnapin, who she subsequently came to respect, as she did Philip himself.

Ransomed in May 1676, she wrote an account of her captivity entitled *The Sovereignty and Goodness of God . . . A Narrative of the Captivity and Restauration of Mrs. Mary Rowlandson.* Published posthumously in 1682, the book became a frontier classic and the best known of all the captivity accounts. Over a period of years it was reissued in many editions.

See also: King Philip's War
Further Reading: Bourne, *The Red King's Rebellion;* Rowlandson, *The Soveraignty and Goodness of God*

S

Sachem

Among the Indian tribes of New England, particularly in what is present-day Massachusetts, a sachem was considered the supreme ruler of his territory, in much the same fashion as was the head of the Powhatan Confederacy. Under the sachem were lesser or subrulers known as sagamores. The position of sachem was hereditary, not elective.

See also: Powhatan Confederacy
Further Reading: Hodge, *Handbook of American Indians*

Sagamore
See Sachem

Sagoyewatha
See Red Jacket (Sagoyewatha)

Samoset
?–ca. 1654

Samoset (literally, he who walks over much) was a sagamore and once the original proprietor of what is today Bristol, Massachusetts. He is reported to have greeted the Pilgrims with the words "Welcome, Englishmen." The story may be apocryphal; since European traders had visited the region prior to the arrival of the Pilgrims, it is conceivable that Samoset acquired a few words of English. The Pilgrims apparently provided Samoset with food and clothing, and he in turn repaid the colonists with his friendship and assistance, remaining a staunch friend of the English for the rest of his life. It was Samoset who introduced Massasoit to the Pilgrims. Friendly though he may have been, his attitude toward the English was likely influenced by a desire to ally with a force capable of resisting the stronger Narragansett tribe to the west.

See also: England; Massasoit
Further Reading: Hodge, *Handbook of American Indians*

San Carlos Reservation, Arizona

Comprising some 1,834,000 acres in east-central Arizona, the San Carlos Reservation was established in 1871 for many of the Western Apache bands. San Carlos played a prominent role in the Apache wars of the 1870s and 1880s. With its harsh climate, San Carlos left much to be desired as a home. Moreover, Apache bands consigned here often were forced to coexist with unfriendly bands. As a consequence, many Apache uprisings occurred, with leaders such as Victorio, Loco, and Geronimo bolting San Carlos to resume old raiding habits.

See also: Apache Wars; Crook, Gen. George; Geronimo; Miles, Gen. Nelson Appleton; Victorio
Further Reading: Clum, *Apache Agent*; Perry, *Western Apache Heritage*

Sand Creek Massacre
29 November 1864

In September 1864, Black Kettle, a known peace chief of the Cheyennes, sent peace feelers to Fort Lyon in response to the proclamation of Colorado Gov. John Evans, issued the previous June. In essence, Evans proclaimed that any group of Indians who detached from known hostile groups would be

Samoset, the Indian Visitor

allowed to set up camp near specified army posts and enjoy military protection.

In the weeks following the proclamation, however, the situation became increasingly tense. Indian raids to the east had virtually isolated Denver, and the June murder of the Hungate family near Denver had fueled public outcry for retaliation. Evans was thus caught in a difficult situation: On the one hand, his offer was on record; on the other, the public was demanding action. So Evans promulgated a second notice in August, which virtually gave citizens a free hand with any hostile Indians. He had also received authorization to form a volunteer cavalry regiment for home defense. In late September, at a parley held at Camp Weld near Denver, Evans washed his hands of the problem by turning it over to the district military commander, Col. John M. Chivington. The June offer was still open, Evans informed Black Kettle, but it would now be necessary to make peace with the military.

Disturbed but still desiring peace, Black Kettle and the other chiefs agreed to the governor's terms. In early October a large band of Arapahos surrendered to Maj. Edward Wynkoop at Fort Lyon, near the site of present-day Lamar, Colorado. Since the Indians were in effect considered prisoners, Wynkoop saw it as his responsibility to feed them, an act for which he was promptly replaced by Maj. Scott Anthony. After collecting the Indians' firearms, Anthony ordered the Arapahos to camp on Sand Creek, some 40 miles distant; when Black Kettle arrived in early November he, too, was directed to set up camp on Sand Creek. Both contingents believed they had acted in good faith and were now under the protection of the troops.

Meanwhile, in Denver, Chivington had been formulating plans for a strike against the Indians. There was a sense of urgency to Chivington's efforts, since the term of enlistment for the Third Colorado, organized during the summer, would soon run out. The regiment had seen no action and had come to be known as the Bloodless Third.

Although there had been some vague talk of a campaign against hostile villages in eastern Colorado, it seems clear that Chivington aimed from the start to strike the Indian encampments on Sand Creek. Accordingly, on 28 November Chivington arrived at Fort Lyon with the Third Colorado, prepared to launch a surprise attack. Some of the officers at Fort Lyon strenuously objected on the grounds that the Indians were under a pledge of protection, a protest that Chivington angrily overruled. That evening, Chivington's command, composed of the Third Colorado and part of the First Colorado, together with four mountain howitzers—some 700 men in all—left Fort Lyon.

By dawn on 29 November the forces were positioned for a surprise attack on Black Kettle's village. Chivington struck. While two battalions cut off and captured the pony herds, the remaining troops attacked the village proper. Unable to accept what he saw was happening, Black Kettle hoisted an American flag above his tipi, reassuring his people there was no need to panic. White Antelope, meanwhile, ran at the attacking troops, urging them not to fire and crying out that this was a peaceful camp. But it was all to no avail, as he was quickly killed.

Elsewhere in the village panic took hold despite Black Kettle's pleas. The troops tore through, shooting or bayoneting any Indian they came across—man, woman, or child. Chivington had ordered that no prisoners be taken, and none were. Perhaps 60 or 70 of the villagers managed to take up a defensive position of sorts and return fire, but it did little to halt the slaughter. When at last it was over, more than 200 Indians—the entire village—lay dead, many of them mutilated.

In the aftermath, cries of indignation echoed from across the country. To his dying day Chivington defended his actions at Sand Creek, but the verdict of history has condemned the act for what it was: one of the most infamous massacres on record, a grim day in the annals of American history. The legacy of Sand Creek was a bloody war that lasted from 1867 until 1869.

See also: Chivington, Col. John M.; Evans, Gov. John; Indian War (1867–1869)

Further Reading: Dunn, *I Stand by Sand Creek;* Hoig, *The Sand Creek Massacre;* Mendoza, *Song of Sorrow;* Schultz, *Month of the Freezing Moon;* Utley, *Frontiersmen in Blue*

Sassacus
ca. 1560–1637

Sassacus (literally, he is wild) was born near Groton, Connecticut, the son of Wopigwooit, the first chief to have contact with the whites and who was killed by the Dutch about 1632. Sassacus was the last major chief of the Pequots and a noted sachem.

During Sassacus's time as chief, his territory extended from Narragansett Bay to the Hudson River. In 1634 Sassacus made an offer of peace and friendship to the governor of Massachusetts Bay Colony. Incredibly, the offer is reported to have included the surrender of all rights to the Pequot lands in exchange for a plantation to be built in the middle of those lands. The offer, if true, must have seemed unbelievable to the English, and surely a man of Sassacus's intelligence could not have believed he would ever be able to deliver on a such a promise. In any case, it did alienate him from Uncas, the Mohegan leader to whom he was related by both blood and marriage.

With the conclusion of the Pequot War and the virtual end of the Pequots as a tribe, Sassacus fled into the land of the Mohawks, where he, his brother, and five Pequot chiefs were subsequently killed and scalped.

See also: Mohawks; Mohegans; Pequot War; Uncas
Further Reading: Hodge, *Handbook of American Indians*

Sassamon
See King Philip's War

Sauks and Foxes

The Sauks (Sacs) were an Algonquian family. Earliest records suggest that their tribal origins began in what is now the Michigan area. Driven out by the powerful Iroquois Confederacy in the early 1600s, they eventually migrated into the area around present-day Green Bay, Wisconsin.

The Mesquakie—called Fox by early French traders—were a Wisconsin tribe that also lived in the Green Bay region. Their particular territory allowed them control over inland waterways in the area, for which they exacted payment from any who sought to use those routes, whether Indian or white. Because of this the Fox earned the enmity of many, leading to continuous adversarial re-

lations with European traders and other tribes. To strengthen themselves, the Fox eventually established an alliance with the nearby Sauks. The alliance was logical, since both tribes had cultural and linguistic ties.

During the eighteenth century and the first half of the nineteenth century, the blending of the two tribal entities produced a single identity. A treaty with the fledgling United States at that time recognized them as Sauks and Foxes, the "Sauk" later being corrupted to "Sac." Treaties entered in the 1830s and 1840s and the outcome of the Black Hawk War resulted in the relocation of the Sauks and Foxes to places west of the Mississippi River.

See also: Black Hawk; Black Hawk War
Further Reading: Edmunds and Peyser, *The Fox Wars*; Hagan, *Sac and Fox Indians*; Jackson, *Black Hawk*

Saybrook, Connecticut

A fortified trading post located on the west bank of the Connecticut River, Fort Saybrook was built by John Winthrop Jr. under authorization granted by the Saybrook Company, a group of English investors. With the Pequots and Western Niantics to the east and the Mohegans to the north, Fort Saybrook was in a vital strategic location during the early years of the English colonies. As such, the post played an important role in the Pequot War.

See also: Mohegans; Pequot War
Further Reading: Jennings, *The Invasion of America*; Steele, *Warpaths*

Scalping and Scalp Bounty

Throughout the history of the Indian wars the scalp of an enemy or victim was regarded as a trophy of triumph by Indians and whites. In some instances, scalping involved the removal of the entire skin of the victim's upper head; in others, just the topknot or crown sufficed.

The practice seems to have been commonplace among many, though not all, Indian tribes long before the arrival of Europeans. However, most frontiersmen and many of the citizen soldiers who fought Indians soon adopted the idea. The practice spread with the introduction of the scalp bounty, which paid the bearer a fixed amount for each scalp turned in, in much the same way a trapper would receive the going price for a fur pelt.

In New England, colonies such as Massachusetts, for example, offered 10 pounds for the scalp of an Indian child and 50 pounds for that of an adult. During the nineteenth century the Mexican provinces of Chihuahua and Sonora offered 100 pesos for the scalp of an Apache warrior over 14 years of age, 50 pesos for a woman's scalp, and 25 for that of a child.

See also: Apache Wars; Mangas Coloradas
Further Reading: Leach, *Arms for Empire;* Steele, *Warpaths;* Worcester, *The Apaches*

Scarlet Point
See Inkpaduta (Scarlet Point)

Schurz, Carl
1829–1906

Born in Germany, Carl Schurz emigrated to the United States in 1852 and became a journalist. He later joined the army and during the Civil War rose to the rank of general and saw considerable action. Following the war he became interested in politics and was elected to the U.S. Senate from Missouri as a liberal. He was named secretary of the interior by Pres. Ulysses S. Grant, taking a strong stand on conservation issues. He also frequently sympathized with the plight of the Indians; he fired Commissioner of Indian Affairs Ezra Hayt for incompetence and irregularities in the administration of the San Carlos Apache Reservation in Arizona.

Schurz's strong stand against further military intervention following the Meeker Massacre, together with the efforts of agent Charles Francis Adams and Ute chief Ouray, helped avoid a full-scale war between the U.S. government and the Utes in 1879.

See also: Meeker Massacre
Further Reading: Utley, *Frontier Regulars*

Seminole

A branch of the greater Creek confederation, the Seminoles moved into Florida early in the eighteenth century. The name is of Spanish derivation and means, literally, runaway or wild. During the eighteenth century the Seminoles absorbed other Indians, such as the Yamasees, who were then fleeing the British. Runaway black slaves also found a home with the Seminoles. Although the Seminoles did not join the Red Stick Creeks during the Creek civil war, they were allied with the Red Sticks both in spirit and cultural styles.

The Seminoles supported the British during the War of 1812, and shortly after its conclusion Andrew Jackson (in 1818) employed the stratagem of Indian fear to drive the Spanish out of Florida and subjugate the Seminoles. Between 1818 and 1842 the United States waged three separate wars with the Seminoles. The third and last (1835–1842) was the costliest Indian war in U.S. history. By 1850 most Seminoles had been relocated to the Indian Territory in Oklahoma.

It is worth noting that the Seminoles never actually surrendered to the United States, the war being concluded by negotiated settlement. In the only such agreement of its kind, some Seminoles were allowed to remain on their own land in Florida. Today the tribe owns less than 10 percent of the lands originally granted to them by treaty.

See also: Dade's Massacre; Seminole War, First; Seminole War, Second; Seminole War, Third
Further Reading: Covington, *The Seminoles of Florida;* Laumer, *Dade's Last Command*

Seminole War, First
1816–1818

The first of three conflicts between the United States and the Seminoles of Florida began in 1816 when U.S. troops, in pursuit of runaway slaves, destroyed an old British post at Prospect Bluff in northwestern Florida known as Negro Fort (so called because it had become a sanctuary of sorts for runaways and a Seminole stronghold). The

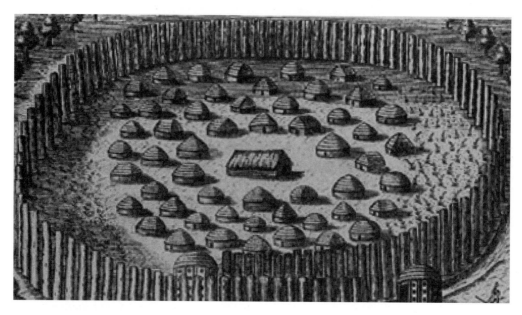

Undated engraving of a Seminole encampment of small huts surrounded by a circular wooden fence

attack touched off a series of raids and counterraids. On 21 November 1817, Maj. David Twiggs attacked a Seminole village at Fowltown, driving the Seminoles deep into the swamp. In retaliation, the Indians ambushed a boatload of troops from Fort Scott on 30 November, killing many.

As a result of this incident, Maj. Gen. Andrew Jackson was ordered to move into the area with regular infantry, militia, and Indian scouts, a force of some 3,500. Jackson wasted little time sweeping through Seminole territory, burning villages and seizing livestock. Possessing a force that heavily outnumbered the Seminoles and their allies, he encountered little resistance.

Jackson continued the march then captured the Spanish garrison at St. Marks on April 6 and the Peter McQueen's Red Stick village six days later, fighting several engagements in the process. Jackson next moved on Nero, a Suwanee River settlement run by a mulatto named Nero who had set himself up as the head of several hundred fugitive slaves. Jackson attacked the settlement on 16 April, and although the inhabitants put up a spirited defense they were finally forced to withdraw.

The concluding phase of the First Seminole War involved the trial and execution of a pair of Englishmen from Nassau, in the Bahamas. A former British army officer, Robert Armbrister, was charged with involvement in a scheme to seize Florida; Alexander Arbuthnot, a Scots trader, was accused of inciting the Indians to war against the United States. The former was executed by firing squad; Arbuthnot was hanged from the yardarm of his own vessel. Jackson's harsh treatment of the two Englishmen created an international incident.

Jackson's campaign had effectively broken the back of Seminole resistance for the time being. The war also led to the U.S. acquisition of Florida from Spain in 1819.

See also: Seminole; Seminole War, Second; Seminole War, Third

Further Reading: Covington, *The Seminoles of Florida*

Seminole War, Second
1835–1842

As a result of agreements signed at Payne's Landing (1832) and Fort Gibson (1833), some Seminoles were relocated from Florida to western lands under the Indian Removal

Massacre of the Motte family during the second Seminole War

Act of 1830. The last of the tribes to be thus relocated under the law, which was passed during Andrew Jackson's administration, the Seminoles' transfer was attended by confusion, misunderstanding, and, in many cases, fierce resistance.

Although some Seminoles did move to the Indian Territory, the majority of the tribe was opposed to relocation, and events moved the U.S. government closer to having to force removal. In August 1835 an effort was made to work out a compromise in which the Seminoles would move provided they be given a reservation separate from that of the Creeks—ironic given that the Seminoles had at one time been a branch of the Creeks. One of the stumbling blocks in reaching an agreement was the disposition of runaway slaves; many had integrated with the Seminoles but were still considered to be the property of the slave owner.

The situation continued to deteriorate when Seminole leader Charley Emathla was killed by a young warrior named Osceola over a disagreement about removal. Minor clashes soon burst into full-scale war. In December 1835 Maj. Francis Dade arrived at Fort Brooke on Florida's western coast. Moving to reinforce Fort King in north-central Florida, Dade's entire command of 108 men was attacked and wiped out in what has come to be known as Dade's Massacre. It was also during this time that Osceola led a devastating attack on the sutler's house at Fort King.

Although Andrew Jackson had personally conducted a campaign against the Seminoles 20 years earlier, mounting a military response was easier said than done. The territory was unmapped. Very few whites were acquainted with the region, which offered many opportunities for concealment. Yet the Seminoles could muster only about 800 warriors, their supplies of powder and lead were limited, and resupply was difficult. The tribe's children were also a problem for the Seminoles, for whom concealment was a primary tactic; some children were actually killed for fear their crying would reveal positions.

As hostilities intensified, the United States increased its troop commitment. Maj. Gen. Winfield Scott, commanding the army's Eastern Department, organized three columns to converge on the Seminoles. The campaign proved a bust, however, and the exhausted troops, short on supplies, returned to Fort Brooke with minimal success.

In February 1836 Maj. Gen. Edward Pendleton Gaines, who commanded the army's Western Department and had been involved in the First Seminole War, brought an 1,100-man force to Tampa on his own volition. Following Dade's earlier route, he was attacked by a large Seminole force at Withlacoochee River, where he withstood an eight-day siege until relieved by a column under Gen. Duncan Lamont Church that finally forced the Seminoles to disperse. While the Seminoles continued to raid settlements the U.S. troops found a second enemy—tropical diseases such as yellow fever, malaria, and others, which decimated the ranks.

At this juncture the army's command structure underwent a change. General Scott was transferred to Alabama to deal with a conflict with the Creeks. Scott's initial replacement was Florida Gov. Richard Call, who promptly launched an all-out campaign against the Seminoles, using the Withlacoochee River as an avenue of supply. Call's lack of experience, however, produced limited results. Next to arrive on the scene was Gen. Thomas Jesup, who launched a vigorous campaign that caused some of the Seminoles to cease hostilities and agree to relocate. This proved short-lived, however, as the Seminoles changed their mind and disappeared into the interior.

On 25 October 1837, Jesup captured Osceola and some 70 followers under a flag of truce. Already ill, Osceola died in captivity several months later. (Jesup was later harshly criticized for his action in taking a prisoner under a flag of truce.) Seminoles who surrendered were immediately deported to the Indian Territory. Blacks unfortunate enough to be captured by Creeks were often sold to white slave owners.

In the fall of 1837 Jesup launched a second campaign with 4,000 regulars and 5,000 volunteers. Again the strategy called for several columns to move against the Seminoles. On Christmas Day, Col. Zachary Taylor, with a force of 1,000, engaged some 400 Seminoles in what may have been the most significant battle of the war, at Okeechobee. Taylor suffered about 150 casualties, the Indians about 24.

During Jesup's 18-month tenure in Florida, nearly 2,000 Seminoles and blacks were captured and several hundred were killed. Perhaps due to the censure incurred as a result of the Osceola incident, Jesup asked to be relieved and was replaced by Taylor in May 1838. Taylor intended to construct a series of forts throughout Seminole territory in order to closely monitor Seminole activity and thereby control the situation. Lacking the necessary manpower, however, he was unable to implement this strategy. Taylor was only moderately successful in his efforts against the Seminoles and was replaced in 1839 by Gen. Alexander Macomb as the army continued to search for a commander who could resolve matters.

Macomb rounded up a few Seminoles, but in the main neither he nor his successor, Gen. Walker Armistead, enjoyed much success. Villages were burned, but the Seminole bands continued to elude the army, who even turned to using bloodhounds imported from Cuba. The dogs had proved useful there in tracking slaves but were largely unsuccessful against the Seminoles.

In 1841 Gen. William J. Worth was appointed commander in yet another change. Worth had at his disposal nearly 5,000 regulars to send against the Seminoles, who maintained strong resistance in central Florida. During 1841 and 1842 Worth pursued and harassed the Seminoles relentlessly, eventually bringing on what proved to be the last battle of the war near Fort King.

The U.S. government came to recognize, finally, that complete removal of the Seminoles was impractical. Negotiations that began in July 1842 eventually allowed some Seminoles to remain in Florida. No other eastern tribe had managed to achieve the objective of remaining on ancestral lands. The victory was not without its price, however. Of the 5,000 or so original Seminoles, only about 600 remained in Florida, the others having been killed or relocated to the Indian Territory. The seven-year war had been an expensive proposition for the United States as well, costing $30 million in addition to the 1,500 casualties, which included 100 civilians.

See also: Dade's Massacre; Seminole; Seminole War, First; Seminole War, Third
Further Reading: Covington, *The Seminoles of Florida;* Laumer, *Dade's Last Command;* Mahon, *History of the Second Seminole War;* Prucha, *Sword of the Republic*

Seminole War, Third
1855–1858

By November 1855 the U.S. Army's presence in Florida had been reduced to about 700 men, down from several thousand during the height of the first two Seminole wars. Even so, the army still outnumbered the remaining male Seminoles by nearly four to one.

On 7 December 1855, Lt. George Hartsuff of the Second Artillery left Fort Myers in command of an 11-man patrol. Hartsuff's mission was to move through Big Cypress Swamp and observe Seminole activity, nothing more. On the morning of 20 December the patrol was attacked by a band of Seminoles led by Billy Bowlegs, whose village it had passed through the previous day. In the ensuing fight, six members of the patrol were killed or wounded. Hartsuff himself was badly wounded but managed to escape; several more were able to find their way back to Fort Myers, where they reported what happened.

The attack on Hartsuff's patrol ushered in the third and final Seminole War. Florida mobilized its militia, which vastly outnumbered the Seminoles when combined with the regular army in the area. This numerical advantage, however, was offset by the regular army's disinclination to aggressively pursue the Seminoles as well as by disorganization in the militia.

The Seminoles, led by Billy Bowlegs, Oscen Tustenuggee, and his brothers, Micco and Old, followed up the initial attack on the Hartsuff patrol with a raid on a Miami River farm and an attack on some woodcutters working out of Fort Denaud, east of Fort Myers. Slave quarters on some of the plantations were also targets. A militia column did manage to surprise a small party of Seminoles led by Oscen, killing a few and wounding some including the leader, who managed to escape.

The raids continued. During the spring of 1856 probes by both the militia and regulars had little luck locating the elusive Seminole bands, except for one encounter in April with the Billy Bowlegs band. The summer of 1856 witnessed several clashes, none of which accomplished much except to illustrate the ineffectiveness of the militia system. That fall, however, Col. William S. Harney was appointed commander of the federal troops in Florida. Harney, a tough regular, had been in the second Seminole War, where he had the humiliating experience of having to escape while wearing only underwear during a surprise Seminole attack.

Harney's strategy was to apply relentless pressure against the Seminoles by sending out constant patrols and utilizing shallow-draft whaleboats to move through Florida's myriad inland waterways. The strategy began to wear the Seminoles down. Clothing grew threadbare, and they were forced to find lead for ammunition by scavenging for expended army bullets.

An increase in army troop strength meant more patrols and continued pressure. Some Seminoles who had been relocated to the Indian Territory were also brought in to persuade their recalcitrant brothers to surrender. The combined strategy proved successful, and the war was finally brought to a close on 19 January 1858; on 27 March a Seminole delegation accepted government terms. Some were removed to the Indian Territory; some who refused removal were allowed to remain in Florida.

See also: Dade's Massacre; Harney, Gen. William Selby; Seminole War, First; Seminole War, Second
Further Reading: Covington, *The Seminoles of Florida*

Senecas

A prominent tribe of the Iroquois Confederacy, the Senecas at one time occupied the territory between Seneca Lake and the Geneva River. By the mid-seventeenth century the tribe had expanded west to the shores of Lake Erie. During Pontiac's uprising, the Senecas ambushed and largely destroyed British columns at Bloody Run and Devil's Hole. By the time of the American Revolution, British efforts, primarily of Sir William Johnson and his son Guy Johnson, had drawn most of the Iroquois Confederacy, including the Senecas, into the British camp. As a result of their taking this pro-British stand, they ceded Iroquois lands west of New York and Pennsylvania to the fledgling United States in the second Treaty of Fort Stanwix (1784).

Descendants of the Senecas and other tribes of the Iroquois Confederacy still reside in New York and Canada.

See also: Devil's Hole Road, Battle of; Pontiac's War/Rebellion/Uprising
Further Reading: Debo, *A History of the Indians of the United States*; Hodge, *Handbook of American Indians*, vol. 2; Josephy, *500 Nations*

Shawnee Council
1775

During the summer of 1775 the Shawnees, a fragmented tribe, managed to achieve a confederation of sorts when a number of their bands convened on the Little Miami River near the site of present-day Chillicothe, Ohio, to address the growing problem of white settlers moving into Kentucky. The great chief Cornstalk, who had sided with France during the French and Indian War, preached neutrality in the American revolutionary struggle that was then unfolding. He was, however, adamantly opposed to white settlements in Kentucky, regarded by the

Shawnees as prime hunting grounds. Accordingly, raids against the settlements increased as Kentucky became the "dark and bloody ground" depicted in history books. Despite the Indian raids the influx of settlers continued unabated.

See also: Cornstalk; French and Indian War
Further Reading: Dowd, *A Spirited Resistance*; Hurt, *The Ohio Frontier*

Shawnees

A tribe of the Algonquian family, the Shawnees originally dwelled in South Carolina, Tennessee, Pennsylvania, and Ohio. One of the foremost opponents of white advancement into the country north of the Ohio River, the Shawnees, led by the likes of Cornstalk, Blue Jacket, and the great Tecumseh, were a formidable foe.

The Shawnees were very much involved in Pontiac's uprising and were the principal component of the pan-Indian alliance that destroyed Josiah Harmar in 1790 and Arthur St. Clair in 1791. This same coalition, however, was badly defeated by Anthony Wayne at Fallen Timbers in 1794. As a result of the Treaty of Greenville that followed their loss at Fallen Timbers, the Shawnees lost much of their territory in what is present-day Ohio.

See also: Blue Licks, Battle of; Clark's Ohio Campaign of 1782; Clark's Ohio Campaign of 1786; Cornstalk; Fallen Timbers, Battle of; Ohio Company (of Virginia); St. Clair's Campaign; Treaties and Agreements, Greenville, Treaty of
Further Reading: Dowd, *A Spirited Resistance*; Hurt, *The Ohio Frontier*

Sheepeater War
1879

The Sheepeater War, the last of Idaho's Indian wars, began in May 1879, when Indians murdered five Chinese prospectors on Loon Creek in the Salmon River country. Shortly thereafter two white prospectors were found dead. The country in which the killings took place is extremely rugged. Speculation as to the killers tended to focus on a splinter group of Bannocks and Shoshones who lived in this country and were known as

Sheepeaters, or Weisers because they mostly lived in the Weiser Valley.

Upon learning of the killings, Gen. Oliver Otis Howard immediately ordered army detachments to pursue the killers. From Fort Boise, Capt. Reuben Bernard took the field with a company of the First Cavalry while a second column of 50 mounted infantry under Lt. Henry Catley moved out from Camp Howard near Grangeville, Idaho. The two columns were later augmented by a third detachment of some 20 Umatilla scouts.

July found the three columns converging on the area where the Indians were expected to be, and they were there. On 29 July Catley's column was ambushed on Big Creek by a small party of hostiles under War Jack. Howard, upset by Catley's defeat at the hands of an inferior force, reinforced the troops in the field with an additional 25 men under Capt. Albert Forse. Closing in on the Big Creek area, the troops skirmished occasionally with the Indians, who managed to keep the army at arm's length while retreating. One soldier was killed by Indian snipers; as it turned out, he was the only soldier to lose his life during this campaign.

The estimated 30 Indians were forced to abandon food and supplies as they fled but managed to avoid capture. As the campaign dragged on, area newspapers expressed outrage that the Indians had not been caught. While Bernard returned to Fort Boise for supplies and replacement horses, Lt. Edward Farrow and Lt. William Brown, in charge of the Indian scouts, maintained pressure on the Weisers, and by early October most of them, now tired and without provisions, surrendered.

Although the Weisers claimed they had not been involved in killing either the Chinese miners or white prospectors, as far as Howard was concerned the guilty parties had been apprehended; the campaign was officially declared at an end. Some of the Weisers were relocated to the Fort Hall Reservation, Idaho, after spending time as prisoners at Vancouver, Washington. Those who had eluded the soldiers remained in re-mote parts of the mountains and eventually developed small homesteads.

See also: Bannock War; Howard, Gen. Oliver Otis; Shoshones (Shoshonis)
Further Reading: Corless, *The Weiser Indians*

Sheridan, Gen. Philip Henry
1831–1888

The place of Philip Sheridan's birth is uncertain; it may have been Ireland or aboard the vessel that carried his parents to the United States. His own accounts vary. In any case, his family moved to Ohio, from where he received his appointment to West Point. Following graduation from West Point there in 1852, Sheridan served on the northwestern frontier for the next eight years. After the outbreak of the Civil War, he rose rapidly in rank, emerging at the close of hostilities with one of the most distinguished careers in the Union Army, ranking behind only Ulysses S. Grant and William T. Sherman.

After the war he first commanded the District of Texas and Louisiana and in 1868 was named to head up the Department of Missouri, an assignment that carried with it the responsibility for meeting Indian conflicts on the Central and Southern Plains. In 1869 Sheridan was promoted to lieutenant general and appointed to the command of the larger Military Division of the Missouri, succeeding Sherman, who became General of the Army upon Grant's election to the presidency.

In his capacity as head of the sprawling Division of the Missouri, Sheridan was responsible for most of the Trans-Mississippi region, where Indian conflicts posed an increasingly serious concern to a westward-expanding nation. It was Sheridan's directive, always with the support of Sherman and Grant, that orchestrated Custer's 1868 campaign on the Southern Plains that resulted in the destruction of Black Kettle's Cheyenne village on the Washita. And it was Sheridan who set in motion the disastrous 1876 campaign that witnessed Custer's stunning defeat on the Little Bighorn.

An energetic, exuberant officer, Sheridan was perhaps better suited to leading troops in the field than directing operations from his distant office in Chicago. Notwithstanding, he must be given credit for at least some of the army's success during his tenure as head of the Division of the Missouri, a post he held until 1883, by which time most of the western Indian conflicts had subsided. Upon Sherman's retirement in 1884, Sheridan was named General of the Army. He was promoted to full general just months before his death in 1888.

Unlike William T. Sherman, who believed Indians needed to be met firmly but fairly, Sheridan tended to be more harsh in his judgment and less sympathetic to the native plight. A difficult man at times, Sheridan made his share of enemies. Brave and aggressive almost to a fault, he was one of the celebrated U.S. military figures of the nineteenth century.

See also: Sherman, Gen. William Tecumseh; Sioux War; Washita, Battle of the
Further Reading: Morris, *The Life and Wars of Gen. Phil Sheridan*

Sherman, Gen. William Tecumseh
1820–1891

Born in Ohio, William Tecumseh Sherman graduated from West Point in 1840. After serving in the second Seminole War he was stationed in California. In 1853 he resigned from the army to pursue business interests, without much success. In 1859 he was named president of the Louisiana State Seminary of Learning and Military Academy (now Louisiana State University).

Sherman was appointed colonel upon the outbreak of the Civil War, and despite an early period during the war when he was accused by the press of mental instability, he became one of the Union Army's great leaders, second only to Ulysses S. Grant, his close friend. After the war he was promoted to lieutenant general and given command of the sprawling Military Division of the Missouri, an area of burgeoning unrest. With Grant's election to the presidency in 1869, Sherman received his fourth

star and succeeded Grant as General of the Army.

As the nation's top-ranking soldier, Sherman oversaw the army's development in the often difficult decade following the Civil War. Drastic reductions in troop strength, coupled with an increasing need to provide military protection in the reaches of the western frontier, made for a formidable challenge. Although not known as an Indian hater, Sherman was nevertheless adamant in his belief that the Trans-Mississippi West needed to be made safe for westward expansion and settlement. Sherman's philosophy was that the Indians needed to be treated firmly but fairly, an objective he worked to achieve. He was indirectly in-

Gen. William Tecumseh Sherman

volved in the important Medicine Lodge Treaty (1867) and was a member of the negotiating council at the Treaty of Fort Laramie (1868).

Often acerbic in his comments, Sherman was a brilliant if sometimes eccentric individual and one of the ablest military leaders of his time.

See also: Sheridan, Gen. Philip Henry; Sioux War

Further Reading: Athearn, *William Tecumseh Sherman and the Settlement of the West*; Marszalek, *Sherman*

Shoshone War
See Bear River, Battle of

Shoshones (Shoshonis)

Shoshones are a member of the Uto-Aztecan family and are divided into two basic divisions: the Eastern Shoshones in Wyoming's Wind River Mountains and the northern Shoshones, Bannocks, and Lemhis living at nearby Fort Hall, Idaho. Shoshones are distantly related to Comanches, from whom they probably first acquired horses in the eighteenth century. By the middle of the seventeenth century the Sioux, Cheyennes, and Blackfeet had driven the Shoshones south from the northern Plains into the northern Rockies; eventually, Shoshone activity east of the mountains was limited to buffalo-hunting excursions.

During Gen. George Crook's Big Horn and Yellowstone Expedition during the Sioux War of 1876, the command was augmented by a large contingent of Shoshones and Crows, who performed bravely in the Battle of the Rosebud on 17 June 1876.

See also: Bear River, Battle of; Indian Scouts and Auxiliaries; Rosebud, Battle of the; Sioux War
Further Reading: Madsen, *The Northern Shoshone*; Trenholm, *The Shoshonis*

Sibley, Gen. Henry Hastings
1811–1891

Born in Detroit, Henry Hastings Sibley, although a lawyer by training, became involved in fur-trade ventures early on. His experience as a frontiersman and trader led to a certain influence among the Eastern Sioux. Later a territorial delegate, he fought unsuccessfully for a new Indian policy. He served as governor of Minnesota from 1858 to 1860.

During the 1862 Minnesota Sioux uprising Sibley was appointed colonel in the state militia and commanded a column that de-

Gen. Henry Hastings Sibley

feated the Indians in the Battle of Wood Lake. Promoted to brevet brigadier general in 1863, he led an expedition into Dakota Territory in pursuit of the Sioux who had fled Minnesota after Wood Lake, defeating them in fights at Big Mound, Stoney Lake, and Dead Buffalo Lake. Although promoted to major general of volunteers in 1865, the conclusion of the 1863 campaign had marked the end of his military career. He was later appointed to a commission to negotiate treaties with the Sioux. He died at St. Paul in 1891.

Henry Hastings Sibley is sometimes confused with Henry Hopkins Sibley, a contemporary army officer to whom he was not related.

See also: Birch Coulee, Battle of; Little Crow; Minnesota Sioux Uprising; Wood Lake, Battle of
Further Reading: Carley, *The Sioux Uprising*; Jones, *The Civil War in the Northwest*; Utley, *Frontiersmen in Blue*

Sieber, Albert
1844–1907

Born in Germany, Albert Sieber emigrated to Pennsylvania as a young boy with his mother and seven siblings. The family later moved to Minnesota, where young Albert enlisted in the First Minnesota Volunteer Infantry upon the outbreak of the Civil War. He subsequently participated in several major battles, including those during the Peninsula Campaign as well as Antietam, Fredericksburg, and Gettysburg, where he was badly wounded.

After the war Sieber moved west to California for a time, then mined in Nevada and handled horses in Arizona. The Southwest, Arizona in particular, evidently appealed to Sieber; he spent the remainder of his life there. When conflicts with the Apaches surfaced he initially signed on as a mule packer, but General Crook soon recognized his skills and in a short time he was named chief of scouts, in which capacity he served throughout the Apache wars. As a scout Sieber had few peers, if any, and was highly respected by army officers, white frontiersmen, and Indians alike. On occasion, he was sent into Mexico by Crook on spy missions to learn the location of Apache bands in the Sierra Madres.

In 1887 Sieber sustained a serious leg wound that left him permanently crippled. In 1889 he was fired as a scout by Capt. John Bullis, whose reasons for doing so were unclear. It may have involved a dispute between Sieber and another man, or it may simply have been a case of bad chemistry between Sieber and Bullis. After his army days ended, Sieber worked as a prospector and at various other enterprises. He was killed by a falling boulder in 1907 while supervising Indian laborers during the construction of Roosevelt Dam.

See also: Apache Wars; Apaches; Crook, Gen. George; Geronimo
Further Reading: Thrapp, *Al Sieber;* ——, *The Conquest of Apacheria*

Sioux

One of the most recognizable of all Indian tribal names, Sioux is actually a corruption of a French word, *nadouessioux,* meaning little snakes.

The Sioux comprised three major divisions: Dakota, Nakota, and Lakota, each of which is further subdivided into smaller entities. Of the three major divisions, the Dakota (Santee) occupied territory in the Upper Midwest—parts of Minnesota, Wisconsin, and Iowa—and was the division mainly involved in the 1862 Minnesota uprising. The Nakota (Yankton and Yanktonai) lived farther west—the prairie country of western Minnesota and Iowa and the eastern portion of the Dakotas. The Lakotas (Teton Lakotas) lived on the northern Great Plains and is the branch best known to history. The consummate buffalo hunters of the Great Plains, the Lakotas battled off and on with whites for nearly a half-century.

The Teton Lakota division was composed of seven bands or council fires: Brulé, Sans Arc, Hunkpapa, Oglala, Miniconjou, Blackfeet (no relation to the Blackfoot of Montana), and Two Kettles. Crazy Horse was Oglala; Sitting Bull was Hunkpapa. A powerful confederation, the Lakotas at first only occasionally annoyed and harassed wagon trains passing over the Great Platte River Trail, but as the advance of civilization came increasingly to threaten their territory and way of life, they resisted fiercely and were the focus of military attention until the final, desperate tragedy at Wounded Knee in 1890. Unquestionably, the zenith of Sioux resistance came on 25 June 1876, when the great Indian coalition composed mainly of Sioux destroyed Lt. Col. George Armstrong Custer and nearly half of his regiment at the Battle of the Little Bighorn.

See also: Crazy Horse (Tashunca Utico, Tashunka Witko); Custer, Lt. Col. George Armstrong; Little Bighorn, Battle of the (Custer's Last Stand); Minnesota Sioux Uprising; Sioux War; Sitting Bull
Further Reading: Hassrick, *The Sioux;* Hyde, *A Sioux Chronicle;* ——, *Red Cloud's Folk*

Sioux War
1876–1877

Sometimes called the Great Sioux War, this is one of the best known of the Indian wars, primarily because its apex—the Battle of the Little Bighorn, or Custer's Last Stand—has assumed mythic status in the American experience.

The Sioux War had its roots in the Treaty of Fort Laramie, signed in 1868. One of the most significant documents of its kind, this treaty contained several important provisions, the most important of which set aside, as unceded hunting grounds, a sprawling tract bordered by the Black Hills on the east, the Big Horn Mountains on the west, the Yellowstone River on the north, and the North Platte River on the south. Additionally, the Black Hills were made off-limits to white development, and the U.S. government agreed to remove its military presence from the Bozeman Trail. In return for these concessions, the tribes agreed to reside on permanent reservations and to allow passage across the hunting grounds.

The treaty was flawed from the outset because the so-called wild bands of Teton Lakotas (the western branch of the Sioux nation) under leaders such as Sitting Bull and Crazy Horse refused to sign it or even acknowledge its provisions. As a consequence, the peace supposedly achieved through the signing of the treaty was tenuous at best, and conditions on the northern Plains were unsettled during the next eight years.

The discovery of gold in the Black Hills in 1874 led to an invasion by hordes of prospectors that the army was unable to thwart. This in turn led to retaliatory raids by Indians. When the hostile bands, as they were then referred to, failed to return to their agencies, the problem was turned over to the War Department for resolution early in 1876. Responsibility for conducting the campaign against the hostiles fell to Lt. Gen. Philip H. Sheridan, who commanded the vast Military Division of the Missouri headquartered in Chicago. Sheridan, long a believer in winter campaigns, immediately directed his senior field commanders, Brig. Gen. George Crook and Brig. Gen. Alfred H. Terry, commanding the Departments of the Platte and Dakota, respectively, to take the field as soon as possible, thereby initiating military action against the recalcitrant Sioux and their northern Cheyenne allies.

During the next 15 months the U.S. Army waged a mostly unsuccessful campaign against the hostile bands, achieving little success until the latter part of 1876 and early 1877. Despite the strong columns that were sent against them, the Indians more than held their own—and scored the resounding victory over Custer and his regiment at the Little Bighorn on 25 June 1876.

In November 1876 a column under Col. Ranald S. Mackenzie destroyed the northern Cheyenne village on the Powder River, and during the winter of 1876–1877 forces under Col. Nelson A. Miles, operating out of Cantonment Keogh on the Yellowstone River (present-day Miles City), inflicted harsh defeats on the remnants of the Sioux coalition at Wolf Mountain and Lame Deer, Montana, that brought the war to a close.

See also: Crook, Gen. George; Custer, Lt. Col. George Armstrong; Little Bighorn, Battle of the (Custer's Last Stand); Miles, Col. Nelson Appleton; Rosebud, Battle of the; Slim Buttes, Battle of; Terry, Gen. Alfred Howe; Wolf Mountains, Battle of
Further Reading: Gray, *Centennial Campaign;* Greene, *Battles and Skirmishes of the Great Sioux War*

Sitting Bull
1831 [1837?]–1890

A Hunkpapa Lakota Sioux leader, Sitting Bull is one of the most celebrated Indian leaders in American history. Tatanka-Iyotanka, literally bull sitting down, was born between 1831 and 1837 in what is now South Dakota near the Missouri River.

A warrior of repute, Sitting Bull counted his first coup at age 14 and through young manhood added to his reputation in numerous raids and encounters with traditional tribal enemies such as the Crows. By age 30 he had come to be regarded as an important leader among his band. In 1863 and 1864 he fought against Gen. Alfred Sully's troops at the Battles of Whitestone Hill and Killdeer Mountain in what may have been the first real demonstration of his opposition to white encroachment.

In the aftermath of the Treaty of Fort Laramie (1868), which he rejected and did not sign, Sitting Bull became the recognized leader of the nontreaty faction that refused to comply with its terms. From this point on, his name, together with that of Crazy Horse,

Lakota Sioux leader Sitting Bull

became more and more synonymous with the hostile bands, as they were then known.

Although his official authority was limited to his own Hunkpapa band, in reality his sphere of influence reached far beyond the pale of his immediate followers. In the Sun Dance celebration immediately preceding the Battle of the Little Bighorn, Sitting Bull claimed a vision in which he saw many soldiers falling into the Indian village upside down; the disaster that later befell Custer seemed to bear it out. After the Little Bighorn triumph Sitting Bull led his followers to the sanctuary of Canada, where they remained until 1881, when Sitting Bull agreed to return to the United States after being granted amnesty. Yet he remained adamant in his opposition to efforts designed to manipulate the Sioux into selling their land. As such, he remained a thorn in the government's side.

Sitting Bull's notoriety, however, worked to his favor. In 1885 he became a member of Buffalo Bill's Wild West Show and one of its most popular attractions. In 1888 he encouraged a burgeoning movement called the Ghost Dance to be held in his camp at Standing Rock Agency, an event that was not welcomed by government officials who feared it might lead to trouble, as indeed it would in the massacre at Wounded Knee.

In 1890 Sitting Bull was shot and killed by an Indian policeman who was attempting to arrest him. The arrest order was ostensibly issued due to the growing popularity of the Ghost Dance, which Sitting Bull continued to support. Beyond that, however, the government viewed Sitting Bull as a real impediment to their future plans for the Sioux. His death, which may or may not have been orchestrated, played an important role in the subsequent Wounded Knee tragedy.

See also: Little Bighorn, Battle of the (Custer's Last Stand); Sioux War; Wounded Knee Massacre
Further Reading: Utley, *The Lance and the Shield*

Slaughter of the Innocents
25–26 February 1643
In this infamous affair, which took place near Pavonia (present-day Jersey City, New Jersey), Dutch soldiers brutally tortured and slaughtered Wappingers—mostly women and children—who had survived an earlier massacre by their traditional Mohawk enemies.

See also: Dutch-Indian Wars; Mohawks; Wappingers
Further Reading: Jennings, *The Invasion of America;* Steele, *Warpaths*

Slim Buttes, Battle of
9 September 1876
Following the Little Bighorn disaster in June 1876, army forces in the field were reinforced, but an earnest pursuit of the hostile Indian coalition that destroyed the Custer battalion was late in getting under way. In August the forces of Gen. Alfred H. Terry and Gen. George Crook, which had earlier come together by chance, separated. Terry's column returned to the Yellowstone River and eventually disbanded. Crook's Big Horn and Yellowstone Expedition, however, continued in pursuit of the rapidly disappearing trail, which led toward the Black Hills of South Dakota.

Pushing on through rain-soaked terrain and running short of provisions, Crook's men were forced to kill their starving horses in order to survive. The episode thereafter came to be called Horsemeat March. Desperate, on 7 September Crook sent Capt. Anson Mills with 150 hand-picked men on the strongest remaining horses to procure supplies from Deadwood, 100 miles distant. En route, Mills discovered a Sioux village at Slim Buttes, an area of large rock formations on the northern edge of the Black Hills. Although a relatively small village compared to the one Custer had the misfortune of discovering, it nevertheless proved strong, and its residents inflicted a number of casualties on Mills's command when it attacked at dawn on 9 September.

The attack dispersed the villagers and caused a number of casualties, including chief American Horse. The fight would have amounted to little more than a skirmish except that by late afternoon Crazy

Horse had arrived with a party of some 200 warriors. In the meantime, however, Crook had also reached the scene with the main body of his column, and the Indian reinforcements were subsequently repulsed. Afterward, the village and its store of supplies were destroyed, thereby ending the otherwise disastrous campaign of 1876 on a somewhat positive note as far as the army was concerned.

See also: Crook, Gen. George; Sioux War
Further Reading: Finerty, *War-Path and Bivouac;* Greene, *Slim Buttes, 1876*

Smith, Capt. John
1580–1631

Like Pocahontas, the Indian woman with whom he will be forever linked, John Smith's niche in history is secure. Born in Willoughby, Lincolnshire, England, John Smith was already a well-traveled soldier and adventurer by the time he arrived in the New World. He had previously soldiered in the Low Countries and fought the Turks in Transylvania, where he was taken prisoner. Escaping, he returned to England and joined the Virginia Company as one of the original Jamestown colonists.

Bold, aggressive, and determined, he served a term as president of the Jamestown colony in 1608, though he much preferred leading expeditions into the interior, dealing with Indians and bargaining for food, especially seed corn, a crop they grew in abundance. Smith's tough brand of leadership stood the colony in good stead during the early days. (For example, while negotiating for a supply of corn with Opechancanough, half-brother of Powhatan, Smith sensed a threat from the leader's followers. Seizing the initiative, he leveled a pistol at Opechancanough's head and held him prisoner until a ransom of corn was paid.)

Smith is best remembered for allegedly being rescued from a cruel death through the intercession of Pocahontas, daughter of Powhatan. His *Generall Historie* of Virginia, published in 1624, provided much information about early Virginia.

See also: Jamestown, Virginia; Opechancanough; Pocahontas (Matawaka, Matoaka); Powhatan; Powhatan Confederacy
Further Reading: Hodge, *Handbook of American Indians;* Rountree, *The Powhatan Indians*

Snake War
1866–1868

In 1866 Yahuskin and Walpapi bands of the northern Paiutes, called Snakes, who lived in southeastern Oregon and southwestern Idaho, raided mines in the area. In response, Gen. George Crook, a Civil War veteran, was sent out to prosecute a campaign against the raiders. The campaign would prove to be one of the longest on record.

With the First Cavalry and the newly reorganized Twenty-Third Infantry, together with a detachment of Shoshone scouts and using trains of pack mules (as he would throughout his Indian-fighting career), Crook doggedly pursued the raiders over the next two years, clashing nearly 50 times. In the end the Indians had lost a reported 329 killed. Recognizing the futility of continued resistance given such losses, the Snakes came to terms with Crook in July 1868 and returned to their reservations.

See also: Crook, Gen. George
Further Reading: Corless, *The Weiser Indians;* Crook, *General George Crook: His Autobiography;* Glassley, *Pacific Northwest Indian Wars*

Solomon's Fork, Battle of
See Cheyenne Campaign

Soto, Hernando de
1500–1542

Hernando de Soto was a Spanish hidalgo who made a fortune while serving as military adviser to Pizarro in Peru. Intrigued by de Vaca's tales and armed with a grant from Charles V, de Soto personally financed a large expedition and set sail for La Florida in 1538, anticipating a repeat of the success he had enjoyed in South America.

Following a sojourn in Cuba that lasted nearly a year, de Soto landed near what is

Hernando de Soto's men committing atrocities against Florida Indians

present-day Fort Myers in May 1539 with an expedition that numbered nearly 600 men and more than 200 horses. De Soto was lucky at the outset by the chance meeting of a Spaniard named Ortiz, sole survivor of a ship that had come searching for the missing Pánfilo de Narváez, whose expedition had passed through more than a decade earlier. Ortiz, it seems, had survived by helping the local Indians and gaining their confidence. His services as guide and interpreter proved an invaluable asset to the expedition. Unfortunately, he would not survive the rigors of the journey that lay ahead.

The de Soto expedition is regarded by some as the most ambitious of the early Spanish efforts to explore that part of the New World. Like Coronado and his conquistadores, who were far-western counterparts, de Soto and his men had also heard tales about places of great wealth (namely, Chisca or Kuska), which drew them ever farther into the interior of this new land, through land comprising present-day Georgia, the Carolinas, Tennessee, and Alabama.

As with other Spanish expeditions, treatment of native inhabitants was harsh and often brutal. De Soto's strategy was to capture the chief or head of each Indian village through which they passed. The captive would then be ransomed to ensure that Spanish demands for food, women, and slaves were met. If the demands were satisfied, the captive would be released when the expedition approached the next village, where the process was repeated.

In one instance, however, the strategy had unexpected repercussions when the captive, a Choctaw chief named Taskaloosa (Tuscaloosa) orchestrated an offensive in response, which at first sent the Spanish reeling. In the ensuing fight, known as the Battle of Mabila (near present-day Selma, Alabama), de Soto's troops eventually regained the initiative, inflicting an estimated 2,500 Indian casualties. Following the Battle of Mabila, de Soto headed northwest, where his winter encampment was attacked and burned by Chickasaws in 1541. The following spring, 1542, the expedition moved west across the Mississippi, where de Soto died of illness. The survivors of the nearly four-year-old expedition were finally driven out of the New World by Indians from the kingdom of Quigualtam.

See also: Mabila (Mobile), Battle of; Spain
Further Reading: Morison, *The European Discovery of North America: The Southern Voyages;* Steele, *Warpaths*

Spain

Spain was the first of the European powers to reach the New World and remained a dominant force for more than a century after the arrival of Columbus. The first of the Spanish arrivals in the New World were primarily Castilian with a threefold mission: God, Spain, and gold, not always necessarily in that order. Theirs was a heritage of conquest or, more correctly, reconquest, the preceding seven centuries having been spent driving the Moors out of Spain. Their goals, particularly the acquisition of personal wealth and glory, were deemed ample justification for subjugating the native inhabitants of the new land, often in brutal fashion not at all in keeping with the directives of the Spanish Crown. But in the far-flung reaches of the New World frontier, it was the hidalgo on the spot who ruled. With few exceptions, this oppressive treatment of native peoples established a pattern of mistrust and hatred that would be passed on to subsequent generations, notwithstanding the sometimes well-intentioned directives of the Spanish monarch.

Spanish conflict with natives in the Americas commenced almost immediately, when the fortified camp of Villa de la Navidad (Town of the Nativity), erected by Columbus on Hispaniola prior to his return to Spain in 1493, was attacked and destroyed by natives of the area in retaliation for brutal treatment. With minor variations, it was a scenario that would repeat in the years to follow.

The success of Pizarro in South America and of Cortés in Mexico led the Spanish to believe that even greater wealth awaited them in the lands to the north. Accordingly, between 1513 and 1563 a dozen expeditions of varying sizes landed along the southeastern and Gulf Coast areas of what is today the United States. Mostly these efforts were directed to La Florida (flowery Easter), named by Juan Ponce de León, who discovered the area on Easter Sunday in 1513. Several other expeditions, however, ranged as far north as Georgia and the Carolinas.

Notwithstanding the presence of women, children, and slave labor and a retinue of friars and priests, these expeditions were decidedly military in character. Typically, they consisted of mounted lancers, armed with both lances and swords, supported by infantry, equipped with pikes, crossbows, and harquebuses (an early matchlock shoulder weapon). In addition, large, vicious dogs of war sometimes accompanied the columns. The expeditions were usually financed and led by a Spanish hidalgo (nobleman). The object of the expedition was to make an armed entrance, or *entrada,* into the interior of the country and create a fortified base camp, called a *presidio,* from which to carry out the mission.

Most of these expeditions clashed with the natives they encountered; in some instances resistance from the latter was fierce and, in view of Spanish behavior, completely understandable. Native villages were plundered, women raped, and people taken into slavery. A favorite Spanish tactic was to lure the chief or village head into a council setting then hold him hostage to ensure that the expedition's needs were met. In one instance, expedition leader Pánfilo de Narváez ordered the nose of a Timucua chief to be cut off, then ordered the chief's

Spaniards battling Indians in California

mother thrown to savage dogs to be torn apart.

Major confrontations between the Spanish conquistadores and natives include fights around San Carlos Bay, Florida, by Francisco de Córdoba in 1517 and Ponce de León in 1521. Hernando de Soto's 1541 clash with Choctaws in the Battle of Mabila (near what is present-day Selma, Alabama) was probably the largest single engagement of the period. Interestingly, de Córdoba, Ponce de León, and de Soto eventually died from wounds sustained during their fights with natives.

Another expedition that had its share of fighting was that of hidalgo Pánfilo de Narváez. Landing on the west coast of Florida in 1527, Narváez, after sending his ships in search of a better harbor, headed overland. After first fighting Timucuas, they clashed with Apalachees. Continuing on, the

hard-pressed and exhausted column was constantly harried by Indians. After discovering that their ships were not waiting at the expected place (the ships had been there and, believing the expedition lost, departed for Mexico), they finally reached Mobile Bay and crossed the Mississippi River. Of the 300 who began the ordeal, only four would survive to finally reach Mexico: Cabeza de Vaca, Alonso del Castillo, Andrés Dorantes, and his black slave, Esteban. The saga of their incredible ordeal, later recounted in de Vaca's journal, became one of the epics of history.

Spanish efforts were not limited to the Southeast. In April 1540 Francisco Vasquez de Coronado set out from Compostela in search of the fabled Seven Cities of Cibola. In large part, Coronado's expedition was inspired by de Vaca's reports. During the two-year expedition, Coronado failed to find the rumored golden cities but did explore much of what is now the U.S. Southwest, penetrating as far east as Kansas. In the process, Coronado managed to capture the Zuni pueblo at Hawikuh as well as other Hopi and Zuni pueblo communities in Arizona and New Mexico. Later Spanish expeditions in the Southwest resulted in Oñate's brutal attack on Acoma pueblo in 1599, followed by the bloody Pueblo revolts of the seventeenth century.

During the last half of the sixteenth century the Spanish continued to send expeditions into the interior of La Florida in an effort to strengthen their position there. As earlier, ill treatment of native peoples, particularly in the form of forced labor, continued to produce clashes between the two cultures, although an increased emphasis on the establishment of missions met with some success. Perhaps the most notable Spanish achievement in the area was the creation of San Augustín (St. Augustine). Spanish presence in La Florida continued until 1763, when the territory was given over to England in exchange for Cuba.

Although the Spanish legacy in the New World is one of harsh treatment and exploitation, its contribution to architecture, the arts, and language should not be overlooked.

See also: Apaches; Ponce de León, Juan; Pueblo Indians; Pueblo Revolt of 1680; Soto, Hernando de
Further Reading: Forbes, *Apache, Navajo, and Spaniard;* Kessell, *Kiva, Cross, and Crown;* Morison, *The European Discovery of North America,* vols. 1 and 2; Steele, *Warpaths*

Spirit Lake Massacre
8–9 March 1857

In 1857 a renegade Wahpekute Sioux named Inkpaduta (Scarlet Point), who had refused to acknowledge the Treaty of Traverse des Sioux (1851), led a group of 14 followers in massacring some 35 to 40 white settlers at Spirit Lake in northwestern Iowa, not far from the Minnesota border. Although perpetrated by outlaws, the Spirit Lake Massacre foreshadowed the bloody uprising in south-

eastern Minnesota five years later. It also proved to be the last incident of Indian-white warfare in Iowa.

See also: Minnesota Sioux Uprising
Further Reading: Carley, *Sioux Uprising of 1862;* Meyer, *History of the Santee Sioux;* Sharp, *History of the Spirit Lake Massacre*

St. Clair, Arthur
1736–1818

Born in Scotland, Arthur St. Clair (pronounced Sinclair) became an ensign in the British army at age 21 serving under Gen. Jeffrey Amherst during the French and Indian War. By the time of the Revolution, St. Clair was a wealthy landowner, largely by virtue of marriage. He allied himself with the Continental cause and was appointed a general officer in 1776. Through the course of the war he served well if not spectacularly. He resigned his commission at the end of the war.

In October 1786 he was appointed governor of the Northwest Territory and was, simultaneously, Superintendent of Indian Affairs. In this latter capacity he negotiated treaties with several tribes, most of which were largely ineffective due to the unremitting advance of settlers into the Ohio country.

In March 1791 he returned to the military, having been appointed major general and charged with breaking the Indians' military power in the Ohio country by establishing a series of outposts. After considerable delay, his expedition finally set forth in early August 1791, advancing west from Fort Washington (Cincinnati). After the force constructed two posts en route, his camp was suddenly struck by a large Indian war party led by Little Turtle and Blue Jacket. The unprepared and poorly defended camp was quickly overrun. St. Clair and others managed to fight their way out, leaving in their wake the U.S. Army's worst disaster in the Indian wars.

St. Clair was exonerated by a congressional committee but resigned his commission the following March. However, he remained active in political life in the Old Northwest until his retirement. A wealthy colonial landowner at one time, he died in poverty.

See also: St. Clair's Campaign
Further Reading: Hurt, *The Ohio Frontier;* Prucha, *Sword of the Republic;* Sword, *President Washington's Indian War*

St. Clair's Campaign
1791

In March 1791 Arthur St. Clair (pronounced Sinclair), governor of the Northwest Territory, was directed to establish a strong military presence in Miami and Shawnee country by building a series of outposts from which Indian activity could be monitored and controlled and the area made safe for settlement.

St. Clair, a general officer during the Revolutionary War but a politician since that time, reverted to his former rank. The mandate under which General St. Clair was to operate also stipulated that Secretary of War Henry Knox would supply ample troops to carry out the assignment. St. Clair officially assumed command of his expedition at Fort Washington (Cincinnati) in May. From the outset things did not bode well for the forthcoming campaign. The additional troops did not arrive, and those on hand were poorly supplied as well as undisciplined.

Most of the summer was lost waiting for reinforcements and supplies and trying to effect a dependable military structure. Accordingly, it was not until early August that the 2,300-man expedition finally got under way; St. Clair had anticipated that 3,000 men would be made available to him. About 200 women and children—wives, laundresses, cooks, and camp followers—accompanied the column.

Progress was slow. By mid-September St. Clair had reached the Miami River, where construction began on Fort Hamilton, the first in the planned series of outposts. The work there consumed a month, so that it was not until 5 October that the expedition resumed its march. En route, the column was reinforced by some 300 Kentucky militia, and to this happy event was added a continuation of glorious autumn weather, although early-morning frosts signaled what lay ahead.

In mid-October St. Clair paused again, some 50 miles beyond Fort Hamilton to build Fort Jefferson, the second outpost. At this juncture St. Clair was in critical need of supplies. A wagon train was reportedly on the way, but some of St. Clair's disaffected militia units, tired and hungry, were pulling out for home and threatening to help themselves to the supply train along the way. Unable to risk the loss of even part of those supplies, St. Clair detached some of his more reliable units to provide an escort for the wagons.

On 3 November a tired, hungry, and dispirited expedition (the supply wagons had not caught up) reached the banks of the Wabash River. To make matters worse, the fine fall weather had finally turned colder, with rain and snow making for miserable conditions. Believing Indians were not in the immediate area and that they would not dare attack so large a force, St. Clair allowed the expedition to bivouac without benefit of a defensive perimeter. The Indians, however, were much closer than St. Clair realized. Scouting parties, which included a rising young warrior named Tecumseh, had been monitoring the column's movements for some time, and St. Clair would soon pay for his lack of caution.

At dawn on 4 November a powerful force of Wyandots, Iroquois, Shawnees, Miami, Delawares, Ojibwas, and Potawatomis, led by Little Turtle, Blue Jacket, and the renegade Simon Girty, fell upon the unsuspecting expedition. The Kentucky militiamen, who had crossed the river, were driven back headlong into the main camp, where chaos came quickly. St. Clair's artillery managed to slow the Indians but only momentarily, as their aim was poor; the Indians soon had the camp enveloped.

Disoriented, the soldiers panicked. Order was nonexistent. St. Clair, who was

Arthur St. Clair battling Indians near Fort Wayne, Ohio, 4 November 1791

in great physical discomfort with the gout, was nearly killed and had two horses shot from under him. He and other survivors finally managed to break through the Indian lines. The Indians, more interested in looting the abandoned camp and mutilating the dead and dying, did not pursue with any real vigor. In the bivouac area, dead and wounded were everywhere. Many were scalped, including all but three of the 200 women and children. By midmorning the survivors had managed to reach Fort Jefferson, some 29 miles distant. However, with no supplies available there, the survivors had to push on to Fort Washington, 79 miles away, which they reached in three days.

The crushing and stunning defeat was the army's worst in all of the Indian wars: 623 killed and 258 wounded—in addition to the nearly 200 women and children. In fact, no battle of the recently concluded Revolutionary War had produced as many casual-

ties. Although a congressional investigation later cleared St. Clair, he would live with the stigma of this defeat for the remainder of his life.

See also: Fallen Timbers, Battle of; Girty, Simon; Little Turtle (Me-she-kin-no-quah); St. Clair, Arthur; Wayne, Gen. Anthony (Mad Anthony)
Further Reading: Hurt, *The Ohio Frontier;* Sword, *President Washington's Indian War*

Staked Plains
See Llano Estacado (Staked Plains)

Standing Rock Reservation, North Dakota and South Dakota

Comprising some 1.8 million acres, Standing Rock was originally part of the Great Sioux Reservation, established by the Treaty of Fort Laramie, signed 29 April 1868. The reservation is home to several bands of the

Sioux nation, including the Blackfeet (no relation to the Blackfoot of Montana), the Hunkpapa, and the Lower and Upper Yanktonai. Standing Rock was the last home of Sitting Bull, who was killed there in 1890 by Indian police who were attempting to arrest him.

See also: Ghost Dance; Sitting Bull
Further Reading: Utley, *The Indian Frontier of the American West*

Steptoe, Col. Edward Jenner
ca. 1816–1865

Born in Virginia, Edward Jenner Steptoe graduated from West Point in 1837. His first assignment was in Florida against the Seminoles, followed by duty in the removal of Cherokees to the Indian Territory. After seeing considerable action in the Mexican War, he returned to Florida for more service against the Seminoles until he was transferred to the Pacific Northwest in the early 1850s, where he completed his military service. He saw considerable action during the 1850s and early 1860s.

The low point of his career occurred during the Spokane Expedition of 1858, when he was soundly defeated by a large force of Spokanes, Coeur d'Alenes, and Palouses, sustaining heavy casualties in what came to be known as the Steptoe Disaster. The colonel has been criticized for failing to undertake the expedition with a greater sense of appreciation for the strength that later overwhelmed him. Steptoe resigned from the army in 1861 due to ill health and died in 1865.

See also: Rogue River War; Seminole War, First; Seminole War, Second; Seminole War, Third
Further Reading: Burns, *The Jesuits and the Indian Wars;* Utley, *Frontiersmen in Blue*

Stevens, Gov. Isaac Ingalls
1818–1862

Born in Massachusetts, Isaac Ingalls Stevens graduated from West Point in 1839. After service in the Mexican War, where he won three brevets for gallantry,

Isaac Ingalls Stevens

he resigned his commission to enter the world of business and politics. After organizing a railroad survey from Minnesota to the Pacific Coast, he was appointed governor of the Washington Territory, serving in that capacity from 1853 to 1857. Like Gov. Arthur St. Clair before him, he simultaneously served as Superintendent of Indian Affairs.

Ambitious and aggressive, Stevens negotiated a number of treaties with tribes in the Northwest. Several were responsible or a key factor in later Indian wars, especially those with the Nez Perce and Yakimas. His twin tenure produced a conflict of interest, and thus his term as governor is regarded as controversial; his accomplishments have been lauded by some, however. Upon the outbreak of the Civil War Stevens returned to the military and was appointed a brigadier general of volunteers. He was killed in a battle at Chantilly, Virginia, in 1862.

See also: Nez Perce War; St. Clair, Arthur; Yakima-Rogue War
Further Reading: Corless, *The Weiser Indians;* Hampton, *Children of Grace;* Utley, *Frontiersmen in Blue*

Stillman's Run, Battle of
12 May 1832

In May 1832 an expedition under Gen. Samuel Whiteside, in pursuit of the Sauk chief Black Hawk, halted at Dixon's Ferry to await the arrival of fresh supplies. Black Hawk was known to be close, some 30 miles ahead, and so Maj. Isaiah Stillman was given permission to scout with a force of 275 Illinois militia. Meanwhile, amid a festive celebration, Black Hawk was told of the approach of a large body of horsemen. Uncertain as to the intent of the mounted men, Black Hawk dispatched three of his warriors under a flag of truce to find out what it was. Shortly after sending the trio, he sent a party of five scouts to observe developments.

The three emissaries had barely reached Stillman's camp when the trailing scouts were spotted. Treachery was immediately suspected. One of the panicky militiamen fired and others followed. Two of the emissaries were killed, but the third, along with the five scouts, fled back to camp. Angry, Black Hawk assembled a small party and headed toward Stillman's camp. Upon seeing the soldiers advancing, Black Hawk hid his warriors. At the right moment, he ordered a charge that promptly threw the untrained militia into confusion. Panicked, they fled to Dixon's Ferry and Whiteside's main body.

Stillman's casualties amounted to 11 killed, but the behavior of untrained militia demonstrated how undependable hastily formed groups of citizen soldiers could be in a crisis. Stillman's Run, as the incident came to be known, together with the Indian Creek Massacre, left the northern Illinois and southern Wisconsin frontiers in a state of near-panic.

See also: Black Hawk; Black Hawk War
Further Reading: Jackson, *Black Hawk;* Prucha, *Sword of the Republic*

Stuyvesant, Peter
1610–1672

Director-general of New Netherlands from 1647 to 1664, one-legged Peter Stuyvesant demonstrated little compassion for the indigenous tribes that dared resist his harsh, often brutal treatment. In so doing he continued the pattern established by his predecessor, Willem Kieft. Perhaps the most deplorable act of Stuyvesant's administration was his decision to sell captured Esopus children into West Indian slavery when the tribe refused to yield to his demands. His proved to be the last Dutch administration in the New World after New Amsterdam was surprised and captured by the English in 1664.

See also: Dutch; Dutch-Indian Wars
Further Reading: Jennings, *The Invasion of America;* Steele, *Warpaths*

Sully, Gen. Alfred
1821–1879

Born in Philadelphia, Alfred Sully graduated from West Point in 1841. He served in the Seminole and Mexican Wars, after which he saw action in the Pacific Northwest against Rogue Indians. From 1860 to 1861 he served on the Great Plains against the Cheyennes. Following Civil War service in the Battles of Antietam, Fredericksburg, and Chancellorsville, he was transferred to the Dakota Territory.

In 1863 and 1864 he conducted campaigns against Sioux, who had been involved in the 1862 Minnesota uprising, defeating them in the Battles of Whitestone Hill (3–5 September 1863) and Killdeer Mountain (28 July 1864). In 1868 he was transferred to the Southern Plains and led an expedition into the Indian Territory against the Cheyennes. Later in the campaign, he was replaced by George Armstrong Custer, who outranked him in the brevet grade of major general.

In 1873 Sully returned to the Northwest, where he was again involved in several Indian campaigns before his death in Vancouver in 1879. A difficult man to get along with, Sully was nevertheless a good soldier with a creditable record.

See also: Killdeer Mountain, Battle of; Minnesota Sioux Uprising; Sibley, Gen. Henry Hastings; Whitestone Hill, Battle of
Further Reading: Sully, *No Tears for the General*

Sully-Sibley Campaigns
1863–1864

Many of the Sioux who had participated in the Minnesota uprising during the summer of 1862 fled west to Dakota to avoid capture by military forces who had gained the upper hand by fall. Concerned that these Indians might again pose a threat to Minnesota settlements, Gen. John Pope, commanding the Department of the Northwest, decided to seize the initiative by sending troops into the Dakota Territory to find and punish these bands.

Accordingly, two columns were ordered to take the field. One, under newly promoted Brig. Gen. Henry Hastings Sibley, commanding the District of Minnesota, was to march northwest to Devil's Lake, North Dakota, with a column composed mainly of infantry. The second and larger of the columns was headed up by Brig. Gen. Alfred Sully, recently arrived from the eastern theater of the Civil War. Sully was directed to march north from Fort Randall, near present-day Pickstown, up the Missouri River valley to a rendezvous with Sibley at Devil's Lake. The idea was to catch the Indians between the two columns, a favorite tactic often used by the army during the Indian wars.

Sibley's column left Camp Pope, near Redwood Falls, Minnesota, on 16 June 1863. Numbering 3,000 men, with a large wagon train, the column stretched out nearly 5 miles. Sibley reached Devil's Lake about mid-July. After establishing a base camp, he took two-thirds of his command and headed off in pursuit of a large band reportedly moving toward the Missouri River in search of buffalo.

On 24 July, Sibley found and engaged a band of some 1,500 Sioux at Big Mound, near Bismarck. The fight lasted most of a day before the Indians finally broke off and headed west. Sibley pursued and fought them again at Dead Buffalo Lake and Stony Lake, near present-day Driscoll, on 26 and 28 July. On 29 July Sibley reached the Missouri near the present-day site of Bismarck. There was no sign of Sully, and as supplies began to run low Sibley elected to return to Minnesota, reaching Fort Snelling on 13 September.

Sully, with a command numbering about 2,000, had been delayed in getting under way with his campaign and did not reach the vicinity of Bismarck until the end of August, when he learned Sibley had returned to Minnesota. Advised that Sioux hunting parties were near the James River, Sully turned southeast in pursuit and on 3 September found and attacked a large body of Sioux at Whitestone Hill, near present-day Ellendale, North Dakota.

The Indian encampment, which turned out to be larger than Sully had anticipated, may have contained as many as 1,000 warriors. As Sully advanced in the waning daylight, the camp attempted to disperse. Sully's troops attempted to encircle the Indians, but in the darkness and confusion most of the Sioux managed to escape, though many were killed before the fighting finally ended. Sully's losses amounted to 20 killed and 38 wounded; Indian casualties were estimated at 150 to 200. After the fight Sully's detachments scoured the countryside, destroying any Indian equipage they could find. Some small bands of Sioux were also rounded up in the process, after which Sully returned to Fort Randall.

Both Sibley and Sully had scored decisive victories. The Sioux, however, were soon back across the Missouri River, resulting in a second campaign the following year. In June 1864 Sully again marched up the Missouri River with a force of 2,000 men. After establishing Fort Rice on the west bank south of present-day Bismarck, he turned his column west and in late July attacked a large Sioux contingent at Killdeer Mountain near present-day Waterford City. In a hard, day-long fight the Indians were finally driven back with heavy losses, reportedly 150 as compared to five for Sully.

After the fight Sully continued west as far as the Yellowstone River without encountering further signs of Indians. Satisfied that his campaign had been a success, Sully turned about and headed east, reaching Fort Ridgely, Minnesota, by early October. The campaigns of 1863 and 1864 were successful, not only in terms of the battles fought and won but also in providing assurance that the Minnesota settlements were now secure and had little to fear from Indian uprisings.

See also: Killdeer Mountain, Battle of; Minnesota Sioux Uprising; Pope, Gen. John; Sibley, Gen. Henry Hastings; Sully, Gen. Alfred; Whitestone Hill, Battle of
Further Reading: Carley, *The Sioux Uprising;* Jacobson, *Whitestone Hill;* Josephy, *The Civil War in the American West;* Sully, *No Tears for the General*

Summit Springs, Battle of
11 July 1869

In the aftermath of the celebrated Beecher Island fight, efforts to subjugate Indian bands on the Central Plains continued. In June 1869 the Republican River Expedition under Col. Eugene A. Carr, consisting of 500 men of the Fifth Cavalry, together with the famous Pawnee Scouts led by Maj. Frank North, marched out of Fort McPherson, Nebraska (near present-day North Platte). Also accompanying the expedition as chief scout was Buffalo Bill Cody.

Near the old Beecher Island battlefield (near present-day Wray, Colorado), Carr's scouts picked up the trail of Tall Bull's band of Cheyenne Dog Soldiers, who were in company with a few Sioux and Arapahos. The band included two white women captives. The Indians, intending to cross the South Platte River and head north into Sioux country, had camped near a place called Summit Springs (near present-day Sterling, Colorado) while waiting for the river to subside.

Meanwhile, undiscovered by the Indians, Carr, with roughly half of his command (some 300 men, including Buffalo Bill) attacked the unsuspecting village on the morning of 11 July, killing a reported 50 and wounding a number of others. Among the dead was Tall Bull himself. Some accounts have Buffalo Bill killing the Cheyenne leader, others have Frank North. One of the captive white women, Susanna Alderdice, was killed in the attack; the second captive,

Maria Weichell, was seriously wounded but survived. The Battle of Summit Springs eliminated the feared Dog Soldiers as a serious military threat on the Central and Southern Plains.

See also: Carr, Gen. Eugene Asa; Cody, William Frederick (Buffalo Bill); Dog Soldiers
Further Reading: Danker, *Man of the Plains;* Grinnell, *Fighting Cheyennes;* J. King, *War Eagle;* Price, *Across the Continent with the Fifth Cavalry;* Russell, *Buffalo Bill*

Susquehannock War
1675–1676

Following a brief war against the Susquehannocks in 1643, Maryland established peace with the tribe. During the so-called Beaver Wars the Susquehannocks and others aligned against the Iroquois Confederacy and welcomed peace with the Marylanders, now regarded as allies. The arrangement deteriorated in 1675, however, when Maryland, hungry for additional land, betrayed the Susquehannocks by making a pact with the Senecas. The net result was the brief Susquehannock War.

See also: Susquehannocks (Susquehannas)
Further Reading: Steele, *Warpaths*

Susquehannocks (Susquehannas)

A tribe of Iroquoian stock, the Susquehannocks were a people of large stature. Capt. John Smith referred to them as giants. They were at one time the principal supplier of pelts to Dutch, English, and Swedish traders along the Delaware and Chesapeake Rivers. Although a powerful, warlike tribe, the Susquehannocks were unable to compete against the mighty Iroquois Confederacy, which continued to raid south, involving the Susquehannocks in hostilities against other tribes in their area and against English settlements in Maryland and Virginia, especially during the period of Bacon's Rebellion.

In 1675 the Susquehannocks were finally defeated by the Iroquois Confederacy. Some were absorbed by the Iroquois; others remained in Pennsylvania, adopting the name Conestoga.

See also: Bacon's Rebellion; Iroquois Confederacy; Smith, Capt. John
Further Reading: Hodge, *Handbook of American Indians;* Jennings, *The Invasion of America;* Steele, *Warpaths*

Sweden

In terms of its impact on indigenous peoples, Sweden was the least influential of the European powers in North America, establishing Fort Christina (Wilmington) on the Delaware River in 1637. New Sweden provided arms to the Susquehannocks during the short-lived Maryland war with that tribe. Swedish presence in North America was largely supplanted by the Dutch and English during the last quarter of the seventeenth century.

See also: Susquehannock War
Further Reading: Wright, *Cultural Life of the American Colonies*

T

Tahkahokuty Mountain, Battle of

See Killdeer Mountain, Battle of

Tall Bull

ca. 1830–1869

A chief of the Southern Cheyenne Dog Soldiers, Tall Bull was one of the most militant Cheyenne leaders. Like many others of his tribe he was stirred to action by the attack on Black Kettle's village at Sand Creek, Colorado, in November 1864; he took part in the two raids on Julesburg in January and February 1865.

Although a signator of the Treaty of Medicine Lodge (1867), Tall Bull almost certainly had only the vaguest notion of what the treaty stipulated, namely, Indian removal to a reservation, and so he continued to lead raids across the Central Plains. Along with Roman Nose and other notable war chiefs, he was at Beecher Island in September 1868.

In July 1869 Tall Bull's camp was surprised at Summit Springs, Colorado, near present-day Sterling, by a detachment of the Fifth Cavalry under Col. Eugene A. Carr. In the ensuing fight Tall Bull was killed and his village essentially destroyed, as was the fearsome military threat posed by his Dog Soldiers.

See also: Carr, Col. Eugene Asa; Cody, William Frederick (Buffalo Bill); Julesburg, Battles of; Summit Springs, Battle of; Treaties and Agreements, Medicine Lodge, Treaty of
Further Reading: Grinnell, *Fighting Cheyennes;* J. King, *War Eagle*

Tecumseh

ca. 1768–1813

A legendary Shawnee Indian leader, Tecumseh (Tekamthi) was born in what is now Ohio. His father, a Shawnee chief, was killed in the Battle of Point Pleasant in 1774. Tecumseh's brother, Tenskwatawa, later known as Prophet, was to play an important role in Tecumseh's future efforts to create a pan-Indian union.

Tecumseh distinguished himself as a warrior at an early age. However, unlike most Indians of his day, he steadfastly opposed torture of captives, a custom widely practiced by both Indians and whites on the frontier of that era. At an early age Tecumseh became imbued with the mission of unifying all Indians in resisting white encroachment. He accepted British support because the British seemed to pose a lesser threat to the Indian way of life than did expansionist American colonists.

In 1811, while Tecumseh was in the South soliciting the support of the Creeks, Tenskwatawa let himself be drawn into battle with the forces of Gen. William Henry Harrison, despite Tecumseh's strict admonition to avoid such an encounter. The resulting Battle of Tippecanoe was a major defeat for the Indians. During the War of 1812 Tecumseh and his followers fought with the British in a number of engagements. Tecumseh himself was killed in the Battle of the Thames, Ontario, on 5 October 1813.

Tecumseh was one of the most powerful and influential Indian leaders in American history.

See also: Harrison, William Henry; Tippecanoe, Battle of
Further Reading: Eckert, *A Sorrow in Our Heart;* Gilbert, *God Gave Us This Country;* Thom, *Panther in the Sky*

Tenskwatawa (Prophet)

ca. 1768–ca. 1836

A Shawnee mystic and brother of Tecumseh, Tenskwatawa was the first of two influ-

Tecumseh saving prisoners during the Northwest Indian War

ential Indians to be called Prophet (Wabokieshiek of the Sauks and Foxes was the other). Tenskwatawa became a self-made prophet in 1805 when he foretold an eclipse that occurred the following year. The prediction firmly established his powers, and he was thereafter known as Prophet. Tenskwatawa's teachings, which promoted a return to the pure Indian way of life with no white contact, were essentially the same as those of Tecumseh; the brothers worked in concert.

In 1811, despite Tecumseh's warning not to battle the white man while he (Tecumseh) was in the South seeking support for the united Indian movement, Tenskwatawa was drawn into battle at Tippecanoe by Gen. William Henry Harrison. Although the battle was not decisive in any tactical sense, the Indians suffered heavy casualties despite Tenskwatawa's pledge that his medicine would protect them. As a result, his credibility suffered a mortal blow. More importantly, the

Battle of Tippecanoe ended Tecumseh's dream of a pan-Indian confederation.

Tenskwatawa later moved to Canada, where he lived until 1826, when he returned to the United States. Unlike his brother, he did not participate in the War of 1812.

See also: Harrison, William Henry; Tecumseh; Tippecanoe, Battle of; Wabokieshiek (Prophet)
Further Reading: Dowd, *A Spirited Resistance;* Eckert, *A Sorrow in Our Heart;* Hurt, *The Ohio Frontier;* Thom, *Panther in the Sky*

Terry, Gen. Alfred Howe
1827–1890

Born in Connecticut, Alfred Howe Terry was commissioned colonel of volunteers upon the outbreak of the Civil War; by war's end he had risen to the rank of major general of volunteers. The high point of his Civil War career was the capture of Fort Fisher. Following the Civil War Terry was appointed brigadier general in the regular army and commanded the Department of Dakota, with headquarters in St. Paul, Minnesota, from 1866 to 1868 and again from 1873 to 1886.

When Lt. Col. George Armstrong Custer was relieved of command of the Dakota Column during the Sioux War of 1876 for injudicious remarks concerning Pres. Ulysses S. Grant's brother, it fell to General Terry, as department commander, to name Custer's replacement. However, at Terry's intercession Grant relented, and so Custer was allowed to participate, but only as commander of a regiment, not the column. Thus, intellectual Alfred Terry, a lawyer by profession, became involved in one of American history's most infamous incidents.

Highly regarded and respected by officers and men with whom he served, Terry was promoted to major general in the regular army in 1886 and named commander of the Military Division of the Missouri. Following retirement Terry returned to New Haven, where he died in 1890.

See also: Custer, Lt. Col. George Armstrong; Little Bighorn, Battle of the (Custer's Last Stand); Sioux War
Further Reading: Darling, *A Sad and Terrible Blunder*

Thayendanega
See Brant, Joseph (Thayendanega)

Tippecanoe, Battle of
7 November 1811

Unhappy with the Treaty of Fort Wayne, dissident Indians of the upper Wabash Valley, notably Tecumseh, argued that the treaty was invalid because it had been signed only by the so-called annuity chiefs, who did not speak for all the Indians. William Henry Harrison, governor of the Indiana Territory, feared that the mood of the Indians would eventually lead to conflict. Although it was

The American flag can be seen flying as Gov. William Henry Harrison leads his troops against the Indians of the upper Wabash Valley during the Battle of Tippecanoe.

Pres. James Madison's wish to avoid a full-blown frontier war, he authorized Harrison to employ force—but only if necessary. In a liberal interpretation of that directive, Harrison decided to seize the initiative at the right time.

The opportunity came when Harrison learned that Tecumseh would be absent from the area while seeking support among southern tribes for his pan-Indian union. Assembling a force of 1,000 regulars and militia, Harrison moved against the Shawnee village known as Prophet's Town, near what is present-day Lafayette, Indiana. With Tecumseh absent the village was headed by his brother, Tenskwatawa, known as Prophet, a quasimystic who lived in his brother's shadow. Although it was Tecumseh's wish that conflict be avoided, some of the other chiefs in the village persuaded Prophet to attack the American "long knives," who were then nearing the village. Tenskwatawa, perhaps sensing his own opportunity for achieving glory, acceded to their wishes, promising the chiefs that his medicine would render the whites helpless and the warriors strong.

Placing his force near the village, Harrison hoped, would entice the Indians to attack, thereby justifying his presence. And attack the Indians did, at dawn on 7 November. Surprised, Harrison's troops were driven back and nearly routed. Harrison's commanding presence, however, helped steady the troops and enabled them to hang on and beat back three furious assaults. In the midst of the battle a small group of Indians—their mission to kill the hated Harrison—penetrated deep enough to kill an officer they mistook for Harrison (the victim rode a mount that resembled Harrison's). After a savage two-hour fight the Indians finally withdrew, angry that Prophet's "magic" had failed to work. The following day, Harrison entered the now-abandoned Prophet's Town, destroying supplies and torching part of the village.

The Battle of Tippecanoe produced some 30 Indian casualties; Harrison incurred losses of about 180, making it a costly if not questionable victory. Although Harrison declared that the destruction of Prophet's Town would break the back of Indian resistance, it merely provoked more Indian raids throughout the territory. But the tarnished glory of Tippecanoe would serve Harrison again; running with vice-presidential nominee John Tyler, he rode the slogan "Tippecanoe and Tyler, too" to the White House in 1840; he died in office soon thereafter.

See also: Harrison, William Henry; Tecumseh; Tenskwatawa (Prophet)
Further Reading: Dowd, *A Spirited Resistance;* Gilbert, *God Gave Us This Country*

Trail of Tears

The Indian Removal Act, which required the tribes of the Five Civilized Nations to leave ancestral homes in the Southeast, caused a split among the Cherokees. One faction, under John Ross, accepted removal as a fact of life; the other faction, led by a Cherokee known as the Ridge (sometimes Major Ridge because he had served under Andrew Jackson), remained steadfastly opposed. Thus, in 1838 Gen. Winfield Scott, with a force of 7,000 troops, was given the unenviable assignment of rounding up the Cherokees and removing them to the Indian Territory. Some 13 groups made the migration west, a horrendous journey that required each group about six months to complete. The route came to be called the Trail of Tears because of the suffering and deaths endured by the Cherokees. It was a disgraceful chapter in American history.

See also: Cherokees; Chickasaws; Choctaws; Creeks; Jackson, Andrew; Seminole
Further Reading: Debo, *History of the Indians of the United States*

Treaties and Agreements

By strict definition, treaties are formal contracts or agreements between political entities. In dealing with many Indian tribes throughout its history, the United States negotiated hundreds of treaties and a number of agreements. Although a treaty is an agreement, so-called agreements were not treaties

Conference of Indians with the U.S. Commissioner of Indian Affairs

per se. The two were similar in many respects, but they differed significantly in that the treaty was formal—it was constitutionally ordained. As historian Francis Jennings has pointed out, a treaty was both a "product and process." It was the act of meeting and simultaneously fashioning details of terms.

During the early colonial period up to the American Revolution, the independent colonies entered into many so-called treaties, agreements, and pacts with various Indian tribes, but none of these had force beyond the pale of the colony or community that negotiated the terms. Yet treaties negotiated by the united colonies introduced arrangements that carried much broader geographical significance, a fact that almost certainly was not fully appreciated by the tribes at the time.

The period of official U.S. treatymaking began in 1778, when federal commissioners consummated a treaty with the Delawares; it ended in 1868 with a Nez Perce treaty. In that 90-year period, 367 treaties were proclaimed and ratified. In 1871 Congress abolished treaties as an official method of dealing with Indian issues. Nevertheless, between 1871 and 1911 the United States entered into a number of "agreements" with Indian tribes, which differed from earlier treaties perhaps only in name.

The following is a sampling of treaties and agreements. The examples given were the outcome of particular Indian wars or campaigns or became one of the root causes of armed conflict.

Casco, Peace of
12 April 1678

The Peace of Casco (Maine), officially ended King Philip's War. Its provisions may have been the simplest of any peace treaty between Indians and European colonists.

Under its terms all captives were to be released without ransom and allowed to return to their respective homes. Additionally, the Indians in Maine were to receive one peck of corn annually for each white family that settled in Maine.

Easton, Treaty of (1758)

The Treaty of Easton (Pennsylvania) was an important agreement between the British army and several of the Indian tribes inhabiting the Ohio Valley during the French and Indian War. The Indians agreed to withdraw their support of the French in exchange for the cancellation of what they regarded as illegal land sales. Additionally, the British made a pledge to withdraw from the area at the Three Forks of the Ohio River, which the British had no intention of doing. Throughout the next half-century Ohio Valley settlements would bear the bitter consequences of its legacy.

Fort Harmar, Treaties of
9 January 1789

This was one of the early post–Revolutionary War treaties, signed at Fort Harmar, near the present-day site of Marietta, Ohio. Representatives of the United States met with members of the Six Nations (the Iroquois Confederacy). The agreement exacerbated tensions in the Ohio frontier by calling for the Indians to cede virtually all of what is present-day Ohio. Indian anger over the Ohio country would lead to much bloodshed during the following several years.

Fort Jackson, Treaty of
9 August 1814

This treaty was signed at Fort Jackson in Alabama in the aftermath of Gen. Andrew Jackson's overwhelming victory over the Red Stick Creeks at Horseshoe Bend the past March. By virtue of this treaty Jackson forced the Creek nation to cede huge tracts of land to the United States.

Fort Laramie, Treaty of
29 April 1868

This was perhaps the most significant treaty between the United States and the Lakota Sioux. The treaty provided for closure of the three Bozeman Trail forts and established the Great Sioux Reservation. Violations of this treaty (by both sides) played a key role in the Sioux War of 1876–1877.

Fort Stanwix, Treaty of
22 October 1784

This was the second treaty council held at this site (near Rome, New York), the first being in 1768. The 1784 treaty was between the United States and the Six Nations (the Iroquois Confederacy) and was an important post–Revolutionary War treaty in that it fixed boundaries for the tribes of the Six Nations.

Fort Wayne, Treaties of
7 June 1803, and 30 September 1809

As with the Treaty of Fort Jackson, the two treaties of Fort Wayne, negotiated by Indiana's territorial governor, William Henry Harrison, resulted in the Indians' surrender of large tracts of land. Harrison's tactics outraged many of the tribes and their leaders, such as Tecumseh.

Greenville, Treaty of
3 August 1795

Between 16 June and 10 August 1795, Delawares, Ottawas, representatives of the Wyandots, Shawnees, Chippewas, Potawatomis, Kickapoos, and Miami and other smaller tribes gathered at Fort Greenville in the Ohio country to negotiate a settlement with Americans. The Indians ceded to the United States a huge tract of land north of the Ohio River, roughly from a point southwest of Cincinnati north to Fort Recovery, thence southeast to near Coshocton and north to Lake Erie. Covering approximately 25,000 square miles, the area represents more than half of present-day Ohio. Although most of the major Indian leaders were signatories to the treaty, a few, such as the rising young Shawnee warrior Tecumseh, refused to sign.

The effect of the Greenville Treaty was far-reaching. First, it established a long-lasting peace in the Northwest Territory. Second, as a result of this treaty as well as Jay's Treaty (1794), the British were finally compelled to abandon key outposts in the Great Lakes country that they had failed to relinquish in accordance with the Treaty of Paris (1783), which ended the Revolutionary War.

Hartford, Treaty of (1638)

The Treaty of Hartford, concluded in 1638, officially ended the Pequot War. The two major provisions stipulated that those Pequots who had survived the final battle in the swamp would be distributed as slaves among England's Indian allies. Additionally, no Pequot would again be permitted to reside in his former territory.

Horse Creek, Treaty of
17 September 1851

Negotiations were actually held at Horse Creek, about 36 miles from Fort Laramie. An estimated 10,000 Indians were present, mainly Sioux; they agreed to be at peace with each other and with whites. The treaty also gave the United States the right to build roads across Indian territory.

Lancaster, Treaty of
June 1744

An agreement between Virginia, Maryland, and Pennsylvania in which the Iroquois Confederacy agreed to give up its claims to all lands within the colony of Virginia. The agreement represented a significant cession because the Indians were unaware that Virginia's boundaries were nearly limitless by virtue of royal charter.

Logstown Treaty (1752)

The Logstown Treaty was an arrangement with Ohio country tribes that essentially allowed the Virginia Company and Ohio Company to lay claim to the coveted lands in this region. Located about 20 miles from the junction of the Monongahela and Allegheny Rivers in Pennsylvania, Logstown (Chininque) was a large village site occupied by Mingos (Ohio Valley Iroquois), Delawares, Shawnees, and others. The treaty was in force only briefly, however, as a result of

the Pickawillany Massacre, which occurred later that year.

Massachusetts Bay–
Pequot Treaty (1634)

The Massachusetts Bay–Pequot Treaty of 1634 was more convoluted agreement than formal treaty. In essence, the Pequot tribe sought to open a channel of trade with the English to replace that lost by the closure (to them) of House of Hope, the Dutch trading post near what is present-day Hartford, Connecticut. The Dutch rejection had come about as a result of Pequot interference with Narragansett efforts to trade with the Dutch. Additionally, the Pequots desired that the English negotiate peace between them and the Narragansetts.

Relations between the Pequots and the Massachusetts Bay Colony were tenuous at best, and the picture was further clouded by the steadily growing struggle for dominance among the neighboring colonies in the region and their mounting appetite for land. The combination resulted in a bloody two-year war with the Pequots.

Medicine Lodge, Treaty of
21–28 October 1867

Actually, three separate treaties were consummated over the course of a week at Medicine Lodge Creek in southwest Kansas, in which the United States entered into an agreement with Kiowas, Comanches, Cheyennes, and Arapahos. It was a most significant agreement with western tribes. It provided for the Indians to reside on two separate reservations in the Indian Territory. The United States agreed to furnish rations and whatever was needed for the tribes to adopt an agricultural way of life. The Indians had little intention of making such a drastic change, as evidenced by the fighting that raged across the Central and Southern Plains during the next several years.

Middle Plantation, Treaty of (1677)

The Treaty of Middle Plantation (Virginia) followed the Indian War of 1675–1676. The basic provisions of the agreement repealed an earlier law passed by the Virginia Council that authorized the taking and selling of Indian lands to underwrite the cost of the war. The treaty also put an end to the practice of Indian slave trade.

Nez Perce, Treaties with (1855, 1863, and 1868)

The Nez Perce War of 1877 had its roots in the steadily shrinking boundaries of reservation lands originally granted to the Nez Perce in 1855. Each succeeding treaty further reduced the size of the reservation in order to grant miners access to rich ore country.

Pettaquamscutt Rock, Treaty of (1675)

This treaty was orchestrated by the Massachusetts Bay Colony to keep the Narragansetts neutral during King Philip's War in 1675.

Traverse des Sioux, Treaty of 23 July–5 August 1851

This was a key treaty in that it established reservation boundaries for the Eastern (Santee) Sioux. Later agreements by certain Sioux leaders to sell part of the reservation produced discontent among the Sioux and became a contributing factor in the Minnesota uprising of 1862.

Further Reading: Kappler, *Indian Laws and Treaties;* Prucha, *American Indian Treaties; other works cited in the bibliography* (where treaties are discussed in some detail)

Tuscarora War
1710–1713

The Tuscaroras were a tribe that dwelled mainly along North Carolina's extensive coastal river system. Since the beginning of European colonization in America, unscrupulous white traders took advantage of the peaceful Tuscaroras, introducing liquor to the tribe and cheating tribe members in business transactions. Many were also captured and sold into slavery. As the British colonies expanded, they encroached more and more on Tuscarora territory. Grievances mounted. In 1711 the Swiss unilaterally attempted to establish a small colony on the site of what is present-day New Bern, in Indian territory; the Tuscaroras struck, killing some 200 settlers. North Carolina was then too thinly populated to fight an Indian war alone; its primary ally was South Carolina, but Virginia also helped by neutralizing the northern branch of the Tuscaroras.

In 1711 Col. John Barnwell led a mixed force of settlers and Yamassee allies against the Tuscaroras, burning many villages. Moving against the stronghold of a Tuscarora king known as Hancock, Barnwell found the resistance too stiff and was forced to fall back. When the Indian request for a peace talk was rejected, the Tuscaroras proceeded to torture some of their captives while Barnwell's men watched. With no other alternative available, Barnwell agreed to withdraw his column from the area in return for the release of the hostages.

Angered at the effrontery of the Tuscaroras, the North Carolina legislature demanded that a second punitive expedition be sent out. In compliance with that directive, Barnwell returned to Tuscarora country with another, larger column, which forced Hancock to capitulate and sign a peace agreement. The peace agreement proved short-lived, however; by the following summer hostilities broke out. Once again, South Carolina provided help. This time, a strong column under Col. James Moore, former governor of South Carolina, attacked the main Tuscarora camp near the present-day site of Snow Hill, North Carolina, in March 1713. The fight, lasting three days, inflicted heavy casualties on the Tuscaroras. Many of the survivors were sold into slavery. Some of those who survived headed north to ally with the Iroquois, thereby making it a confederacy of six nations. Those who remained had little choice but to sign the peace treaty of 11 February 1715.

See also: England; Iroquois Confederacy
Further Reading: Leach, *Arms for Empire*

⇒ U ⇐

Uncas
?–ca. 1682

Uncas was the "Last Mohican" made famous in the works of James Fenimore Cooper, but in real life he was someone less admirable than the noble literary figure. Uncas was married to the daughter of Sassacus, chief of the Pequots. Rebellious, he was finally banished from the Pequots but evidently had developed a following that enabled him to establish his own tribal group—the Mohegans. Ruthless and ambitious, he sided with the English during the Pequot War and King Philip's War. After capturing Miantonomo he carried out an English order to execute the Narragansett chief, who was technically beyond England's jurisdiction. In 1847 the citizens of Norwich, Connecticut, erected a monument to Miantonomo's memory.

See also: Miantonomo (Miantonomi); Pequot War; Sassacus
Further Reading: Hodge, *Handbook of American Indians;* Jennings, *The Invasion of America;* Steele, *Warpaths*

Underhill, Capt. John
1597?–1672

An English soldier of fortune, John Underhill made a reputation for himself as an Indian fighter during the Pequot War. In the attack on the Pequot village at Mystic Harbor, Underhill surrounded the village then set fire to it, slaughtering the inhabitants as they attempted to escape. The brutal act had severe political repercussions for Underhill when he returned to Massachusetts. On the basis of his "success" against the Pequots, the Dutch hired Underhill in 1643 to retaliate against the various Indian tribes who had been raiding Dutch settlements throughout New Netherlands.

However, by 1660 Underhill, who had clashed with Gov. Peter Stuyvesant, had turned to privateering, raiding Dutch shipping out of Providence, Rhode Island. Underhill's piracy was an example of the restlessness felt by the growing number of English living in New Amsterdam. In fact, Underhill played a key role in the English takeover of New Amsterdam in 1664. He later was named high constable and undersheriff of North Riding, Yorkshire, Long Island.

See also: Dutch; Pequot War
Further Reading: Axelrod, *Chronicle of the Indian Wars;* Jennings, *The Invasion of America;* Steele, *Warpaths*

Upper Sioux Agency, Minnesota

The Upper Sioux Agency was one of two agencies created by the U.S. government to administer to the needs of the Wahpeton and Sisseton bands of the Eastern (Santee) Sioux. Sometimes called Yellow Medicine Agency, it was located near the mouth of the Yellow Medicine River not far from Granite Falls, Minnesota. The Lower Sioux Agency, also known as the Redwood Agency, was located along the Minnesota River near Redwood Falls.

See also: Minnesota Sioux Uprising
Further Reading: Carley, *The Sioux Uprising of 1862*

Ute War
See Meeker Massacre

Utes

A member of the Shoshonean linguistic family, the Utes occupied territory that ranged from northern New Mexico to central Utah, including all of western Colorado. Like many other tribes, the Utes were subdivided into smaller groups or bands, each of which traditionally occupied its own area within the larger tribal territory. Although the Utes regularly traveled onto the Plains to hunt buffalo, they were more at home in the mountains and high desert plateaus of their territory. They were often raided by neighboring Cheyennes, Arapahos, and Comanches.

During the 1850s, the Utes clashed with the Mormons, and in 1879 a band of angry northern Utes perpetrated the Meeker Massacre, which subsequently resulted in many Utes being relocated to a new reservation in Utah; a sizable group did remain in southwestern Colorado.

See also: Meeker Massacre; Ouray
Further Reading: Rockwell, *The Utes;* Smith, *Ouray;* Sprague, *Massacre*

⇒ V ⇐

Victorio
ca. 1825–1880

A noted Apache war chief, Victorio was born in southwestern New Mexico, probably about 1825. He was a member of the Mimbres band of the Eastern Chiricahua Apaches. Victorio's band was sometimes referred to as the Warm Springs Apaches because its home territory was around the hot springs at Ojo Caliente, New Mexico.

Victorio may also have been known as Lucero, but in any case his skills as a warrior and leader of men in battle came to the fore early on. He was a trusted lieutenant of the great Mangas Coloradas. After the death of Mangas in 1863, Victorio became the dominant leader of the Eastern Chiricahuas. Victorio was involved in numerous clashes with whites during the Civil War period and was probably with Mangas Coloradas and Cochise at the Battle of Apache Pass in July 1862.

During the 1870s Victorio led at least two successful breakouts from the San Carlos Reservation (where his band had been sent), raiding south into Mexico as well as up and down the Rio Grande Valley in New Mexico. The object of numerous but unsuccessful U.S. Army pursuits, Victorio was killed at the Battle of Tres Castillos, Mexico, in October 1880, reportedly by a Tarahumara scout in the employ of Mexican troops. Victorio's biographer, Dan Thrapp, has called him "America's greatest guerrilla fighter."

See also: Apache Pass, Battle of; Apache Wars; Mangas Coloradas
Further Reading: Sweeney, *Cochise;* Thrapp, *The Conquest of Apacheria;* ———, *Victorio;* Worcester, *The Apaches*

W

Wabokieshiek (Prophet)
ca. 1794–1841

A Sauk and Fox medicine man, Wabokieshiek, known as Prophet, was a confidante of Black Hawk and an influential figure in the Black Hawk War. Wabokieshiek prophesied that if the Sauks and Foxes resisted the white man help would come from some vague quarter. Black Hawk reportedly accepted this teaching and as a result took a militant stand against the whites.

After the Black Hawk War, Wabokieshiek was held for a time as a prisoner at Fortress Monroe, Virginia. The prophecy having failed, his credibility as a diviner was diminished, and he spent his last years among the Winnebagos, somewhat of an exile. Prophet's village was located on the Rock River, near the present-day site of Prophetstown, Illinois. Wabokieshiek was one of two prominent Indians to be known as Prophet, the other being Tenskwatawa, brother of Tecumseh.

See also: Black Hawk; Black Hawk War; Dodge, Col. Henry; Tecumseh; Tenskwatawa (Prophet)
Further Reading: Dowd, *A Spirited Resistance;* Jackson, *Black Hawk*

Wagon Box Fight
2 August 1867

A celebrated engagement during Red Cloud's War (1866–1868), the Wagon Box Fight took place about 20 miles south of what is present-day Sheridan, Wyoming, on 2 August 1867. Angry over the military presence in the Powder River country, the Sioux sought to drive the army out by continually harassing patrols and working parties.

Wood-cutting details traveling back and forth from the cutting area to Fort Phil Kearny, some 5 miles away, were a favorite target of the Sioux.

On 1 August, Company C of the Twenty-Seventh Infantry, commanded by Capt. James Powell, took over the duties of providing escort and protection for the civilian woodcutters during the month of August. At the cutting area in the foothills of the Big Horn Mountains, the wagons used to haul supplies and equipment were detached from their wheel assemblies and arranged to form an oval-shaped corral, approximately 60 feet by 25 feet, inside of which the livestock was placed at night to keep them from being run off by Indian raiders. The canvas tops were also removed from most of the wagon boxes or tops. Supplies were stored inside the boxes. From this base camp, small wood-cutting parties fanned out into the nearby timber to cut logs, which were then hauled from the cutting area back to Fort Kearny on the wheel assemblies, or running gear, of the wagons.

Early on the morning of 2 August a large war party of Sioux attacked the camp, forcing the 26 soldiers and six civilians to take up defensive positions inside the wagon circle. After several mounted charges were repulsed, the Indians attempted to overrun the corral on foot, but that effort also failed. The ability of the defenders to turn back each Indian assault was primarily due to their new breech-loading rifles, which enabled them to deliver a much heavier and more sustained volume of fire than the Indians had previously experienced.

After several hours a relief column from Fort Kearny arrived to disperse the Indians.

The number of Indians in the attacking party has been estimated at anywhere from 300 to several thousand. Estimates of Indian casualties vary wildly, from two to 1,500. Three defenders were killed and two were wounded.

See also: Bozeman Trail; Fetterman Disaster; Forts, Camps, Cantonments, Outposts, Phil Kearny
Further Reading: Keenan, *The Wagon Box Fight*

Wahunsonacock, Wahunsenacawh

See Powhatan (Wahunsonacock, Wahunsenacawh)

Walking Purchase
1737

The so-called Walking Purchase was a treaty with the Delawares by which the tribe granted William Penn land that extended from the forks of the Leigh and Delaware Rivers as far into the woods "as a man can go in one day and a half." In later years, as settlements expanded, whites wanted access to the land above the forks of the river, but the Delawares refused. Government officials pressured the tribe until it reluctantly agreed to a realignment of the original boundaries.

Three athletes were hired, and on 19 September, after the route had been cleared of obstacles, they began to walk off a new treaty, using the original starting point. By the time the walkers had completed their trek on the second day, they had covered 66 miles. When the boundary lines were redrawn the new tract was larger by approximately 1,200 square miles. The Delawares angrily protested but to no avail.

Further Reading: Debo, *History of the Indians of the United States;* Jennings, *Empire of Fortune*

Wampum

The word wampum is taken from a New England Algonquian word, *wampompeag,* itself one of several variants, which early English colonists shortened to refer to strings of beads made from several kinds of shells found along the coast of the Atlantic Seaboard. Usually white or violet, the shells were highly valued by Indians, who used them as a medium of exchange and to seal pacts or agreements. The introduction of new tools by the English colonists enabled the Indians to increase production of wampum, which also proved to have economic value for the colonists, who were able to use it in trade with England. An exorbitant payment of wampum was demanded by the Massachusetts Bay Colony from the Pequot tribe in their agreement of 1634.

See also: Treaties and Agreements, Massachusetts Bay–Pequot Treaty
Further Reading: Jennings, *The Invasion of America;* Steele, *Warpaths*

Wamsutta (Alexander)
?–ca. 1662

Wamsutta became chief of the Wampanoag upon the death of his father, Massasoit, in 1661. Massasoit's death marked the end of an era in which relations between English colonists and Indians had been relatively stable. Wamsutta, who took the Christian name Alexander, was accused of conspiracy by Plymouth authorities, probably as a result of real estate transactions he entered with Massachusetts Bay or Connecticut colonies, who were vying to become the dominant power in the region.

In any case, Wamsutta was brought to Plymouth under arrest and charged with conspiracy. While there he became ill and was then released. He died from the effects of his illness en route home. Many, including his younger brother Metacomet (Philip), who succeeded him as chief, were convinced that Wamsutta's illness and death had been brought on by harsh treatment by English. Thus, Wamsutta might be thought of as the first casualty of King Philip's War.

See also: King Philip's War; Massasoit; Philip (King Philip, Metacom, Metacomet)
Further Reading: Jennings, *The Invasion of America;* Steele, *Warpaths*

Wappingers

An Algonquian-speaking tribe, closely related to the Mahicans and Delawares, the Wappingers were part of an Indian confederacy that occupied the east bank of the Hudson River from approximately Poughkeepsie to Manhattan and east beyond the Connecticut River. In 1643 the powerful Mohawk nation came down the Hudson River to exact a heavy tribute from the Wappingers, who fled to the Dutch for protection. The Dutch, however, refused the requested sanctuary and indeed permitted the Mohawks a free hand in inflicting heavy casualties among the Wappingers. Later, Dutch soldiers killed many of the survivors. Lacking the numbers to compete against either their stronger neighbors or the growing European presence, the Wappingers eventually merged with the Delaware nation.

See also: Dutch; Dutch-Indian Wars; Mohawks; Slaughter of the Innocents
Further Reading: Hodge, *Handbook of American Indians;* Steele, *Warpaths*

War Belt

A large belt of wampum measuring about nine feet by six inches and covered with vermilion paint, the war belt represented a symbolic call to arms for many of the eastern woodland tribes. Acceptance of the belt by a tribal leader indicated his support of the war effort.

Further Reading: Dowd, *A Spirited Resistance*

Warren Wagontrain Raid
18 May 1871

In May 1871 an army supply train of 12 wagons under the command of Capt. Henry Warren left Fort Richardson, Texas, for Fort Griffin, carrying a supply of shelled corn. On 18 May the train was attacked by a Kiowa war party. The entire wagon train was captured and seven of the teamsters were killed. The survivors managed to return to Fort Richardson, where they reported the attack. Although a minor incident, it is interesting in that Gen. William T. Sherman, on an inspection tour of the Southwest, had passed along this same route just hours earlier—with no sign of hostile Indians. The attack served as a wake-up call to U.S. troops on the frontier.

Further Reading: Athearn, *William Tecumseh Sherman and the Settlement of the West;* Capps, *The Warren Wagontrain Raid*

Washita, Battle of the
27 November 1868

On the morning of 23 November 1868, the Seventh Cavalry, under the command of Lt. Col. George Armstrong Custer, marched out of Camp Supply in northwestern Oklahoma. Custer's mission was to locate and attack Cheyennes believed responsible for raids on Kansas settlements. The strategy for a winter campaign came from Maj. Gen. Philip H. Sheridan, commanding the Department of the Missouri, who believed that striking while Indians' mobility was limited by winter weather offered better chances for success than did a summer campaign.

The Seventh Cavalry, more than 800 strong and supported by a large wagon train, moved south through a foot of fresh snow, following the trail of a Cheyenne war party returning from raids in Kansas. Late on 26 November Custer located the Cheyenne village along the Washita River, northwest of what is present-day Elk City, Oklahoma. At dawn on 27 November Custer launched an attack on the village to the martial strains of "Garryowen," which was played by the regimental band until the instruments froze in the bitter-cold air.

The village turned out to be that of Black Kettle, whose village had been wiped out in the infamous Sand Creek Massacre. In that catastrophe his village had been composed mostly of peaceful Indians living (or so they thought) under the protection of the U.S. flag. Although Black Kettle himself remained peaceably inclined, he was now elderly and exercised little influence on the young warriors in the Washita village who

U.S. cavalry led by Custer entering a Cheyenne village

had been terrorizing frontier settlements in Kansas and Colorado.

Caught completely by surprise, the Indians were driven from their lodges. Some of the warriors recovered and fought back, but most who survived fled down the river valley. Black Kettle and his wife were killed while attempting to escape. After securing the village Custer put it to the torch, burning most of the winter food supply and clothing; he slaughtered more than 800 ponies. As the day progressed, however, increasing numbers of warriors from other villages downstream, whose presence Custer had not suspected, arrived to open fire on the soldiers.

By late afternoon the Indians had managed to encircle most of the village, though not enough to overwhelm the soldiers. After establishing a defensive perimeter, Custer feinted as though to move against the other villages downstream then suddenly withdrew to his supply train, bringing along his wounded and a number of captives. The Indians, fearing a second attack on their villages, did not pursue.

Custer returned to Camp Supply on 2 December, reporting losses of 22 killed and 14 wounded. Indian losses were estimated at more than 100. Although a decisive victory for the army, the Battle of the Washita proved controversial, given that Sand Creek was still fresh on the public's mind. Notwithstanding, the destruction of the village, including the supplies and large pony herd, represented a significant loss for the Indians, who no longer could count on winter to protect them from the bluecoats.

The Battle of the Washita was significant for two other reasons. First, Maj. Joel Elliott and a detachment of 15 men, all of whom were killed by the Indians, had been abandoned, which created a rift in the regiment that remained until the Battle of the Little Bighorn eight years later. However, Custer's decision to abandon Elliott was probably necessary for the overall security of the regiment. Second, an Indian captive taken at the battle was a young Cheyenne woman named Monaseetah; she reportedly shared Custer's tent and bed during the return march to Camp Supply and is said to have later given birth to a yellow-haired boy.

Further Reading: Grinnell, *Fighting Cheyennes;* Keim, *Sheridan's Troopers on the Border;* Utley, *Cavalier in Buckskin*

Wayne, Gen. Anthony (Mad Anthony)
1745–1796

Born in Pennsylvania of Irish descent, Wayne was employed first as a surveyor and then as a tanner in his father's business. Elected to the Pennsylvania legislature in 1774, he resigned upon the outbreak of the Revolution to raise a regiment of volunteers. Wayne's Revolutionary War record included service at Trois Rivieres (Canada), Fort Ticonderoga, Brandywine, Germantown, Valley Forge, Monmouth, and Stony Point.

In 1781 he very ably defused a mutiny among troops of the Pennsylvania line. During the latter stages of the Revolution he campaigned in Georgia and negotiated treaties with the Cherokees and Creeks. From the end of the Revolution until 1792 he was a largely unsuccessful rice planter. He was elected to Congress from Georgia, but the election was subsequently declared invalid due to voting irregularities.

In April 1792 Pres. George Washington appointed Wayne to command the American Army of the Northwest. He eventually rebuilt and trained the army, leading it to decisive victory against allied Indian forces in the Battle of Fallen Timbers in August 1794. The following year he brought the same tribes together for a grand council of peace, resulting in the significant Treaty of Greenville.

He died suddenly at Presque Isle (Erie), Pennsylvania, in 1796. Bold, flamboyant, and often eccentric, Wayne was one of the ablest American soldiers of his era, but his accomplishments are often overlooked. His most notable achievements were the Battle of Stony Point, New York, during the Revolution and the Battle of Fallen Timbers.

See also: Fallen Timbers, Battle of; Treaties and Agreements, Greenville, Treaty of
Further Reading: Gilbert, *God Gave Us This Country;* Prucha, *Sword of the Republic;* Sword, *President Washington's Indian War*

Gen. "Mad Anthony" Wayne

Wayne's Campaign
1794

After two years spent organizing and training an army—now officially designated the Legion of the United States, Gen. Anthony (Mad Anthony) Wayne, a famous Revolutionary War veteran, was finally prepared to take the field against Indians in the Northwest Territory. Efforts to reach a settlement with the tribes had proven unsuccessful, and it now became Wayne's task to accomplish militarily what the government had been unable to achieve through negotiation.

On 28 July 1794, Wayne's mixed force of some 3,500 men marched out of Fort Greenville and Fort Recovery. Near the junction of the Maumee and Auglaize Rivers in northwestern Ohio Wayne paused briefly to erect Fort Defiance, the last in a string of outposts stretching from Fort Washington (Cincinnati) north, to a site close to the present-day site of Toledo. After building Fort Defiance Wayne continued his advance to within a few miles of the British post at Fort Miamis. Increasing Indian signs prompted Wayne to erect a defensive structure for his supplies before resuming his advance on the morning of 20 August.

Moving through an area of dense underbrush and downed trees known as Fallen Timbers, Wayne was attacked by the Indians and after a somewhat muddled opening sent the attackers reeling in headlong flight. Many of the Indians sought safety at the walls of the British post at Fort Miamis, but the British commander refused to grant them entry, fearing the serious political repercussions that would likely follow. Wayne then retraced his steps along the Maumee River and, after reinforcing Fort Defiance, set to work erecting yet another post on the Wabash River, which was named Fort Wayne.

By early November Wayne was back in Greenville, having led the campaign that finally erased the stigmas of the earlier Harmar and St. Clair disasters.

See also: Fallen Timbers, Battle of; Harmar, Gen. Josiah; St. Clair, Arthur; Wayne, Gen. Anthony (Mad Anthony)
Further Reading: Gilbert, *God Gave Us This Country;* Prucha, *Sword of the Republic;* Sword, *President Washington's Indian War*

Weapons, Indian
Bow and Arrow

The bow is perhaps the most identifiable of all North American Indian weapons. There were several variations over the years, depending on the geographic location of the tribe using the weapon. Generally, the bow was approximately four feet in length, made from ash, mulberry, or osage orange. Bows were sometimes backed with laminations of animal bone or horn from deer or mountain sheep. Bow strings were made from the sinew of deer and, later, from that of domestic animals.

The arrows were made of cane or other woods. They were fletched with hawk or eagle feathers and were usually painted with a color code for tribal designation. Length varied from three to four feet. The arrowheads were made from flint or obsidian; steel products were introduced later. The maximum effective range of a bow and arrow was about 150 yards.

Knife

Knives were not original Indian weapons. They were introduced by Europeans and were found in a wide range of types and sizes.

Lance

A spear reaching lengths up to 14 feet and with a steel tip, the lance was primarily used by horseback tribes for hunting buffalo; they were also employed as a weapon of war.

Shield

Usually made of buffalo hide, the war shield was handsomely decorated and capable of deflecting arrows but not bullets.

Tomahawk

Next to the bow and arrow, the tomahawk is probably the most recognizable Indian weapon. Actually a light ax, the original tomahawk had a head fashioned from stone or bone. The introduction of iron trade goods from the Europeans changed the design of the tomahawk to its more recognizable form.

War Club

War clubs varied in size and style, ranging from a small club with a stone head attached to the handle by animal-skin thongs to large, beautifully crafted, all-wood clubs fashioned from a burl. Some also carried a spike for splitting skulls. Many were ornately decorated with bright color schemes, identifying the owner or his tribe.

Further Reading: Hurley, *Arrows Against Steel;* Time-Life, *People of the Lakes;* ———, *People of the Plains;* Utley and Washburn, *The Indian Wars*

Weapons, White
See Firearms

Weroance (Werowance)

In the political hierarchy of the Powhatan Confederacy, the weroance, or werowance, functioned as a lesser chief or subchief of the principal ruler, known as the mamanatowick.

See also: Powhatan Confederacy

Further Reading: Hodge, *Handbook of American Indians;* Rountree, *The Powhatan Indians*

Western Reserve

As part of the Peace of Paris signed in 1783, the United States acquired the so-called Western Lands. States that had standing claims to parts of this region surrendered those claims, thereby making the area the exclusive domain of the federal government. As payment for surrendering its claims, however, Connecticut reserved a tract of 3 million acres in the northeastern corner of what is present-day Ohio. That tract thus came to be known as the Western Reserve.

Further Reading: Hurt, *The Ohio Frontier*

White Bird Canyon, Battle of
17 June 1877

The Battle of White Bird Canyon, the opening clash of the Nez Perce War, had its genesis on 14 June 1877, when three young Nez Perce men, perhaps under the influence of liquor and angry at being forced to move to a new reservation, killed several white settlers. Gen. O. O. Howard, commanding the Department of the Columbia, was on an inspection tour of the area and learned of the killings when he reached Fort Lapwai, near the site of present-day Lewistown, Idaho. Wasting no time, Howard immediately sent a detachment of 100 cavalry under Capt. David Perry into the area to protect settlers and apprehend the guilty parties. The column was augmented by a contingent of citizen soldiers.

However, when he arrived in the area on 16 June, Perry discovered that the trouble had already escalated. Some 17 Nez Perce warriors, allegedly under the influence of liquor, had killed another 15 white settlers. Despite chief Joseph's council to work out a peaceful resolution with white authorities, the nontreaty bands—including those of Joseph and Yellow Wolf—feared reprisal and so opted to flee to the Salmon River country. Joseph reluctantly agreed.

Perry, a Civil War veteran and experienced Indian fighter who had seen action in the Modoc War, lost no time taking up the chase. By daylight on 17 June Perry and his tired troopers (they had ridden some 70 miles over two nights and a day), followed the Nez Perce trail along White Bird Creek through the deep gorge of White Bird Canyon, which eventually emptied into the Salmon River, along which the Nez Perce were camped.

The Nez Perce, meanwhile, had learned of Perry's approach on the night of 16 June. Some wished to negotiate with the soldiers; if this failed to produce satisfactory results then they would fight. The militant faction, however, including a number of warriors allegedly still under the influence of liquor, opted to fight now. Accordingly, some 60 warriors, perhaps one-half of the camp's fighting strength, took up positions in the ravines and on the high ground above the village. As Perry's column descended the canyon it was unable to see the village, concealed beyond a ridge. When the war party suddenly appeared, the advance guard opened fire, despite Perry's orders not to fire until fired upon.

Perry immediately formed his command for battle. The Nez Perce, however, were able to pour a heavy and deadly fire upon Perry's entire line from their positions in the ravines and on the heights. The citizen soldiers quickly lost their courage and fled back up the canyon. With their departure, Perry's position disintegrated. Many of his regulars, themselves lacking experience, panicked and followed the volunteers up the canyon, despite efforts by the officers to halt the flight. One detachment of 18 men under Lt. Edward Theller was wiped out.

Having little choice but to save their skins, the remainder of Perry's fractured command fought a continuous withdrawal to Mount Idaho. Perry's losses totaled 34 killed—nearly one-third of his command. Coming only a year after the disaster at the Little Bighorn, the setback at White Bird Canyon was particularly disturbing. This was only the beginning, however. The army would know more humiliation before the Nez Perce War ended in October.

See also: Big Hole, Battle of the; Howard, Gen. Oliver Otis; Joseph; Nez Perce War
Further Reading: Brown, *The Flight of the Nez Perce;* Hampton, *Children of Grace;* McDermott, *Forlorn Hope*

Whitestone Hill, Battle of
3 September 1863

In the summer of 1863, Gen. John Pope, commanding the Department of the Northwest, ordered a two-pronged campaign against the Sioux in the Dakota Territory. The objective was to find and punish the Sioux who had been involved in the 1862 Minnesota uprising. Pope was also concerned that unless soundly defeated these Indians might attack the Minnesota frontier a second time.

One column—3,000 men commanded by the recently promoted Brig. Gen. Henry Hastings Sibley—marched west from Camp Pope, Minnesota, in June. The second column, under the command of Brig. Gen. Alfred Sully, would march north from Fort Randall, South Dakota. The two columns were to rendezvous in the vicinity of present-day Bismarck, North Dakota, to support and compliment each other. However, the late arrival of troops and low water on the Missouri River delayed Sully's force until 21 August. With a column of some 2,000 men composed of volunteer cavalry units from Iowa and Nebraska supported by some artillery, Sully marched up the Missouri River valley.

Sully did not reach Bismarck until the end of the month, only to discover that Sibley, low on supplies, had returned to Minnesota. Sully, having learned some Sioux were in the vicinity of the James River southeast of Bismarck, moved in pursuit. On 3 September Maj. Albert House, with four companies of the Sixth Iowa Cavalry commanding Sully's advance, was alerted to the presence of Indians by scout Frank LaFrambois. Ordering his command to advance, House found the Sioux camped near a small lake. The nearby hills were dotted with white rocks—thus Whitestone Hill.

House soon discovered that the camp was considerably larger than expected, containing an estimated 300 to 600 lodges, with perhaps as many as 1,000 warriors. After sending LaFrambois back to inform Sully of the development, House learned he had been discovered. Deploying his battalion, House ordered a reconnaissance, sending two companies to the left and a second pair to the right. While some of the Sioux prepared for battle, several leaders approached House to negotiate, offering the surrender of some. House, who was biding time while waiting for Sully, pondered the offer then rejected it, saying that all must surrender.

LaFrambois reached the main body late that afternoon. Upon being advised, Sully immediately advanced with the Second Nebraska on the right, the Sixth Iowa on the left, and the Seventh Iowa, together with the artillery, in the center. It was sundown as Sully approached; seeing the arrival of more soldiers, the Indians began to disperse, abandoning equipment and supplies. Sully quickly issued orders to cut off the Indians and round them up. A battalion of the Second Nebraska under Col. Robert Furnas swung to the right while Major House's battalion moved left. Sully, with the remainder of the command, moved through the center of the disintegrating camp, collecting any Sioux who surrendered.

Meanwhile, a large body of Sioux fleeing from Furnas and House collected in a large ravine about a half-mile from the village. Although it was now nearly dark, Furnas advanced his troops in two lines, joined shortly by House's command. As the troops advanced the Indians opened fire. Oddly, and for some unexplained reason, some of the Sixth Iowa went into battle with their weapons unloaded.

In the gathering darkness the firing continued, though it was becoming increasingly difficult for either side to see. Some of the Iowans, in fact, wound up firing at the Nebraskans. Troopers were also having difficulty controlling the cavalry horses. The Battle of Whitestone Hill was fast becoming one of the most chaotic on record. Many of the Indians managed to escape in the darkness, noise, and confusion.

From a tactical point of view, the battle was inconclusive. However, Sully's command did destroy most of the Indian supplies, including a large store of dried buffalo meat, a devastating blow to the Sioux.

See also: Minnesota Sioux Uprising; Pope, Gen. John; Sibley, Gen. Henry Hastings; Sully, Gen. Alfred; Sully-Sibley Campaigns
Further Reading: Carley, *The Sioux Uprising of 1862;* Jacobson, *Whitestone Hill;* Josephy, *The Civil War in the American West*

Whitman Massacre
29 November 1847

In 1834 Marcus Whitman, a 32-year-old missionary doctor, and his 26-year-old wife, Narcissa Prentiss Whitman, were in company with a small group of immigrants crossing the Rockies to Oregon. Narcissa and the other woman in the group, Mrs. Henry Harmon Spalding, became the first two white women to cross these mountains.

In Oregon the Whitmans established a mission near the site of present-day Walla Walla, Washington. In 1842 the couple returned to the East, where they promoted emigration to Oregon. They later helped guide the first wagon train of notable size into Oregon. Both Marcus and Narcissa were dedicated to promoting Christianity by providing medical attention and spiritual guidance. They were devoted likewise to the new Oregon country.

In 1847 the Cayuses, who had been marginal neighbors, grew increasingly uneasy as more settlers arrived in the region. Shamans were also uneasy over the Whitman's medical practice, fearing it would undermine their own authority. As a consequence, when a measles epidemic struck the shamans, believing it had been brought on by the white doctor, urged that the missionaries be destroyed.

The Whitmans had been alerted of the danger of Indian attack, but they chose nevertheless to go about their business. The attack came on 29 November, when Cayuse warriors murdered the Whitmans and a dozen others. In addition, 47 whites were taken captive but later released. The massacre led in part to legislation that eventually created the Oregon Territory in 1848.

Further Reading: Jeffrey, *Converting the West*

Williams, Roger
1603–1683

A clergyman during New England's early years, Roger Williams was banished from Massachusetts Bay Colony by the Puritans for his heretical beliefs. He subsequently established a haven in what is today the state of Rhode Island for new religious voices. Highly regarded by Indians, it is ironic that the Massachusetts Bay Colony later called on him to persuade the Narragansetts to maintain their pledged neutrality during the Pequot War. He accepted the mission out of a sense of responsibility to his fellow Englishmen and was successful in keeping the tribe out of the conflict.

See also: Pequot War
Further Reading: Jennings, *The Invasion of America;* Steele, *Warpaths*

Winnemucca, Sarah
1844–1891

A northern Paiute, Sarah Winnemucca was born in the area around Humboldt and Pyramid Lakes, Nevada. Her Indian name, Thocmetony, means shell flower. Although Sarah claimed to have been the daughter of chief Winnemucca, this is disputed. As a girl she attended Catholic school—but only briefly because of the bias against Indians. Sarah quickly developed fluency with languages. During the Bannock War of 1878 she served the U.S. Army as both a scout and an interpreter. She married three times, twice to U.S. Army officers and once to a Paiute man. Sarah Winnemucca was the first Indian woman to author a book, writing about the mistreatment of her people. During the 1880s she lectured in the East and founded the Peabody School for Indian children in 1884. She died in Montana in 1891.

See also: Bannock War
Further Reading: Canfield, *Sarah Winnemucca of the Northern Paiutes*

Wolf Mountains, Battle of
8 January 1877

This was one of the last military actions of the Great Sioux War of 1876–1877. By late 1876 the village of Crazy Horse, estimated to contain some 3,500 individuals including the survivors of Dull Knife's Cheyenne village (destroyed by Col. Ranald S. Mackenzie in November), was located on the Tongue River in the Wolf Mountains near what is present-day Birney, Montana.

After efforts to peacefully resolve the year-old conflict had been undermined by some overaggressive Crow scouts of the U.S. Army, Sioux who had been inclined toward settlement lost credibility. As a consequence, the Sioux resumed hostile action, which included raids in the area around Cantonment Keogh, later Fort Keogh and, eventually, the site of Miles City, Montana. Here the Sioux employed a favorite tactic—enticing troops out of the post and into a trap. Col. Nelson A. Miles, commanding the Fifth Infantry at Cantonment Keogh, obliged and in late December 1876 took the field with a force of some 350 men of the Fifth and Twenty-Second Infantry and two field pieces.

On 7 January 1877, anxious Indians inadvertently revealed their trap early, thereby alerting Miles, who took precautions to protect his camp. Three feet of snow blanketed the ground when Crazy Horse attacked with a war party of 500 on the overcast morning of 8 January. Miles was prepared, however, so that the attack was not as effective as it might have been. The fighting waged throughout the morning as snow continued to fall from leaden skies. The two field pieces kept the Indians from concentrating, but neither side was able to gain any real advantage, despite heavy firing on both sides.

By midday the weather worsened. As blizzard conditions set in, the forces withdrew from the field, recognizing the futility of continuing the fight. Although a great deal of ammunition had been expended, casualties were light. A victory there might have meant an end to the war; Miles would have to take the field again in the spring.

See also: Crazy Horse (Tashunca Utico, Tashunka Witko); Kelly, Luther S. (Yellowstone); Miles, Col. Nelson Appleton; Sioux War
Further Reading: Greene, *Yellowstone Command;* L. Kelly, *Yellowstone Kelly;* Wooster, *Nelson A. Miles*

Wood Lake, Battle of
23 September 1862

During the late summer and early autumn of 1862, military forces mobilized in response to the Sioux uprising that left hundreds dead in southern Minnesota. In September, Col. Henry Hastings Sibley of the Minnesota militia moved against the Sioux with a mixed force of citizen rangers, militia, and Civil War volunteer units that included the Third, Sixth, Seventh, and Ninth Minnesota Regiments. There were also nearly 300 men of the Third Minnesota who had surrendered at the Battle of Murfreesboro, Tennessee; they had been paroled and allowed to return home to fight Indians. Altogether, Sibley had more than 1,600 men plus some artillery.

On 19 September Sibley's column marched out of Fort Ridgely and headed up the Minnesota River valley. Three days later, 22 September, the command bivouacked on the east shore of Lone Tree Lake, near today's Echo, Minnesota. At the time it was believed they had reached Wood Lake, which was actually a few miles to the west. Also believing there were no Indians in the immediate vicinity, Sibley posted only a few pickets. Unknown to Sibley, however, there was a large Sioux village on the Chippewa River near Montevideo—much closer than he had suspected. Alerted to the presence of the soldiers, a war party numbering about 1,000 moved down the river that night and prepared to attack Sibley's camp.

An ambush planned for the morning of 23 September was foiled, being accidentally discovered by several members of the Third Minnesota who had gone off on an unauthorized mission to steal additional food from the Upper Agency, just across the Yellow Medicine River. The Sioux were thus forced to attack, and Sibley, hearing the firing, quickly advanced, momentarily forcing the

Indians to fall back. An attempt to flank the troops was subsequently repulsed by the Sixth and Seventh Minnesota, supported by the artillery.

Driven back a second time, the Sioux did not renew their attack—nor did Sibley pursue. Sibley suffered losses of seven killed and 33 wounded; Indian casualties numbered 14, including chief Mankato, who was killed in the fighting. Although tactically the battle could be considered a standoff, it later resulted in the release of civilian hostages held by the Sioux since the outbreak of hostilities.

See also: Birch Coulee, Battle of; Minnesota Sioux Uprising; New Ulm, Battles of; Sibley, Gen. Henry Hastings; Sully-Sibley Campaigns
Further Reading: Carley, *The Sioux Uprising of 1862;* Josephy, *The Civil War in the American West*

Wool, Gen. John Ellis
1784–1869

Born in New York, Wool was appointed captain in the Thirteenth Infantry Regiment during the War of 1812, compiling a fine record during that conflict. Later he was involved in the removal of Cherokees to the Indian Territory. Following an outstanding record in the Mexican War, Wool was appointed to head the Department of the Pacific in 1854.

During 1855 and 1856 he was forced to deal with two Indian wars, one against the Yakimas, the other against the Rogue Indians. In a sense, there was a third: territorial politics and the bureaucracy of the War Department. Wool was outspoken and highly critical of both. Although the Indian conflicts eventually ended, the resolution of issues that had provoked the war in the first place was unsatisfactory and pleased no one. In the end, Secretary of War Jefferson Davis, weary of the turmoil in Wool's department, reassigned the argumentative general.

Further Reading: Burns, *Jesuits in the Indian Wars of the Northwest;* Glassley, *Pacific Northwest Indian Wars;* Utley, *Frontiersmen in Blue*

Worth, Gen. William Jenkins
1794–1849

Born in New York, William Jenkins Worth was appointed a lieutenant in the Twenty-Third Infantry Regiment in 1813. He served as an aide to Gen. Winfield Scott, and by the end of the War of 1812 he had compiled a fine record, receiving the brevet rank of major. Following a term as commandant of West Point, he was involved in the Black Hawk War, though not in a particularly notable way. He was promoted to colonel of the Eighth Infantry in 1838, and in 1840 he was sent to Florida with orders to bring the Second Seminole War to a successful conclusion.

Although he did capture a great many Seminoles, his strategy and tactics proved no more successful against the elusive Seminoles than had those of his predecessors. He was awarded the brevet rank of brigadier general for his Florida service and later that of major general for service in the Mexican War. He died of cholera in Texas in 1849.

See also: Seminole War, Second

John Ellis Wool

Further Reading: Covington, *The Seminoles;* Mahon, *History of the Second Seminole War*

Wounded Knee Massacre
29 December 1890

The Ghost Dance, a nonmilitant quasireligious movement among most tribes, had a reverse effect on the Lakota Sioux. Militant leaders among the Sioux, angered by the plight of their people, suffering from hunger and sickness, capitalized on the Ghost Dance fervor by preaching the overthrow of the white man and his rule. They promised that the sacred ghost shirt would protect them from soldiers' bullets.

Government officials watched with growing concern. At the Pine Ridge Agency and the Rosebud Agency emotions ran high, and nearby settlements feared an uprising.

In response to settlers' cries for military protection, Pres. Benjamin Harrison ordered the War Department to take control of a rapidly deteriorating situation. Accordingly, in mid-November 1890 army troops occupied both agencies.

Within the Sioux tribe two factions had emerged: friendlies (those not wanting trouble) and hostiles (the militants). In December the hostile ghost dancers, numbering perhaps 500 or 600, had come together in the northwest corner of the Pine Ridge Reservation. Elsewhere, other Sioux bands, notably that of Sitting Bull, also appeared threatening. One in particular, that of Big Foot, steadfastly refused the army's efforts at pacification.

Meanwhile, Gen. Nelson A. Miles, having recently assumed command of the Military Division of the Missouri, ordered the arrest

Indians' bodies frozen in the ice the morning after the Wounded Knee Massacre, South Dakota, 1891 (photo by W. H. Rose)

of Big Foot and Sitting Bull. Much to Miles's chagrin, however, the death of Sitting Bull, killed by Indian policemen attempting to arrest him, further provoked a charged situation, which was now beginning to receive considerable media attention. Most of Sitting Bull's Hunkpapa band agreed to be relocated, but a few hardliners joined Big Foot's band. Lt. Col. Edwin Sumner, with orders to arrest Big Foot, deemed it more prudent to temporarily hold off on the execution of his orders to avoid trouble. His delay led to trouble nevertheless.

Although militant, Big Foot had a reputation as a peacemaker and had been asked by some of the Oglalas to come down from his Cheyenne River camp to Pine Ridge to help ease tensions. When Colonel Sumner finally decided to carry out his orders, he found that Big Foot and his band had quietly slipped away under cover of night for Pine Ridge. On 17 December an angry Miles took personal charge of a situation he felt had been bungled. His troops were still trying to persuade the militants to come in from the remote corner of Pine Ridge where they had been holding out, and Miles now sought to keep Big Foot from joining them. Accordingly, elements of the Sixth and Ninth Cavalry were directed to prevent such a union.

Big Foot, however, managed to elude the cavalry patrols, making his way toward Pine Ridge by way of the Badlands. Along the way, the Oglala leader was stricken with pneumonia. Meanwhile, a frustrated Miles ordered Custer's old regiment, the Seventh Cavalry, now commanded by Col. James W. Forsyth, to intercept the elusive Oglalas. Forsyth succeeded where the others had failed. On the night of 28 December 1890, his advance units had located and surrounded Big Foot's camp along Wounded Knee Creek.

Surrounded by 500 soldiers and four field pieces, the Sioux, numbering about 100 men and perhaps 200 women and children, readily agreed to be escorted to the railhead for transfer to Omaha. However, when Forsyth demanded surrender of all weapons the Sioux grew angry and refused to comply.

Soldiers, understandably nervous, were sent in among the throng of murmuring Indians to search for concealed weapons. It was a volatile situation. In a disagreement between one of the soldiers and a Sioux, a rifle was discharged. Suddenly both sides were firing at each other. Brutal, close-in fighting ensued, with shooting and stabbing.

As the fighting broke off and the two sides gradually separated, Forsyth's Hotchkiss guns began firing into the camp with deadly effect, scattering the Indians. When the shooting finally ended some 150 Sioux including Big Foot lay dead, and another 50 were wounded. Army losses amounted to 25 killed and 40 wounded.

Miles was furious. He considered the massacre totally unnecessary, a blunder, and relieved Forsyth of command (that decision was later overturned). Wounded Knee was a genuine tragedy, but as historian Robert Utley has pointed out it was not a massacre in the sense that Sand Creek was a massacre, being neither deliberate nor indiscriminate. Further violence was averted, due mainly to General Miles's avoidance of dangerous situations. The power and attraction of the Ghost Dance waned after that. For all intents and purposes, Wounded Knee marked the end of organized Indian resistance to the white culture that had arrived in the New World four centuries earlier.

See also: Forsyth, Col. James William; Ghost Dance; Miles, Gen. Nelson Appleton; Sioux; Sitting Bull; Wovoka
Further Reading: Brown, *Bury My Heart at Wounded Knee*; Utley, *Last Days of the Sioux Nation*

Wovoka
ca. 1856–1932

Wovoka—known as Jack Wilson to whites—was a Paiute mystic whose teachings had a profound impact on many Indians, particularly the Lakota Sioux, during the latter part of the nineteenth century. Wovoka claimed to be the son of Tävibo, an earlier mystic, and promoted his teachings, which held that whites would be swallowed up by the earth and that dead Indians would return to harvest the legacy left by the departed whites. Claiming the gift of contact with departed Indian spirits, Wovoka urged his followers to dance their traditional circle dance; because of his ability to contact the spirit world, the dance became known as the Ghost Dance.

In 1889 Wovoka suffered a fever during a solar eclipse. In his delirium he reported being taken to the Supreme Being, who directed him to promote the practice of working in harmony with whites. If Indians followed this teaching and continued to dance the circle dance, whites would disappear. As Wovoka's teachings spread they found a ready audience among the vanquished Teton Lakota Sioux, the end result being the tragedy at Wounded Knee, South Dakota.

Wovoka was disheartened by Wounded Knee, since his teachings had stressed nonviolence. Nevertheless, for the remainder of his life he continued to believe in his vision and urged peace between Indians and whites.

See also: Ghost Dance; Wounded Knee Massacre
Further Reading: Bailey, *Wovoka*

Wright, Gen. George
ca. 1801–1865

Born in Connecticut, George Wright graduated from West Point in 1822. Appointed a second lieutenant in the Third Infantry, he first saw action against the Seminoles in Florida, for which he received the brevet rank of major. After distinguished service in the Mexican War, he was appointed colonel of the Ninth Infantry in 1855. He was named commander of the District of Columbia in the Pacific Northwest in 1856, the unsettled years of the Yakima and Rogue River Wars.

In 1856 he conducted what has been termed a "bloodless campaign" against the Yakimas. Lacking provisions to feed prisoners, he grouped them in temporary locations where they could be self-supportive. To ensure his orders were followed he took hostages from each group. Citizens and territorial officials tended to be unhappy not only with Wright's campaign but also with the army's overall prosecution of the war, believing that a firmer hand had been called for.

A quiet but generally able officer of substantial experience, Wright's style did not fit the mood of the territory. Promoted to brigadier general upon the outbreak of the Civil War, he commanded the Department of the Pacific until 1864. He drowned following a shipwreck on the Pacific Coast in 1865.

See also: Kamiakin; Rogue River War; Steptoe, Col. Edward Jenner; Yakima-Rogue War
Further Reading: Burns, *Jesuits in the Indian Wars of the Northwest;* Glassley, *Pacific Northwest Indian Wars;* Utley, *Frontiersmen in Blue*

Y

Yakima-Rogue War
1855–1856

At the great council held at Walla Walla in May 1855 the Walla Wallas, Cayuses, Umatillas, Yakimas, and Nez Perce agreed to exchange much of their land for cash and other annuities. Of the participating tribes, the Nez Perce alone remained generally amenable to the treaty's provisions. The other tribes, especially the Yakimas, led by brothers Kamiakin and Skloom, were unhappy and voiced their displeasure with the terms.

Although the treaty was yet to be ratified by Congress, word was that the land east of the Cascade Mountains was open for settlement. Coincidentally, the discovery of gold along the Columbia River in northeastern Washington, near the Canadian border, heightened interest in the territory—and increased tension, since prospectors had to cross Yakima territory to reach the goldfields.

At the same time, tension was rising in Yakima country, and there was another flare-up with the Rogue Indians. Although some remained on the Table Rock Reservation established for them after the Rogue War of 1853, others, dissatisfied with conditions, continued raiding targets of opportunity. Angry citizens were not inclined to make a distinction between the guilty and the innocent. In this climate, a group of volunteers attacked an Indian camp in October 1855, killing 23 women, children, and old men. The Indians promptly retaliated with a strike of their own, which fueled tensions even more. Some of the Rogues detached themselves from those who argued for war and placed themselves under military protection. Others simply moved into the mountains, seeking refuge there. White cries for extermination echoed throughout the area. Additional volunteer groups were quickly formed and ranged throughout the country, skirmishing several times with the Indians.

In the spring of 1856 Gen. John E. Wool, commanding the Pacific Department, put three columns of troops in the field with orders to converge on the Rogue River country from Forts Humboldt, Orford, and Lane. Wool's primary concern was farther north, where conflict was expected among the Yakimas. Yet the Rogue threat would still have to be met, and so Wool faced war on two fronts.

After unsuccessfully campaigning for two months, one column found that its toughest foes were the weather and the terrain. In late May, however, another column under Capt. A. J. Smith was attacked by Indians led by a defiant chief named Old John at Big Meadows on the north bank of the Rogue River. The Indians had agreed to surrender then changed their minds, and Smith's command soon found itself surrounded, occupying a small rise of ground. There was hard fighting for 24 hours until a relief column under Capt. C. C. Augur arrived to drive off the attackers. Smith's command suffered losses of 11 killed and 20 wounded. Despite this near-victory, the arrival of additional contingents of volunteers persuaded the Indians that further resistance was futile, and in June most surrendered.

Meanwhile, the Yakimas were growing increasingly restless, urged on by their eloquent spokesman, Kamiakin, who was trying to forge an Indian alliance—much as Tecumseh, Black Hawk, and others had tried before him. The Yakima War was precipitated by the murder of two prospectors. This incident was followed by the murder of an Indian agent who arrived to undertake an investigation of the first murders.

As a result, one army column under Maj. Granville Haller marched from Fort Dalles on 3 October while a smaller column of about 100 regulars and volunteers under Capt. Maurice Maloney moved in from the west. On 6 October, Haller encountered Kamiakin and a force of 500. Surrounded for two days, Haller broke out and fought his way back to Fort Dalles.

Kamiakin's victory breathed life into the Indian cause—and brought more white volunteers. At Fort Dalles, a mixed force of regulars and volunteers under Brig. Gen. Gabriel Rains took the field against the Yakimas at the end of October. Rains's command merely skirmished with Indians. The failure of both Rains and Maloney to accomplish much prompted General Wool to take personal charge of the situation. Wool's strategy was to station garrisons throughout Yakima territory. To implement this strategy he had a force of about 1,000, and he requested additional troops.

Both sides of the Cascades saw Indian attacks, including Seattle, which was defended by townspeople and a contingent of U.S. sailors and Marines who came ashore from their warships. Winter weather largely curtailed offensive troop movements, but in December a volunteer force under Lt. Col. James Kelly had a fight with a mixed force of Walla Wallas, Cayuses, and others. In a peace parley following the fight, the famous Walla Walla chief Peo-Peo-Mox-Mox was killed trying to escape.

In January reinforcements arrived from the Ninth U.S. Infantry, commanded by tough veteran Col. George Wright. Wool's objective, as soon as weather permitted, was to restore peace to the area near Puget Sound and to occupy the Walla Walla and Yakima Valleys. He assigned Lt. Col. Silas

Casey to the first task; Wright was given the second. Casey accomplished his mission after two fights with the Indians, and by March Wright was finally under way, having moved up the Columbia to Fort Dalles, after which he headed east toward Yakima country.

While Casey and Wright were going about their business, another column of volunteers marched through the country between the Snake and Palouse Rivers in southeastern Washington but found no Indians. In late March 1856 a mixed force of Indians attacked settlements along the Columbia River known as the Cascades. Wool responded by sending Lt. Philip H. Sheridan and 40 men upriver by boat. Sheridan's force drove the Indians out of the Lower Cascades. Meanwhile, Wright, who had now returned to Fort Dalles, was alerted to this new development and moved in to clear the Upper Cascades, then linked up with Sheridan.

In late April Wright headed back to Yakima country with three companies of infantry, a company of dragoons, and a company of the Third Artillery. Following Wright was an additional force of three companies under the command of Lt. Col. Edward J. Steptoe. Two additional companies under Maj. Robert Garnett marched from Puget Sound, bringing Wright's total force to ten companies when the three columns united in late May.

While Wright paused to construct a log bridge over the Naches River, north of present-day Yakima, the Indians watched, arguing among themselves as to the wisdom of fighting such a large force. The subsequent consensus was to surrender. Some chiefs crossed the river to confer with Wright. Kamiakin, not surprisingly, refused to negotiate. At any rate, the chiefs agreed to surrender all hostiles in five days, a pledge that soon proved hollow.

Leaving Steptoe and three companies to guard his supplies and complete the construction of Fort Naches, Wright took the remainder of his command on a sweep through Yakima country. The march gave Wright the clear impression that the Indians had calmed down and backed off of their hostile posture, and so by late July he had returned to Fort Dalles. The treaties negotiated by Governor Isaac I. Stevens had not yet been ratified, so the situation remain unsettled.

For his part, Stevens, unhappy that the army had failed to prosecute its campaign against the Indians more vigorously, decided to act and ordered two volunteer forces to move against the Yakimas. One column of 400 volunteers under Lt. Col. B. F. Shaw encountered a similar-sized war party in the Grande Ronde Valley in mid-July. In a brief but hard fight the Indians were defeated and their village destroyed.

Meanwhile, General Wool was concerned about protecting peaceful Indians from the vengeful volunteers. He was thus waging a war within a war, in a way. Accordingly, Wright was ordered back to the Walla Walla Valley with orders to build a fort and remove unauthorized volunteers from the area, under arrest if necessary.

Wright sent Lieutenant Colonel Steptoe as his deputy along with Governor Stevens to hold a great council with the Indians that Shaw's volunteers had collected. The Indians, some 4,000, were in an uncertain mood. Stevens, meanwhile, had released his volunteers and, sensing that trouble might be afoot, asked Steptoe for protection. Steptoe, then in the process of building his fort, refused the request on the grounds that his small force needed to remain intact. As the council disintegrated some of the young warriors threatened Stevens while he left to join Steptoe. Advised of this development, Steptoe provided a small escort for the governor as far as the Columbia River. An angry Stevens felt that his powers as territorial governor had been usurped by the military, whose authority in this particular situation was supported by the U.S. government over the governor's mighty protests.

The Yakima War resolved nothing to speak of, although it did result in the creation of two forts in Yakima country. The end of the war was not brought about by military success in the field. Rather, it seemed to simply sputter and die. More than anything it set the stage for the next conflict.

See also: Kamiakin; Stevens, Gov. Isaac Ingalls; Wool, Gen. John Ellis
Further Reading: Bischoff, *The Yakima Indian War;* Josephy, *The Nez Perce and the Opening of the Northwest;* Utley, *Frontiersmen in Blue*

Yamasee War
1715–1716

Like the Tuscaroras, their neighbors to the north, the Yamasee of South Carolina had long suffered at the hands of unscrupulous traders and some settlers. On Good Friday, 15 April 1715, a mixed Indian force, mainly Yamasee but including some Catawbas and other tribes, attacked settlements north of Savannah, burning buildings and killing more than 100. Some believed the attack was incited by the Spanish, who feared British expansion into their territory. The French, who saw British efforts to establish trade with the Choctaws, a Mississippi tribe, as a threat to their own economic well-being, may also have persuaded the powerful Creeks to interdict British trade routes, thereby indirectly aiding the Yamasee.

In the wake of the Yamasee attack, Gov. Charles Craven quickly assembled the militia and launched a punitive strike in June, burning villages and killing many. Relentlessly, Craven pursued the Yamasee as they fled south, seeking sanctuary in Spanish Florida. So thorough was Craven's pursuit that the Yamasee almost ceased to exist as a tribal entity thereafter. What had been Yamasee territory now became part of James Oglethorpe's new colony of Georgia. The Yamasee War made Britain aware of France's increasing determination to compete for control of North America.

Further Reading: Axelrod, *Chronicle of the Indian Wars;* Leach, *Arms for Empire*

Year of Sorrow (Year of Blood)

Defending the Kentucky frontier against Indian raids was always costly, but it was especially so in 1781. During this period, which came to be known as the Year of Sorrow, or Year of Blood, the British increased their support and encouragement of Indian raids in the Kentucky region.

Further Reading: Bakeless, *Background to Glory*

Yellow Medicine Agency
See Upper Sioux Agency, Minnesota

Yuma War
1851–1852

In the mid-nineteenth century, the crossing of the Colorado River at its junction with the Gila was an important entry point to southern California. At that time the region was inhabited by Yumas and Mohaves, kindred tribes who proved hostile to travelers from time to time. When the first white travelers began to arrive in 1849, the Yuma operated what eventually proved to be a profitable ferry operation. When a band of opportunistic whites commandeered the operation, this set the stage for conflict.

Biding their time, the Yuma waited until the whites were not expecting trouble, then surprised and killed most of them, retaking the ferry operation. In light of this, the army built Fort Yuma at the crossing in 1850. However, the difficulty of supplying the post led to its abandonment the following year.

Late in 1851 a large war party of Yuma attacked a band of sheepherders but were driven off, largely because of the determination of the leader, a Mexican War veteran who employed his howitzer to good advantage. Other Indian attacks resulted in military action by Maj. Samuel P. Heintzelman, who led a Christmas Day attack on one village. Reinforced by troops who arrived in February 1852, Heintzelman launched a second campaign, burning more villages along the Colorado River; a second column under Lt. Thomas Sweeney attacked villages in Baja.

During the summer and early fall of 1852, there were several unsuccessful attempts to negotiate a peaceful settlement. On 29 September Heintzelman surprised a Yuma village near present-day Blyth, California. The Yuma offered no opposition, and by October a peace had been arranged ending the war.

Further Reading: Sweeney, *Journal of Lieut. Thomas Sweeney;* Utley, *Frontiersmen in Blue;* Woodward, *Feud on the Colorado*

References and Selected Readings

Literature pertaining to the Indian wars exists in such abundance that any bibliography seeking to be comprehensive would fill at least a sizable volume, if not more. Such a work (or works), it is hoped, will one day be available to scholars, researchers, and writers.

For those so interested, primary source materials exist in a variety of forms and include letters, journals/diaries, government reports, and unpublished manuscripts. These materials may be found in a variety of repositories, ranging from federal archives to various state and local historical societies, university libraries, and private institutions such as the Huntington and Newberry Libraries. The researcher interested in exploring these sources will find that the *Handbook for Research in American History* by Francis Paul Prucha (Lincoln: University of Nebraska Press, 1987) provides an excellent overview.

Newspapers and periodicals also contain a wealth of material on the Indian wars. In addition to various commercial publications such as *American Heritage,* nearly every state historical society has now, or has in the past, regularly published a journal, many of which contain articles relevant to research on the Indian wars.

In the bibliography that follows, no attempt was made to be all-inclusive. Nevertheless, there was a conscientious effort to cover as much ground as was deemed appropriate and practical given the necessary limitations of space. In any event, here is a list of selected readings that will guide the reader toward other works that may shed further light on topics of particular interest.

Afton, Jean, David Fridtjof Halas, and Andrew Masich. *Cheyenne Dog Soldiers: A Ledgerbook History of Coups and Combat.* Niwot: University Press of Colorado, 1997.

Alberts, Donald E. *Brandy Station to Manilla Bay: A Biography of General Wesley Merritt.* Austin: Presidial Press, 1980.

Ambrose, Stephen E. *Undaunted Courage: Meriwether Lewis, Thomas Jefferson, and the Opening of the American West.* New York: Simon and Schuster, 1996.

Anderson, Gary Clayton. *Little Crow: Spokesman for the Sioux.* St. Paul: Minnesota Historical Society Press, 1986.

Anderson, Gary Clayton, and Alan R. Woolworth, eds. *Through Dakota Eyes: Narrative Accounts of the Minnesota Indian War of 1862.* St. Paul: Minnesota Historical Society Press, 1988.

Arnold, R. Ross. *The Indian Wars of Idaho.* Caldwell, ID: Caxton Printers, 1932.

Athearn, Robert G. *William Tecumseh Sherman and the Settlement of the West.* Norman: University of Oklahoma Press, 1956.

———. *Forts of the Upper Missouri.* Lincoln: University of Nebraska Press, 1967.

Axelrod, Alan. *Chronicle of the Indian Wars from Colonial Times to Wounded Knee.* New York: Prentice-Hall, 1993.

Bailey, Paul. *Wovoka: The Indian Messiah.* Los Angeles: Westernlore Press, 1957.

Bakeless, John. *Background to Glory: The Life of George Rogers Clark.* Lincoln: University of Nebraska Press, 1992.

———. *Daniel Boone.* Harrisburg: Stackpole, 1965.

Baker, Robert Orr. *The Muster Roll: A Biography of Fort Ripley, Minnesota.* St. Paul: Smyth, No Date.

Ball, Eve. *In the Days of Victorio: Recollections of a Warm Springs Apache.* Tucson: University of Arizona Press, 1970.

Bandel, Eugene. *Frontier Life in the Army, 1854–1861.* Glendale, CA: Arthur H. Clark, 1932.

Beecher Island Association. *The Battle of Beecher Island.* Wray, CO: The Beecher Island Battle Memorial Association, 1985.

Bennett, James A. *Forts and Forays: A Dragoon in New Mexico, 1850–1856.* Ed. Clinton E. Brooks and Frank D. Reeve. Albuquerque, University of New Mexico Press, 1996.

Berthrong, Donald J. *The Southern Cheyennes.* Norman: University of Oklahoma Press, 1963.

Berton, Pierre. *The Invasion of Canada, 1812–1813.* Markham, Ontario, Canada: Penguin Books, 1980.

———. *Flames Across the Border: The Canadian-American Tragedy, 1813–1814.* Boston: Little Brown, 1981.

Billington, Monroe Lee. *New Mexico's Buffalo Soldiers, 1860–1900.* Niwot: University Press of Colorado, 1991.

Billington, Ray Allen. *Westward Expansion: A History of the American Frontier.* New York: Macmillan, 1960.

Bischoff, W. N., S.J. "Yakima Campaign of 1856." 31 *Mid-America* (1949), pp. 162–208.

Bolton, Herbert Eugene. *Spanish Exploration in the Southwest, 1542–1706.* New York: Charles Scribner's Sons, 1916.

———. *Coronado on the Turquoise Trail: Knight of Pueblo and Plains.* Albuquerque: University of New Mexico Press, 1949.

Bourke, John G. *An Apache Campaign in the Sierra Madre.* New York: Charles Scribner, 1958.

———. *On the Border with Crook.* New York: Charles Scribner's Sons, 1891.

Bourne, Russell. *The Red King's Rebellion: Racial Politics in New England, 1675–1678.* New York: Atheneum, 1990.

Brimlow, George F. *The Bannock Indian War of 1878.* Caldwell: Caxton Printers, 1938.

Brookhiser, Richard. *Founding Father: Rediscovering George Washington.* New York: Free Press, 1996.

Brown, D. Alexander, *The Galvanized Yankees.* Urbana: University of Illinois Press, 1963.

———. *Bury My Heart at Wounded Knee.* New York: Holt Rinehart, 1970.

———. *Grierson's Raid.* Urbana: University of Illinois Press, 1954.

Brown, Mark H. *The Flight of the Nez Perce: A History of the Nez Perce War.* New York: G. P. Putnam, 1967.

———. *The Plainsmen of the Yellowstone: A History of the Yellowstone Basin.* New York: G. P. Putnam, 1961.

Burns, Robert Ignatius, S.J. *The Jesuits in the Indian Wars of the Northwest.* New Haven: Yale University Press, 1966.

Canfield, Gae W. *Sarah Winnemucca of the Northern Paiutes.* Norman: University of Oklahoma Press, 1983.

Capps, Benjamin. *The Warren Wagontrain Raid.* Dallas: SMU Press, 1989.

Carley, Kenneth. *The Sioux Uprising of 1862.* St. Paul: Minnesota Historical Society Press, 1976.

Carpenter, John A. *Sword and Olive Branch: Oliver Otis Howard.* Pittsburgh: University of Pittsburgh Press, 1964.

Carrington, Frances C. *My Army Life: A Soldier's Wife at Fort Phil Kearny.* Boulder: Pruett Publishing, 1990.

Carrington, Margaret I. *Absaraka: Home of the Crows.* Lincoln: University of Nebraska Press, 1983.

Carroll, John M., ed. *The Black Military Experience in the American West.* New York: Liveright, 1971.

Carter, Harvey Lewis. *"Dear Old Kit": The Historical Christopher Carson.* Norman: University of Oklahoma Press, 1968.

Carter, Robert G. *On the Border with Mackenzie.* New York: Antiquarian Press, 1961.

Chalfant, William Y. *Cheyennes and Horse Soldiers: The 1857 Expedition and the Battle of Solomon's Fork.* Norman: University of Oklahoma Press, 1989.

———. *Without Quarter: The Wichita Expedition and the Fight on Crooked Creek.* Norman: University of Oklahoma Press, 1991.

Clum, Woodworth. *Apache Agent: The Story of John P. Clum.* Boston: Houghton Mifflin, 1936.

Comfort, Will Levington. *Apache.* Lincoln: University of Nebraska Press, 1986.

Conkling, Roscoe P., and Margaret B. Conkling. *The Butterfield Overland Mail, 1857–1869*. 3 vols. Glendale, CA: Arthur H. Clark, 1947.

Conner, Daniel Ellis. *Joseph Reddeford Walker and the Arizona Adventure*. Norman: University of Oklahoma Press, 1956.

Corless, Hank. *The Weiser Indians: Shoshoni Peacemakers*. Salt Lake City: University of Utah Press, 1990.

Covington, James W. *The Seminoles of Florida*. Gainesville: University Press of Florida, 1993.

Craig, R. S. *The Fighting Parson: The Biography of Colonel John M. Chivington*. Los Angeles: Westernlore Press, 1959.

Crampton, C. Gregory, ed. *The Mariposa Indian War, 1850–1851. Diaries of Robert Eccleston: The California Gold Rush, Yosemite, and the High Sierra*. Salt Lake City: University of Utah Press, 1957.

Cremony, John C. *Life among the Apaches*. Tucson: Arizona Silhouettes, 1954.

Crook, George. *General George Crook: His Autobiography*. Ed. Martin F. Schmitt. Norman: University of Oklahoma Press, 1946.

Custer, George Armstrong. *My Life on the Plains: Personal Experiences with Indians*. New York: Sheldon, 1875.

Danker, Donald F., ed. *Man of the Plains: Recollections of Luther North, 1856–1882*. Lincoln: University of Nebraska Press, 1961.

Darling, Roger. *A Sad and Terrible Blunder: Generals Terry and Custer at the Little Bighorn*. Vienna, VA: Potomac-Western Press, 1990.

Dary, David A. *The Buffalo Book*. Athens: Ohio University Press, 1974.

De Mallie, Raymond J., ed. *The Sixth Grandfather*. Lincoln: University of Nebraska Press, 1985.

DeBarthe, Joe. *Life and Adventures of Frank Grouard*. Norman: University of Oklahoma Press, 1958.

Debo, Angie. *And Still the Waters Run: The Betrayal of the Five Civilized Tribes*. Princeton: Princeton University Press, 1991.

———. *A History of the Indians of the United States*. Norman: University of Oklahoma Press, 1970.

———. *Road to Disappearance: A History of the Creek Indians*. Norman: University of Oklahoma Press, 1941.

Denig, Edwin T., and John C. Ewers, eds. *Five Indian Tribes of the Upper Missouri*. Norman: University of Oklahoma Press, 1961.

Derleth, August. *Vincennes: Portal to the West*. New York: Prentice-Hall, 1968.

Dixon, David. *Hero of Beecher Island: The Life and Military Career of George A. Forsyth*. Lincoln: University of Nebraska Press, 1994.

Dixon, Olive K. *Life of Billy Dixon*. Dallas: n.p., 1927.

Dowd, Gregory Evans. *A Spirited Resistance: The North American Indian Struggle for Unity, 1745–1815*. Baltimore: Johns Hopkins University Press, 1992.

Downes, Randolph C. *Council Fires on the Upper Ohio: A Narrative of Indian Affairs in the Upper Ohio Valley until 1795*. Pittsburgh: University of Pittsburgh Press, 1940.

Drips, J. H. *Three Years among the Indians in Dakota*. New York: Sol Lewis, 1974.

Dunlay, Thomas W. *Wolves for the Blue Soldiers: Indian Scouts and Auxiliaries with the United States Army, 1860–1890*. Lincoln: University of Nebraska Press, 1982.

Dunn, Jacob. *Massacres of the Mountains*. New York, 1886.

Dunn, William R. *I Stand by Sand Creek: A Defense of Colonel John M. Chivington and the Third Colorado Cavalry*. Fort Collins, CO: Old Army Press, 1985.

Eckert, Allan W. *The Frontiersmen: A Narrative*. Boston: Little Brown, 1967.

———. *Wilderness Empire: A Narrative*. Boston: Little Brown, 1969.

———. *The Conquerors: A Narrative*. Boston: Little Brown, 1970.

———. *The Wilderness War: A Narrative*. Boston: Little Brown, 1978.

———. *Gateway to Empire: A Narrative*. Boston: Little Brown, 1983.

———. *Twilight of Empire: A Narrative*. Boston: Little Brown, 1988.

———. *A Sorrow in Our Heart: The Life of Tecumseh*. New York: Bantam Books, 1992.

———. *That Dark and Bloody River: Chronicles of the Ohio River Valley.* New York: Bantam Books, 1995.

Edmunds, R. David, and Joseph L. Peyser. *The Fox Wars: The Mesquakie Challenge to New France.* Norman: University of Oklahoma Press, 1993.

Ege, Robert J. *Tell Baker to Strike Them Hard: Incident on the Marias.* Bellevue, NE: The Old Army Press, 1970.

Ellis, Richard N. *General Pope and U.S. Indian Policy.* Albuquerque: University of New Mexico Press, 1970.

Emmitt, Roger. *The Last War Trail: The Utes and the Settlement of Colorado.* Norman: University of Oklahoma Press, 1965.

Ewers, John C. *The Blackfeet: Raiders of the Northern Plains.* Norman: University of Oklahoma Press, 1958.

Faragher, John Mack. *Daniel Boone: The Life and Legend of an American Pioneer.* New York: Henry Holt, 1992.

Fehrenbach, T. R. *Comanches: The Destruction of a People.* New York: Da Capo Press, 1994.

Finerty, John. *War-Path and Bivouac or the Conquest of the Sioux.* Norman: University of Oklahoma Press, 1961.

Flexner, James Thomas. *Mohawk Baronet: Sir William Johnson of New York.* New York: Harper and Bros., 1959.

Forbes, Jack D. *Apache, Navaho, and Spaniard.* Norman: University of Oklahoma Press, 1994.

Foreman, Grant. *The Five Civilized Tribes.* Norman: University of Oklahoma Press, 1934.

Fort Phil Kearny/Bozeman Trail Association Members. *Portraits of Fort Phil Kearny.* Sheridan, WY: Fort Phil Kearny/Bozeman Trail Association, 1993.

Fox, Richard Allan Jr. *Archaeology, History, and Custer's Last Battle.* Norman: University of Oklahoma Press, 1993.

Gaff, Alan, and Maureen Gaff, eds. *Adventures on the Western Frontier: Major General John Gibbon.* Bloomington: Indiana University Press, 1994.

Gilbert, Bil. *God Gave Us This Country: Tekamthi and the First American Civil War.* New York: Atheneum, 1989.

Glassley, Ray Hoard. *Pacific Northwest Indian Wars.* Portland: Binfords and Mort, 1953.

Gordon-McCutchan, R. C., ed. *Kit Carson: Indian Fighter or Indian Killer?* Niwot: University Press of Colorado, 1996.

Graham, Col. William. *The Custer Myth: A Source Book of Custeriana.* Harrisburg: Stackpole, 1953.

Gray, John S. *Centennial Campaign: The Sioux War of 1876.* Fort Collins, CO: Old Army Press, 1976.

———. *Custer's Last Campaign: Mitch Boyer and the Little Bighorn Reconstructed.* Lincoln: University of Nebraska Press, 1991.

———. "On the Trail of Lonesome Charley Reynolds." 14(8) *Chicago Corral* (October 1957).

Graymont, Barbara. *The Iroquois in the American Revolution.* Syracuse: Syracuse University Press, 1972.

Greene, Jerome A. *Slim Buttes, 1876: An Episode of the Great Sioux War.* Norman: University of Oklahoma Press, 1982.

———. *Yellowstone Command: Colonel Nelson A. Miles, and the Great Sioux War, 1876–1877.* Norman: University of Oklahoma Press, 1991.

———. *Battles and Skirmishes of the Great Sioux War, 1876–1877: The Military View.* Norman: University of Oklahoma Press, 1993.

———. *Lakota and Cheyenne Indian Views of the Great Sioux War, 1876-1877.* Norman: University of Oklahoma Press, 1994.

Grinnell, George Bird. *The Fighting Cheyennes.* Norman: University of Oklahoma Press, 1956.

———. *Two Great Scouts and Their Pawnee Battalion.* Cleveland: Arthur H. Clark, 1928.

Hafen, LeRoy R., and Ann W. Hafen, eds. *Powder River Campaigns and Sawyers Expedition of 1865.* Glendale, CA: Arthur H. Clark, 1965.

Hagen, William T. *The Sac and Fox Indians.* Norman: University of Oklahoma Press, 1980.

Haines, Aubrey L. *An Elusive Victory: The Battle of the Big Hole.* West Glacier, MT: Glacier Natural History Association, 1991.

Haley, James. *The Buffalo War.* Garden City: Doubleday, 1976.

Hampton, Bruce. *Children of Grace: The Nez Perce War of 1877.* New York: Henry Holt, 1994.

Hassrick, Royal B. *The Sioux: Life and Customs of a Warrior Society.* Norman: University of Oklahoma Press, 1964.

Hebard, Grace Raymond, and E. A. Brininstool. *The Bozeman Trail.* 2 vols. Lincoln: University of Nebraska Press, 1990.

Hedren, Paul. *Fort Laramie, 1876: Chronicle of a Frontier Post at War.* Lincoln: University of Nebraska Press, 1988.

Heidler, David S., and Jeanne T. Heidler. *Old Hickory's War: Andrew Jackson and the Quest for Empire.* Mechanicsburg: Stackpole Books, 1996.

Heyman, Max L. *Prudent Soldier: A Biography of Major General E.R.S. Canby, 1817–1873.* Glendale: Arthur H. Clark, 1959.

Hodge, Frederick Webb, ed. *Handbook of American Indians North of Mexico.* 2 vols. Washington, D.C.: U.S. Government Printing Office, 1912.

Hoig, Stan. *The Sand Creek Massacre.* Norman: University of Oklahoma Press, 1963.

———. *The Battle of the Washita.* Lincoln: University of Nebraska Press, 1976.

Howard, Oliver O. *My Life and Experiences among Our Hostile Indians.* New York: Da Capo Press, 1972.

Hoxie, Frederick E. *Parading through History: The Making of the Crow Nation in America, 1805–1935.* Boston: Houghton-Mifflin, 1996.

Hunt, Aurora. *Major General James Henry Carleton, 1814–1873: Western Frontier Dragoon.* Glendale, CA: Arthur H. Clark, 1958.

———. *The Army of the Pacific: Its Operations in California, Texas, etc....., 1860–1866.* Glendale, CA: Arthur H. Clark, 1961.

Hurley, Victor. *Arrows against Steel: The History of the Bow.* New York: Mason/Charter, 1975.

Hurt, R. Douglas. *The Ohio Frontier: Crucible of the Old Northwest, 1720–1830.* Bloomington: Indiana University Press, 1996.

Hutton, Paul Andrew. *Phil Sheridan and His Army.* Lincoln: University of Nebraska Press, 1985.

Hutton, Paul Andrew, ed. *Soldiers West: Biographies from the Military Frontier.* Lincoln: University of Nebraska Press, 1987.

Hyde, George E. *Life of George Bent, Written from His Letters.* Ed. Savoie Lottinville. Norman: University of Oklahoma Press, 1967.

———. *Pawnee Indians.* Norman: University of Oklahoma Press, 1973.

———. *Red Cloud's Folk: A History of the Oglala Sioux Indians.* Norman: University of Oklahoma Press, 1937.

———. *Spotted Tail's Folk: A History of the Brule Sioux.* Norman: University of Oklahoma Press, 1961.

———. *A Sioux Chronicle.* Norman: University of Oklahoma Press, 1956.

Innis, Ben. *Bloody Knife.* Fort Collins, CO: Old Army Press, 1973.

Iverson, Peter. *Navajo Nation.* Albuquerque: University of New Mexico Press, 1981.

Jacobson, Clair. *Whitestone Hill: The Indians and the Battle.* LaCrosse, WI: Pine Tree Publishing, 1991.

Jackson, Donald, ed. *Black Hawk: An Autobiography.* Urbana: University of Illinois Press, 1964.

Jeffrey, Julie Roy. *Converting the West: A Biography of Narcissa Whitman.* Norman: University of Oklahoma Press, 1991.

Jennings, Francis. *The Invasion of America: Indians, Colonialism, and the Cant of Conquest.* Chapel Hill: University of North Carolina Press, 1975.

———. *Empire of Fortune: Crowns, Colonies, and Tribes in the Seven Years War in America.* New York: W.W. Norton, 1988.

———. *The Founders of America.* New York: W.W. Norton, 1993.

John, Elizabeth A. H. *Storms Brewed in Other Men's Worlds: The Confrontation of Indians, Spanish, and French in the Southwest, 1540–1795.* College Station: Texas A&M University Press, 1975.

Jones, Robert H. *The Civil War in the Northwest: Nebraska, Wisconsin, Iowa, Minnesota, and the Dakotas.* Norman: University of Oklahoma Press, 1960.

Josephy, Alvin M. Jr. *The Civil War in the American West.* New York: Alfred Knopf, 1992.

———. *500 Nations: An Illustrated History of North American Indians.* New York: Alfred Knopf, 1994.

———. *The Nez Perce Indians and the Opening of the Northwest.* New Haven, CT: Yale University Press, 1965.

Kammen, Robert, Frederick Lefthand, and Joe Marshall. *Soldiers Falling into Camp: The Battles at the Rosebud and the Little Bighorn.* Encampment, WY: Affiliated Writers of America, 1992.

Kane, Lucile M., ed. *Military Life in Dakota: The Journal of Philippe Regis de Trobriand.* Lincoln: University of Nebraska Press, 1982.

Kappler, Charles J., comp. *Indian Laws and Treaties.* Washington, DC: U.S. Government Printing Office, 1904.

Keenan, Jerry. *The Wagon Box Fight.* Boulder: Lightning Tree Press, 1992.

———. "Yellowstone Kelly: From New York to Paradise." 40(3) *Montana: The Magazine of Western History* (Summer 1990), pp. 14–27.

Keim, DeB. Randolph. *Sheridan's Troopers on the Border: A Winter Campaign on the Plains.* Lincoln: University of Nebraska Press, 1985.

Kelly, Lawrence C. *Navajo Roundup: Selected Correspondence of Kit Carson's Expedition against the Navajo, 1863–1865.* Boulder: Pruett Publishing, 1970.

Kelly, Luther S. *Yellowstone Kelly: The Memoirs of Luther S. Kelly.* Ed. Milo M. Quaife. Lincoln: University of Nebraska Press, 1973.

Kelsey, Harry. *Frontier Capitalist: The Life of John Evans.* Denver: State Historical Society of Colorado, 1969.

Kessell, John L. *Kiva, Cross, and Crown: The Pecos Indians and New Mexico, 1540–1840.* Albuquerque: University of New Mexico Press, 1990.

Killoren, John., S.J. *"Come Blackrobe": De Smet and the Indian Tragedy.* Norman: University of Oklahoma Press, 1994.

King, Charles. *Indian Campaign Sketches of Cavalry Service in Arizona and on the Northern Plains.* Ed. Harry H. Anderson. Fort Collins, CO: Old Army Press, 1984.

King, Duane H., ed. *The Cherokee Indian Nation: A Troubled History.* Knoxville: University of Tennessee Press, 1979.

King, James T. *War Eagle: A Life of General Eugene A. Carr.* Lincoln: University of Nebraska Press, 1963.

Knaut, Andrew L. *The Pueblo Revolt of 1680: Conquest and Resistance in Seventeenth-Century New Mexico.* Norman: University of Oklahoma Press, 1995.

Knight, Oliver. *Following the Indian Wars: The Story of Newspaper Correspondents among the Indian Campaigners.* Norman: University of Oklahoma Press, 1960.

Kuhlman, Charles. *Legend into History and Did Custer Disobey Orders.* Harrisburg: Stackpole Books, 1994.

Laumer, Frank. *Dade's Last Command.* Gainesville: University Press of Florida, 1995.

Lavender, David. *Let Me Be Free: The Nez Perce Tragedy.* New York: Harper Collins, 1992.

———. *The Way to the Western Sea: Lewis and Clark across the Continent.* New York: Harper and Row, 1988.

Leach, Douglas Edward. *Arms for Empire: A Military History of the British Colonies in North America, 1607–1763.* New York: Macmillan, 1973.

———. *Roots of Conflict: British Armed Forces and Colonial Americans, 1677–1763.* Chapel Hill: University of North Carolina Press, 1986.

Leckie, William H. *The Military Conquest of the Southern Plains.* Norman: University of Oklahoma Press, 1963.

Leckie, William H., and Shirley A. Leckie. *Unlikely Warriors: General Benjamin H. Grierson and His Family.* Norman: University of Oklahoma Press, 1984.

Long, E. B. *Saints and the Union.* Urbana: University of Illinois Press, 1981.

Madsen, Brigham D. *The Shoshoni Frontier and the Bear River Massacre.* Salt Lake City: University of Utah Press, 1985.

———. *Glory Hunter: A Biography of Patrick Edward Connor*. Salt Lake City: University of Utah Press, 1990.

Mahon, John K. *History of the Second Seminole War, 1835–1842*. Gainesville: University Press of Florida, 1967.

———. *The War of 1812*. Gainesville: University Press of Florida, 1972.

Mails, Thomas E. *Mystic Warriors of the Plains: The Culture, Arts, Crafts, and Religion of the Plains Indians*. New York: Mallard Press, 1991.

Mangum, Neil C. *The Battle of the Rosebud: Prelude to the Little Bighorn*. El Segundo: Upton and Sons, 1987.

Marquis, Thomas. *Memoirs of a White Crow Indian*. New York: Century, 1928.

Marsh, Charles S. *People of the Shining Mountains: The Utes of Colorado*. Boulder: Pruett Publishing, 1982.

Marszalek, John F. *Sherman: A Soldier's Passion for Order*. New York: Free Press, 1993.

Mattes, Merrill J. *The Great Platte River Road*. Lincoln: Nebraska State Historical Society, 1969.

McCann, Lloyd E. "The Grattan Massacre." 37 *Nebraska History* (1956), pp. 1–26.

McChristian, Douglas C. *The U.S. Army in the West, 1870–1880*. Norman: University of Oklahoma Press, 1995.

McDermott, John D. *Forlorn Hope: The Battle of White Bird Canyon and the Beginning of the Nez Perce War*. Boise: State Historical Society, 1978.

McDermott, John Francis, ed. *Frenchmen and French Ways in the Mississippi Valley*. Urbana: University of Illinois Press, 1969.

McGinnis, Anthony. *Counting Coup and Cutting Horses: Intertribal Warfare on the Northern Plains, 1738–1889*. Evergreen, CO: Cordillera Press, 1990.

McNitt, Frank. *Navajo Wars: Military Campaigns, Slave Raids, and Reprisals*. Albuquerque: University of New Mexico Press, 1992.

McWhorter, Lucullus V. *Hear Me My Chiefs*. Caldwell, ID: Caxton Printers, 1952.

Mendoza, Patrick M. *Song of Sorrow: Massacre at Sand Creek*. Denver: Willow Wind Publishing, 1993.

Meyer, Roy W. *History of the Santee Sioux: United States Indian Policy on Trial*. Lincoln: University of Nebraska Press, 1967.

Mid-America Productions. *The Fort Laramie Treaty of 1868*. Collectors' Edition. Rapid City: Mid-America Productions.

Milanich, Jerald T., and Susan Milbrath. *First Encounters: Spanish Explorations in the Carribean and the United States, 1492–1570*. Gainesville: Florida Museum of Natural History, 1989.

Miles, Nelson A. *Personal Recollections and Observations of General Nelson A. Miles*. 2 vols. Lincoln: University of Nebraska Press, 1992.

Mills, Charles K. *Harvest of Barren Regrets: The Army Career of Frederick William Benteen*. Glendale: Arthur H. Clark, 1985.

Moller, George D. *American Military Shoulder Arms, Volume 1: Colonial and Revolutionary War Arms*. Niwot: University Press of Colorado, 1993.

———. *American Military Shoulder Arms, Volume 2: From the 1790s to the End of the Flintlock Period*. Niwot: University Press of Colorado, 1993.

Monnett, John H. *The Battle of Beecher Island and the Indian War of 1867–1869*. Niwot: University Press of Colorado, 1992.

Mooney, James. *The Ghost Dance Religion and the Sioux Outbreak of 1890*. Lincoln: University of Nebraska Press, 1991.

Morison, Samuel Eliot. *The European Discovery of America: The Northern Voyages, A.D. 500–1600*. New York: Oxford University Press, 1971.

Morris, Roy. *Sheridan: The Life and Wars of General Phil Sheridan*. Dayton, OH: Morningside Books, 1993.

———. *The European Discovery of America: The Southern Voyages, 1492–1616*. New York: Oxford University Press, 1974.

Murray, Keith A. *The Modocs and Their War*. Norman: University of Oklahoma Press, 1959.

Murray, Robert A. *Military Posts in the Powder River Country of Wyoming*. Buffalo, WY: The Office, 1990.

Nabokov, Peter, ed. *Native American Testimony: A Chronicle of Indian-White Relations from Prophecy to the Present*. New York: Penguin Books, 1991.

Nearing, Richard, and David Hoff. *Arizona Military Installations, 1752–1922: Presidios, Camps, and Forts.* Tempe, AZ: Gem Publishing, 1995.

Nichols, Roger. *General Henry Atkinson: A Western Military Career.* Norman: University of Oklahoma Press, 1965.

Nye, W. S. *Bad Medicine and Good: Tales of the Kiowas.* Norman: University of Oklahoma Press, 1962.

O'Donnell, James H. III. *Southern Indians in the American Revolution.* Knoxville: University of Tennessee Press, 1973.

Olson, James C. *Red Cloud and the Sioux Problem.* Lincoln: University of Nebraska Press, 1975.

Paher, Stanley W., ed. *Fort Churchill Nevada Outpost of the 1860s.* Las Vegas: Nevada Publications, 1981.

Peckham, Howard H. *Pontiac and the Indian Uprising.* Detroit: Wayne State University Press, 1994.

Pelzer, Louis. *Henry Dodge.* Iowa City: State Historical Society of Iowa, 1911.

Perry, Richard J. *Western Apache Heritage: People of the Mountain Corridor.* Austin: University of Texas Press, 1991.

Peters, Joseph P., comp. *Indian Battles and Skirmishes on the American Frontier, 1790–1898.* Ann Arbor: University Microfilms, 1966.

Pfaler, Louis, O.S.B. "The Sully Expedition of 1864." 31 *North Dakota History* (1964), pp. 1–54.

Phelps, McKinnie L., M.D., comp. *The Indian Captivity of Mary Kinnan, 1791–1794.* Boulder: Pruett Publishing, 1967.

Pierce, Michael D. *The Most Promising Young Officer: A Life of Ranald Slidell Mackenzie.* Norman: University of Oklahoma Press, 1993.

Potoma Corral of Westerners. *Great Western Indian Fights.* Lincoln: University of Nebraska Press, 1970.

Powell, Peter J. *Sweet Medicine.* 2 vols. Norman: University of Oklahoma Press, 1969.

Price, George F. *Across the Continent with the Fifth Cavalry.* New York: Antiquarian Press, 1959.

Prucha, Francis Paul. *Guide to Military Posts of the United States.* Madison: State Historical Society of Wisconsin, 1964.

———. *The Sword of the Republic: The United States Army on the Frontier, 1783–1846.* Lincoln: University of Nebraska Press, 1969.

———. *American Indian Treaties: The History of a Political Anomaly.* Berkeley: University of California Press, 1994.

Remini, Robert V. *Andrew Jackson and the Course of American Empire, 1767–1821.* New York: Harper and Row, 1977.

Rickey, Don Jr. *Forty Miles a Day on Beans and Hay: The Enlisted Soldier Fighting the Indian Wars.* Norman: University of Oklahoma Press, 1963.

Roberts, David. *Once They Moved Like the Wind: Cochise, Geronimo, and the Apache Wars.* New York: Simon and Schuster, 1993.

Roberts, Kenneth. *Northwest Passage.* Garden City, NY: Doubleday, 1937.

Robinson, Charles M. III. *A Good Year to Die: The Story of the Great Sioux War.* New York: Random House, 1995.

Robinson, Doane. *History of the Dakota or Sioux Indians.* Minneapolis: Ross and Haines, 1956.

Rockwell, Wilson. *The Utes: A Forgotten People.* Denver: Sage Books, 1956.

Rountree, Helen C. *The Powhatan Indians of Virginia.* Norman: University of Oklahoma Press, 1989.

Rowlandson, Mary. *The Soveraignty and Goodness of God . . . A Narrative of the Captivity and Restauration of Mrs. Mary Rowlandson.* Boston: n.p., 1682.

Russell, Don. *The Lives and Legends of Buffalo Bill.* Norman: University of Oklahoma Press, 1960.

———. *One Hundred and Three Fights and Scrimmages: The Story of General Reuben F. Bernard.* Washington, DC, 1936.

Sandoz, Mari. *Crazy Horse: Strange Man of the Oglalas.* New York: Hastings House, 1942.

———. *Cheyenne Autumn.* New York: Hastings House, 1953.

Schellie, Don. *Vast Domain of Blood: The Story of the Camp Grant Massacre.* Los Angeles: Westernlore Press, 1968.

Schultz, Duane. *Month of the Freezing Moon: The Sand Creek Massacre, November 1864.* New York: St. Martin's Press, 1990.

Sharp, Abbie Gardner. *History of the Spirit Lake Massacre.* Des Moines: Iowa Printing, 1892.

Turner, Frederick Jackson. *The Significance of the Frontier in American History.* Ed. Harold P. Simonson. New York: Continuum, 1991.

Smith, P. David. *Ouray: Chief of the Utes.* Ridgway, CO: Wayfinder Press, 1990.

Sprague, Marshall. *Massacre: The Tragedy at White River.* Boston: Little Brown, 1957.

Stands-in-Timber, John, and Margot Liberty. *Cheyenne Memories.* New Haven: Yale University Press, 1967.

Starr, Emmet. *History of the Cherokee Indians and Their Legends and Folklore.* Oklahoma City: n.p., 1921.

Steele, Ian K. *Warpaths: Invasions of North America.* New York: Oxford University Press, 1994.

———. *Betrayals: Fort William Henry and the Massacre.* New York: Oxford University Press, 1990.

Stern, Theodore. *The Klamath Tribe: A People and Their Reservation.* Seattle: University of Washington Press, 1966.

Stewart, Edgar I. *Custer's Luck.* Norman: University of Oklahoma Press, 1956.

Stone, W. L. *Life of Joseph Brant.* 2 vols. Reprint, St. Clair Shores, MN: Scholarly Press, 1970.

Strait, Newton A., comp. *Alphabetical List of Battles, 1754–1900: War of the Rebellion, Spanish-American War, Philippine Insurection, and all Old Wars with Dates.* Washington, D.C.: U.S. Government Printing Office, 1902.

Stratton, Royal. *Captivity of the Oatman Girls.* New York: 1858.

Sully, Langdon. *No Tears for the General: The Life of Alfred Sully, 1821-1879.* Palo Alto, CA: American West Publishing, 1974.

Sweeney, Edwin R. *Cochise: Chiricahua Apache Chief.* Norman: University of Oklahoma Press, 1991.

Sweeney, Lt. Thomas W. *Journal of Lt. Thomas W. Sweeney, 1849–1853.* Los Angeles: Westernlore Press, 1956.

Sword, Wiley. *President Washington's Indian War: The Struggle for the Old Northwest, 1790–1795.* Norman: University of Oklahoma Press, 1985.

Terrell, John Upton, and George Walton. *Faint the Trumpet Sounds.* New York: David McKay, 1966.

Thom, James Alexander. *From Sea to Shining Sea.* New York: Ballantine Books, 1984.

Thrapp, Dan L. *Al Sieber: Chief of Scouts.* Norman: University of Oklahoma Press, 1995.

———. *The Conquest of Apacheria.* Norman: University of Oklahoma Press, 1967.

———. *General Crook and the Sierra Madre Adventure.* Norman: University of Oklahoma Press, 1972.

———. *Victorio and the Mimbres Apaches.* Norman: University of Oklahoma Press, 1980.

Time-Life Books, *People of the Lakes.* Alexandria, VA: Time-Life Books, 1994.

———. *Tribes of the Southern Plains.* Alexandria, VA: Time-Life Books, 1995.

Trenholm, Virginia C., and Maurine Carley. *The Shoshonis: Sentinels of the Rockies.* Norman: University of Oklahoma Press, 1964.

———. *The Arapahoes, Our People.* Norman: University of Oklahoma Press, 1970.

Urquhart, Lena M. *Colorow: The Angry Chieftan.* Denver: Golden Bell Press, 1968.

Urwin, Gregory J. *Custer Victorious: The Civil War Battles of General George Armstrong Custer.* East Brunswick, NJ: Associated University Presses, 1983.

Utley, Robert M. *Cavalier in Buckskin: George Armstrong Custer and the Western Military Frontier.* Norman: University of Oklahoma Press, 1988.

———. *Frontier Regulars: The United States Army and the Indian, 1866–1890.* New York: Macmillan, 1973.

———. *Frontiersmen in Blue: The United States Army and the Indian, 1848–1865.* New York: Macmillan, 1967.

———. *The Indian Frontier of the American West.* Albuquerque: University of New Mexico Press, 1984.

———. *The Lance and the Shield: The Life and Times of Sitting Bull.* New York: Henry Holt, 1993.

———. *Last Days of the Sioux Nation.* New Haven: Yale University Press, 1963.

———. *A Clash of Cultures: Fort Bowie and the Chiricahua Apaches.* Washington, D.C.: National Park Service, 1977.

Utley, Robert M., ed. *Life in Custer's Cavalry: Diaries and Letters of Albert and Jennie Barnitz, 1867–1868.* New Haven: Yale University Press, 1977.

Utley, Robert M., and Wilcomb E. Washburn. *The American Heritage History of the Indian Wars.* New York: Barnes and Noble Books, 1992.

Vaughan, Alden T. *New England Frontier: Puritans and Indians, 1620-1675.* Boston: Little, Brown, 1965.

Vaughn, J. W. *With Crook at the Rosebud.* Harrisburg, PA: Stackpole, 1956.

———. *Indian Fights: New Facts on Seven Encounters.* Norman: University of Oklahoma Press, 1966.

———. *The Battle of Platte Bridge.* Norman: University of Oklahoma Press, 1963.

Vestal, Stanley. *Warpath: The True Story of the Fighting Sioux.* Lincoln: University of Nebraska Press, 1984.

Wainright, Nicholas B. *George Croghan: Wilderness Diplomat.* Published for the Institute of Early American History and Culture. Chapel Hill: University of North Carolina Press, 1959.

Wallace, Ernest, and E. A. Hoebel. *The Comanches: Lords of the South Plains.* Norman: University of Oklahoma Press, 1988.

Ware, Eugene F. *The Indian War of 1864.* Ed. Clyde F. Walton. Lincoln: University of Nebraska Press, 1994.

Warren, William Whipple. *History of the Ojibway People.* St. Paul: Minnesota Historical Society Press, 1984.

Weeks, Philip, ed. *The American Indian Experience: A Profile, 1524 to the Present.* Arlington Heights, IL: Forum Press, 1988.

Weibert, Hank. *Sixty-six Years in Custer's Shadow.* Billings, MT: Bannack Publishing, 1985.

Weigley, Russell F. *History of the U.S. Army.* New York: Macmillan, 1967.

Welch, James, with Paul Stekler. *Killing Custer: The Battle of the Little Bighorn and the Fate of the Plains Indians.* New York: Norton, 1994.

White, Lonnie J., ed. *Hostiles and Horse Soldiers: Indian Battles and Campaigns in the West.* Boulder: Pruett Publishing, 1972.

Wilfong, Cheryl. *Following the Nez Perce Trail: A Guide to the Nee-Me-Poo National Historic Trail with Eyewitness Accounts.* Corvallis: Oregon State University Press, 1990.

Wood, W. J. *Battles of the Revolutionary War, 1775–1781.* New York: Da Capo Press, 1995.

Woodward, Arthur. *Feud on the Colorado.* Los Angeles: Westernlore Press, 1955.

Woodward, Grace. *The Cherokees.* Norman: University of Oklahoma Press, 1963.

Wooster, Robert. *Nelson A. Miles and the Twilight of the Frontier Army.* Lincoln: University of Nebraska Press, 1993.

———. *The Military and United States Indian Policy, 1865–1903.* Lincoln: University of Nebraska Press, 1988.

Worcester, Donald E. *The Apaches: Eagles of the Southwest.* Norman: University of Oklahoma Press, 1992.

Wright, Louis B. *The Cultural Life of the American Colonies.* New York: Harper and Row, 1956.

Index

Abenakis. *See* Abnakis
Abnaki War. *See* King William's War
Abnakis (Abenakis), 1, 67, 68, 116–117, 120–121, 167, 195
Abraham Lincoln, Fort, 61, 82
Acoma Pueblo, 1, 181, 220
  fight at, 1
Adams, Charles Francis, 138, 162, 203
Adobe Walls
  First Battle of, 2, 104
  Second Battle of, 2, 164, 188
Aix-la-Chappelle, Treaty of, 117
Albany (NY). *See* Orange, Fort
Alden, Capt. Bradford, 195
Alderdice, Susanna, 106, 226. *See also* Allen, Samuel, Jr.; Dustin, Hannah; Oatman family; Rowlandson, Mary White; Weichell, Maria
Alexander. *See* Wamsutta
Algonquian, 3, 22, 42, 120, 147, 159
Allen, Samuel, Jr., 3. *See also* Dustin, Hannah; Oatman family; Rowlandson, Mary White
Alliances, Indian-white, 3–4, 59
American Horse, 215
Amherst, Gen. Jeffrey, 4, 40, 172, 195, 220
Amherst's Decree, 4, 172. *See also* Pontiac's Uprising
Anjou, Philip of, 183
Anthony, Maj. Scott, 201
Apache, Fort, 45, 82
Apache Pass, Battle of, 4, 7, 136
Apache scouts, 55, 87, 104
Apache wars, 5, 6, 45, 48, 55–56, 104, 135–136
Apacheria. See Apaches
Apaches, 4, 5, 6, 7, 13, 31, 34, 37, 42, 48, 50, 55, 58, 66, 81, 87, 91, 95, 101, 123, 135, 136, 139, 150–151, 159, 169, 175, 180, 199, 203, 212, 239

Apalachees, 149, 219
Arapahos, 6, 7, 16, 52, 105–106, 113, 201, 238
Arbuthnot, Alexander, 204
Arikaras, 7
Arizona, Department of, 45
Arizona Territory, 58
Armbrister, Robert, 204
Armistead, Gen. Walker, 206
Artillery, 7, 81. *See also* Military units, white
Arundel, 1
Ash Hollow. *See* Blue Water, Battle of
Assiniboine, Fort, 82
Assowamset Swamp, 119
Athapascan, 6, 7
Atkinson, Fort (IA), 82
Atkinson, Fort (NE), 7, 82
Atkinson, Gen. Henry, 7, 10, 20, 66
Auglaize, Council on the, 55
Augur, Gen. C. C., 7, 8, 255

Baker's attack on the Piegans, 10–11
Berkeley, Gov. William, 9, 10. 17, 178
Bernard, Capt. Reuben, 12, 19, 209
Bienville, Jean Baptiste Le-moyne Sieur de, 149
Big Bend, Battle of, 17
Big Foot, 253
Big Hole, Battle of, 17, 18, 31, 131, 154
Big Horn and Yellowstone Expedition, 195, 215–216
Big Horn Mountains, 213
Big Mound, Battle of, 211, 225
Billy Bowlegs, 207
Birch Coulee, Battle of, 18, 143
Birch Creek, Battle of, 12, 19
Bitterroot Valley. *See* Nez Perce War
Black Bear, 51
Black Fish, 192

Black Hawk, 10, 19, 20, 21, 116, 224, 241, 256
Black Hawk War, 7, 19, 20, 21, 53, 66, 97, 103, 116, 202, 224, 241, 251
Black Hills (SD), 21, 51, 61, 81, 213, 215
  as cause of Sioux War of 1876, 212–215
Black Kettle, 21, 75, 104, 199, 201, 209, 229, 243–244
Black Robes, 21, 160
Blackfeet. *See* Sioux
Blackfoot, 22, 210
Blackfoot Confederation, 10
Bliss, Fort, 83
Block Island. *See* Pequot War
Blockhouses, 22
Bloodless Third. *See* Third Colorado Cavalry
Bloody Knife, 7
Bloody Run, 208
Blue Jacket, 77, 127–129, 208, 220, 221
Blue Licks, Battle of, 22, 23, 46, 193
Blue Water, Battle of, 22, 41, 97
Blunt, Gen. James, 104
Bogus Charley, 146
Boise, Fort, 209
Boone, Daniel, 22–24, 23, 37, 44, 46, 192–193
Boone, Squire, 23
Boonesboro, 23–24, 192
Bosque Redondo, 24, 34, 36, 39, 136, 151
Bouquet, Col. Henry, 29, 175
Bow and arrow. *See* Weapons, Indian
Bowie, Fort, 5, 83
Bowman, Col. John, 44, 192
Boyer, Minton (Mitch), 24
Bozeman, John, 25
Bozeman Trail, 24, 37, 53, 99, 185–187, 195, 234
  Indian resistance to, 78–79, 185–187, 99–100, 241–242. *See also* Red Cloud's War

Index

Brackett, Maj. Alfred, 116
Braddock, Gen. Edward, 25–26, 87, 159
Braddock's campaign, 25–26, 87. *See also* French and Indian War
Brant, Joseph, 26–27, 110, 112, 147, 160, 187, 189–193
Brant, Molly, 27, 110
Breechloading weapons. *See* Firearms, breechloader
Bridger, Fort, 83
Bridger, Jim, 24, 37
British. *See* England
British Band, 19–20
Brodhead, Col. Daniel, 27, 191
Broken Arrow, 48
Brooke, Fort, 65, 206
Brown, Capt. Fred, 79
Brown, Lt. William, 209
Brown, Maj. Joseph, 18
Brulé. *See* Sioux
Buchanan, Fort, 13–14
Buell, Col. George P., 188
Buffalo, 6, 27, 48
Buffalo Bill. *See* Cody, William F.
Buffalo Bill's Wild West Show, 155
Buffalo Horn, 12–13, 27–28
Buffalo soldiers, 16, 28
Buffalo War. *See* Red River War
Buford, Fort, 83
Burgoyne, Gen. John, 191
Burnt Corn Creek, Battle of, 28, 57
Bushy Run, Battle of, 29, 175
Butler, Col. John, 191
Butterfield Overland Mail Route, 29–30
Butterfield Stage Line. *See* Butterfield Overland Mail Route
Butterfield Trail. *See* Butterfield Overland Mail Route

C. F. Smith, Fort, 25, 83, 99, 187
Caddoan, 7, 164
Cahokia, 45, 173, 192
Calhoun, Lt. James C., 126
California, Department of, 176
California Volunteers, 34
Calusas, 53, 149, 172
Camas Meadows, Battle of, 31, 154
Camp Charlotte, Treaty of, 132
Camp Grant Massacre, 6, 11, 31, 137, 165
Camp supply, 243–244
Campbell, Capt. Donald, 174

Canby, Gen. E.R.S., 31–32, 34, 136, 145–146, 165
Canby's campaign, 32
Cannibalism, 33
Canonchet, 33, 119
Cantonments. *See* Forts
Canyon de Chelly, 13, 33–34, 36, 151
Captain Jack, 32, 34, 144–146, 165
Carillon, Fort. *See* Ticonderoga, Fort
Carleton, Gen. James H., 2, 24, 34, 36, 39, 151
Carleton's campaign, 36, 151
Carpenter, Capt. Louis, 16
Carr, Gen. Eugene A., 37, 45, 106, 226, 229
Carrington, Col. Henry B., 37, 78–79
Carrington, Frances, 37
Carrington, Margaret, 37
Carson, Christopher (Kit), 2, 13, 24, 34, 36, 37–39, 38, 104, 136, 151
Casey, Lt. Col. Silas, 256
Casco, Peace of, 119, 233
Casper, Fort, 83
Castillo, Alonso del, 149, 219
Catawbas, 40, 192
Catholicism, 21, 120
Catley, Lt. Henry, 209
Catskills, 74
Cavalry. *See* Military units, white; *specific units*
Cayugas, 107
Cayuses, 249, 255–256
Cherokee campaign, 39
Cherokee War, First, 39–40
Cherokees, 10, 39–40, 41, 43–44, 55, 57, 101, 103, 104, 110, 131, 147–148, 157, 183, 192, 223, 232, 240, 251
Cherry Valley Massacre, 27, 191
Cheyenne campaign, 1857, 41
Cheyenne Trail of Tears. *See* Dull Knife Outbreak
Cheyennes, 6, 16, 25, 41–42, 44, 51–52, 61, 67–68, 80, 99, 104, 105–106, 112–113, 121, 129, 134, 163–164, 170, 188, 195, 199–201, 209, 211, 213, 224, 229, 235, 238, 243–244
Chickamaugas, 42–43
Chickasaws, 41, 43, 44, 57, 104, 110, 157, 183
Chillicothe (OH), Battles of, 44–46, 192
Chippewas. *See* Ojibwas
Chiricahua. *See* Apaches

Chivington, Col. John, 21, 44, 75, 104, 113, 165, 201
Choctaws, 41, 43–44, 57, 104, 133, 150, 157, 183, 217, 257
Christianity, 179, 249. *See also* Catholicism
Church, Benjamin, 119, 121
Churchill, Fort, 83
Cibecue Creek, incident at, 37, 45
Cibola, Seven Cities of, 54, 219
Claiborne, Gen. F. L., 57
Clark, Ann Rogers, 45
Clark, Fort, 83
Clark, George Rogers, 44–47, 127, 169, 190, 192
Clark, John, 45
Clark, William, 45–47. *See also* Lewis and Clark
Clarke, Gen. Newman, 50
Clark's Garrison, Battle of, 46
Clark's Ohio campaign (1782), 46
Clark's Ohio campaign (1786), 47
Clinch, Fort, 83
Clinch, Gen. Duncan Lamont, 47–48, 206
Clinton, Gen. James, 27, 191
Cobb, Fort, 83, 106
Cochise, 4, 6, 13, 14, 48, 101, 165, 239
Cody, William F. (Buffalo Bill), 37–39, 48, 106, 226
Coeur d' Alene War, 50
Coeur d' Alenes, 50, 223
Coffee, Gen. John, 100–101
Cole, Col. Nelson, 51–53, 195
Collins, Fort, 83
Collins, Lt. Casper, 170
Colorow, 50
Colt "Dragoon." *See* Firearms, handgun
Columbia, Department of, 12, 101, 153, 247
Columbia, District of, 254
Colville, Fort, 83
Comancheros, 2, 129
Comanches, 2, 4, 39, 42, 50–51, 61, 104, 121, 134, 139, 151, 163–164, 188, 235, 238
Compa, Juan Jose, 5. *See also* Mangas Coloradas; Scalp bounty
Compostela, 54, 219
Concho, Fort, 83
Conestoga, 164, 227
Connecticut Colony, 179, 242
Connor, Gen. Patrick E., 15, 24, 51, 155
Connor's Powder River Expedition, 51, 155
Conquering Bear, 94–95

Conquistadores, 53, 217, 219
Cooke, Col. Philip St. George, 53
Cooper, James Fenimore, 88, 147, 237
Coppermine Apaches. *See* Apaches
Cordoba, Francisco de, 53, 219
Cornplanter, 53–54, 112
Cornstalk, 54, 131–132, 148, 192, 208
Cornwallis, Lord Charles, 193
Coronado, Francisco Vasquez de, 54–55, 217, 219
Covenant Chain, 55
Cow Island, 154
Coyoteros. *See* Apaches
Craig, Fort, 83
Craven, Gov. Charles, 257
Crawford, Col. William., 193
Crawford, Fort, 83
Crawford, Lt. Emmet, 55
Crazy Horse, 56, 78, 96, 197, 213, 215–216, 250
Creek campaigns (1813–1814), 56–57
Creeks, 40–41, 43–44, 55–57, 100–101, 109–110, 157, 183, 189, 193, 205, 234, 245, 257
Croatans, 57
Crockett, Davy, 22
Croghan, George, 57–58, 131, 159, 173
Crook, Gen. George, 49, 56, 58–59, 91–92, 96, 104, 195, 197, 212–213, 215–216
Crown Point, 89, 111, 117
Crows, 4, 59, 104, 121, 152, 154, 197, 210, 213, 250
Crows Nest. *See* Little Bighorn, Battle of the
Cullen Guards, 18
Cumberland Gap, 23–24
Curly, 59–60
Curly Headed Doctor, 145–146
Curtis, Gen. Samuel, 104
Custard, Sgt. Amos, 170
Custer, Boston, 126
Custer, Capt. Thomas, 126
Custer, Elizabeth Bacon, 61–62
Custer, Lt. Col. George Armstrong, 7, 16, 21, 24, 49, 56, 60–63, 91, 93, 106, 123–126, 189, 193, 209, 212, 215, 224, 231, 243–244
Custer's Black Hills Expedition, 194
Custer's Last Stand. *See* Little Bighorn, Battle of the

D. A. Russell, Fort, 83

Dade, Maj. Francis L., 65, 162, 205
Dade's Massacre, 65, 162, 205
Dakota Column. *See* Little Bighorn, Battle of the
Dakota, Department of, 93, 213, 231
Dalles, Fort, 83, 256
Davidson, Lt. Col. John (Blackjack), 188
Davis, Fort, 83
Davis, Gen. Jefferson C., 145
Davis, Jefferson, 22, 41, 251
Dead Buffalo Lake, Battle of, 211, 225
Dearborn, Fort, 83
Deerfield (MA), attacks on, 3, 65–67, 117, 121, 183
Defiance, Fort (NM), 32–33, 36, 83, 136
Defiance, Fort (OH), 245–246
Deganawida, 107
Delawares, 3, 15, 29, 58, 77, 88, 93, 147–148, 175, 192, 221, 234–235, 242–243
Delgadito, 66
Denaud, Fort, 207
Deposit, Fort, 100
DeSmet, Father Jean Pierre, 21. *See also* Black Robes
Detroit, Fort, 83, 173, 175, 194
Devil's Hole Massacre. *See* Devil's Hole Road, Battle of
Devil's Hole Road, Battle of, 66, 208
"Digger" Indians, 66. *See also* Shoshones
Dixon, Billy, 3
Dodge, Col. Henry, 20, 66–67, 136
Dodge, Fort, 83
Doeg. *See* Nanticokes
Dog Soldiers, 16, 67, 80, 105–106, 155, 226, 229. *See also* Cheyennes
Doniphan, Alexander, 136
Dorantes, Andres, 219
Douglas, Fort, 15, 51, 83
Dudley, Gov. Joseph, 67
Dull Knife, 42, 67–68, 129, 134, 155, 250
Dull Knife Outbreak, 68
Dunmore, Lord, 54, 130
Duquesne, Fort, 25, 87, 89, 172
Dustin, Hannah, 121. *See also* Alderdice, Susana; Allen, Samuel, Jr.; Oatman family; Rowlandson, Mary White; Weichell, Maria
Dutch, 53, 69–71, 86, 120, 147, 165, 185, 215, 224, 235, 243

oppressive treatment of Indians, 70–71
Dutch West India Company, 69–70
Dutch-Indian wars, 70–71

Eagan, 12
East, Department of, 106
Eastern Sioux. *See* Sioux
Easton, Treaty of, 89, 175, 234
Edge Hill. *See* Bushy Run, Battle of
Egushawa, 77
Eighteenth U.S. Infantry, 78
Eighth U.S. Infantry, 251
El Popé. *See* Popé
Eleaser, Thomas, 145
Eleventh Ohio (Volunteers) Cavalry, 51, 170
Eliot, John, 179
Elliott, Maj. Joel, 16, 244
Ellis, Fort, 83
Encomienda, 73
Endecott, John, 166
England, 1, 3, 4, 17, 53, 73, 86–87, 89, 95, 100, 104, 117–119, 120–121, 127–129, 147, 159–160, 165–167, 168, 171–172, 176, 179–180, 183, 189–193, 199, 201–202, 208, 224, 234–237, 242, 245, 257
Eries, 15
Esopus, 71, 74, 224
Estevan (Esteban), 149
Evans, Gov. John, 74–75, 104, 199–201
Evans, Maj. Andrew, 106

Fallen Timbers, Battle of, 43, 46, 77–78, 93, 98, 104, 126, 129, 208, 245–246
"Far" Indians, 78
Farrow, Lt. Edward., 209
Fetterman, Capt. William J., 78–79
Fetterman Disaster, 37, 42, 56, 129, 137, 186–187
Fetterman, Fort, 83, 195
Fetterman Massacre. *See* Fetterman Disaster
Fifteenth Kansas (Volunteers) Cavalry, 51
Fifth U.S. Cavalry, 37, 49, 229
Fifth U.S. Infantry, 14, 33, 139, 188, 250
Fillmore, Fort, 83
Finney, Fort, 47, 127
Firearms, 79
    breechloader, 79
    carbine, 79

handgun, 79
harquebus, 80
muzzleloader, 79
rifle, 80
snaphance, 80
First Colorado Volunteers, 44
First Dragoons, 189
First U.S. Cavalry, 12, 41, 207, 216
First Virginia War. *See* Powhatan
    War
Five Civilized Tribes. *See*
    Cherokees; Chickasaws;
    Choctaws; Creeks;
    Seminoles
Five Nations, 15
Flandrau, Charles, 152
Fleming, Lt. Hugh, 94
Floyd, Gen. John, 57
Forbes Expedition, 39
Forbes, Gen. John, 39, 88
Forse, Capt. Albert, 209
Forsyth, Col. James W., 81, 253
Forsyth, Maj. George A., 15, 16,
    80–81, 106
Fortieth Volunteer Infantry, 139
Forts, 81–86. *See also specific forts*
Fourth U.S. Cavalry, 34, 123, 134,
    188
Fox Wars, 86
France, 25–26, 39, 43, 50, 73,
    86–87, 104, 110–111,
    116–117, 120–121, 150, 159,
    168, 172, 183, 191, 202, 208,
    234, 257
Fred Steele, Fort, 83
Free, Mickey, 87
Fremont, John C., 39
French and Indian War, 4, 87–89,
    93, 159, 167, 170, 174, 208,
    220
Frontenanc, Comte de, 120–121
Frontenanc, Fort, 88
Furnas, Col. Robert., 248

Gage, Gen. Thomas., 175
Gaines, Gen. Edward P., 206
Galbraith, Thomas, 143
Gall, 56, 91
Garland, Fort, 83
Garnett, Maj. Robert, 256
Gatewood, Lt. Charles B., 91
Geoffe (Goffe), Gen. William,
    117
George II, King, 157
George III, King, 179–180
Geronimo, 55, 91–92, 123, 139,
    199
Ghent, Peace of, 73
Ghost Dance, 92, 150, 215,
    252–254

Gibbon, Col. John, 17–18, 24, 59,
    61, 93, 123–124, 126, 131,
    154
Gibson, Fort, 83, 204
Gila River, 91
Gillem, Col. Alvin, 145
Girty, Simon, 22, 93, 94, 169,
    192–193, 221
Gladwin, Maj. Henry, 174
"Glaize," the, 55, 93, 245
Gnaddenhutten Massacre, 93,
    147, 193
Good Friday Massacre, 160, 178
Grand Duke Alexis of Russia, 193
Grand Glaize. *See* "Glaize," the
Grant, Capt. Hiram, 18
Grant, Fort, 45, 84
Grant, Lt. Col. James, 40
Grant, Orville, 61, 231
Grant, Ulysses S., 10, 61, 134,
    164–165, 188, 203, 209–210,
    231
Grattan, Lt. John L., 94–95
Grattan Massacre, 22, 94–95, 97,
    185
Gray Beard, 188
Great Commoner. *See* Pitt,
    William
Great Law of Peace of the
    Longhouse, 95, 107
Great Meadows (CT), attack on,
    117
Great Overland Trail. *See*
    Overland Trail
Great Platte River Road. *See*
    Overland Trail
Great Sioux Reservation, 95, 169,
    234
Great Sioux War. *See* Sioux War,
    1876
Great Swamp Fortress, 95
Greenville, Fort, 77, 234, 245
Greenville, Treaty of, 78, 93, 123,
    126, 208, 234–235
Grierson, Col. Benjamin, 95, 99
Griffin, Fort, 84, 243
Grinnell, George Bird, 155
Grouard, Frank, 95–96
Grummond, Lt. George, 37

Hadley Mountain, Battle of, 117
Hale, Capt. Owen, 14
Hall, Fort, 11, 13, 84, 209
Haller, Maj. Granville, 256
Hamilton, Fort, 84, 221
Hamtramck, Col. John, 77
Hancock, 236
Hancock, Gen. Winfield Scott,
    105
Hand, Gen. Edward, 192

Harker, Fort, 84
Harmar, Fort, 54, 84
    treaties of, 234
Harmar, Gen. Josiah, 77, 97, 128,
    208, 246
Harney, Gen. William S., 22, 37,
    41, 97, 207
Harrison, Benjamin, 252
Harrison, Fort, 82, 84
Harrison, William Henry, 77,
    97–98, 123, 180, 229–230,
    231–232, 234
Harrod, James, 99
Harrod, William, 99
Harrodsburg, 23–24, 99, 131
Hartford (CT). *See* House of
    Hope
Hartford, Treaty of, 138, 167, 235
Hartsuff, Fort, 84
Hartsuff, Lt. George, 207
Hatch, Col. Edward, 99
Haverhill (MA), raid on, 121
Hawikuh, 54
Hayfield fight, 99–100, 187
Hays, Fort, 16, 84
Hazen, Gen. William B., 106
Heintzelman, Maj. Samuel P., 258
Herkimer, Gen. Nicholas, 191
Hermitage, the, 109
Hirrihigua, 149
Hooker, Jim, 145–146
Hopis, 54, 151, 220
Horse Creek, Treaty of, 235
Horse Meat March. *See* Slim
    Buttes, Battle of
Horseshoe Bend, Battle of, 57,
    100–101, 109, 234
House, Maj. Albert, 248
House of Hope (CT), 69, 235
Howard, Camp, 209
Howard, Fort, 84
Howard, Gen. Oliver Otis, 12, 14,
    18–19, 31, 101, 112, 153–154,
    165, 247
Howitzer, 2, 5, 7
Huachuca, Fort, 84
Hudson, Henry, 69
Hudson River Valley, 70–71
Humboldt, Fort, 255
Hungate family, murder of, 104,
    200
Hunkpapa. *See* Sioux
Hurons, 4, 15, 29, 86, 107, 174

Illinois, 15
Indian Creek Massacre, 103, 224
Indian Removal Act, 43, 103, 109,
    232
Indian scouts and auxiliaries, 103.
    See also Cibecue Creek,

incident at; Crook, Gen.
    George; Pawnee scouts;
    Rosebud, Battle of the
Indian Territory, 41, 43–44, 57,
    103, 129, 203, 251
Indian War of 1675–1676. *See*
    Susquehannock War
Indian War of 1864, 6, 104
Indian War of 1867–1869, 105, 107
Indian warfare
    pre-battle practices, 78
    religious ceremonies, 92, 195
Infantry. *See* Military units, white;
    specific units
Inkpaduta, 107, 126, 142, 220
Iroquois Confederacy, 15, 55, 73,
    86, 88, 95, 107, 110, 112, 117,
    120–121, 130–131, 147,
    159–160, 183, 187, 191, 202,
    208, 221, 226, 234–236
Isa-Tai, 3

Jackson, Andrew, 48, 57, 67, 97,
    100–101, 103, 109, 203–205,
    232, 234
Jackson, Capt. James, 144
Jackson, Fort, Treaty of, 101, 234
Jacobs, John, 25
James I, King, 109
James II, King, 120
Jamestown, 9, 80, 109, 110, 171,
    176, 178, 216
Jefferson Barracks, 84
Jefferson, Fort, 221–222
Jeffords, Thomas, 48
Jenkins, Robert, 110
Jenkins's Ear, War of, 110
Jessup, Gen. Thomas, 162, 206
Johnson, Sir Guy, 111, 191, 208
Johnson, Sir John, 111–112
Johnson, Sir William, 27, 73, 88,
    110–111, 117, 131, 147, 157,
    174–175, 191, 208
Johnson's campaign, 111
Johnston, Lt. Col. Joseph E., 41
Jones, John Gabriel, 192
Jones, Sgt. John, 143
Joseph, 14, 112, 131, 153–154, 247
Joseph, Fort, 174
Juh, 6
Julesburg (CO), Battles of,
    104–105, 112–113

Kamiakin, 115, 255–256
Kaskaskia, 45, 192
Kearney, Fort (NE), 84, 104
Kearny, Gen. Stephen Watts, 39
Keepers of the Eastern and
    Western Door, 107
Kelly, Lt. Col. James, 256

Kelly, Luther S. (Yellowstone), 28,
    115, 250
Kenton, Simon, 128
Keogh, Fort/Cantonment, 14, 81,
    84, 154, 213, 250
Keokuk, 19, 20, 115–116
Kickapoos, 3, 134, 234
Kieft, Willem, 70, 116, 224
Kieft's War. *See* Dutch-Indian
    wars
Killdeer Mountain, Battle of, 116,
    144, 213, 224–225
King George's War, 3, 116–117
King Philip's War, 9, 33, 104,
    117–120, 137, 198, 233,
    236–237, 242. *See also*
    Philip, King
King William's War, 1, 120, 183
King's Fort, 65, 205–206
Kingston (NY). *See* Wiltwyck
Kintpuash. *See* Captain Jack
Kiowa-Apaches, 2
Kiowas, 2, 39, 42, 61, 95, 104, 106,
    121, 134, 139, 163, 188, 235,
    243
Klamath, Fort, 34, 84, 146
Klamath Reservation, 146
Knife. *See* Weapons, Indian
Knox, Henry, 221

Lachine Massacre, 120
LaFrambois, Frank, 248
Lake Okoboji, 107
Lakes, Department of, 176
Lakota. *See* Sioux
Lame Deer Agency, 68
Lame Deer, Battle of, 213
Lancaster (MA), raid on, 119
Lancaster, Treaty of, 235
Lance. *See* Weapons, Indian
Lane, Fort, 255
Lane, Joseph, 195
Langlade, Charles Michel de, 59,
    168
Lapwai, Fort, 84, 153, 247
Laramie, Fort, 22, 24, 42, 51–52,
    84, 94, 104, 235
    Treaty of, 21, 25, 61, 67, 97, 169,
    187, 210, 213, 222, 234
Larned, Fort, 84, 104
Last of the Mohicans, 88
Lava beds. *See* Modoc War
Lawton, Lt. Henry Ware, 123
Leavenworth, Fort, 22, 84
Legion of the United States, 77,
    245
Lemhis, 11, 211
Lewis, Col. Andrew, 132
Lewis, Meriwether, 45, 77. *See also*
    Lewis and Clark

Lewis and Clark, 7, 22, 152–153
Lincoln, Abraham, 20, 75, 143
Little Bighorn, Battle of the, 16,
    24, 42, 56, 62–63, 91,
    123–126, 129, 137, 189, 194,
    197, 209, 212–213, 215, 244,
    247
Little Carpenter, 40
Little Crow, 126, 142–144
Little Otter, 77
Little Turtle, 77, 126, 127–129,
    220–221
Little Turtle's War, 127–129
Little Wolf, 42, 67–68, 129
Llano Estacado, 2, 129, 163, 188
Loco, 199
Lodge Trail Ridge, 78–79
Logan, Col. Benjamin, 47, 128
Logan, Fort (CO), 84
Logan, Fort (MT), 84
Logan, John, 130–131
Logstown Treaty, 58, 159, 235
Long Tom. *See* Firearms, rifle
Long Walk. *See* Bosque Redondo
Longhouse, 130
Looking Glass, 131, 153–154
Lord Dunmore's War, 131–132
Los Indios. *See* Native Americans
Loudoun, Fort, 39–40
Louis XIV, King, 120
Louisborg, Nova Scotia, capture
    of, 117
Lowell, Fort, 84
Lower Pimeria Alta, 168
Lower Sioux Reservation, 142
Lower Town Creeks, 57
Lucero, Capt. Blas, 33
Ludlow, Capt. William, 194
Lyon, Fort, 84, 104, 199–201
Lyttleton, Gov. William Henry, 40

Mabila, Battle of, 133–134,
    218–219
Mackenzie, Col. Ranald Slidell,
    67, 99, 129, 134, 135, 155,
    163, 188, 213, 250
Macomb, Gen. Alexander, 206
Madison, Fort, 84
Madison, James, 56, 103, 232
Mahicans, 15, 69, 74, 126, 134,
    191, 243
Maloney, Capt. Maurice, 256
Mamekotings, 74
Mangas Coloradas, 4, 6, 66, 92,
    135–136, 239
Manifest destiny, 136
Mankato, Chief, 18, 251
Mankato (MN), 152
Manuelito, 136
Marcos, Fray, 54

Index

Marias Massacre. *See* Baker's attack on the Piegans
Mariposa War, 136
Mariposas, 136
Marsh, Capt. John, 143
Massachusetts Bay Colony, 118, 179, 201, 235–236, 242, 249
Massachusetts Bay–Pequot Treaty, 165, 235
Massacre, 137
Massasoit, 118, 137, 167, 179, 242
Matowaka (Matoaka). *See* Pocahontas
Mather, Cotton, 69
McDowell, Fort, 84
McKee, Alexander, 127
McKinney, Fort, 91
McLaws, Capt. Lafayette, 33
McLeave, Col. William, 36
McPhail, Col. Samuel, 18
McPherson, Fort, 84
McQueen, Peter, 28, 57
Mdewakanton, 126, 142
Meacham, Alfred, 145
Meade, Fort, 84
Medicine Lodge, Treaty of, 2, 6, 8, 105, 210, 235
Meeker Massacre, 50, 99, 137–138, 141, 162, 238
Meeker, Nathan, 50, 137–138, 141
Memeskia. *See* Old Briton
Meriwether, David, 136
Merritt, Gen. Wesley, 138, 141
Mescaleros. *See* Apaches
Mesquakie. *See* Sauks and Foxes
Metacom. *See* Philip, King
Miamis, 77, 126, 168, 221–222, 234
Miamis, Fort, 77–78, 174, 245–246
Miantonomo, 33, 138, 237
Michilimackinac, Fort, 84, 174, 194
Micmac, 116, 120, 139
Micmac raids on Nova Scotia, 139
Middle Plantation, 109
Middle Plantation, Treaty of, 10, 235
Miles, Capt. Evan, 12
Miles, Gen. Nelson A., 6, 13–14, 27, 56, 81, 92, 115, 123, 129, 131, 139–140, 153–154, 188, 213, 250, 252–253
Milk Creek, Battle of, 138, 141
Military units, white, 140–141
Mills, Capt. Anson, 215
Mimbres. *See* Apaches
Mims, Fort, 57
    Massacre, 57, 100
Mingos, 29, 130, 235
Miniconjou. *See* Sioux

Minisinks, 71
Minnesota, District of, 225
Minnesota Sioux Uprising, 107, 116, 126, 141–144, 152–153, 176, 211, 224–225, 236, 248, 250
Missoula, Fort, 84
Missouri, Department of, 105
Missouri, Division of the, 10, 176, 209–210, 213, 231, 252
Mitchell, Gen. Robert, 104, 113
Modoc War, 144–145, 247
Modocs, 32, 34, 144–146, 165
Mohave, Fort, 84, 146
Mohave War, 146
Mohaves, 146, 258
Mohawk Valley, 110, 112
Mohawks, 69–70, 104, 107, 115–117, 146–147, 160, 187, 191, 193, 201, 215, 243
Mohegan, 33, 118, 134, 147, 166
Mohican, 134, 147
Monaseetah, 61, 244
Montana Column. *See* Gibbon, Col. John
Montana, District of, 93, 154
Montcalm, Marquis de, 89
Montgomery, Col. Archibald, 40
Montreal, Fort, 117
Moore, Col. James, 236
Moravians, 74, 93, 147, 193
Motte family, massacre of, 205
Moultrie, Fort, 162
Munsees, 74
Muscle Shoals, Grand Council on, 147–148, 192
Muskogean Nation, 57
Myers, Fort, 207, 217
Myrick, Andrew, 143
Mystic River Massacre, 148, 166–167

Naches, Fort, 256
Nanticokes, 9
Narragansetts, 33, 95, 118–119, 138, 165–167, 199, 235
Narváez, Panfilo de, 149, 217, 219
Natchez Revolt, 149–150
Native Americans, 150
Nativism, Indian, 150, 189, 229
Navajo War, 150–151
Navajos, 2, 7, 13, 24, 32–34, 36, 39, 121, 136, 150–152
Negro Fort, 48, 204
Neolin, 150, 174
Nevada, District of, 51
New Amsterdam, 69
New Mexican Volunteers, 2, 33–34, 36, 151

New Mexico, Department of, 2, 32, 34, 99, 150
New Mexico, District of, 134
New Orleans, Battle of, 109
New Ulm (MN), Battles of, 143, 152
New York City. *See* New Amsterdam
Nez Perce, 11–14, 16–18, 27, 31, 50, 93, 101, 112, 115, 131, 139, 152–154, 223, 236, 247, 255
    treaties with, 236
Nez Perce War, 153–154, 247
Niagara, Fort, 66, 89, 172, 175
Niantics, 165
Ninety-six, 40
Ninth Minnesota (Volunteers), 250
Ninth U.S. Cavalry, 99, 138, 253
Nocadelklinny, 45
Non-treaty Nez Perce, 153
North brothers, 106, 154–155, 164, 226
North, Luther. *See* North brothers
North, Maj. Frank. *See* North brothers
Northern Pacific Railroad, 61, 193
Northwest, Department of, 248
Northwest Ordinance, 123, 128
Northwest Passage, 194

Oacpicagigua, Luis, 168–169
Oatman family, 157
Oatman, Olive, 157, 158
O'Beel, Captain. *See* Cornplanter
Occaneechees, 9–10, 157
Odeneal, Thomas, 144
Ogelthorpe, Gov. James, 110, 157, 257
Oglala. *See* Sioux
Ohio Company, 157
Ojibways, 86, 159, 174, 221, 234
Ojo Caliente (NM), 159, 239
Old Briton, 159, 168
Old Hickory. *See* Jackson, Andrew
Old John, 255
Old Northwest, 97, 127–128, 159, 220, 245
Oñate, Don Juan, 1
One-Eyed John, 198
Oneidas, 107, 159–160, 189
Onondagas, 107, 160
Opechancanough, 17, 160, 176, 178, 216
Orange, Fort, 69–71
Oregon, Department of, 97
Oregon-California Trail. *See* Overland Trail

Oriskany, Battle of, 160, 191
Ormsby, Maj. William, 17
Ortiz, Juan, 133
Osceola, 160, 161–162, 205–206
Oswego, Fort, 88, 175
Ottawas, 3, 15, 55, 77–78, 86, 147–148, 159, 173–174, 192, 234
Ouiatenon, Fort, 174
Ouray, 50, 138, 162, 203
Outposts. *See* Forts
Overland Trail, 25, 94–95, 162
Oytes, 12

Pacific, Department of, 251, 254
Pacific, Division of, 93, 176
Paha Sapa. *See* Black Hills
Paiutes, 11–12, 17, 58, 216, 249, 253
Palo Duro Canyon, Battle of, 123, 134, 163, 188
Palouses, 50, 223
Pamunkeys, 9, 163, 176
Papagos, 31, 169
Paris, Treaty of, 89, 127, 235
Parker, Cynthia Ann, 3, 164
Parker, Eli, 164
Parker, Quanah, 3, 163–164, 188
Pawnee Battalion. *See* Pawnee scouts
Pawnee scouts, 155
Pawnees, 4, 51, 67, 104, 164, 185
Payne, Capt. J. Scott, 141
Paxton boys. *See* Paxton Riots
Paxton Riots, 164
Peabody School, 249
Peace Policy, Grant's, 10, 145, 164–165, 188
Peach War. *See* Dutch-Indian wars
Pecos Pueblo, 181
Pemaquid, Fort, 119
Penn, Gov. John, 164
Penn, William, 74, 242
Pennacooks, 120
Penobscots, 120
Peo-Peo-Mox-Mox, 256
Pequot War, 117, 147, 165–167, 201, 235, 249
Pequots, 165–167, 201, 235, 237, 242
Perry, Capt. David, 153, 247
Peskeompskut Massacre, 119, 167
Peta Nocona, 164
Petite Guerre, La, 167
Pettaquamscutt Rock, Treaty of, 236
Phil Kearny, Fort, 25, 37, 56, 78–79, 81, 84, 99, 187, 241

Philip, King, 33, 137, 167–168, 242
Phips, Sir William, 120
Pickawillany Massacre, 58, 159, 168, 235
Picuris Pueblo, 54
Piegans, 10, 22, 165
Pima Revolts, 168–169
Pimas, 168
Pine Ridge Reservation, 68, 169, 252
Piqua Town, Battles of, 44–46, 169, 192
Pistol. *See* Firearms, handgun
Pitt, Fort, 58, 84, 174–175
Pitt, William, 169–170
Pizarro, Francisco, 133, 218
Platte Bridge, Battle of, 52, 170, 195
Platte Bridge Station, 84
Platte, Department of the, 8, 53, 59, 195, 213
Plymouth Colony, 118, 179, 242
Pocahontas, 170, 171–172, 176, 178, 216
Pocasset, 118
Point Pleasant, Battle of, 54, 130, 229
Ponce de León, Juan, 172, 218
Pontiac, 58, 168, 172, 173–175
Pontiac's Uprising, 27, 66, 159, 173–175, 208
Popé, 175, 180–181
Pope, Camp, 225
Pope, Gen. John, 18, 52, 175–176, 225, 248
Potawatomis, 3, 15, 77, 103, 174, 221, 234
Powder River, 80, 186, 213
Powder River, Battle of, 96
Powder River Country (WY), 25, 37, 99
Powell, Capt. James, 241–242
Powhatan, 160, 170–171, 176, 177, 216
Powhatan Confederacy, 17, 109, 160, 170, 176, 178, 199
Powhatan War, 9, 17, 109, 176–178
Praying Towns/Praying Indians, 178–179
Price, Maj. William, 188
Proclamation of 1763, 179–180, 189
Prophet. *See* Tenskwatawa
Prophet's Town, 180, 232
Prince George, Fort, 39–40
Protestant Revolt, England, 120
Providence (RI), burning of, 119
Pueblo Revolt, 175, 180–181, 220
Pueblos, 175, 180

Queen Anne's War, 67, 183
Queen's Rangers, 194
Quinnapin, 198
Quivara, 55

Rains, Gen. Gabriel, 256
Raleigh, Sir Walter, 57
Randall, Fort, 85, 225
Rangers, 185
Ransom, Fort, 85
Raritans, 69–70, 185
Recovery, Fort, 85, 234, 245
Red Cloud, 185–186, 186
Red Cloud's War, 25, 53
Red Jacket, 187–188
Red River War, 2, 51, 107, 163–165, 188–189
Red Sleeves. *See* Mangas Coloradas
Red Stick Creeks, 28, 56–57, 189, 203, 234
Reed, Armstrong, 126
Rehoboth (RI), burning of, 119
Reno, Fort, 25, 187
Reno, Maj. Marcus, 16, 61, 91, 124–126, 189, 194
Revolutionary War, 43, 45, 73, 93, 111, 126, 160, 170, 189–194, 208, 220, 245
Revolver. *See* Firearms, handgun
Reynolds, Charles Alexander, 193–194
Richardson, Fort, 243
Ridge, Major, 232
Ridgely, Fort, 18, 85, 126, 143, 225, 250
Riley, Fort, 85, 104
River Raisin massacre, 56
Roberts, Capt. Thomas, 4, 36
Roberts, Kenneth, 1, 194
Robertson, James, 131
Robinson, Fort, 56, 67–68, 85, 96, 99, 129
Rogers, Joseph, 169
Rogers, Robert, 58, 172, 173, 185, 194
Rogers's raid on St. Francis, 194–195
Rogers's Rangers, 185, 194
Rogues, 7, 58, 251, 255
Rolfe, John, 171, 178
Roman Nose, 16, 195, 196, 229
Rosalie, Fort, 149–150
Rosebud Agency, 252
Rosebud, Battle of the, 55–56, 59, 96, 211
Ross, John 41, 232
Rowlandson, Mary White, 119, 197–198. *See also* Alderdice, Susanna; Allen, Samuel,

Jr.;, Dustin, Hannah;
Oatman family; Weichell,
Maria
Royal Greens. *See* Oriskany,
Battle of
Ruddell's Station, 192
Ryswick, Treaty of, 121

Sachem, 33, 199
Sachem's Plain, 138
Sackville, Fort, 45
Sagamore. *See* Sachem
Sagoyewatha. *See* Red Jacket
Salmon Falls (NH), raid on, 120
Samoset, 199, 200
San Carlos Reservation, 55, 92,
115, 199, 203
Sand Creek Massacre, 11, 21, 42,
75, 104–105, 112, 165, 176,
195, 199–201, 229, 243–244,
253
Indian reaction to, 105–107,
111–112
Sandusky, Fort, 174
Sans Arc. *See* Sioux
Santa Fe Trail, 41, 193
Sappa Creek, Battle of, 189
Saratoga, Fort, 117
Sassacus, 147, 166, 201–202, 237
Sassamon, John, 118
Sauks and Foxes, 3, 7, 10, 19–21,
55, 116, 201, 241
Sawyers, James A., 52–53
Saybrook, Fort, 85, 166, 202
Scalp bounty, 5, 202–203
Scarlet Point. *See* Inkpaduta
Schlosser, Fort, 66
Schurz, Carl, 162, 203
Scott, Fort, 85
Scott, Gen. Winfield, 97, 116, 206,
232, 251
Second Artillery, 207
Second California (Volunteer)
Cavalry, 51
Second Dragoons, 33, 41, 138
Second Missouri Light Artillery,
51
Second Nebraska (Volunteer)
Cavalry, 248
Second U.S. Cavalry,10
Sedgwick, Maj. John, 41–42
Seekaboo, 150
Seminole War, First, 48, 109
Seminole War, Second, 32, 97,
103, 162, 204–205, 210,
251
Seminole War, Third, 207
Seminoles, 41, 43–44, 50, 57, 65,
93, 97, 109, 162, 203,
204–207, 223, 251, 254

Senecas, 58, 107, 112, 115, 164,
175, 187, 208
Seven Cities of Cibola, 54–55
Seventh Iowa (Volunteer)
Cavalry, 51
Seventh Minnesota (Volunteer)
Infantry, 250
Seventh U.S. Cavalry, 14, 16,
60–61, 81, 123–126, 154,
189, 243, 253
Seventh U.S. Infantry, 17, 33
Shaw, Fort, 85
Shaw, Lt. Col. B. F., 257
Shawnees, 3, 23, 29, 39, 44, 46–47,
54–55, 58, 77, 88, 99,
127–128, 130–133, 147–148,
192–193, 208, 221–222, 229,
232, 234–235
Sheepeater War, 208–209
Sheridan, Gen. Philip H., 10,
15–16, 61, 80–81, 106, 188,
193, 209–210, 213, 243, 256
Sherman, Gen. William
Tecumseh, 58, 209–210, 243
Shield. *See* Weapons, Indian
Shoshones, 4, 152, 211
Sibley, Col. Henry Hastings, 18,
143, 176, 211, 225–226, 248,
250–251
Sibley, Col. Henry Hopkins, 32
Sieber, Albert, 211–212
Sill, Fort, 95, 106, 164, 188
Silverheels, 131, 192
Sioux, 6, 10, 16, 22, 25, 37, 42, 51,
55, 59, 67, 97, 104, 112–113,
115–116, 124–126, 140, 152,
155, 159, 164, 170, 195,
211–213, 225–226, 234–236,
241, 248, 252–253
Sioux War, 1876–1877, 59, 68, 107,
212–213, 231, 234, 250
Sisseton, 237
Sisseton, Fort, 85
Sitting Bull, 56, 91, 96, 213–214,
215, 223, 252
Six Nations. *See* Cherokees;
Creeks; Ottawas; Sauks
and Foxes; Shawnees
Sixteenth Kansas (Volunteer)
Cavalry, 51
Sixth Iowa (Volunteer) Cavalry,
248
Sixth Michigan (Volunteer)
Cavalry, 51
Sixth Minnesota (Volunteer)
Infantry, 18
Sixth U.S. Cavalry, 37, 91, 188, 253
Sixth U.S. Infantry, 41–42, 53, 146,
188
Skloom, 255

Slaughter of the Innocents, 116,
215
Slim Buttes, Battle of, 59, 96,
215–216
Smallpox, 7, 147, 164–165, 172,
175
Smith, Capt. A. J., 255
Smith, Capt. John, 160, 170–171,
216, 226
Snake War, 216
Snakes. *See* "Digger" Indians;
Shoshones
Snow Hill, Battle of, 236
Sokokis, 15, 119
Soldier Spring, 106
Solomon's Fork, Battle of. *See*
Cheyenne campaign
Soto, Hernando de, 43, 133–134,
216, 217, 218
Southern Cheyennes. *See*
Cheyennes
Spain, 1, 5, 28, 39, 50–51, 53,
54–56, 73, 86, 109, 133–134,
149, 168–169, 183, 204,
216–220, 257
oppressive treatment of
Indians, 1, 2, 53–55, 133,
149, 168, 172, 175, 180–181,
183, 204, 216–220
Spalding, Mrs. Henry Harmon,
249
Spencers. *See* Firearms,
breechloaders
Spirit Lake Massacre, 107, 126,
220
Spokanes, 50, 223
Springfield-Allin breechloader.
See Firearms, rifle
St. Augustine (FL), 10, 172, 183,
220
St. Clair, Fort, 85
St. Clair, Gen. Arthur, 77, 128, 208,
220–223, 246
St. Clair's campaign, 221–222
St. Leger, Gen. Barry, 160
St. Vrain, Fort, 41
Staked Plains. *See* Llano Estacado
Standing Rock Reservation, 91,
215, 222–223
Stanton, Fort, 36, 85
Stanwix, Fort, 54, 160
Treaty of, 111, 131, 188, 208,
234
Steck, Michael, 66
Steele, Fort Fred, 137, 141
Steptoe, Lt. Col. Edward J., 50,
223, 256–257
Steptoe Disaster, 50
Stevens, Gov. Isaac Ingalls, 223,
223, 257

Stillman, Maj. Isaac, 224
Stillman's Run, Battle of, 20, 103, 224
Stone Calf, 188
Stone, John, 165
Stoney Lake, Battle of, 211, 225
Stratton, Royal, 147
Strother, Fort, 100
Stuart, Lt. J.E.B., 41, 53
Sturgis, Col. Samuel D., 154
Stuyvesant, Gov. Peter, 71, 116, 224
Sullivan, Gen. John, 27, 187, 193
Sully, Fort, 85
Sully, Gen. Alfred, 116, 144, 176, 213, 224, 225–226, 248
Sully-Sibley campaigns, 225–226
Summit Springs, Battle of, 37, 48, 67, 106, 226, 229
Sumner, Col. Edwin V., 41–42, 253
Sumner, Fort, 24, 36
Susquehannock War, 226
Susquehannocks, 9, 15, 71, 74, 226
Swansea (MA), 118
Sweden, 73, 227
Sweeney, Lt. Thomas, 258
Swiss. See Tuscarora War

Table Rock Reservation, 255
Table Rock, Treaty of, 195
Tahkahokuty Mountain. See Killdeer Mountain, Battle of
Taos Pueblo, 54, 181
Tall Bull, 37, 106, 155, 226, 229
Tascaloosa (Tuscaloosa), 133, 217–218
Taylor, Col. Zachary, 206
Tecumseh, 20, 56, 128–129, 150, 168, 180, 189, 208, 221, 229–230, 234, 256
Tenskwatawa, 98, 150, 180, 229–230, 232, 241
Tenth U.S. Cavalry, 95
Tenth U.S. Infantry, 33
Terry, Gen. Alfred, 61, 123–124, 126, 213, 230–231
Texas and Louisiana, District of, 209
Texas, Department of, 8
Thames, Battle of, 98, 229
Thayendanega. See Brant, Joseph
Theller, Lt. Edward, 247
Third Colorado Cavalry (Bloodless Third), 201
Third Minnesota (Volunteer) Infantry, 250
Third U.S. Cavalry, 55
Third U.S. Infantry, 254

Thornburg, Maj. Thomas, 137, 141
Ticonderoga, Fort, 88–89, 191
Tiffany, J. C., 45
Timucuas, 172, 219
"Tippecanoe and Tyler, too," 98, 232
Tippecanoe, Battle of, 180, 229–230, 231, 232
Tiquex Pueblo, 54
Tobaccos, 15
Tomahawk. See Weapons, Indian
Tracy, Spencer, 194–195
Trail of Tears, 103, 232. See also Dull Knife Outbreak
Trap door Springfield. See Firearms, carbine
Traverse des Sioux, Treaty of, 107, 126, 142, 220, 236
Tres Castillos, Battle of, 239
Turkey Foot, 77
Turner, Capt. William J., 119, 166–167
Tuscarora War, 236
Tuscaroras, 107, 160, 189, 236, 257
Tustenuggee, Oscen, 207
Twelfth Missouri (Volunteer) Cavalry, 51
Twenty-Seventh U.S. Infantry, 241
Twenty-Third U.S. Infantry, 216, 251
Twiggs, Maj. David, 203
Tyler, Capt. George, 14
Tyler, John, 98, 232

Umatillas, 11–12, 209, 255
Uncas, 138, 147, 166, 237
Underhill, Capt. John, 71, 237
Union, Fort (ND), 85, 86
Union, Fort (NM), 85
United Colonies, 118–119
Upper Sioux Reservation, 142, 237, 250
Upper Town Creeks, 57
Utah, District of, 53
Ute War. See Meeker Massacre
Utes, 2, 33, 36, 50, 121, 137, 141, 151, 162, 203, 237
Utrecht, Treaty of, 183

Vaca, Cabeza de, 54, 149, 219
Van Rensselaer, Gen. Robert, 112
Victorio, 91, 99, 159, 199, 239
Villa de la Navidad, 218
Vincennes (IN), 45, 47, 66, 192
Virginia Company, 109

Wabokieshiek, 230, 241
Wagon Box fight, 99, 186–187, 241

Wahpekute, 107, 142, 220
Wahpeton, 237
Wahunsonacock. See Powhatan
Walk-a-Heaps, 140
Walker, Col. Samuel, 51–53, 195
Walking Purchase, 242
Walla Walla, Fort, 50
Walla Wallas, 256
Wallace, Fort, 16
Walpapi. See Snake War
Wampanoags, 46, 118–119, 137, 167–168
Wampum, 242
Wamsutta, 118, 168, 242
Waoranex, 74
Wappingers, 70, 116, 215, 243
War belt, 243
War club. See Weapons, Indian
War Department, U.S., 123, 213
War Dogs, Spanish, 149
War Jack, 209
War of the Austrian Succession. See King George's War
War of the League of Augsburg. See King William's War
War of the Spanish Succession. See Queen Anne's War
Waranawonkongs, 74
Warasinks, 74
Ward, John, 13, 87
Warm Springs Apaches. See Apaches
Warm Springs (NM). See Ojo Caliente
Warren wagontrain raid, 243
Warren, Capt. Henry, 243
Warrior, the, 10, 20–21
Washakie, Fort, 86
Washington, Fort, 86, 97, 128, 220–222, 245
Washington, George, 25–27, 191, 245
Washita, Battle of the, 16, 21, 42, 61, 106, 209, 243–244
Wayne, Gen. "Mad" Anthony, 46, 77–78. 98, 104, 126, 128–129, 140–141, 208, 245–246
Wayne, Fort, 86, 128
Treaty of, 231, 234
Wayne's Legion. See Little Turtle's War
Weapons, Indian, 246
Weapons, white. See Firearms
Weatherford, William, 56
Weetamo, 118
Weichell, Maria, 106, 226, 106, 226. See also Alderdice, Susanna; Allen, Samuel, Jr.; Dustin, Hannah; Oatman

family; Rowlandson, Mary
   White
Weisers. *See* Sheepeater War
Wells (MA), raid on, 121
Western Reserve, 247
Western Shoshones. *See* "Digger"
   Indians
Wethersfield (CT), raid on, 166
Wheaton, Col. Frank, 145
Whipple, Capt. Stephen, 153
White Antelope, 201
White Bird Canyon, Battle of, 247
White Stick Creeks, 56
Whiteside, Gen. Samuel, 224
Whitestone Hill, Battle of, 144,
   213, 225, 248–249
Whitman Massacre, 249
Whitman, Narcissa Prentiss, 249
Wilkinson, Gen. James, 47, 77,
   129
William Henry, Fort, 81, 86–87,
   137, 192
William of Orange, 120
Williams, Roger, 166, 249
Williamsburg, 109
Williamson, Col. David, 93, 193

Wiltwyck (NY), 69–71
Wingate, Fort, 36, 86, 136
Winnebago, Fort, 86
Winnebagos, 20, 66
Winnemucca, Sarah, 249
Winslow, Gov. Josiah, 119
Wintermoots, Fort, 191
Winthrop, John Jr., 202
Wisconsin Heights, Battle of, 66
Wolf Mountains, Battle of, 213, 250
Wolfe, Gen. James, 89
Wood Lake, Battle of, 143, 211,
   250–251
Wool, Gen. John E., 251, 255–256
Worth, Gen. William J., 206, 251
Wounded Knee Massacre, 37, 81,
   91, 92, 104, 150, 169, 212,
   215, 251, 252–254
Wovoka, 92, 150, 253
Wright, Gen. George, 50, 254, 256
Wyandots, 3, 147–148, 159, 221,
   234
Wynkoop, Maj. Edward, 201
Wyoming Valley Massacre, 191

Yahuskin. *See* Snake War

Yakima-Rogue War, 195,
   254–257
Yakimas, 7, 58, 115, 223, 251, 254
Yamasee War, 257
Yavapais, 157
Year of Sorrow, 257
Yellow Hair. *See* Custer, Lt. Col.
   George A.
Yellow Hair (Cheyenne), 49
Yellow Hand (Cheyenne). *See*
   Yellow Hair (Cheyenne)
Yellow Medicine Agency. *See*
   Upper Sioux
   Reservation
Yellowstone National Park
Yellowstone River, 61, 80, 93, 123,
   213, 225
Yuma Crossing, 146. 258
Yuma, Fort, 86, 258
Yuma War, 258
Yumas, 146, 258

Zaldivar, Juan de, 1
Zarah, Fort, 86
Zia Pueblo, 181
Zunis, 36, 54, 151, 180, 220